15

MEN AND MEMORIES

D. S. MacCOLL, CHARLES FURSE, MAX BEERBOHM
WILSON STEER AND WALTER SICKERT (1894)

MEN AND MEMORIES

RECOLLECTIONS

OF

WILLIAM ROTHENSTEIN

1872–1900

✱

'*Man is born passionate of body, but with an innate
though secret tendency to the love of good in his
main-spring of mind. But, God help us all!
it is at present a sad jar of atoms.*'

BYRON

NEW YORK
COWARD-McCANN, INC.
1935

PRINTED IN THE UNITED STATES OF AMERICA
BY THE POLYGRAPHIC COMPANY OF AMERICA, N.Y.

TO
MY WIFE

CONTENTS

Contents

vii

ILLUSTRATIONS

Unless otherwise stated, the paintings and drawings reproduced are by the writer.

ix

*Illustrations
continued*

xi

CHAPTER I

EARLY DAYS IN BRADFORD

MY earliest memory: the house in which we lived. *First memories*
I vaguely recall only two of its rooms—the drawing
room, the least used, more clearly, on account of its pinkish
grey carpet with a yellow pattern, and a black cabinet, 'hand-
painted' with flowers and birds. Of the other, the dining
room, I remember little, except its red-covered chairs and red
curtains. But once out of the house, my memory grows
stronger: there was the small front garden, with a laburnum
tree near the gate, and to the left of the house a path leading
to the backyard, stone-flagged, with a stone 'ash-pit', a small
building for rubbish. In the next house lived some wild,
venturous boys of whom we were rather afraid. I remember
the ash-pits and their acrid smell, because these boys used to
set rat-traps in them, and set on their terrier to worry the rats
they caught. The house itself stood in a private road, but had
gates into Manningham Lane. The houses hereabouts had
gardens and were of unequal size; ours was the smallest of all.
A queer kind of caste separated the families living in Spring
Bank; we played with some children, who lived in certain
houses, but not with others. A superior caste showed itself
among girls in the form of very high laced boots.

I clearly remember, too, the stories my father told me in
bed—Jack and the Beanstalk, and the Giant saying 'Fee fi fo
fum, I smell the blood of an Englishman', and Big Claus and
Little Claus, and the Ten Swans. A nurse called Olive, whose
clothes always had an unpleasant, acrid odour, told me more

I

stories, which gave me nightmares, and every evening I dreaded going to bed. She used to tell us that God was everywhere. This was puzzling; was God in the trees in Lister Park, I asked? She was sure He was there too. Every Sunday we walked in Lister Park, myself dressed in a black velvet suit and a Scotch cap, my three sisters in maroon-coloured dresses; Sunday was strictly kept; games were forbidden, and our toys remained in the cupboards. But my sister had a little tin kitchen which stood on a chest of drawers, and we saved fruit and nuts and biscuits from the midday meal and with these we pretended to cook various dishes, which we enjoyed at tea-time. I used to think the nut-shells too beautiful to throw away, and treasured them up, but never quite knew what use to make of them.

The Park played an important part in our young lives. Everything in it seemed familiar but yet romantic. There was a wide space of grass in the Park, where, on certain Saturday afternoons, red-coated volunteers drilled, first marching along Manningham Lane, with spiked helmets, headed by a major on a horse, whose officers wore real swords—a glorious event. One might know them in ordinary clothes, but on these occasions they were like people in church, whom it was not proper to recognise. Even more glorious were the circus processions through the streets, with wild beasts in cages, and ladies, splendidly arrayed, sitting high up in great gilded and painted cars. Sometimes, too, there came strange men with dancing bears, and men carrying on their persons whole orchestras—drum, trumpets, bells, cymbals and all, which they manipulated with wondrous skill. Punch and Judy shows were frequent, and of course German bands; for all of these we extracted pennies from patient, or impatient, parents.

Of my first Kindergarten school, kept by two Misses Gregory, to which I was sent when I was seven years old (this would be in 1879), I remember little, save knitting a bright woollen scarf on a rake-like frame, and that I shied at learning to dance. I have a talent for forgetting, and what

2

I most clearly retain up to the age of ten are the unusual things I have mentioned. But the most exciting, the most important event was the Christmas pantomime. There were afternoon and evening performances, and I was allowed to go with my older brother and sisters in the evening, so I was put to bed in the afternoon, needlessly, I thought, for I was too excited to sleep. We were all eager to go to the pantomime when the season first started, well before Christmas that was, but each year our parents said that the performance was poor at first but improved later, a reason that never convinced us. Other children went earlier, much envied, and told us the plot; while the joke-motif, which the funny man carried through all the scenes, was repeated for weeks at school without ever palling. At last the great night was come. We were ready dressed an hour before the time—surely the cab was late! But we reached the theatre well before the orchestra began to tune up, settled in our seats in the dress circle, looked round and recognised acquaintances and examined the drop curtain, in its great gold proscenium frame, covered with local advertisements. At last the music began, and slowly the curtain went up to reveal yet another curtain, of glorious scarlet with huge yellow tassels. Would the music never finish? At last the second curtain rose, and the pantomime began. The first scene represented the underworld; there was a crowd of small devils; then the villain, who appeared and vanished through a trap door and made fire and lightning and thunder come at his will; the lovely heroine; and the funny men—only I wished these last wouldn't interrupt the 'London' accent, which to our ears sounded so refined, of the lovely lady in tights who played the hero. At the end was a transformation scene, and finally, and almost best of all, the harlequinade. Yes, I think this was my favourite part, with the clown, toes in and frills out, stealing from the shops and fooling the passers-by, and then himself being fooled by the pantaloon, that bent and aged figure of fun. Then came the scene when clown and pantaloon, after many mishaps and much quarrelling, got into bed, when awful things

3

happened, grandfather-clocks moved about, ghosts appeared, and finally the whole room rocked and tumbled, and the bed fell in on top of them, while through all the fun and noise Harlequin and Columbine danced and glided noiselessly and elegantly. Oh, that it ever should end! But end it did, and we drove home in the ample cab, smelling of old leather, with a favourite cabman, red-faced, whiskered Henry Maiden. If we had a cab, we must always have Henry Maiden. He was a permanent institution, immortal as Jehu. At home cocoa was waiting; and for weeks afterwards we talked and acted all we had seen.

Besides the real theatre, there was the toy one. I don't know if this is still an habitual plaything of the modern child; it certainly was a constant one with me, an absorbing toy, with its brightly coloured proscenium, and its back-scene and wings representing a forest and an architectural perspective, still in the early tradition. The figures were of cardboard, mounted on wooden bases, with horizontal wires attached; but these figures were never the ones I needed, so I painted and cut out others. I discovered also the surprising effects to be got by holding a candle behind painted paper scenes. The Tay bridge disaster, which befell about my eighth year, was a favourite representation; a storm at sea, the bombardment and burning of a town, were others. German relatives used to send us broadsheets of Busch's delightful series as they appeared; and my brother and I collected soldiers—we had between us an army of close on a thousand men, to be shot at from toy cannons. Toys were beautiful in those days: the Noah's Arks, with Noah and Mrs Noah, and the farms with their bright green trees, fleecy sheep and brindled cows, shepherds, farmers, farmers' wives, were all hand-carved and hand-coloured, smelling superbly of paint. Before the 14th of February we bought, or else painted, Valentines, sending atrocious ones, representing future husbands, to our nurse and the servants, and various girl friends. Valentine's Day and April Fools' Day were important festivities then, besides the 5th of November. Acting and painting,

4

these are the two natural forms of expression for children, for all children surely. At home we all painted, sitting round the table, colouring pages of *The Illustrated London News*, pictures of the Zulu War, and later of Arabi Pasha's revolt; and I can still remember a double-page drawing of Victor Hugo lying on his death-bed, crowned with a chaplet of leaves. When we acted plays, each of us wanted to be the hero who saves someone else's life and then—but not before making a long and heart-rending valedictory speech—dies of his wounds. My eldest sister, who had an angelic nature, always gave way, willing to be the inglorious saved. There were five of us, four very quarrelsome, but with this sister the rest of us never quarrelled; she was our counsellor and peacemaker; we trusted her judgment implicitly, and she never deceived us. Much is written of the problem of evil. Children know that some among them are born good all through, while others have ugly streaks in them. Calvin's doctrine may well be roughly true; happily he used it to paint his repulsive picture of man's future life, and bitter though his teaching was, had he applied it to our span of life on earth it would have been more cruel still.

Other memories: the delicious smell of new bread on Fridays, the household baking day. This meant, besides fresh bread, oven-cake, which only a Yorkshire cook can bake, for tea. An oven-cake is large and flat, like a big, thin muffin, eaten hot and buttered. My mother was a perfect housewife. I still remember her in a blue apron, busy about the house, seeing to everything, as her own mother did. Not a speck of dust escaped her searching eyes. She became too delicate later, and could do little then, but she trained cook and maid to her ways. When I was nine years old there came as nurse a young girl, fair, sweet-tempered and, like my eldest sister, perfectly trustworthy. After her there was no further change. I have met many women endowed with beautiful natures, but none with a more radiant character than that of Nurse Adkins; indeed it is a matter of family pride that we won the lasting devotion and friendship of this noble Yorkshire soul. Independent, enlightened and scrupulously honest, she came from Doncaster, of a family of farmers. Her brother was long one of the most respected and influential men among Yorkshire miners. There is no finer stock than Yorkshire stock, to my belief. The natural independence of the Yorkshire character is shown, even under the detrimental conditions of factory life, by the energy and wage-earning capacity of each member of a family. Half a century ago, something of the relation of squire and villager existed between the head of the firm and the warehousemen in a manufacturing town. In our case everyone who helped in the house was, in one way or another, connected with my father's warehouse. They seemed to us children an integral part of the family.

My mother's character inclined to be strict; but her deep-rooted, carefully trained sense of household order and economy was helpful to everyone under her. For her there was a right way and a wrong way of doing things, and she insisted, undisturbed by doubt, on things being done in the way she thought right. As she was with the maids, so she was with us children. I could not abide cold beef or rice pudding; what I left on my plate was sent up for tea, to be finished before tea proper, with its generous home-made preserves and cakes, might be taken. My father was milder and less determined; from him we could get more concessions; but his trust in my mother's judgment was absolute; her word was law, and he consulted her on everything. I heard not only no cross word spoken between them but no impatient one. As my mother was the stronger character, she loved to dwell on my father's just and generous nature; to her he was the perfect husband. Such indeed he was; but in those innocent days we didn't suspect there were any imperfect husbands. My father had a large repertory of stories. Grimm, on whose stories he had himself been brought up in Germany, he knew from cover to cover; also Hans Andersen and the stories from Homer. He had a natural gift for telling stories.

Every morning my father went to his 'business'; it was

PACKING ROOM AT MY FATHER'S WAREHOUSE, BY ERIC GILL

always, in Bradford, called so, never 'the office'. The business was a big warehouse, a place, to us children, of endless interest. There was an engine room, in which was a great steam-engine, and a man who looked after it. There were rooms full of machines for cutting and measuring cloth, and other rooms piled up to the ceiling with bales; and one room where beautiful labels, richly ornamented with gold, were attached to patterns. There were trucks, on which we could ride, and a lift—it was called a hoist—on which bales of cloth were lowered to the packing room; while outside, in the yard, lorries drawn by great horses with harness and heavy collars ornamented with brass, stood waiting to take the packing-cases to the railway. The warehousemen were patient and good-natured; we adored them all: the clerks, engine-man, liftman and packers, and we grieved if anyone left the firm. Every Christmas a deputation from the warehouse came to the house to wish us a Merry Christmas. For good or for ill there were no unions in those days, and my father was responsible for the welfare of everyone at the warehouse. Most of the houses employed foreigners, chiefly Germans and Swiss, as travellers abroad. My father offered to employ certain members of his staff as foreign travellers and agents, if they would learn French or Spanish; in consequence, his firm was one of the few in Bradford which finally sent Englishmen, instead of foreigners, abroad. My father had a passionate admiration for England, for the English character, and for the spirit of liberty for which, in his eyes, England stood. A staunch Liberal and free-trader, he admired the principles of Gladstone, Cobden and Bright; and he had read much of Carlyle, Ruskin, Darwin and Huxley.

Being an indifferent scholar, I thoroughly disliked my school-days. The Bradford Grammar School was a dreary building, inside and out. We assembled in a hall of stained pitchpine, its single decoration a framed wooden tablet, on which were inscribed the names of holders of university scholarships. To see my name among these was an honour I knew would never be mine. The class-rooms, with their shabby, bare walls, ugly stained desks and hot pipes, smelt close and stuffy. Once a day, at eleven in the morning, we could buy freshly baked buns, and this, for a brief spell, brought a pleasant odour into the school. Yet the school had a great reputation for the number of university scholarships won there each year, and it attracted many boys from the neighbouring towns. This was an advantage, for through school friends I became familiar with many picturesque Yorkshire towns, which otherwise I might not have seen, such as Halifax, Sowerby Bridge, Haworth, Carverley, Lightcliffe and Todmorden. These small manufacturing towns, beautifully set on hills or in valleys, had a severe and uncommon charm all their own. Many of the old mills had attached to them the dwelling-houses of the owners, much as farms have their farm-houses attached. Often a single mill lay in a remote valley or on a moorside, and the building, being plain and dignified, took nothing from the poetry of the scene. I can remember many such mills near my home; few of them are likely to have survived the rapid extension of the manufacturing towns.

In my first year I gained a prize, which I received from the hands of W. E. Forster, then Member for Bradford, and being an undersized lad, I got a round of applause. It was my only success—I never won another. The headmaster, known to generations of boys as 'Old Rusty', used to call out—'Stand up, Sir. You will have to earn your living with your hands, you will never do it with your head!' Only in English History did I show any capacity. Happily there came to the school, early in my career, an admirable master, Arthur Burrell. Burrell knocked a hole, as it were, in the stale, drab walls of the schoolroom and let in the fresh air. He was an excellent reader, and encouraged us to read Shakespeare and other poets aloud for ourselves. He asked me often to his room, talked of books and authors, and encouraged my love for reading which, since my eyes gave me trouble, was discouraged at home. My brother and I shared a bedroom on the attic floor, and we were expressly forbidden to read in

bed by gas light. My father would call up as he put out the
lights on his way to bed, and at the sound of his voice we
would spring out of bed and turn down the gas; but often, after
hearing him shut the door of his room, we would turn up the
gas again. Another practice of which I was guilty was saving
the pennies I got for the daily school bun, to spend them on
old books. There was a second-hand bookstall in the covered
market where noble folios and quartos could be acquired for
a few pence. I used my bun money and most of my pocket-
money in this way, and spent much time copying the old
prints I acquired, and often the title-pages too, which I thought
beautiful. I was a voracious and undiscriminating reader,
swallowing book after book, enjoying Harrison Ainsworth
as much as Scott, and Talbot Baines Reed, Rider Haggard
and Anstey as much as Dickens and Thackeray. But in youth
nothing equals the joy of the theatre. No one, I thought,
understood the subtlety of the actors as I did on the rare and
rapt occasions when I went to the play. The first play, apart
from the pantomime, which I saw was *Hans the Boatman*;
a rubbishy play, no doubt, but wonderful to me. I saw
Edward Compton and Kate Vaughan in *The School for
Scandal*, when Compton as Charles Surface seemed all that
was handsome, generous and manly; I was told too that he
was in real life what he appeared to be on the stage. And
I remember Mary Anderson as Galatea, and Barry Sullivan
as Richard III; this must have been late in his life, for he belonged to the school of 'barn-stormers', and was born in
1828. I rather think he modelled himself on Hogarth's picture of Richard starting up from a couch, which later I saw
at Saltaire. Then there was Hamilton's Panorama: painted
scenes, showing many parts of the world, which moved
slowly and continuously across the stage. One especially I
remember, a scene representing Rotten Row, wherein Mr
Gladstone was seen conversing with Lord Hartington, with
Mrs Langtry and other fashionable beauties near by. Gilbert
and Sullivan operas came to Bradford as well, a delight to
everyone, children and grown-ups. Above all I enjoyed the

9

Mikado. Japan was then a remote and mysterious country; the dresses and characters were novel and fantastic, and, unmusical though I was, so tuneful were the songs I could even join in singing them at home. But I couldn't ever sing a bar in tune. My mother played the piano by ear, I believe quite brilliantly—her eyes were not good enough to read music—and my eldest brother and one of my sisters were musical. Frederick Delius, as a boy, used to play with my mother—his parents were friends of my parents—but this was during my childhood. Unfortunately, I was made to learn the violin, much against my inclination. My master used to say I would make the saints in Heaven swear; no doubt I did. I would cut the strings of the fiddle half through, so that one of them was sure to snap in the middle of my practising. Still, I was always a little hurt when the family groaned at my rendering of some mild sonata on my parents' birthdays. Happily I was able to convince them of the hopelessness of the pursuit, and I was allowed to give up torturing myself and others; and the language of the saints in Heaven became seemly again!

Having no taste for music, I never went to concerts; but I went, whenever I could, to the lectures at the Philosophical Society. Here I was able to see and hear great men from London, men like Andrew Lang and H. M. Stanley. Nothing excited me more. It is difficult for a Londoner to realise how cut off we were from art and literature, and how eventful a lecture was. I was all ears at these lectures. Often, when my father and others in the audience would suddenly laugh, I would fail to know why, and feel ashamed of not having laughed too.

Most of my school friends collected stamps; I had a passion for 'curiosities', and a set of book-shelves became my museum. My mother's sanitary sense was disturbed by the old books and other objects I brought home; happily I had Arthur Burrell's support, and so long as I did not keep my 'smelly old things' in my bedroom, my collection grew.

One day the local art master, to whom I confided my interest in old things, told me it was the sign of an artistic

DESERTED QUARRY NEAR BRADFORD

temperament. This remark made me glow all over, and I re- *Early friends*
peated it triumphantly on my return home. It was the first
time I had heard the cliché; I considered it a final answer to
my mother's disapproval.

I had one friend who shared my tastes, Austin Meade. His
father and his grandfather were both well-known doctors at
Bradford, direct descendants of the famous Dr Meade, Queen
Anne's physician. At the Meades' I was aware of an atmosphere of culture unusual in Bradford, and Austin had
treasures much more varied and precious than mine: butter-
flies, moths, old weapons and fine books. He gave me a
Breeches Bible, and an old Georgian pistol from the Tower,
a rare treasure in my eyes. The Binnies were then also settled
in Bradford. Mr Binnie, afterwards Sir Alexander Binnie,
Chief Engineer to the L.C.C., had a small private observatory
in his garden at Heaton, with a fine large telescope, through
which he let us gaze at the stars when the sky was clear.

Other friends were the Fairbairns, who lived at the Pres-
byterian College, of which their father was Principal; later
he became Head of Mansfield College at Oxford. John, his
son, now a distinguished physician in Harley Street, was
senior to me at school, and Andrew, his younger brother, was
my chosen companion.

One of my father's most intimate friends was our old
doctor, Dr Bronner, the first eye and ear specialist, I believe,
in the north of England. He was an exile from Baden, a man
of 1848, who escaped with Karl Blind to England, settled at
Bradford, and founded the Eye and Ear Hospital there. He
was a German of the old school, gentle, and kind, whom as
children we adored. He never failed, if he passed any of us
in his carriage, to stop and take us up for a ride, a rare treat
in those simple days when there were not, I think, more than
half a dozen private carriages in the town. He had grey side
whiskers, like the old Kaiser Wilhelm I, and was very pale,
with deep-set blue eyes. There was always a faint odour
of iodine about him. To us children he was The Doctor,
able, directly he was sent for, to set everyone right. What

11

confidence children have in the infallibility of men! If we lose
some of it with the years, we still remain children in idealising
men in high places for the rest of our lives, Generals and
Prime Ministers and Royal Academicians, and such. When
the good old doctor died, it was my first experience of death.
His funeral, attended by great numbers of people, for he was
universally beloved, sobered and rather frightened me. I had
never thought about death before. Then a young cousin, a slip
of a child, a constant companion, developed diphtheria, and,
her poor throat swelling, she too died. This brought the surprising knowledge of death still closer. The idea of death used
to bring me nights of terror, so that I dreaded going to bed.

A great friend of my father was Sir John Cass, to whose
family, as to the Bronners', we were closely attached. The
youngest daughter was at school with my sisters; the eldest
daughter had married Weetman Pearson, afterwards Lord
Cowdray, while another, Gertrude (now Mrs Kinnell), had
been to school in Brussels. She had a mind like a sword, yet
she encouraged my childish drawing and writing. She had
a wide knowledge of books and of pictures, was a sparkling
talker and a shrewd and witty observer of things and of
people. Other girl friends of the family with whom we
were intimate were the Ahronses. If a play was to be written,
a prologue composed, Elizabeth Ahrons and her sisters were
called in; none so fertile in ideas for new games and adventures, none so dashing in carrying them through. As class-
mates I had J. L. Hammond and Frank Dyson. Hammond
as a schoolboy was already an ardent Liberal and a student
of history; he and I were the fiery Radicals in the school
Debating Society. I was a passionate admirer of Gladstone,
and I remember going down to Manningham station to watch
a train pass, without stopping, in which the great man was
supposed to be travelling to Edinburgh! Among the older
boys were two who coached me in classics, J. B. Firth, later
leader-writer on *The Daily Telegraph*, and H. Ward, with
whom I was again to be associated at the Board of Education.
Other Grammar School boys, all my seniors, were Woodford

Sallitt, Arthur Colefax, A. Dufton, Charles Harris, and
A. C. R. Carter.

In my form were two young Wades, sons of the Vicar of Haworth, whom I visited sometimes at the vicarage, the old home of the Brontës. Haworth was but a four mile walk across the fields from our home; it had changed little since the days when that strange, gifted, tragic family lived there. The vicarage, the church and churchyard, the Black Bull close by, and the steep grey street with the austere stone-roofed houses were all much as they were in the Brontës' time. Even the mill girls, in their brass-tipped clogs and with shawls over their heads—only on Sundays did they wear hats and boots—had an old-world look.

There were still old people in the village who had known Miss Charlotte. Of Emily and Anne I then knew nothing, but *Jane Eyre* was the local classic. There was a big, square, Georgian house at Guiseley, a village still nearer than Haworth, the house, it was said, where Jane Eyre had first taught as a governess.

The relations of a town-bred Bradford lad with the country must have been similar to those of a London boy a century ago. I knew little of country life or ideas, little of the open drama of the year; but I was familiar with its scenes. Ten minutes' walk took one into the open country. No hedges separated the fields, only rough stone walls.

> The pliant harebell swinging in the breeze
> On some grey rock,
> The single sheep and the one blasted tree
> And the bleak music from the old stone wall

applied perfectly to the landscape. The farm-houses and barns were austere in character, stone-built and stone-roofed, with stone-flagged yards in front. The stone for these, and for the walls, came from neighbouring quarries, still worked with simple derricks, like the Romans used. Once enough stone for immediate needs was obtained, the quarries were abandoned. These old quarries had a great fascination for me; there was a haunting stillness and a wildness about them, which stimulated my boyish sense of romance. A deserted old quarry, not more than fifteen minutes' walk from our home, was a favourite playground. It lay off a path, a hundred yards from a canal, among black and stunted trees; there hung about it that haunted atmosphere peculiar to places where men have once been quick and busy, but which, long deserted, are slowly re-adopted by the old earth. To climb among the ledges of these old quarries within sight of the canal, with its locks and bridges and painted barges, was like climbing among cliffs and rocks by the sea.

Kirkstall and Bolton Abbeys had a like fascination. I doubt whether I ever quite realised that once they were actual churches, with smooth colour-washed walls and timbered roofs and stalls, carved saints and painted altar-pieces, and beds in the monks' cells; still less did I see them as centres of busy life, with monks active in mills and barns and orchards and fields. To me they were ruins, and natural features as such, which had never been different. I remember no reference to these abbeys in our history lessons at school; I only knew that, during the civil war, blankets were hung round the parish church in the town to protect it against Cromwell's, or else against Charles's cannon-balls. Again, no one told us that this church contained some of William Morris's finest windows. It was many years later when I came to Bradford with May Morris and Arthur Clutton-Brock to plead for the encouragement of local talent, that I saw them in the parish church.

Of old buildings, which appealed to me strongly as a boy, there was no lack around Bradford. At Bingley the stocks still stood in the market place, and above Bingley there stood a noble Tudor farm-house with big stone balls topping the gate-posts; there were others between Bingley and Keighley; but Kirkstall, then unrestored, and Bolton Abbeys, were the most exciting landmarks near Bradford. At Bolton Abbey was the famous 'Strid', across the Wharfe; and when I found that Wordsworth had written a poem about this very spot, it became almost sacred in my eyes. Further afield were Malham Cove and Gordale Scar, beyond Skipton Castle, where Turner and Ward had painted; and further off still lay Furness Abbey. I made childish drawings of all these places, which my schoolfellows thought wonderful.

In winter, when the lake in the Park was frozen, we skated, using wooden skates strapped to our boots. They were not very comfortable; but only grown-ups or much older boys· had 'acme' skates. There were two islands in the lake, and when the lake was frozen, these could be explored. There wasn't much to explore; still, islands, however small, have a fascination for boys. We sometimes skated on a mill-beck, so deep that the ice was a dark green colour; but it had a bad name, for more than one lad had been drowned there. Beck and tarn and gill, how sweet these names still sound in my ears! A pond near my home was called Chellow Dene, a lovely name, I thought, though there were many as lovely—Malham Cove, Gordale Scar, Ben Rhydding, Guiseley, Hawksworth. I was reminded of these many years later when Mr Stanley Baldwin, speaking of W. H. Hudson, thanked God that English flowers and villages were given names before popular education arose. I am thankful, too, that though we lived in a manufacturing town, the open country was so near. Above Saltaire, a couple of miles from home, were the moors, and one could walk, I was told, as far as Scotland, without taking the road. In winter sometimes, when the moors lay under snow, no footmarks were to be seen; one walked through a landscape strange, white and virginal, while above one's head the peewits wheeled and uttered their haunting cry. The low stone walls on the moors looked coal black against the snow, and these moorside boundary walls were centuries old, men said. On my way home the mill chimneys along the valley, rising up tall and slender out of the mist, would look beautiful in the light of the setting sun. When I first read Whistler's *Ten O'Clock* it at once evoked the Shipley Valley I knew as a child; I had not then seen the Thames chimneys of Battersea Reach, the chimneys which were in Whistler's mind when he described them as looking like campaniles in the air.

15

CHAPTER II

SCHOOL-DAYS

A Greek play
at school My talent for drawing was recognised at school; instead of writing so many lines for misconduct, I was made to draw and paint lantern slides. My Greek master, Frank Colson, the one other master beside Arthur Burrell who won my whole-hearted devotion, was editing one of the books of Thucydides, and for this I made a map which was used, after being redrawn, of course, by a professional draughtsman, for the published text-book. Colson was a true scholar, probably the finest who ever came to Bradford, and though not a strict disciplinarian, he was an admirable schoolmaster. For those who cared for Greek he spared himself no trouble; so far he aroused my interest in the Greek dramatists, I would go to the Free Library after school hours to read the Greek plays in translation. But I did this secretly, and in constant fear; thinking that were I discovered I should be expelled for reading cribs. It is true we were construing the text of *Alcestis*; but it took a term to get through a single scene; and I wanted to read the play throughout.

I enjoyed the comic scene in English, when Herakles, ignorant of what was going on in Admetus' house, prepared to feast himself; and I got my first glimpse of the Greek spirit in the description of Alcestis preparing to die—'and then she washed her white self before the altar'; I seemed to *see* a Greek statue, warm and radiant.

But I showed little aptitude for scholarship when I reached my fifteenth year, and no inclination for commerce. I was

16

constantly playing with pencils or paints, and was bent on becoming an artist. *Punch* had taken the place of *The Illus-* *trated London News* as a weekly inspiration. John Tenniel, Linley Sambourne, Harry Furniss and Charles Keene were to me equally masters of drawing; I copied their drawings with uncritical ardour. To Harry Furniss, whose drawings of Mr Gladstone I particularly relished, I sent a batch of my own pen drawings. In returning them he wrote that I had wit of a certain, but drawing of a very uncertain kind; the latter sentiment was sound, but my ardour was unquenched. About the same time W. P. Frith's *Autobiography* was lent me to read. It was just the kind of book to kindle a boy's fancy for an artist's life. Accounts of the Bushey School of Painting had reached Bradford—accounts likely to dazzle a provincial lad—a sort of Bushey-Bayreuth with acting, music and painting centring round the figure of the Bavarian wood-carver's son, Hubert Herkomer. My father, proud enough of my drawings, and of the praise they won from his friends, hoped that I would nevertheless do as most solid merchants' sons then did, and follow in his footsteps. But he was a man of large views. Seeing my little zeal for anything save drawing and reading, he probably had doubts concerning my fitness for business, for he finally agreed to let Herkomer decide whether my drawings showed sufficient promise to justify serious study. A collection of my drawings was sent to Bushey; I anxiously awaited the verdict. Within a few days Herkomer wrote that, in view of my youth, I should work for a year at a local art school, and then come to Bushey. Crude indeed my drawings must have been; I marvel that Herkomer accepted this responsibility. However, there was his decision. My father had promised to abide by it.

My headmaster was informed of what was intended; hence-forward I was allowed to spend a great part of my time in the art rooms of the school. In the chief art room a succession of boys practised perspective, and what was then called 'free-hand' drawing, from copies issued from South Kensington. The two or three hours weekly devoted to 'art' had until

The art then filled me with gloom. The principles of perspective I
room was unable to grasp. I am unmusical, so I have always been
unmathematical. Indeed, the only person who suspected any
unusual talent in me was my mathematical master, who
habitually said that anyone so stupid as myself must have
some hidden genius of which he was unaware.

Happily there was, besides the large art room, a small
inner room little used, full of casts of fruit and leaves and
floral ornament, one or two casts of Roman heads, and the
figure of the *Dancing Faun.* The art master wanted me to
keep to cubes and triangles, shading them carefully with
stump and charcoal; my fancy was for black conté chalk and
for drawing the head and figure. I was by no means a credit
to the art master. The Science and Art Department, which
rained green and white certificates on my elder brother, regularly withheld them from me. Notwithstanding the aloofness
of the South Kensington authorities, the masters who wanted
maps or lantern slides drawn and coloured selected me for
the task, and had my caricatures of the French master been
carried through the streets of Bradford they would, I
verily believe, have been received with something of the
enthusiasm shown for Cimabue's Madonna by the citizens of
Florence!

Meanwhile my elder brother, Charles, had left school and
was working at the Technical College, recently opened by
the Prince of Wales. The year 1887 was a momentous one in
the history of the town. It was Jubilee Year, and at Saltaire,
two miles from our home, an exhibition was held where for
the first time I saw some famous pictures. The painting which
impressed me most, indeed the only one that I remember
clearly, was Hogarth's portrait of Garrick as Richard III,
starting up from his couch. This I copied in chalk; but my
desire to sketch certain other pictures was nipped in the bud
by the attendant: I must first get the permission of the artists.
For this sanction I was advised to write, and I actually sent
letters to Leighton and Alma Tadema, and received replies
from both these eminent painters.

18

Besides the picture gallery there was a Japanese village, where a native painter and a potter were busily at work. With both of these craftsmen I made friends, watching their skilful ways. I still have a Japanese book, given me by the painter, my first introduction to Eastern art. There was a case full of Japanese objects, weapons, enamels and boxes, in the local museum, and Japan seemed a land of mother-of-pearl and lacquer, and of feudal romance.

But a greater experience was in store for me. I was invited to Manchester to spend a week with my cousins, while the Exhibition was on, which included the most important collection of pictures ever brought together in the North of England. I had never been to London. There was not yet an art gallery in Bradford, but only a small museum, containing some pictures, mostly (except for a few by James Charles, Sichel and Buxton Knight) of the kind one sees in cheap auction rooms. The effect of the Manchester Exhibition was profound. I went from room to room, bewildered at first by the number and variety of the paintings; but gradually certain works emerged from the rest—by Frith, Faed, Fred Walker and Alma Tadema; then Burne-Jones' *Wheel of Fortune* and his series of *Pygmalion and Galatea*; and no doubt many others, which I now forget. Pictures, after all, are meant to be looked at; even the clearest recollection of a painting is not worth two minutes in front of it. But if I have forgotten most of the canvases I saw, the pictures I admired there were naturally not those I would now prefer. Still, I remember the excitement and glow of discovery. I felt as a colonial might feel when he visits the home of his forbears: everything was new and strange, yet there was a secret sense of kinship; the paintings seemed suddenly to throw light on a hundred things I had always known, but known hesitatingly. I returned home in a state of exaltation; but exaltation, I have noticed, not infrequently shows itself in the form of conceit and ill manners. School, where I rarely was happy, became still more distasteful, and my itch to be drawing more persistent.

19

It happened that there came to Bradford at this time, to assist in the Art Department of the newly-opened Technical College, a Mr Durham, who had been on the staff at the Slade School. He was not, I think, a very good draughtsman, but he upheld me in my dislike of stump and charcoal, and taught me to use sanguine. His special subject was anatomy—he had been assistant to Professor Thane, the great anatomist at University College, who gave lectures for many years to Slade students. Mr Durham held evening classes in anatomy, and these I attended. Living models were used in the demonstrations, and in this way I gained my first experience of drawing from the life.

I also had the advantage of frequenting the studio of Ernest Sichel, the gifted son of a wealthy Bradford merchant. Young Sichel had lately returned to Bradford after studying at the Slade School for many years. He was now at work on a portrait of Sir Jacob Behrens, one of Bradford's most public-spirited citizens; a friend, too, of my father. Sir Jacob was then 86 years old, a fine looking Jew, whom Rembrandt would have liked to paint, I thought. I longed to paint old men; youth excited me much less. Sichel was a fine draughtsman and a sensitive painter and modeller. Shy and reticent, a man of uncommon modesty, he had already made a place for himself in a distinguished circle in London—he was a close friend of William Strang and of John Swan—but he preferred to work quietly in his native town, though there were few to appreciate the sensitive sincerity of his drawings and pastels. I was fortunate to get thus early into touch with a true artist. Sichel's father was also a man of unusual taste and judgment. At his house I first saw drawings by Legros, Strang and John Swan. He was sternly critical of my attempts, rightly deeming me careless and inaccurate. My brother's still-life paintings he rated more highly, and considered his prospects of becoming a painter were more likely than mine. My brother thought otherwise, and chose a business career; but throughout his life he was devoted to the arts, and was a discerning friend and patron to many artists. Sichel advised my father

to send me to the Slade School rather than to Bushey. I was
only too willing the plan should be changed, for the glowing
account of the students' life at Herkomer's school, which
had turned my head, was soon forgotten when I saw Strang's
and Sichel's drawings; and the hope that under Legros'
tuition I might some day do similar work made me long for
the day when I might set my face towards London.

Came the longed-for last days at school. My years at
school, which then seemed flat and unprofitable, were pleasant
only in retrospect. It was arranged that I should enter University College at the beginning of the coming session. My
father was to take me up to London. My excitement was
intense. We travelled with one other person in the compartment, who soon got talking to us, a tall man with dark
moustaches, who looked like a stage hero. He explained,
I thought unnecessarily, that being in the army he did not
usually travel third-class. The journey then took close on five
hours; it seemed endless. The seats in the third-class carriages
were higher than they are now, and my feet did not quite
reach the floor. This failure to achieve the dignity of a
'grown-up' person distressed me. We reached King's Cross
at last, and spent the first night in the Great Northern Hotel.
For me it was a restless one; the thought that I was actually
in the same city as Watts and Leighton (and how many
others?) kept sleep away.

The next morning we went to Gower Street. There we
found a Bradford friend, Bertram Priestman, likewise with
his father, waiting outside the Professor's door. Charles Holroyd introduced us to Legros, and we were both directed to
the Antique room.

CHAPTER III

THE SLADE AND LEGROS

Early days at the Slade THE Slade School in my time had much the same appearance it has at present, but the atmosphere then was very different. At that time there were not many more than a hundred students, of whom the greater number were men. Men and women worked together in the Antique rooms only, but rarely met after working hours. I doubt whether the women were as brilliant as many of the women students are now; they were certainly more austere, as was the atmosphere of the whole school. The older students who worked in the Life rooms had little or nothing to do with the freshers in the 'Antique'. During my time at the Slade, scarcely one of the older students ever spoke to me.

We drew on Ingres paper with red or black Italian chalk, an unsympathetic and rather greasy material, manufactured no longer I think. The use of bread or indiarubber was discouraged. From morning till late afternoon, day after day, we toiled over casts of Greek, Roman and Renaissance heads, of the *Discobolus* and of the *Dancing Faun*. However, we did *draw*, at a time when everywhere else in England students were rubbing and tickling their paper with stump, chalk, charcoal and indiarubber. Legros himself was first and foremost a great draughtsman. He was a disciple of Mantegna, Raphael and Rembrandt, of Ingres and Delacroix, of Poussin and Claude. He taught us to draw freely with the point, to build up our drawings by observing the broad planes of the model. As a rule we drew larger than sight-size, but

ALPHONSE LEGROS

Legros would insist that we studied the relations of light and
shade and half-tone, at first indicating these lightly, starting
as though from a cloud, and gradually coaxing the solid forms
into being by super-imposed hatching. This was a severe and
logical method of constructive drawing—academic in the
true sense of the word, and none the worse for that. It was
not Legros' fault that the standard of drawing in England
during his tenure of the Slade professorship was not a high
one. William Strang was perhaps his ablest student. Charles
Furse, another of Legros' pupils, a very gifted painter
whose early work showed evidence of Legros' teaching, soon
came under other influences. He was strongly attracted first
to Whistler, finally to Sargent. There were no students of the
stature of Strang and Furse working during my year. At
heart I was disappointed; I had expected a great stream of
talent; I found only a thin trickle.

Legros himself, with his grey hair and beard and severe
aspect, appeared to us an old man, though he was then not
much more than fifty. A Burgundian, born near Dijon, he
had early been drawn into the more advanced group of artists
in Paris, though he was by nature a traditionalist rather than
an experimenter. A pupil of Lecoq de Boisbaudran, he used
to say that one of the first tasks set him was copying Holbein's
portrait of Erasmus at the Louvre, going and returning until
he had perfected his copy from memory, and that this had a
lasting influence on his own methods of work. The training
of the memory was an essential part of Lecoq's teaching. But
he also drew his students' attention to the earlier masters like
Giotto, Mantegna and Masaccio, at a time when their paintings were little studied, and their effect on Legros was evident.
From Millet and from Courbet he also learned much. He was
fortunate in that his first exhibited work attracted the notice
of Baudelaire. Through Baudelaire's admirable translations
he was able to read Edgar Allan Poe's *Tales*. Their *macabre*
character appealed to something in his own nature, and the
early etchings they inspired are among the most personal of
Legros' plates. It was as an etcher, perhaps, that he found

23

most encouragement. Though his prints have never reached the prices achieved by other modern etchers, the best of them show a dignity of design and a solid draughtsmanship which many collectors of prints fail to appreciate. Like most of his contemporaries, Legros found it difficult to make a living by his etching and painting in Paris. Whistler, one of his earliest friends, advised him to try his fortune in England; so he came to London, and was introduced to Rossetti by Whistler. Dante Gabriel, with his usual quick generosity, put him into touch with Lady Ashburton, who had already commissioned Fantin-Latour to make copies of old masters. She now employed Legros in the same way. This unhappily led to a misunderstanding between the two artists that was never healed. When later, being in Paris with Legros, I was anxious to bring the two old friends together again, Legros was willing, but Fantin held back, and the meeting never took place. Edward Poynter, who had been friendly both with Legros and Whistler in Paris, admired Legros' scholarly work. Poynter had been elected the first Slade professor of painting in London, after a period as head of the Government School of Art at South Kensington, and he now offered to retire from the Slade in Legros' favour. This extremely generous action on Poynter's part enabled Legros to settle permanently in London, sure at last of a regular income. Though he married an Englishwoman and his children were all born in England, he never learnt to speak English, and this was awkward for those among us who knew no French. His assistants, however, on whom we depended, translated whatever he said, although in the Antique room they had little need, since his criticisms there were usually laconic and somewhat bleak. None the less, Legros' personality commanded great respect. If he kept me and others for a whole year in the Antique room, Legros' estimate of our abilities was probably shrewd enough. He urged us to train our memories, to put down in our sketch books things seen in the streets. We were also encouraged to copy, during school hours, in the National Gallery and in the Print Room of the British Museum.

I fancy we used the Print Room more assiduously than the students of other schools. It is not easy to decide how far copying, the method by which most of the old masters learned their trade, is necessary to the modern student, whose work is based more on direct drawing and painting than was usual in the past; copying freely is certainly the best means of understanding the methods and outlook of good artists. Moreover, to do so is natural, it seems, since most young poets and painters begin by imitation. Legros, as a student of Lecoq, had no doubt of the wisdom of this. He used to say 'Si vous volez, il faut voler des riches, et non pas des pauvres'. And to work at the National Gallery was indeed a relief from the uneventful hours I spent in the cast room. I copied Rembrandt's head of an old man with a turban, Raphael's Pope Julius, and filled more than one book with drawings after Michael Angelo, Raphael, Dürer, Leonardo, Holbein, Signorelli and others. In the engraving room at the Slade School I etched plates after Rembrandt, Dürer, Van Dyck, Paul Potter and Callot.

It was a stirring event for us students when Legros, once a term at least, painted a head before the whole school. Practical demonstration is unquestionably the most inspiring method of teaching. Legros had a masterly way of constructing a head by the simplest means. He worked on a canvas previously stained a warm neutral tone, beginning by brushing in the shadows, then the half-tones, finally adding the broad lights. He had a particular objection to any undue insistence on reflected lights, and this is the part of his teaching I remember most clearly. Legros' views were impressed on us chiefly by old Mr Slinger and Charles Holroyd. We knew and respected Holroyd's able drawings and etchings; of Mr Slinger, as an artist that is, we knew nothing. With his large nose, grey beard and shaky, stooping frame, he was an easy target for caricature. Whether or not he was a legacy from Poynter's reign I do not know. Though later I became intimate with Legros, I recall no reference to poor Mr Slinger's career. Of Charles Holroyd Legros was especially fond.

A handsome, upstanding Yorkshireman, blunt in his speech, but most courteous in manner, young though he was when Legros first chose him as his assistant, Holroyd won our confidence and affection. His devotion to Legros remained constant throughout his life. It was largely through Holroyd and Strang that I came to appreciate fully Legros' teaching. The opening of the New Gallery in 1888 gave me a chance of seeing two of Legros' paintings, a dead Christ, and the *Femmes en Prière*, now hanging at Millbank, both notable examples of direct painting. The heads and hands of the latter are beautifully drawn. When, some years later, I spent an evening with Legros at Degas' home in the rue Victor Massé, Degas showed us, in his bedroom, hung between two drawings by Ingres, a gold-point study of hands by Legros.

Legros was a supporter of both the Grosvenor and the New Gallery. He took no trouble to hide the critical spirit in which he regarded the Royal Academy. He had little respect for most of the Academicians, not because they were academic, but for the reason that they represented neither tradition nor scholarship; on this account he never encouraged his students to exhibit at Burlington House, and in this way he fostered the independence for which the Slade School has been famous since. The essential tradition of the Slade School has, however, been one of constructive drawing, brilliantly carried on, after Legros' time, by Frederick Brown and Henry Tonks. Augustus John was to raise the standard of drawing among Slade students in dazzling fashion; but this time was not yet. Since Strang's and Sichel's day drawing there had declined and there was no outstanding draughtsman during my year at Gower Street.

It was from my companions at University Hall, then a students' hostel, that I got my keenest mental stimulus. The Hall, of which Henry Morley was Warden, was shared by students of University College and Unitarian students belonging to Manchester New College. I confess I found the atmosphere there warmer and kindlier than at the Slade. Perhaps because I was a very small boy among much older

YOUNG WOMEN BY THE THAMES SIDE

men, I found everyone welcoming and helpful. I enjoyed the communal life, the keen talk and the varied interests. Henry Morley himself was a wide-viewed scholar and the kindest of men. In his family circle at Haverstock Hill I was warmly received. A familiar figure at the Hall was Dr Martineau, whose portrait by Watts hung in the library. Older students of University College were Frank Heath, Gregory Foster, Digby Besant, William Jellie and G. F. Hill. I was a raw provincial lad, ignorant, ill-disciplined but eager for knowledge, and these patient friends opened my eyes to many aspects of *dichtung* and *wahrheit*. Of Slade students I saw most of Frank Carter and a young Scotsman, J. P. Downie. Arthur Studd, Harry Furse and Alfred Thornton I got to know more intimately later. I enjoyed meeting men who were following other pursuits, medicine, science, history, philosophy and theology. There was much good talk after dinner in men's rooms, and good talk is a thing I have always enjoyed. When I wanted other society I went to the Weetman Pearsons', at Durham Villas. There I was sure of a welcome; Annie Pearson, knowing my taste for 'curiosities', would ask me to draw Christmas cards for her. This brought an addition to my pocket money with which I could add to the bare amenities of my room.

I used to take a bright green bus to get to Kensington, a bus which stopped, cadging for passengers, many times on the way; it must then have taken nearly an hour to get from Piccadilly Circus to Kensington Church. Sometimes I walked through Hyde Park, to watch the carriages, in which young ladies sat very erect, facing their mothers, as they were driven up and down. Fashionable people, in those days, must regularly show themselves in the Park. It was one of the sights of London to see the horses and carriages there, and the fine people, who were on exhibition every afternoon.

We had our meals in the large dining room of University Hall. In this dining room was a mural decoration of Crabb Robinson and his friends, done by Edward Armitage. This I greatly admired. I have not seen it since, nor heard

27

it referred to, yet it must be one of the rare direct wall paintings in London, and contains portraits of Blake, Lamb, Wordsworth and others of Crabb Robinson's circle.

Another painting, long since destroyed, I hope, was done at University Hall. The subject was Marius on the ruins of Carthage, an atrocity I had the impudence to paint on the door of my room. This room came to be a kind of show-room to which Professor Henry Morley used to bring visitors. It was full of casts, prints, swords and cheap bric-à-brac, which I collected in my furtive wanderings in Cumberland Market and round old furniture and print shops. I say 'furtive', for London being new and strange to me, I could never resist exploring old streets and old shops, wasting many hours, which should have been virtuously occupied in drawing casts at the Slade. I had read most of Dickens' books, and the ghosts of his characters seemed to haunt those old streets that lay between Holborn, Oxford Street, Fleet Street and the Strand. The old Inns of Court, Clare Market, Drury Lane, Holywell Street, one of the oldest London streets surviving at the time, a narrow lane with overhanging gabled houses monopolised by bookshops, were endlessly interesting; ragged boys, without shoes and stockings, sold newspapers or turned catherine wheels for pennies; young girls in tight black bodices, wearing big feathered hats, with aprons around their slender waists, danced mournfully and stiffly round Italian organs in the roadway. There was something hieratic in their expressionless faces and in their steps. Dull-eyed men, and women in shawls, many carrying babies, unkempt save for their elaborately arranged low-fringed hair, swarmed outside and inside the numberless public houses. Most of these streets have long since been destroyed to make room for Aldwych and Kingsway. The booksellers of Holy-well Street have migrated to Charing Cross Road—cleaner but more prosaic quarters. Zola, Rabelais and even Boccaccio were in those days taboo, and while books of every kind were to be found in Holywell Street, it was there alone that

28

unlicensed literature might be bought. For this reason this
street had, in some measure, a doubtful reputation.

People who know only the neat modern antique shop, with its few pieces carefully shown behind plate-glass, can scarcely realise the rich confusion of the old curiosity shops, with their deep, dark, dusty interiors choked and crowded with articles of every kind. Things which would excite the envy of modern buyers were to be purchased for what would now appear trifling sums. In the print shops one might find precious studies by old masters among the heaps of miscellaneous drawings in portfolios; drawings by Blake, Gainsborough and Rowlandson were by no means uncommon and could be purchased for a few shillings.

There was little or no bohemianism among the Slade students, either in dress, manners, or habits, at least among those I consorted with. I cannot remember going to a restaurant, café or music hall, during this first year in London. We went religiously to the Lyceum to see Irving and Ellen Terry in *Macbeth*, also, less religiously, to see *Faust-up-to-date* at the old Gaiety Theatre, with Nelly Farren and Fred Leslie in the principal parts. If I saw any other plays, I have forgotten them.

I remember one incident: while going for an evening walk with two French students from University College we came to a house, in what street I know not, and the Frenchmen suddenly shouted 'vive Floquet'. They then informed me that General Boulanger was staying in the house we had just passed.

Through the acquaintance of a then well-known novelist, Miss Adeline Sargent, I came into touch with the People's Palace. I may have helped with the classes there, under the direction of Sir Edward Currie. I went often to Toynbee Hall, where I was welcomed by Canon Barnett. Here also Llewellyn Smith and others were studying pauperism, and C. R. Ashbee was teaching metal-work. The Barnetts were also beginning to organise exhibitions of paintings with the warm support of Watts, Burne-Jones and Holman Hunt, who

29

freely lent their pictures. The Barnetts had, I fancy, but slender funds at their disposal, on which account we acted by turn as warders while the exhibitions were on. I was given charge of one of the rooms in which Holman Hunt's *Massacre of the Innocents* was hung, so I had plenty of time to examine this strange picture. I found it difficult to understand the literal representation of a subject so remote from credible human experience. Its cruelty had no appropriate symbolic excuse, and might well cause doubt in the mercy of Providence. It was not until later in life that Breughel's profound interpretation of this subject gave it, for the first time in my eyes, a human quality.

I also spent an evening each week in a boys' club in Leman Street, the Whittington Club, where I taught drawing and modelling. To become a worker in Whitechapel seemed an adventure; the East End was a part of London remote and of ill repute, which needed missionaries, it appeared, and it flattered my self-esteem to be one of these. I really liked some of the lads at the Whittington Club, and being liked in return gave a value to what had been vanity otherwise. I made good friends with some of the youths there. They had a cadet corps, and suggested I should join as an officer. I fancied myself in uniform, with a sword, and I drooped when the drill-sergeant looked me critically up and down. He found nothing to encourage any martial notions I cherished.

These activities were rather worrying to my parents; it was the time of the murders by Jack the Ripper, and Whitechapel had a sinister sound to provincial ears. As a matter of fact I came into touch, in this way, with many fine and enlightened people. A letter home at this time describes a visit to Cyril Flower's house at Marble Arch—a house full of paintings by old masters and objects of art. This was somehow in connection with East End activities. Another letter gives an account of Stopford Brooke's house in Manchester Square. There was no Tate Gallery in those days, and I was anxious to see all I could of Legros' paintings. There were one or two of his portrait studies (one of Browning among them) in the South Kensington Museum, but no pictures. So Charles Holroyd gave me an introduction to Stopford Brooke, who owned several works by Legros. Brooke was not in when I called, but I was shown over the house by Miss Honor Brooke.

The house had the rich air, the profusion, of the Victorian interior. Large prints of Rome and huge Italian woodcuts filled the hall. Prints and drawings covered the walls from bottom to top as one climbed up flight after flight of staircase, prints and drawings hung close together in passages, bed-rooms and bathrooms. In the dining room and drawing room were paintings by Legros, Giovanni Costa, Lord Carlisle and Walter Crane; water-colours by Turner and Blake; drawings by Burne-Jones and Rossetti. Also a drawing by Rossetti hung high up outside the drawing room, an early study for *Found*. I happened to mention this drawing with particular enthusiasm in a letter home. Later, when visiting Stopford Brooke, I used often to beg for a chair, to get close to this lovely drawing. After his death I found he had left it to me in his will.

I saw some more of Legros' work at the opening of the New Gallery, to which I have already referred. At the Egyptian Hall, where the exhibitions of the New English Art Club were held, I first saw paintings by Wilson Steer and Walter Sickert, with both of whom I was later to be inti-mately associated. The exhibition of paintings at the New Gallery was followed by the first exhibition of Arts and Crafts, inspired by William Morris and Walter Crane. I can recall the general effect of the rooms, but no particular works. And there was a visit to a girls' school where, oddly enough, Whistler chose to show a number of his paintings. While I was there classes were being held, and it was somewhat embarrassing to walk about and look at the pictures hung in the class-rooms. This was my first acquaintance with Whistler's work, of which I had heard but vaguely before. Full of excitement I returned to the Slade to discover that Legros strongly disapproved of Whistler's influence; so there was an added fascination in the taboo.

With a taste quite unformed I liked many bad pictures equally with good ones. My appetite, like a child's, was a healthy one, I think, whereby I was able to digest and absorb what was needful for my artistic growth. I was greatly attracted by the Dyce and Forster collections at the South Kensington Museum, then housed in a less princely way than they are at present. The Museum always seemed a particularly friendly place, with its unpretentious entrances, and E. F. Strange, who was then looking after the library and prints, was kind and helpful. The Dyce collection being a small one, I became more familiar with the pictures and drawings there than with those in the larger galleries. On Sunday afternoons I frequently went to Little Holland House, when Watts threw open his studios to visitors.

The veneration we felt for George Frederick Watts may to-day seem as misplaced as our admiration for George Meredith. It is doubtful whether peptonised taste is more sustaining than peptonised food. Knowledge of works of art can be honestly earned by hard work alone. An artist learns, not through books or the opinions of others, but by hourly struggle with the difficulties of actual drawing and painting. Appreciation runs parallel with experience. The understanding of works of art must of necessity be a slow growth, like the wisdom we gain in our dealings with life. Youth is quick to respond to what seems daring and novel, and doesn't look deeply into what dazzles it. So it sees at least with a generous eye, and its praise never waits on expert opinion. Whistler's gibe at Oscar Wilde, that he had the courage of the opinions—of others, is apt enough when applied to the connoisseurs whose weakness is a wish to be right. Looking back, every artist can remember enthusiasms which have quickly or slowly faded. But when they were active they were honest and potent, and need no apology.

Our high estimate of Watts and his paintings I still feel to be justified. Some of his large compositions may be vulnerable enough. As with many English artists, Watts' vision was over-much influenced by painting—in his case by Vene-

tian painting. His construction is often faulty and his subjects are admittedly didactic; yet he is likely to take his
place finally as one of the most richly endowed artists of the
English school. To-day the epic spirit is under a cloud, because
it does not now come naturally to modern painters. But to
Watts it did come naturally, and the mention of his name
evokes a luminous world of his own creation. This in itself
is a proof of his genius. Carlyle said, of great talkers, that
they may talk more nonsense than other men, but they may
also talk more sense. So Watts may have painted more tedious
pictures than men less copiously endowed, but he painted
more splendid ones. Certainly, in the early days of which
I am writing, Watts spoke to me more eloquently than did
any other living artist. I was soon—too soon perhaps—to
find other loves, some lighter, some equally worth devotion;
but the impression the great compositions and portraits together made upon me at Little Holland House is unforgettable.
At Millbank to-day, and the same applies to the Guildford
Galleries, much of this impressiveness is lost by over-
crowding. At Little Holland House one saw great compositions in carefully chosen places; among these hung smaller
studies and groups of portraits: Ellen Terry and her sister,
Mrs Langtry in a delicious quaker bonnet, Lady Lytton
golden-haired, and Mrs Senior bending over her plants, the
grave Joachim with his fiddle, William Morris and other
blue-eyed, fresh-complexioned English men and women.
There was a racial quality in all these portraits, a spirit remote from the model-stand, from Louis XV settees and
Coromandel screens. For Watts could still paint men and
women in surroundings which belong to their own time.
Victorian furniture, Victorian carpets and curtains, were
not borrowed from other ages; 'period' furniture had not
yet come in, nor had the fashion for furnishing homes
through dealers in antiques. Watts represented the flower of
Victorian beauty and culture with a distinction which nobody
since has been able to recreate. In Watts' studio all these
pictures seemed thoroughly at home. Times have changed;

his ample manner of living, the noble circle of men and women to which he belonged no longer survive; but for a youngster to get a glimpse of this great world each time one went to Melbury Road was an exhilarating privilege. The memory of these visits to Little Holland House remains as something rich and precious, unlike any other experience.

Ernest Sichel had given me a letter to William Strang. I knew and admired his drawings and etchings, had indeed copied some of them while still at Bradford, and myself owned an original drawing by Strang, given me by Sichel, of which I was very proud. Strang was a short, ruddy, broad-shouldered, thickset Lowlander with a strong Scottish accent and a forehead like a bull, above which the hair grew stiff and strong like a southern Frenchman's. He was a staunch admirer of Legros; this was evident in his drawings and etchings. He had much of Legros' remarkable power of design; his drawing was solid and energetic, and he showed a grim and lusty inventiveness in the composition of his subjects. He was an admirably equipped artist, and at a time when the Glasgow school was becoming fashionable, he was for long under-estimated. In spite of a real curiosity for life, and a fertile invention, an element of pastiche sometimes crept into his work, an infection caught, perhaps, from Legros. He was an ardent experimenter in many materials and methods—what he admired he at once attempted to do himself.

Strang gave me much good advice; he was hospitable and always ready to talk—about artists, about drawing and painting, and of his own opinions. And I was all ears. He had just ccompleted a set of etchings for *The Pilgrim's Progress* and complained that no publisher would take them: they all wanted prettier things. He said he never used models for his subject etchings. I told him of my intense love for J. F. Millet's art, and he sent me to an exhibition at Dowdeswells, where, besides paintings by Millet, I first saw canvases by Ingres, Delacroix, Corot, Daubigny, Diaz, and James and Mathew Maris. I was greatly excited by these

34

artists, especially by Millet and Delacroix, who were, incidentally, introduced in a preface by W. E. Henley, from
which I quoted in a letter home. The only paintings I disliked, it seems, were Gérôme's—and Ingres'!

Towards the end of the session I was given an introduction to Solomon J. Solomon, then a rising young artist whose
first exhibited pictures had made something of a stir at the
Paris Salon and the Royal Academy. Solomon showed himself to be an exceptionally capable painter of the big Salon
'machine'. Immoderate labour and skill were, year by year,
spent on these immense fabrications—historical, biblical or
oriental—signifying little. Solomon's *Samson* was perhaps
the most efficient example of this type of picture in England.
Students were rather dazzled by his power of painting nude
figures. He was all for French methods, and thought little
of the teaching they gave at the Slade. He strongly urged
me to go to Paris. Legros was clearly getting tired of
teaching; there were whispers of a certain Frederick Brown
at Westminster, who was drawing a new class of student by
new methods, some, even, from the Slade; and Paris had a
magical appeal. I found that Studd was thinking of going
to Julian's Academy. I therefore persuaded my father, to
whom Solomon had written, to consent to my going at the
same time.

My father had a brother living in Paris, to whose care
I was now confided. But for this I should scarcely have been
allowed, at the early age of seventeen, to leave the safe rule
of University Hall. I had no regret at leaving the Slade; and
though Legros told me later that he had kept me back to
gain a sound basis for my drawing, it was natural enough that
the daily copying of casts for a whole year became irksome.
Nor was my departure any loss, in their eyes, to the staff.

CHAPTER IV

PARIS AND 'JULIAN'S'

I arrive in Paris IN Paris I was met by my uncle; but on the way an incident occurred which caused much amusement whenever we told it.

Between the compartments in the French carriages were small triangular-shaped peepholes with rings in front of them, which served for stopping the train in case of emergency. Believing that a lady in the adjoining compartment was looking through and laughing at me, I pulled down the ring, thinking it would close a shutter, when to my horror the train began to slow down, and finally came to a standstill, and a group of officials came running along the line and stopped at the carriage in which I was sitting. There was an excited pow-wow; it was perhaps as well that I had no French. The officials finally withdrew, and the train went on. I was relieved to find myself unmolested on reaching Paris.

My uncle had taken a room for me, all bed and divan and arm-chair, in a respectable quarter near the rue Lafayette. He meant well, but I determined to change both the room and the quarter as soon as possible. Next morning I found my way to the rue du Faubourg St Denis.

The Académie Julian was a congeries of studios crowded with students, the walls thick with palette scrapings, hot, airless and extremely noisy. The new students were greeted with cries, with personal comments calculated, had we understood them, to make us blush, but with nothing worse.

Perhaps this was still to come. Wild rumours were current
about what students had sometimes to undergo.

To find a place among the closely-packed easels and tabourets was not easy. It seemed that wherever one settled one was in somebody's way. Happily Studd, who had arrived at Julian's before me, took me under his wing and found me a corner in which I could work. He also proposed I should join him at his hotel, just across the river, opposite the Louvre. This was in the rue de Beaune, a little old street, parallel to the rue du Bac, running into the rue de Lille. Nothing could have suited me better. First of all there was the hotel itself—the Hôtel de France et de Lorraine—established at the time of the first Empire, and little changed since. The hotel belonged indeed to descendants of the original proprietors—old-fashioned, courteous people. It was largely frequented by military men and Royalist families. Here I found a modest room, at the price of 60 francs monthly; modest, but delightful in character. Bed, chest of drawers, chairs, carpet, even the curtains were pure 'Empire'. A valet, François, looked after us, an imposing figure with bushy side-whiskers, looking as though he had walked straight out of a Gavarni lithograph. Excellent François! as intelligent as you were attentive and good-natured, I think of you still with gratitude and affection.

Living at this hotel, besides Studd, there was Kenneth Frazier, a gifted American painter who had been at Bushey under Herkomer and was now also working at Julian's, and Herbert Fisher, a young and learned history don from New College, who was attending lectures at the Sorbonne, sitting at the feet of Taine and Renan.

Studd himself, before coming to the Slade, had been at Cambridge. Although several years older than I, he had preserved a delightfully child-like nature, an affectionate simplicity which endeared him to everyone, man, woman and child. His manners were frank and unconventional, with an engaging diffidence. To Frenchmen he appeared the traditional *Milord*, whose eccentricities, however extravagant,

37

Paris streets were to be accepted without surprise. Much better off than most of us, he occupied two of the largest and best-furnished rooms in the hotel, and his sitting room served as a sort of common-room for us all. We were soon joined by a German artist who was also studying at Julian's—Ludwig von Hofmann. J. K. Stephen was then attending Julian's irregularly. He couldn't draw, but he was a fascinating person, and a brilliant talker. But his health became a source of anxiety to his friends, and he did not stay long in Paris. A cousin of Herbert Fisher, William Vaughan, now headmaster of Rugby, was living at a pension near by, kept by Madame Casaubon, well known to English university men who were studying French. It was a pleasant circle in which to find oneself. These first days in Paris seemed like paradise after a London purgatory.

First and foremost there was Paris itself. To cross one of the bridges over the Seine was each morning and evening an event. The tall buildings along the quays, dove-grey, or sparkling white in the sun, the trees leaning over the river, the bath houses, the barges loading and unloading below the bridges—so many things happening in so small a space, made the quays a source of perpetual interest. Every day I enjoyed the walk through the high narrow streets to the rue du Faubourg St Denis, itself swarming with life. The *concierges* in their white caps, the Auvergnats slouching along in huge hats, and wide, baggy trousers, the red and blue soldiers and cloaked policemen, Algerians, Bretons, and the infinite variety of French types one saw—English fashions for men had not then become general—all appeared novel, yet, through picture books probably, queerly familiar. And following on the orderliness of the Slade, and the aloofness of the students, the swarming life at the Académie Julian seemed vivid, exhilarating and pregnant with possibilities.

Students from all over the world crowded the studios. There were Russians, Turks, Egyptians, Serbs, Roumanians, Finns, Swedes, Germans, Englishmen and Scotchmen, and many Americans, besides a great number of Frenchmen. By

38

CARICATURE OF M. JULIAN (1889)

what means Julian had attracted all these people was a
mystery. He was said to have had an adventurous career, to
have been a prize-fighter—he looked like one—and to have
sat as a model. He himself used to tell the story of how, at
his wits' end for a living, he hired a studio, put a huge
advertisement, 'Académie de Peinture', outside, and waited
day after day, lonely and disconsolate; but there was no
response. One day he heard a step on the stairs; a youth
looked in, saw no one, was about to retire, when Julian
rushed forward, pulled him back, placed an easel before him,
himself mounted the model-stand——'et l'Académie Julian
était fondée!' More students followed; another studio was
added, and finally the big ateliers in the rue du Faubourg
St Denis were taken, and a separate atelier for ladies was
opened.

Julian himself knew nothing of the arts. He had persuaded
a number of well-known painters and sculptors to act as
visiting professors, and the Académie Julian became, after
the Beaux-Arts, the largest and most renowned of the Paris
schools.

The most famous of the professors was Bouguereau, whose
name was a household word in Europe and America. His
name also typified, among those we now call high-brows, all
that was most false and sentimental in popular painting—
peinture léchée, the French called it. I avoided the studios he
visited, and chose to work under Jules Lefebvre, Benjamin
Constant and Lucien Doucet.

Lefebvre, a skilful but thoroughly conventional painter of
the nude, was personally straightforward and unaffected.
Doucet, a suave and polished Parisian, had more sympathy
for the experimental eccentricities current in the studios.
There was something enigmatic in his character. It was
puzzling to find a man, obviously intelligent and, in his way,
a brilliant draughtsman, entirely dominated by the Salon
conventions of the time. Constant, a powerful but brutal
painter, with a florid taste, one of the props of the old Salon,
I remember as a less regular visitor.

At the Académie there were no rules, and, save for a *massier* in each studio who was expected to prevent flagrant disorder, there was no discipline. I believe the professors were unpaid. You elected to study under one or more of these, working in the studios they visited. Over the entrance to the studios were written Ingres' words 'Le dessin est la probité de l'art'; and 'Cherchez le caractère dans la nature'.

We drew with charcoal on Ingres paper; the system in vogue was to divide the figure into four parts, measuring with charcoal held at arm's length, and using a plumb line to get the figure standing well on its feet. No one attempted to draw sight-size, but the figure would usually fill the sheet of paper. So great was the number of students, two models, not always of the same sex, usually sat in each studio. Our easels were closely wedged together, the atmosphere was stifling, the noise at times deafening. Sometimes for a few minutes there was silence; then suddenly the men would burst into song. Songs of all kinds and all nations were sung. The Frenchmen were extraordinarily quick to catch foreign tunes and the sounds of foreign words. There was merciless chaff among the students, and frequently practical jokes, some of them very cruel.

Although I had never drawn from the life at the Slade, the professors seemed to find some character in my drawing, complimenting me on my good fortune in having been a pupil of Legros. Legros was still remembered in Paris: a painting by him hung in the Luxembourg Gallery, and his etchings were often to be seen in the windows and portfolios of the print shops. Doucet was exceedingly kind to me. He frequently asked me to his studio, and gave me introductions to artists, among others to Rochegrosse, Bracquemond and Forain.

Forain was then working chiefly for *Le Courier Français*, week by week producing the mordant drawings and legends which were afterwards published as *La Comédie Parisienne*. On an auspicious day, armed with Doucet's letter, I set out to find him. On reaching his studio, I noticed a quantity of furniture, including one or two easels, in the street. Before I could ring, a youngish man with a brown, fan-like beard, appeared at the entrance; he turned out to be the admired artist himself. The furniture in the street was his; he was being sold up. This, I found out later, not infrequently happened. Forain is now, I am told, one of the wealthiest artists in Paris. Such changes of fortune are not unusual, but there was little to show in those days that Forain would arrive at his present eminence.

Doucet had told me to show Forain my own drawings. These were done on thin brown paper in sketch books specially made by Newmans for John Swan. Forain's comments on the drawings were no doubt appropriately polite, but for the sketch books, bound in pleasant green cloth strengthened by leather, he expressed unstinted admiration. Could I get him some? Yes indeed; I was only too proud and ready. How many? Three or four. Four were ordered. Needless to say, the good Forain never thought of asking for the account, and I was far too shy to proffer it. My finances, in consequence, were crippled for a month.

It was probably on account of my liking for Japanese art that Doucet invited me to meet Rochegrosse, who was a keen collector of Japanese prints and paintings. Rochegrosse (who was a son of Théodore de Banville) was a pleasant enough person, but I was not greatly attracted by his work; he painted immense canvases not unlike Solomon's, but still more sensational and bizarre—I had seen a *Vitellius dragged through the streets of Rome* at the Exhibition, a characteristic work of his. Bracquemond was an artist of a more modest character. Like Frank Short, he was a master craftsman, and an admirable interpreter on copper. He gave me valuable advice on the subject of etching. I did not however continue etching in Paris; direct drawing attracted me more.

The Paris Exhibition of 1889 is confused, in my mind, with the Exhibition of 1899. Whether it was there or at Durand-Ruel's Galleries in the rue le Pelletier that I first saw paintings by Courbet and Manet, Degas, Monet, Pissarro and Puvis de Chavannes, I cannot now recollect; but I soon became a convert to Impressionism, and a more ardent one than either Studd or Frazier. Fisher also declared himself a convinced disciple! We all admired Bastien-Lepage, Dagnan-Bouveret, and especially Cazin; and even quite pedestrian artists like Eliot and Aman-Jean. Watts and Rossetti were, for the time, obscured. But not Millet; his two paintings at the Louvre were strangely moving. *Le Printemps* seemed to me then, as it has ever since, a perfect painting; and *L'Église à Gréville* more austere, and equally complete.

Delacroix I did not understand; though I didn't then know the word 'baroque', his paintings, compared with others at the Louvre, appeared somewhat as those of Tiepolo or Le Brun would appear in a church to a lover of Giotto or Piero della Francesca. Response to Delacroix' genius came later.

The great Rubens' decorations were also above me then; I was unable to see the superhuman qualities of the painting on account of the falseness of the heroics. Ingres seemed to me the fine flower of academic painting—I was told I ought to admire him, but he failed to stir me.

Botticelli was to us then what I suppose El Greco to be to youngsters to-day; Rembrandt's *Butcher's Shop* seemed to me the last word in realistic painting; and his picture of *The Good Samaritan*, the slight indication of blood on the ground to show where the wounded man had lain before being lifted up and carried away, opened my eyes to Rembrandt's almost biblical imagination.

Another picture which moved me strangely was Fra Angelico's *Coronation of the Virgin*—those beautiful women, with their pure necks and virginal persons, whose colour alone, so clear and spotless in its delicate purity, gave one a glimpse of paradise.

I noticed, when I went to the Louvre after returning from Giverny, that many pictures seemed to smell too much of the workroom, of actual paint and varnish. But Fra Angelico's and some others among the primitives, never.

PAGE FROM A SKETCH BOOK (1889)

Sometimes, both in the country and in my studio, I would
feel that nothing had ever been perfectly painted, that everything remained still to be done, despite the genius of the old
painters. Hence one's interest in Manet and Courbet, who
at least, I thought, saw the world with fresh eyes. But when
I saw the life of the fields, the passion of the harvest, men and
women reaping and binding, and the great carts and horses
being led to and fro in the fields, loaded with corn and hay,
I marvelled how completely Millet had expressed one side of
human life. I felt dimly even then that he was the best
balanced among French artists, uniting perfectly colour, design and draughtsmanship with exactitude of observation,
heightened by the inspiration of a great subject matter.

I remember Frazier saying that Watts held the painting of
hair and beard to be the most difficult part of a portrait, and
my ridiculing this statement; when Frazier rightly asked
what experience gave me the right to judge the conclusions
of a ripe painter like Watts.

Meanwhile I was getting acclimatised to the life at Julian's,
though not to the stifling atmosphere. After the monotony
of work at the Slade, the variety of the drawing and painting
at Julian's was highly stimulating. Puvis de Chavannes and
Monet were the prevalent influences among the more intelligent students; but the Salon conventions were still active,
and especially affected the painting of the nude. I was overawed by the aptitude for this shown by many of the students,
and consequently never ventured to paint a nude, but restricted myself to drawing. A nude drawn at Julian's during
my first year turned up at Sotheby's lately; it was not quite
so incompetent as I would have expected; but the growing
friendliness shown me by many of the students was probably
due to drawings I made outside the studio.

At first I was shy of the French students, and my limited
knowledge of French kept me within the Anglo-American
fold. But Frenchmen are generous in their appreciation of
any sign of promise in a foreigner, perhaps because they fear
no rivals; for then, as now, everyone looked to France, as

43

France herself once looked to Italy, as the natural home of painting. But the promiscuity of the studios brought me into contact with several among the French students. Bataille, who later gave up painting to become a successful playwright, d'Espagnat, and a student named Thévenot, were the first French friends I made.

Another student to whom I became attached was Charles Duvent. Duvent, noted for his mordant wit and keen esprit, was one of the most influential among the students at Julian's. Zuloaga, Maurice Denis and Bonnard were, I believe, then working at Julian's, but I did not meet them until later. The studios were full of Americans. Paris has always been the Mecca of American painters. Not only young students, but older painters came to work there. Some of the Americans who joined our circle at the rue de Beaune—Humphreys Johnston, Philip Hale, Sargent Kendall, and Howard Hart— had already had pictures hung at the Salon, in my eyes a wonderful feat. Once, I remember, when I heard some of them discussing the places given to their works, I marvelled how anyone could mind how and where he was hung, so great a thing did the acceptance of a picture at the Salon seem to me. We used to dine with our American friends at a little restaurant called Thirion's on the Boulevard St Germain, going on from there to various studios and rooms in the rue de Seine and adjacent streets, to endless discussions on Courbet, Manet and Monet, Puvis de Chavannes and Besnard.

Besnard was our latest discovery. He stood between the more skilful of the Salon painters and independent artists like Degas, Monet and Renoir. He was not popular among the Impressionists, who regarded him as a Salon painter who had adopted the colour, but was incapable of the heat, of their fire. 'Besnard, vous volez de nos propres ailes,' Degas had said to him. But we knew little of Degas or his work, having seen only the small pastels then in the Caillebotte collection of the Luxembourg, while Besnard's effects of light and lamp-light on nudes were a fascinating novelty, much imitated at Julian's.

44

My fellow student, von Hofmann, had discovered Besnard's wall paintings at the École de Pharmacie, and took me
to see them. So much did he admire these decorations that,
with Besnard's permission, he made careful copies of them.
This devotion naturally gained him Besnard's acquaintance,
to whom he showed one of my sketch books, and one evening,
a great event for us, Besnard, out of the kindness of his heart,
invited von Hofmann and myself to dinner to meet Puvis de
Chavannes, whom he knew we both worshipped from afar.
The great day arrived; but could this rubicund, large-nosed
old gentleman, encased so correctly in a close-fitting frock-
coat, looking more like a senator than an artist, be the
Olympian Puvis? The only other guest was Forain, who
took the lead in the conversation, and made havoc not only
of the dishes before him, but of reputations which to us were
sacrosanct. Puvis himself had an alarming appetite; we
heard later that it was his habit to work all day with no break
for luncheon.

After dinner we adjourned to the studio, where Besnard's
latest canvases stood about on easels. We waited breath-
lessly to hear Puvis' comments, but it was always Forain
who played the critic. Puvis was discreetly genial, and said
little that was remarkable.

An occasion like this was rare. French family life is
notoriously intimate, and strangers are not readily admitted
into the family circle. Usually I dined with Studd, Frazier
and Fisher at a quiet restaurant in the rue de Lille, where
éperlans frits was a favourite dish. Sometimes at the beginning of the month, when the monthly allowance was intact, we went to Sylvain's, a more luxurious restaurant behind
the Opéra. To me the cooking there seemed perfect, and we
got a glimpse of the gayer side of the Paris restaurants. Then
perhaps we would sit outside the Café de la Paix, and watch
the stream of people passing, bearded Frenchmen, English
tourists, *rastaquouères* and *cocottes*, the shabby and overdressed, sinister-looking newspaper men, *camelots* shouting
'voilà le Soir, la Bataille', and others who left little toys on

the marble tables. Or we walked along the Boulevard des Italiens between the Opéra and the Madeleine, admiring the shadows of the plane trees thrown by the tall electric lights on the broad pavement, or down the more crowded Boulevards, past the Café Riche, and the Café Americain, and Tortoni's, with the dandies leaning on the railings. I looked with curiosity as I passed the Café Americain, where sat enormous, overdressed women, in great feathered hats and boas, painted and powdered, usually a black woman amongst them, by whom I marvelled that anyone could be attracted. But the gross pleasure of eating was not, for us, a vain illusion. During the first weeks in Paris our gastronomic exaltation quite equalled our aesthetic enthusiasm. The discovery of *vol au vent, cœur à la crème*, of omelettes of many kinds, within the measure of one's pocket, made luncheon and dinner a daily adventure. It was no form of dissipation which had to be paid for then or thereafter; so these golden hours spent at French tables were taken as a gift of the gods, accepted gratefully, and with modest libations. Even the grave Fisher grew lyrical over the *éperlans frits*, the *truite de rivière*, the *rouget*; and where in England, save in private houses, can one find the fat, juicy steaks, the *choux à la crème*, the young and melting carrots, the *aubergines*? Was it not my friend Eric Gill who wrote that while God doesn't particularly approve of luxury, at least he wants it in good taste? To French people cooking is a serious matter, and to be particular about one's food seems to them right and reasonable. That an ill-cooked dish should at once be rejected is, in France, taken for granted. An active critical faculty is applied in Paris to art and literature and the drama as well as to cooking. I remember J. W. Clark coming to Paris from Cambridge with Arthur Shipley on purpose to see a performance of one of Victor Hugo's plays—I think it was *Le Roi S'Amuse*—at the Théâtre Français. He appeared to have been present at every representation of Victor Hugo's plays for almost half a century, and he knew how every actor had filled and interpreted each particular rôle. He declared this knowledge to be general among a French audience; that at the Théâtre Français any new departure from the traditional delivery of Racine and Molière is detected and commented on; that it may once have been so in the English theatre, but now it was so no longer.

Besides J. W. Clark we had other visitors at the rue de Beaune: Percy Mathieson, George Duckworth, Arthur Shipley and Villiers Stanford. I also met P. G. Hamerton—well known at one time as an art critic and writer on etching, and as the editor of *The Portfolio*, and immortalised by Whistler in *The Gentle Art*. He was then an old gentleman with a French wife and a French family, living just outside Paris, at Boulogne-sur-Seine. One day he insisted on taking me to the Louvre to show me exactly where the old buildings had stood. With the touching, unsteady gait of an old man, he walked carefully over the ground plan of all the buildings, while I stood coldly watching him, little interested in this peripatetic demonstration. Poor Mr Hamerton! he little knew how small was my knowledge of history, and how slight my curiosity for buildings which no longer existed. The Louvre as it stood was good enough for me. I was beginning to distinguish the buildings that remained since the days of François Premier, adorned with the long, elegant figures of Jean Goujon, from those of the time of Louis XIV and XV, and from the later Napoleonic additions, as we passed every day on our way to Julian's. But how tired I got of the florid Garibaldi memorial. I understood the jeers of Claude and his friends, in Zola's *L'Œuvre*, as they, too, walked by the stupid and pretentious sculpture so common in Paris.

Herbert Fisher gave me some idea of the history of Paris, and took me to the Sainte-Chapelle and to Notre-Dame. Fisher used to attend Taine's and Renan's lectures at the Collège de France, or the Sorbonne; at times, too, he would meet them personally, when Studd, Frazier and I would wait his return, to hear all he had to tell about these great men. On one of these occasions Taine advised Fisher to study

47

medicine for three years!—a historian should know something of mental effects on human action. Fisher didn't take
Taine's advice. Fisher met Renan when Déroulède was
preaching *la revanche*; Renan thought Déroulède a dangerous influence. Let France not risk a decision by the
sword; rather let her, like Greece, lead the world as a great
civilising power. She can have no more glorious future.
Fisher returned from these interviews aglow with enthusiasm.
Despite a somewhat grand manner, he had a very human and
affectionate character, and we valued his company among us.
He shared, too, our enthusiasm for French art and literature;
so perhaps he gained something from his association with us
painters.

What plays I saw during my first year I have forgotten,
all save one. I went with Duvent to the Gymnase to see a
new play by Alphonse Daudet, *La Lutte pour la Vie*. I could
follow it fairly well, but one word, constantly repeated,
puzzled me—*strugforliffeur*—what did it mean? I asked
Duvent. 'Why,' said Duvent, 'it is an English word.'
'Surely not,' I said. But he insisted, and finally I realised
that *struggler for life* was intended!

I had read parts of *Les Misérables* at school, also parts of
Tartarin de Tarascon; now I could read them for myself.
But with a knowledge of Monet and Courbet came a zest for
Tolstoi and Zola. I read *War and Peace*, writing home with
enthusiasm of this great book, which was hardly fit for home
reading, I loftily added. Fisher declared it to be the greatest
novel ever written. Studd introduced me to Thomas Hardy,
lending me *Far from the Madding Crowd*. But for the time
my head was filled with French and Russian literature.

Dostoievsky's *Idiot* and Stendhal's *Le Rouge et le Noir*
were two books that fascinated me; they impressed me so,
I can still remember the scene in which the Prince smashes
the china vase when he comes to the party, his heart full of
love for them all; and Julien Sorel's dilemma, when he felt
he ought to caress Mme de Rénal's hand, impressed me too.
All this was an important part of my Paris experience; it was

not studying at Julian's only; it was a new dynamic sense of the fullness of life, of which I was daily becoming aware.

During my first winter in Paris I was taken by an American friend to Giverny, a village near Vernon, famous now as the place where Claude Monet lived and painted, and where he died. I had never before been in the country during the winter; nor indeed among villagers. A new aspect of life was opened to me. There was a pleasant inn at Giverny, kept by Monsieur and Madame Baudy. The little café was fitted with panels, half of which were already filled by painters who had frequented the inn; and there was a billiard room whose white plastered walls had also tempted them. I, too, tried my first mural decoration on one of its walls, the subject forsooth! a man hanged on a gallows. Attached to the inn was a typical village shop, where I purchased a pair of wooden sabots—not altogether an affectation, for sabots make useful wear for painting out-of-doors, especially in winter. They keep out the damp and the cloth footwear worn with them keeps the feet warm. Only at first they make walking uncomfortable; one has to take long sliding steps to avoid friction at the bend of the foot.

It was at Giverny that I painted my first landscapes. I had never seen either Gauguin's or Van Gogh's painting, but a short time ago, when I came upon some of the panels I painted then, I was surprised to find a queer likeness in these to their works.

I know nothing so exhilarating to the spirit as painting out-of-doors. Indeed, I often wonder how anyone can feel the full beauty of a landscape unless he has tried to paint it. This was the first of my many excursions to paint in the country, and the intense delight it gave me brought me nearer to understanding a religious attitude to life; for one's very being seems to be absorbed into the fields, the trees and the walls one is striving to paint; an experience which, in later years, gave me an insight into the poetry of the great mystics, European and Eastern. This winter at Giverny is unforgettable. I had never before realised the beauty of winter

49

landscape, the shapes of the bare trees, and the austere contours of the fields. It was the first of many visits. For the
heat of the studios at Julian's, after a few weeks, became
unendurable, and a few days at Giverny were a respite from
this. For exercise in Paris I joined a number of students at
a riding school, and, when sufficiently expert, I was able to
join Fisher, Studd and Frazier in excursions to 'Robinson',
a wooded district near Paris, where a horse could be hired
very cheaply. One day I was thrown, when I fell on my
head and sprained my ankle!

CHAPTER V

A VISIT TO GERMANY

Early in the summer I returned to England, staying with *Oxford and* Fisher at Oxford on my way to the north. One day Fisher *Germany* came in and threw a book on the table, saying he wished me to read it: *it was by a nephew of Burne-Jones*. He was curious to know my opinion of its merits. The book was *Plain Tales from the Hills*.

Von Hofmann had pressed me to join him in Germany. Would I visit his people in Berlin first, see some of the galleries, and then go on to Rügen to work? Being greatly attached to von Hofmann, I at once agreed.

I found his people delightful. His father, who had been one of Bismarck's young men and the first German Colonial Minister, was a typical German of the old school, scrupulously honest, outwardly severe, but actually gentle, courteous and extremely simple in his habits. He had been called to Versailles as one of the German legal advisers during the peace discussions in 1870, and so came under the old Kaiser's notice. Frau von Hofmann was equally typical of the earlier generation; she managed the house herself, with the help of two unmarried daughters, and kept no maids. The daughters did the cooking and then came in and sat down to table. The little interior was generally full of brilliant young officers, for von Hofmann's younger brother was in the Guards.

I did not much care for Berlin. The old parts were well enough, but that genius for building which the Germans had formerly shown, and which was to assert itself again, was then in abeyance. The houses were pretentious and over ornate; but the blocks of new buildings, because of their greater height, looked impressive at sundown. I remember also the beauty of the gardens at night, gardens full of magnolias and flowering shrubs, many of them running down to the edge of the canals, which are among the attractive features of Berlin.

I missed the old streets and the curio shops of London and Paris; Berlin seemed new, cold and rather parvenu; especially pretentious was the Sieges Allee, the construction of which the Kaiser himself had directed. The museums were very impressive, while the Zoo was enchanting, and far ahead of our own in those days in the provision of natural conditions.

Von Hofmann's uncle, Herr von Kekulé, was head of the Greek department in the museum. He had been the Emperor's tutor at Bonn. His wife was a very beautiful and stately lady, of a classical mould not uncommon among German women, and there were two lovely young daughters.

Von Hofmann, newly arrived from Paris, with his copies of Besnard, seemed, to museum circles, a very revolutionary artist. The Emperor actually sent a message to his father, ordering him to discourage his son from painting in this modern manner! It seemed to me incredible that anything of the kind could happen; but I knew nothing of Court life, and was told this was characteristic of the Kaiser.

Von Hofmann had a copious imagination, and poured out compositions remarkable for their lyrical quality. He himself was proud and reserved, and expected little from life. He was not one of those whom the daily combat rouses to action. The anticipation of having to pack a trunk or catch a train upset his balance. He was shy, a little awkward, very diffident about his work; but his spirit poured itself out in novel designs and lovely vision, bright and clear as a mountain stream, the source of some hidden lake. Von Hofmann slowly won for himself a foremost place among German painters; but of late years the money changers have driven

the true worshippers from the Temple; and Hofmann's gifts
are, for the moment, unappreciated.

Among the German artists I met, I was most struck by
Max Liebermann. Liebermann was a wit, and a notable figure
in Berlin society. An unashamed Jew, he was notoriously
unpopular; but he was clever enough, instead of trying to
minimise his characteristics, to exaggerate them. His talent
could not be ignored, nor indeed could his tongue be bridled,
and being possessed of large private means, he could afford
to indulge it fearlessly. He was a resourceful and adventurous artist, a solid painter and draughtsman, standing head
and shoulders above the other German realists. His work
was uneven, but being a man of strong personality, it was
easier for his friends to flatter than to speak frankly, and he
allowed too much careless work to leave his studio. He had
the gifts of a vital eye and hand; he was a sound painter of
what was before him; but he had little or no imagination, and
a *Samson and Delilah* which I saw in his studio shocked me
by the crudity of its conception, and its raw execution. In
spite of the praise of sycophantic painters, I persuaded him
not to show it at the forthcoming 'Secession'. When lately
I saw it again, in the Frankfort Gallery, I saw no reason to
change my judgment.

The artist whose work I most admired was Adolf
Menzel. This surprised the younger men, and the advanced
critics whom I met. The German painters seemed to me to
be neglecting the solid bourgeois qualities that had always
distinguished German work, to be losing faith in their own
culture and snatching at every latest fashion from France,
Sweden and Norway. Menzel alone was not ashamed of the
genial *bürgerlich* spirit which is the soul of German art.
I saw an astonishing set of gouache drawings at the print
room of the Kaiser-Friedrich Museum—heads of statesmen
and soldiers, studies for the historical pictures he had painted
for the old Emperor William, and a number of drawings
at the Zoological Gardens, also in gouache, which Degas
might have been proud to sign. Indeed, at his best, Menzel

53

was Degas' equal in draughtsmanship. As a painter in oils he was more commonplace, though no less accomplished.

The von Hofmanns frequently supped at the Zoo, in the most fashionable restaurant there, or, indeed, in Berlin, when dear old economical Frau von Hofmann would bring food for us all; we would sit at a table, brilliant with glass and silver, and beer would be ordered, while the Frau Excellenzin drew forth from her basket *belegtes brödchen* and other such delicacies. In those days such things could be done in Berlin —by Excellencies.

The von Hofmanns and the Kekulés were close friends of Cosima Wagner, whose son, Siegfried, entreated von Hofmann and myself to pay them a visit at Bayreuth after we returned from Rügen. I looked for Bayreuth in the German Bradshaw, found that it was a long way from Berlin, and a biggish fare, and made excuses. Bayreuth to one so unmusical as myself meant nothing. When I returned home, and told my parents of this invitation, they were amazed and indignant. How stupid I was! Of course they would have been only too willing to pay my expenses.

But we had a marvellous summer at Rügen; fine weather, and much work done. So beautiful was the landscape that if, on rare occasions, we saw an uninteresting effect, we used to shake hands in mutual congratulation—a momentary respite from ecstacy!

CHARLES CONDER

CHAPTER VI

A SECOND YEAR IN PARIS

IN October I returned to Paris. At Julian's during my first day some students were looking over a brown-paper sketch book I had filled during the summer. They were joined by a blond, rather heavily-built man, blue-eyed, bearded, with long hair parted in the middle and falling over his eyes. Later he came up to me and said kind things about the drawings. He spoke with a soft voice, and walked with a peculiar, rather shuffling gait. There was something oddly attractive about him. I saw the drawing he was doing, which was not very capable. After work that day we lunched together. He was an Englishman, he said, but had been sent out as a youth to Australia, where at first he had led an adventurous life in the Bush as a surveyor; later he had done drawings for newspapers, and finally he had become a painter. His name was Charles Conder. I felt a little shy with him; he knew so much more of the world than I did, or, I thought, than did any of my friends. We continued to meet at Julian's. He was living in Montmartre, a part of Paris then unknown to me. He took me to see his work, pale panels of flowers, and blonde Australian landscapes; a little weak and faded in colour, I thought, but with a delicate charm of their own. His studio contained little else save a divan covered with fine Indian materials—soft white muslins, with faint primrose and rose-coloured stains. Other muslins hung across the windows. Whistler, he said, was his favourite painter, and with him Puvis de Chavannes. He read me verses from

55

Omar Khayyam, then entirely new to me. I was enchanted by the boldness of the verses as well as by their beauty. Disbelief can claim close kinship with religious convictions; for doubt too comes from the gods, opening out shining new vistas, inspiring as those of a new faith. In Conder I also found an ardour for Browning which equalled my own. He talked to me of Ibsen, of whose plays I knew nothing, and of Janet Achurch, whom he had known in Australia, and of her wonderful acting in *The Doll's House*. I had not yet met anyone who was familiar with actors and actresses, and there, in his studio, was a beautiful photograph of Miss Achurch, signed by her hand and with his name on it. I was fascinated, but also a little disquieted, by his suggestive and oddly wandering talk. His painting too grew on me. But lovely colour meant less to me than good drawing, and strength and shrewd observation more than charm. There was no doubt, however, that Conder had unusual gifts. With an outlook in art so different from mine, it surprised me he cared, as he seemed to do, for my drawings. What impressed me most was his faculty for seeing quality and romance in people and things that I would pass by.

Studd, too, admired Conder's work, but was a little suspicious of his influence, and was inclined to dissuade me from seeing too much of him. But Conder seemed to have singled me out as a friend; and when he pressed me to join him at Montmartre, the idea of sharing a real studio was a formidable temptation. The left bank was very well for poets and scholars, but Montmartre was essentially the artists' quarter. Puvis de Chavannes had a studio on the Place Pigalle, while Alfred Stevens lived close by, and in the rue Victor Massé lived Degas. At Montmartre also were the Nouvelle Athènes and the Père Lathuille, where Manet, Zola, Pissarro and Monet, indeed, all the original Impressionists, used to meet. The temptation, therefore, to cross the river and live on the heights was too strong to resist. So I left my beautiful Empire room, and my safe, solid friends for a land unknown. I was only seventeen years old, and though in many ways

timid by nature, I had a blind faith in my star. Dangerous
things might happen to other people, but somehow I should
be protected.

The rue Ravignan lies above the Place Pigalle and the
Boulevard de Clichy. At the top of the street is an irregular
open space, bounded on the north by a flight of steps and
railings, just below which are the studios. Above the steps
was the pavilion of an eighteenth-century country house;
beyond lay old quiet streets, scattered villas with deserted
gardens and *terrains vagues*. In a low, rambling building,
which probably still exists (I went there some years later
with Augustus John to call on Picasso), were the studios,
mere wooden sheds with large windows; but great was my
pride at working in any place which could so be called.

Sharing a workroom was not, however, without grave
drawbacks. Conder's personality proved very attractive to
ladies; I found myself often in the way; there were difficulties
which led to quarrels, soon mended but often repeated.

I had not been long in Montmartre, however, when Phil
May arrived from Australia. He had made his name, and
some money too, as a cartoonist on *The Sydney Bulletin*; but
he wanted to improve his drawing, and at the same time
carry on fresh work for *The St Stephen's Review*, an illustrated
London weekly long extinct. Conder had known May in
Australia; so had Longstaff, an Australian painter with a
charming wife, then struggling to keep a roof over their heads
at Montmartre. Phil May and his wife were living in an
apartment at Puteaux. To us May seemed a man of wealth,
who could afford all the models he needed. He hoped to do
other work besides illustration, even to paint. May being extremely modest and having been so long away from Europe,
thought more of my drawings than they deserved. He pressed
me to share a studio with him, where he could come and
work from time to time. He would, of course, pay half the
rent, and would be delighted to have me share his models.
One of the studios in the rue Ravignan was to let, and he
proposed I should take it. Conder must have been as anxious

to get rid of me as I was to have a studio of my own. A camp-bed, a wooden table and two beautiful Louis XVI chairs (I had bought them near by for six francs each!), some draperies I had from Liberty's, and a cheap stove, sufficed for furniture. Such a stove, with its inside chimney fixed high up in the wall, was usual in every French studio. Delacroix painted a similar stove in a corner of his, and Degas and Forain have made it familiar in many pastels and drawings. The rent was modest—400 francs a year. Phil May in fact made little use of the studio; his failing was already noticeable, and the influence of Conder, who shared it, was detrimental to regular work. Poor Mrs May was often in despair. Phil somehow managed each week to get his weekly drawings done for *The St Stephen's Review*, and sometimes he sketched at night in cafés and *café-concerts*, but he did little else. There was no vice in him. He had a touchingly simple and affectionate character, but unfortunately he wasted himself and his means on a crowd of worthless strangers, who settled round his table like flies; while his terrible weakness for drink sapped his will and his physical strength.

May was illustrating a serial called *The Parson and the Painter*, for *The St Stephen's Review*, and later Whistler used to pretend that the figure of the parson was taken from me, and always called me 'the Parson' in consequence. Whistler praised Phil May's drawings very highly, a little to my surprise; for though I admired their precision and felicity, they did not seem to me to be in the same rank with those of Charles Keene and Forain.

Julian had recently opened a branch of his school in the rue Fontaine at Montmartre; Charles Duvent and several of my friends came there to work. Moreover, being no longer a 'nouveau', I found it much easier to make new friends. Montmartre, which of recent years has become a lure for Russian emigrants and foreign tourists, was, in the early 'nineties, essentially French.

At the rue Ravignan I found Henri Royer and Lomont, whom I had known slightly at Julian's; Royer, who came

CARICATURE OF HIMSELF, BY CHARLES CONDER

from Nancy, was a friend and pupil of another Nancy painter,
Émile Friant, already well known as a careful and capable
artist. Royer, Friant, Duvent, Louis Picard, and Major
Charvot, a retired army doctor, with a passion for painting,
lunched together at a restaurant on the Place Pigalle—le Rat
Mort, where I often joined them. The Rat Mort by night had
a somewhat doubtful reputation, but during the day was frequented by painters and poets. As a matter of fact it was a
notorious centre of lesbianism, a matter of which, being very
young, and a novice to Paris, I knew nothing. But this gave
the Rat Mort an additional attraction to Conder and Lautrec.
It was there that I first met Toulouse-Lautrec, Anquetin and
Édouard Dujardin. Friant, a bachelor of austere habits, who
had a studio on the Boulevard de Clichy, was a meticulous
and orderly painter, and though his work was somewhat cold
and literal, I greatly respected his deliberate thoroughness.
During the three years I was to stay in Paris, we continued
on intimate terms.

To the Rat Mort there often came the Belgian painter,
Alfred Stevens, a magnificent old ruin, broad-shouldered,
white-haired, with a fine head and a powerful frame still erect
in spite of his years. He was charming to young people, often
taking us across to his studio close by in the rue Alfred
Stevens (named after him), where he showed us his pictures.
Poor Alfred Stevens! he had been one of the great figures of
the Second Empire; all the great ladies of that glittering
period had passed through his studio. A great lover of
women, he had lived splendidly, earning largely; he had been
wildly extravagant and although he had once owned a whole
street, he was now reduced to living in a modest atelier and
a couple of rooms. More unfortunate still, he had debts, and
was driven to paint numbers of small pictures for dealers.
His instinct was for highly-wrought painting, for precious
and delicately handled pigment. Still, everyone treated 'le
Père Stevens' with great respect, for not only had he been a
great figure, but he had been a great painter as well. All that
remained of the treasures he had lavishly collected was a small

picture which he told us was by Holbein, the portrait of a
man, clean-shaved, against a green background. He would
fetch it out, and drawing aside a little curtain which protected the surface, he would say each time: 'We are going to
see whether his beard has grown over-night,' so living did
he feel this work to be. One day he climbed up to the rue
Ravignan to see my drawings. Le père Stevens was a great
talker and it was a privilege to hear him hold forth in his
powerful old voice on the Flemish masters, or to hear his
comments on contemporary painters. He had a particular
dislike for Carrière's work—'Il peint comme un cochon, cet
homme-là'—but he was the first French painter whom I
heard give high praise to Whistler. The distance between
eminent French artists and youngsters was much less in
Paris, I fancy, than it was in London, where, forty years ago,
Academicians were regarded as high Olympian figures.

The luncheon at the Rat Mort cost two francs, which was
rather a large sum for me, and towards the middle of the
month I was driven as a rule to lunch at more modest
restaurants. There were many such at Montmartre, frequented
by working-men, cabmen, and by struggling painters and
poets, and by women of the quarter. In one of these, kept by
a good, stout lady named Madame Bataille, close to the rue
Ravignan, we got excellent peaspudding, and there was always fresh, creamy cheese. Another small restaurant, where
the lunch cost little more than a franc, was a favourite resort
of Steinlen and Léandre. Steinlen was already making his
name as an illustrator, but was still very poor. There was a
natural gentleness, with a strain of melancholy, in his character, perhaps not unexpected in the illustrator of Bruant
and of the sinister characters of the exterior Boulevards; when
some years later I met George Gissing, he put me in mind of
Steinlen; there was a strong physical, as well as a spiritual,
likeness between the two. Léandre, then an obscure and
struggling painter, amused himself by drawing caricatures of
his friends after dinner; but he had not yet thought of becoming a professional caricaturist. Later he wisely gave up

painting and won fame, and fortune too I hope, with his caricatures in *Le Rire*. He was a charming fellow, gay and amusing, of whom Conder and I were very fond.

Conder felt himself more in sympathy with Frenchmen than with his own countrymen; he had a natural understanding for the genius of French art, especially for the art of the seventeenth and eighteenth centuries, which was beginning to have a marked effect on his outlook. He greatly admired Chèret's posters, then enlivening the Paris hoardings and kiosks, and Willette's drawings and paintings. Even when he came under Anquetin's influence he never ceased to admire Willette's wall-painting of the Moulin de la Galette, with its marionette-like figures, Pierrots and Pierrettes whirling round the sails of the mill, at a certain café—I knew it well, but the name now escapes me—a café presided over by a brother of Rudolph Salis. Willette was a refined and witty draughtsman, the creator of the contemporary Pierrot, a kind of Montmartre Watteau, careless of fame and money, with something of Murger's faithfulness to *la vie de Bohême*. Maurice Donnay and Xanrof were also familiar figures at Montmartre; they were to be met with constantly at the famous Chat Noir, where Rudolph Salis ruled over a tiny republic of poets, where they improvised and recited witty poems. Charles de Sivry, Verlaine's brother-in-law, provided the music. Close by was Aristide Bruant's Cabaret—Aristide, what a name! It will always be associated in my mind with a swaggering, massive figure, a broad-brimmed hat, blue-black hair, piercing, sombre eyes, and a cloak, a red muffler and top boots. Bruant was the poet of the exterior boulevard, of the Paris stews, of the bully and the harlot. People flocked to his café to hear him sing his sinister songs —sing is scarcely the word, he shouted them in a rough harsh voice, while he walked up and down the floor. Incidentally he made his hearers pay handsomely for their *consommations*. To us artists he liked to play the generous host, and in Lautrec's company one was sure of a welcome. Lautrec's poster of Bruant is now famous. Then there was

Rivière's *Marche à l'Étoile*, a beautiful little shadow play, at the Chat Noir. Can anyone wonder that youths like Conder and myself were fascinated by this strange and vivid life? To Conder it meant more, even, than to me; for it was in the night life of Paris that he found a great part of his inspiration. He found it too in the flowering orchards and the white cliffs of Normandy—a contrast indeed!

No place gave Conder so much as the Moulin Rouge. Here was an open-air *café-concert*, where one could watch people sitting and walking under coloured lamps and under the stars. Inside the great dancing hall, its walls covered with mirrors, he loved to study the crowds of men and women, moving round and round. Above all, there was the dancing of the *cancan*. Since those days much has been written about the dancers of the Moulin—the strange, forbidding figure of Valentin, hollow-eyed, hollow-cheeked, with his flat-brimmed, tall hat and his emaciated frame clad in an ungainly frock-coat and tight, wrinkled trousers; and La Goulue, Nini Pattes-en-l'air, and Rayon d'Or, and the rest of Zidler's extravagant pensioners. In most places dancers performed on a stage; at the Moulin they mixed with the crowd, or sat at tables and drank with admirers and friends. Then suddenly the band would strike up, and they formed a set in the middle of the floor, while a crowd gathered closely round them. It was a strange dance; a sort of quadrille, with Valentin and the other men twisting their legs into uncouth shapes, making gross gestures with hands and arms opposite their partners, their partners in the attitude of Vishnu, one leg on the ground, the other raised almost vertically, previous to the sudden descent—*le grand écart*. The most notorious of the women was La Goulue, an arresting blonde, short and plump, with a handsome, insolent face. She wore her yellow hair piled on top of her head, with a thick, low fringe and curling love locks, and a black ribbon tied round a full, strong throat. She was always bare-headed, while Rayon d'Or—surely a splendid name for a woman—tall and hard-featured, wore an enormous open-work hat on her bright red hair. Nini Pattes-en-

'CHEZ LUI LE MARDI' BY ANQUETIN

l'air was small and light on her feet; Grille d'Égout and La Môme Fromage were more than usually *canaille*, but skilful performers, while to me the single attractive figure was Jeanne Avril, called La Folle, a wild, Botticelli-like creature, perverse but intelligent, whose madness for dancing induced her to join this strange company. Conder painted many pictures of these dancers, in their foamy lace, black stockings and flaming skirts. He went almost nightly to watch them. I still remember the night when, Conder, May and I having drunk more than was good for us, Conder proposed we should each paint, there and then, a picture of the Moulin; and the wild results I remember, too, when we saw them in the cold morning light. It was at the Moulin that we became familiar with three *habitués*, Lautrec, Anquetin and Édouard Dujardin.

Toulouse-Lautrec and Anquetin were at this time the two leaders among the younger independent painters. Anquetin, of whom great things were expected—he was looked on as the most gifted and promising of the group that founded the Salon des Indépendants—was a man of magnificent physique. Broad-chested, with a powerful head and crown of thick, tufted hair, strong neck and ruddy complexion and a broken nose, he put one in mind at once of Michael Angelo. He was then doing striking pastels of men and women, vigorously coloured and amply drawn. They recalled the later work of Manet, with something of the Italian primitives. He made superb studies of the nude, and was probably the best equipped among the younger artists of the time. He was a profound student of the Louvre. Beginning as a naturalistic painter, he gradually became absorbed in the methods of Rubens, Poussin and Delacroix. Among the first to revive an understanding of baroque art, he was himself a baroque artist, unfortunately both after and before his time, with something of the superhuman nature of a character from Balzac. It was in part owing to Anquetin that Daumier was finally recognised as one of the supreme artists of the nineteenth century. Quietly sure of his own powers, physically

Painting the Moulin

and intellectually he moved among us all with a certain aloofness and proud indifference, his superiority tacitly acknowledged by all who knew him. If a visitor wished to see what he was doing he would point towards piles of canvases leaning against the walls and say: 'Look at anything you wish.' He saw so much more of what was needed to make a great artist than did any of us, and was arrogantly indifferent about his own work. It was for his conceptions, and his understanding of great painting, that he most valued his own gifts; his paintings and pastels were to him merely counters representing values known to himself alone. Like the artist in Balzac's *Chef d'Œuvre Inconnu* he became more and more absorbed in this inner vision. He had no great admiration for contemporary painting, believing that we had lost our way, and could only find it again by returning to the methods of the great masters. Meanwhile, like Lautrec, he had a searching eye for character, and chose for his models women who frequented places like the Moulin Rouge and the Moulin de la Galette. A study of one of these women, a pastel, hanging in the Tate Gallery, gives a good idea of the character of Anquetin's slighter work at this period.

Closely associated with Anquetin was Toulouse-Lautrec. There was nothing romantic about Lautrec. He was a frank, indeed a brutal, cynic. Human weaknesses lay naked and unprotected before his eyes. While he had a sincere respect for genius, for men and women themselves and for their ways he had none. Endowed with a keen intellect, he was quick to recognise intellectual gifts in others, but while he believed in the true and the beautiful, for the good he had neither belief nor understanding. Poor Lautrec! He was born under an unpropitious star. Dropped by his nurse while a baby, he had suffered arrest in the growth of his arms and legs, while his head and body were disproportionately large. With a broad forehead, fine and extremely intelligent eyes, he had lips of a startling scarlet, turned as it were outwards, and strangely wide, which gave a hideous expression to his face—a dwarf of Velazquez, with the genius of a Callot. Where

Conder saw in the Moulin and its dancers a glowing shim-
mering dream of Arabian Nights, Lautrec's unpitying eyes
noted only the sinister figures of *fille* and *souteneur*, of de-
generate and waster. A descendant of one of the noblest
families of France, since he could not live in the social world
to which he belonged, he would at least not deceive himself
and others about the company in which he chose to spend his
life. Balzac wrote that the artist, like the physician, must be
regarded, in his search for truth, as being above suspicion.
Lautrec explored a society which even a physician hesitates
to enter—an underworld whose existence is more frankly
acknowledged in France than in England. In *La Fille Elisa*,
Edmond de Goncourt had already probed deeply into the life
of a prostitute; but no artist has ever shown so brutally, so
remorselessly, as Lautrec, the crude ugliness of the brothel.
Nor can I imagine anyone else ready to face what Lautrec did
in order to get material for his studies. He seemed proof
against any shock to his feelings, and he deemed others
equally indifferent. He wanted to take me to see an execution; another time, he was enthusiastic about operations performed before clinical students, and pressed me to join him
at the hospital. I *did* often go with him to the Cirque Fernando, a circus then established at Montmartre, which Lautrec
used to visit assiduously, as he did the Moulin Rouge and
less reputable places.

One evening Lautrec came up to the rue Ravignan to tell
us about a new singer, a friend of Xanrof, who was to appear
at the Moulin Rouge for the first time. Anquetin, Dujardin,
Victor Jose, and some others were coming, and he wanted us
to join them to give her a good send off; she was intelligent,
not ordinary, and might easily fail to please a public fed on
Paulus. Besides, she was to come on early, and the early
turns were given to sparsely filled seats. We went; a young
girl appeared, of virginal aspect, slender, pale, without rouge.
Her songs were not virginal—on the contrary; but the fre-
quenters of the Moulin were not easily frightened; they
stared bewildered at this novel association of innocence with

Xanrof's horrific *double entente*; stared, stayed and broke
into delighted applause. Her success was immediate; crowds
came nightly to the Moulin to hear her, and the name of
Yvette Guilbert became famous in a week. Later she went
to the Divan Japonais, where Lautrec was able to watch her
more closely; he was very much alive to the piquancy of her
appearance and her rendering of the songs she chose. It
amused Lautrec to find formulas for a person's appearance,
which he reduced to the simplest expression; he had one for
Rodin, another for Degas, and one, as cruel as any, for himself. But, for some perverse reason, his drawings of Yvette
were among the most savage he ever made.

Nearly forty years afterwards—going to see Yvette in her
dressing room after one of her recitals in London, I reminded
her of her first appearance that night at the Moulin. She
looked quite startled to hear again of Lautrec and Willette—
'mais ils sont tous morts,' she said, in a tragic voice. Yvette
herself remains the great artist she was, but with something
ampler and richer in her interpretations. But it was not easy
to recognise in the stately matron the slim little *chiffonnée*
Yvette of the Moulin.

The lithographs Lautrec afterwards made of circus life are
perhaps the most remarkable of the records he has left. He
regarded Degas as his master, but he looked on Puvis de
Chavannes as the greatest living artist. The single picture on
his studio walls was a large photograph of Puvis' *Bois
sacré*. In startling opposition to this were a huge Priapic
emblem over his door, and an immense divan placed against
the wall. Lautrec undoubtedly deserves a niche to himself in
late nineteenth-century art. It is futile to assign the place an
artist is likely to take in the future. There are fashions in
immortality as there are trivial fashions. Some men may be
called life-classics. To say that an artist's work will live is not
to say that its life will be constant. Some works have an
inherent beauty and energy which may remain latent over
long periods, but are able to blossom again in the warmth of
renewed understanding. This later flowering may look very

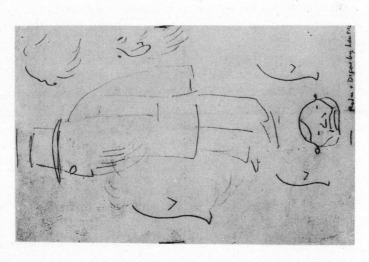

different to men's eyes from the original bloom. Books and
pictures read differently to different generations. Shakespeare
is not the same to us, neither on the stage nor in our studies,
as he was to the Elizabethans. It is not likely that every
generation will have the taste that we have for certain aspects
of life. To-day we incline, in our judgment of art, to make
saints of sinners and sinners of saints; our taste is for works
that are intense rather than profound. Not for a moment
would Lautrec have claimed equality with men like Degas or
Puvis de Chavannes, nor had he the puissant hand or great
mind of a Daumier. But with his misanthropy and his personal excesses, he had the spirit of an epicure—he saw the
artistic refinement of many revolting elements of human life.
In his drawings, his paintings, his posters and lithographs
there is a nervous refinement of design, a crisp sensitiveness
of contour, the fruit of his discernment and daring. Both
Lautrec and Anquetin recognised the loveliness of Conder's
paintings. Conder was, indeed, becoming one of the notables
of Montmartre. Though his French was inaccurate and vague
as his painting, like his painting it revealed a rich and discerning mind.

CHAPTER VII

PARIS INFLUENCES AND SOME LADIES. WHISTLER

Three artists LAUTREC, like Conder, was destined to die early, a victim
of dissolute habits. Very different characters, all three of
them wise and sober youths, were Bonnard, Lomont and
Vuillard, this last a gentle creature with a fierce red beard,
whom I first met at the Coquelins'. Lomont had a very tender
and beautiful nature. With fair hair, blue eyes and slight fair
whiskers, he looked the typical French painter or poet of the
'thirties. He painted tranquil and intimate interiors. Bonnard
was not yet painting interiors, he was doing work which was
influenced by Chèret, and by Japanese prints. For just as there
was later a movement towards the cube, towards exaggerated
volumes, so at this time a new interest in the primitives, and
the vogue for the Japanese print, led to a flattening of tones
and a hardening of contours. Full modelling appeared almost
vulgar. 'Jamais je ne voterai pour un homme qui sait modeler
un œil,' Manet was reported to have said when he had
abandoned his early solid *matière* for a lighter vehicle. This
simplified approach was, in many cases, a mere formula. True
simplification comes after the gradual shedding of much one
would like to retain; it is a radiant fullness, from which needless detail has been removed. Simplicity is the final candour
of things.

The Japanese print cut across the sound French tradition
of *la bonne peinture*, away from the luminous and nacreous
handling of Chardin and Watteau. Most of us were seduced

by this novelty, which, incidentally, led us away from the
pursuit of form. We thought flat pictures more 'artistic' than
solidly painted ones; Gauguin and Seurat had shown new
and exciting canvases of this sort, and the younger painters,
ignoring the trend of a true painter like Renoir, were doing
work halfway between the primitives and the Japanese. But
there was an empty simplicity that was merely baldness; the
effect of poverty of invention or affectation.

Anquetin foresaw the menace of alien influences, and returned to the great European tradition of painting. But others,
like Vuillard, Maurice Denis and Bonnard (Matisse was then
doing quite pedestrian work), never attained the solid practice of older men like Degas, Renoir and Fantin-Latour, and
were among the first to show signs of the decline that was
to infect French painting. French culture flourished while it
remained true to itself, an essentially French self. While
French painters were too absorbed in their work to trouble
about alien cultures all was well; but when they began to
turn towards strange gods from the East and from Africa,
weakness came on them. The twentieth century was to see
the disappearance of that probity which was the glory of
nineteenth-century French painters; while a limited objective,
with a certain success, which enables painters to supply
picture-dealers with canvases in such quantities, was to take
the place of the far-reaching achievement of the older
painters.

Gauguin, a friend of Toulouse-Lautrec, was then working
in Brittany. When later I passed his house at Pont-Aven, on
the door of which he had carved some strange, primitive
figures, I found it shut up; he had gone to Tahiti.

Edouard Dujardin, a Wagner propagandist, and associated
with the symbolist movement in literature, was a close friend
of Anquetin and of Toulouse-Lautrec, and a frequenter of
Montmartre. How much better off he was than most of us
I cannot say, but he had the appearance and manners of a
French dandy. With full brown beard and eye-glass, well-
cut clothes and spotless linen, he looked a figure apart; indeed,

he was a figure apart from his kind, and associated with painters more than with writers and poets. He was something of an Anglophile, and he and Conder became fast friends—a friendship which was destined to become clouded. From Dujardin I first heard of George Moore.

After the quiet and sheltered life at the rue de Beaune, the Montmartre days ran into many late nights. Happily, young people can stand late hours without any serious effects on their health or work. I was up early enough in the morning, however late to bed. The Moulin Rouge, with its dancers, was a constant source of inspiration to Conder; to me it was not; but a sense that I was somehow very close to life in these places took me often there, as well as to the Moulin de la Galette, a more plebeian dancing hall little known to strangers, frequented only by the working-girls and youths of the quarter. The Moulin Rouge was full of colour, this other Moulin had a dark and dusty interior. The quarter of Montmartre where it stood had in fact an evil reputation, and knives and pistols were sometimes in use. Much of the life of the quarter was indeed repellent, unnatural and rather frightening, but I affected indifference and the ways of a person thoroughly seasoned to adventure and to the company of shady people. Goethe says somewhere that young men of spirit are apt for a time to turn their backs on their true selves, to which they are bound to return later. It is true that youth loves to masquerade in mind as in body; but I had been pitchforked into a society more abnormal than most.

It is the fashion at present to scoff at any association of morality with art. It is true that an artist often puts his best self into his work, and in active life may show the weaker side of his nature. Theoretically, art and morals are undoubtedly two different things. Whether there are golden threads running through the warp and woof of the fabric of life which, when seen from afar, form a moral pattern, is matter of eternal dispute among poets and philosophers. But although the reality of this pattern has been questioned by some, its recognition by human eyes is of great practical value. A strong man is likely to regard anything which weakens his will as immoral. It is not perhaps so much a moral as a practical question. Renoir, Cézanne, Whistler, Degas, Puvis de Chavannes, Fantin-Latour, all lived to practise their art to a ripe age. Many of the younger artists I knew died before they could develop their powers to fruition. They wasted their strength in drink and other excesses. The night life at Montmartre, which mesmerised so many of us, was stupidly futile. Men fished for women, and women for men, in muddy water, and drink was the bait they used.

We looked to the older men, of course, for guidance. The days were not yet when it was the fashion to over-estimate the work of our own generation. But our battle on their behalf was not yet won. Their artistic integrity was still challenged by most people. The official Salon remained, like the Royal Academy, the focus of popular interest. Manet's *Olympia* was about to be bought, in the teeth of furious opposition, for the Louvre. At Durand-Ruel's, paintings which now fill the European galleries and the great private collections, on which vast sums are now spent, could be purchased forty years ago for a very few thousand francs. Old Monsieur Durand-Ruel, his son and assistants, would always allow us artists to indulge in their treasures. Most of the work of the older generation of Impressionists passed through their hands. Their gallery, between the rue le Pelletier and the rue Lafitte, was to me a kind of second Louvre.

In the meanwhile I was working at Julian's, where my aims were somewhat confused. If there was the incredible draughtsmanship of Ingres and Degas, was there not Whistler's as well, which with less knowledge and skill achieved results which seemed to me equal to theirs? Puvis himself was a naive and somewhat clumsy draughtsman, and I saw that for all their dexterity Meissonnier, Carolus Duran and Bonnat, men of great abilities, were far inferior to painters of genius like Puvis and Whistler. It was my misfortune that, compared with Conder and other of my friends, I appeared

71

to be a fairly efficient draughtsman; but my drawing was far
from being thorough, and I wish that someone had taken me
to task and shown me what knowledge and skill, how much
will-power and intense application, are needed to make a
good artist. But many young men were in like case. We were
living then, as we are now, at a time of shifting standards.
Capable work that was unintelligent and lacking in any sense
of beauty was rightly condemned; but we were too apt to
believe that an interesting contour and liveliness of handling
condoned other shortcomings. On the other hand, to distrust
the pretentious and showy Salon picture was sound. At least
the men I was with were trying to say what they meant in
their painting.

Whereas in England Whistler's disciples, the youthful élite,
cared little for either Morris or Burne-Jones, the younger
French painters, among them Lautrec, Seurat and Gauguin,
all revered Puvis de Chavannes. For Puvis, while profoundly
influenced by both the Greeks and the early Italians, brought
a fresh vision to bear on the contemporary world. His mural
paintings at the Panthéon and the Sorbonne, his *Pauvre
Pêcheur* at the Luxembourg, were accepted as classics during
his lifetime. I remember the enthusiasm with which his decorations, *L'Été* and *L'Hiver*, for the Hôtel de Ville were
received when they were shown at the Champ de Mars.
Puvis' work had the flavour of naivety, both of form and
design, which we were beginning to relish. Gauguin and
Van Gogh were to insist still more on the primitive, on the
passionate, element in painting, which modern refinement,
they believed, must destroy. But this insistence on a particular and partial aspect of painting had not yet emerged; the
older men like Puvis were able to relate to the whole their
preoccupation with the parts. Although not aware of it then,
we were seeing the last of the heroes. It was the swan-song
of an epoch when discipline and genius went lovingly arm in
arm. I was to see them parted, alas! and coldly estranged; and
although there are some whose interest it is to keep them
apart, as is always the case in quarrels, and others who side

with the one, or with the other, yet their mutual interest,
their ancient, deep need of each other, will once more unite
those true, lusty lovers, if not to-day, then to-morrow, or,
surely, soon after.

I doubt if I foresaw this estrangement; nor was I aware
of the practice necessary to become a good artist. When I saw
pictures like Manet's *Olympia*, or Degas' *Leçon de Danse*,
or Fantin-Latour's portrait group in the Luxembourg, I did
not ask myself whether I was preparing myself for such
efforts as theirs; I blindly took it for granted that, since I
belonged to the advanced school, all would be well.

While Conder had a natural gift for expressing the charm
and radiance of women, my inclination was in the direction
of character. I probably made myself a nuisance by bothering
all my friends to sit to me for drawings. With these I filled
many sketch books. I made them not only during the day,
but also on most evenings in the cafés wherever we met.
Conder worked largely from memory, and the time we spent
in places like the Moulin Rouge was, for his purpose, well
spent. For me it was largely wasted; for the artistic appeal,
so strong to Conder, was slight in my case. Associating with
men all of whom were older than myself, I was living in a
world to which I had not really grown up. That I was also
living, in the eyes of my soberer friends, rather perilously,
flattered my vanity. There is a dangerous attraction in a sense
of exile, in a feeling of separation from the herd, even in the
disapproval of sober people; there is also a charm to be living
in circumstances which wear a character of romance, to be
reading Balzac and Stendhal, Barbey d'Aurevilly and Villiers
de l'Isle-Adam, and to find oneself at supper parties among
poets and painters and their women friends, the Esthers and
Coralies of the day. The time was not yet when artists found
easy companionship among women who belonged to their
own social circle; moreover, something unusual in dress and
appearance will always quicken the interest of artists; and
since breadth and radiance of form move an artist deeply, his
model, to whatever class she belongs, once she is sitting, is

73

near to perfection. That artists often find their inspiration in
men and women at whom the world looks askance does not
mean that they are unaware of the fine qualities of tact and
conduct of women of delicate breeding. There is also this to
be said: men like Conder are able to see in women whom
others would pass by, elements of profound beauty; and
by making these women more aware of their beauty they are
able to bring them a new and joyful pride in what they
themselves have to give. In return for such gifts of beauty
Conder was a spendthrift of time. Often he would disappear
for days, and his paints and brushes would lie idle. Then in
pressing need, he would emerge, and panels would be produced to be turned into bread and butter. The metamorphosis
was not always easily accomplished. So sometimes he sat
alone; for Aline has her rent to pay and Yvonne needs pretty
dresses.

I was often called upon for sympathy when Conder was
in difficulties. Sober men are, alas, poor comforters, and
sorry companions for men crowned with vine leaves. 'Will,
don't look so sensible,' said Oscar Wilde one evening, as I sat
with him and Conder and Max at the Café Royal. I looked
too often at my watch; perhaps a sitter was waiting, and
Conder's dreamy eyes would become mocking. 'Oh, Will,
do stay; the Bird of Time has but a little way to flutter, and
the Bird is on the wing.' But sensible at bottom I was. The
wine that was red did not call up visions in me as it did in
Conder. So I used to say that half my friends disapproved
of me because I sat with wine bibbers, and the other half
because I did not drink.

Poor Phil May got little from looking into the cup. With
him it was but a stupefying and pernicious habit, which gave
him nothing save headache and remorse. Though Conder
knew that his terrible infatuation would one day destroy him,
it did at least set free in him a thousand fancies; his mind was
never more fertile than it was *à l'heure verte*. Rather sleepy
and tongue-tied in these early days, when prompted by wine
he became radiant, joyous and talkative. He could give en-

74

chanting expression to fantastic and lovely ideas, which ran
through his brain; and when we had quarrelled he knew very
well how to win me back. There was a strong feminine strain
in his nature, soft and feline. When he was away he wrote
letters which, in their wandering way, were as charming as
his talk. He talked much to me about style, and counted,
then and afterwards, for much in my imaginative education.

How many poor things to my eyes seemed possessed of
style—precisely that which they lacked! I can understand the
attraction for youngsters to-day of such deceptive work.
I imitated Louis Legrand, Lunel, even the German Schlittgen.
Youngsters naturally sow their artistic wild oats. Looking at
old sketch books it is easy to see what influence had taken
possession of me. The old Slade copies of Michael Angelo,
Leonardo and Dürer had left no traces. Conder was always
trying to influence me in the direction of a romantic, suggestive manner of drawing, admirably suited to his temperament, but foreign to mine. He never aimed at precision of
form, and had little natural power of constructive drawing;
he had, however, a fine sense of material quality. Similarly
with his painting: his form was weak, but he had remarkable
gifts for composition and movement. He was able to do what
many more accomplished artists never achieved, to make his
figures act on paper or on canvas precisely as he wished them
to act, like a *maître de ballet* with his eager pupils. His figures
were all playing parts, but they were parts perfectly made for
them, and directed by Conder himself. It was this power to
evoke an ideal world peopled with lovely figures, which I
admired in Conder so much.

But actual life he also saw as a dream world. He would sit
night after night, at the Abbaye de Thélème or the Rat Mort,
storing his memory with scenes which afterwards served him
well for his lithographs. Sometimes drink made him very
quarrelsome, and more than once he got into difficulties; but
he could never keep away from the night-life of Montmartre
while his money lasted. I could understand the fascination
of many of the women who frequented the night restaurants,

75

but the men we met there were, some of them, sinister and repugnant, foolish wasters of life. But at times I, too, got a glimpse of the poetry which Conder extracted from this society of night-hawks. I can still see a beautiful young girl —Yvonne she was called—standing by the French window under the lamp-light, dressed in red, wearing a large grey hat with a drooping ostrich feather, tired and startlingly pale, against the deep blue lapis sky. And Conder himself when his face was flushed, his eyes bright, looked magnificent; though by day he looked tired and heavy-eyed.

Yvonne, Juliette, Aline, Germaine, even now I can visualise your charm and your beauty very clearly. Can it be that you have grown old, like others I have known since, once fair like you! But not having seen you again since the days of your careless youth, time seems to have left your comely looks and lovely limbs unchanged; though I know you must be old and wrinkled now, who were once so smooth and young.

I stayed but a few months in the rue Ravignan; I found a more convenient studio lower down the hill, in the rue Fontaine, almost opposite Julian's. Soon after I moved, a number of students arrived from England, among them Walter Russell, William Llewellyn, Pegram, Townsend, Ronald Grey and Arthur Blunt. This year Roger Fry also came from Cambridge, where he had been at King's College with Studd. He had done very little drawing; I gathered that he had moved chiefly in scientific and philosophical circles; but he had a quiet attractiveness, and he was clearly very intelligent. He did not stay long in Paris; he was not much of a figure draughtsman and he was somewhat shy and uneasy at first in the free atmosphere of Julian's. He had rather the habits and reserve of the student, and was more at home in the quieter atmosphere of Cambridge and London. Lowes Dickinson, a man who instantly won my regard and affection, came to stay with Fry for a time.

The only English students who lived in Montmartre were Curtis and Warrener. Warrener flung himself into the most

advanced movements then prevalent in Paris. He usually
painted nude figures out-of-doors, set against a background
of the shrillest chrome yellow and viridian green the colour
merchant provided. I don't remember his painting any other
subjects, or working with a more subdued palette, although
he was a keen admirer of Lautrec, who drew him more than
once: a good portrait of him appears in one of Lautrec's well-
known posters. I thought Warrener would carry the chrome
flag back to England, and lead a revolution, but he apparently
gave up painting. He is now a distinguished citizen of Lincoln, guiding public taste in his native city.

If there were few English artists, there were many Americans—Alexander Harrison, Frederick Macmonnies, J. W.
Alexander, Gari Melchers, Paul Bartlett and Walter Gay,
were then all living in Paris. Harrison enjoyed a great
reputation among Frenchmen. He was a *plein air* painter,
and had made his name with a painting of nude figures sitting
about among trees. To paint figures *en plein air* was then the
fashion. His sea-studies were prominent features in every
salon, and well liked. He was on intimate terms with Monet
and Rodin, and wore the ribbon of the Legion of Honour in
his buttonhole. I was inclined to a rather extreme attitude in
my landscape work, though my painting was sober enough
by the side of Warrener's, and Harrison challenged the violet
I used too freely in my shadows. He urged me to see things
soberly and gave me much sound advice. I joined him once
on a walking tour along the coast of Brittany, starting from
Quimper and walking through Pont-Aven, then a famous
artists' village where Gauguin had lately worked, to Concarneau. The Breton women and girls have a simple gravity
which many years later I recognised in the faces of Indian
peasant women, a gravity with which their dress and *coiffes*
are in keeping. And how subtle are the cut and shape of the
peasant dress! England has shed her local costumes entirely,
even the ordinary smock has disappeared. We are losing a
great inheritance of beauty. But in France, and yet more in
Germany, one still sees the old dresses worn. At this time

every Breton village had its own *coiffe*, and both men and women wore the traditional dress.

As we walked into Concarneau a fleet of little fishing boats was coming into the harbour. Beautiful these looked, with their slanting sails in the evening light. It was amusing to see a crowd of women wade into the sea to meet the boats as they came into the harbour, carrying their husbands on their backs from the boats to the shore. Harrison was a charming companion. He spoke French perfectly and understood the French character. Alexander, who had recently come to paint portraits in Paris, was more typically American. I knew his work, having seen his portraits reproduced in the American magazines, notably one of Walt Whitman. He had a studio on the Boulevard Berthier, where he and his wife entertained. He painted life-size portraits in one or two sittings, very skilfully; among others he did was one of myself in exchange for a pastel I made of him. He had much success with these portraits at the Salon du Champ de Mars; for the English tradition of portraiture, which American painters generally followed, was admired in Paris.

A much abler painter was Anders Zorn, who lived at Montmartre, a genial Swede, then winning his way to fame as a painter and etcher. His work was coarse and literal, but extraordinarily skilful and well constructed. He showed me a little wood-carving, a head of his mother, more tender and sensitive than any of his painting. Zorn was a noble trencherman; he rarely dined out, but meals at his table, presided over by Mme Zorn, were on a grand scale, as were Thaulow's later at Dieppe. I marvel now at the kindness of all these men, to a youngster still in his teens.

Another friend was Paul Bartlett, the sculptor, whose beautiful wife Alexander was painting. They lived outside Paris, at Passy, I think. Then there was Walter Gay. Both he and his wife were people of exceptional charm, whose house was full of beautiful pictures and furniture. I still saw much of Studd and Frazier, who had left the rue de Beaune and were now in the rue Madame, where Dermod O'Brien, who

THE WRITER ÆT. XIX, BY EMILE FRIANT

was working at Julian's too, often joined us. Frazier had relations living in Paris, and he and Studd knew a good many people.

To meet someone who shares one's admirations, to unpack one's mind and have one's convictions reinforced by a fresh intelligence, in short the discovery of artistic affinity, is a pleasure which youth alone can enjoy to the full. And in any company of people seemingly commonplace and unreceptive, how delicious to sit down in a corner with a woman of finer clay than the rest, whose sympathy flatters and caresses. Certain figures remain still radiant in my memory: Miss Hope Temple, a singer, golden-haired, who first spoke to me of Delius; Mlle D'Anethan, distinguished-looking, with a finely tempered intelligence which had gained her the friendship of Alfred Stevens, of Puvis de Chavannes and of Whistler. How proud I was of her encouragement! I recollect that Puvis painted her portrait, which he exhibited together with one of Georges Rodenbach, a Belgian poet of great promise, who died young. I thought Puvis' portraits beautiful, very simple, almost naïve; but I have seen none since those early days. Besides Mlle D'Anethan, Marie Baschkirtseff's friend, the painter Mlle Breslau, was kind and encouraging. So was Miss Lee Robbins, a favourite pupil of Carolus Duran, at whose studio I met the hyacinthine-locked *maestro* himself. Others studying painting, Miss McGinnes, who became Mrs Albert Herter, and Mrs Frederick Macmonnies, were the centre of an attractive circle. Mrs Macmonnies, herself like a Florentine portrait, was making copies of the newly found Botticelli frescoes in the Louvre, frescoes which still seem to me among Botticelli's loveliest works. Other friends were the Misses Kinsella, one of whom, Miss Kate Kinsella (now the Marchesa Presbitero), was, and still is, a highly gifted painter. All three were striking looking, Miss Louise being one of the reigning beauties. I had the temerity to ask her to sit, making a Holbeinesque full-length portrait in pastel, and.beginning a large oil painting. Later she sat to Whistler who could, and did, do her beauty justice.

The portrait he painted bid fair to be the most distinguished
work of his later years; but, as often with his portraits, he
scraped out, repainted, and lost his way. I thought Miss
Kinsella one of the noblest women I had ever seen; her placid
and ingenuous nature gained her many devoted friends, in
England as well as in Paris. But I was from the first aware
that both in my drawing and painting, charm, which came
naturally to Conder, evaded me. Conder painted a lovely
portrait of Louise Kinsella, seated in an orchard, holding a
bright green apple in her hand. She, with her large heart,
tried to save Conder from habits that hurt him; but though
he struggled hard, he could not make the sacrifices that were
needed, and they finally trod different paths.

To the Kinsellas' came often Logan Pearsall Smith, a young
American fresh from Oxford, with all the American's interest
in the latest phases of art and literature, and a weakness, not
uncommonly associated with the Puritan temperament, for
probing, a little indiscreetly, into the character and habits of
his friends and acquaintances. In his case it was easy to forgive a curiosity which incubated a fruitful delineation of the
vagaries of human nature. With an analytical mind delighting
in intellectual discussion, he had a true respect for the integrity of the artist; further, he proved a generous and loyal
friend.

And of course besides all these charming people, one had
to endure some intolerable bores and their work, and the
need to comment on, and admire, one canvas after another,
pushed in front of one. There were so many men copying
the Impressionists and Symbolists; men with little talent or
none imagined that they were doing interesting work, when
they lacked the ability to paint a single figure, a simple landscape or a piece of still-life with the capacity of the ordinary
student working in the ateliers. Nothing so lowers one's
vitality as a false relation with some other person; one can
scarcely look a bore in the face, or find a word for one's
tongue; the mind becomes stagnant, the circulation slow and
thick, as canvas after canvas is thrust before one; and then to

be asked to say exactly what one thinks! good gracious, one's
only thought is to rush outside into the clean air and to rid
one's soul of such poison. Paris was then as full of pseudo-
geniuses as is London to-day; men angling for notice with
sorry, pretentious bait. No kinship with these! Heaven
forbid! With men who, fighting, fail—yes, but not with
charlatans or self-deceivers; their society is poisonous; bad
spiritual food is a poison no less than bad fish or bad meat.
Yet how pathetic these men who cling to the fringe of the
arts! feebly imagining, since they know in their hearts they
can never be *good* artists, that somehow they may prove to
be *interesting* ones. They drug themselves with the hope that
what was done without conviction, may yet convince others.

Conder suffered these parasites gladly. He had more
patience perhaps, or was better-natured than I; or maybe he
liked someone to drink with rather than drink alone.

The most notable personality among the Americans I met
with in Paris was Miss Ruebell, granddaughter of a Ruebell
who had been one of the Consuls during the Revolution.
She was a striking figure, with her bright red hair crowning
an expressive but unbeautiful face, her fingers and person
loaded with turquoise stones. In face and figure she reminded
me of Queen Elizabeth—if one can imagine an Elizabeth
with an American accent and a high, shrill voice like a parrot's.
All that was distinguished in French, English and American
society came at one time or another to her apartment in the
Avenue Gabriel; she was adept at bringing out the most
entertaining qualities of the guests at her table. She would
often ask us to meet people whom she felt we would like, or
who she thought might be of use. A maiden lady, with a
shrewd and original mind, she permitted anything but dull-
ness and ill manners, delighting in wit and paradox and adventurous conversation. It was at her house that I first met
Henry James, and later—a momentous event in my life—
I was introduced there to Whistler. She was also a great
friend and admirer of Oscar Wilde, to whom she was constantly loyal, despite Whistler's jibes.

81

Henry James often came to Paris, where he had numerous
friends. He was *persona grata* among French writers, as well
as among his own compatriots. He took a great fancy to
Frazier, and often wandered into the studio in the rue
Madame. He was charming to all of us; he liked young
people, and all his life he had been closely associated with
painters and sculptors. I was amused by his slow and exact
way of speaking. He was not in those days so massive as he
became later, either in person or manner, but he was already
elaborately precise and correct. He always carried his silk
hat, stick and gloves into the room when he paid a call, laying
hat and gloves across his knee. I had not read his writings,
and knew him only as a discerning lover of Paris, who delighted in its old streets and houses, and as an arresting talker,
of course.

One night, when some of us dined with Miss Ruebell, she
told us that Henry James had brought a young Englishwoman to see her, a Mrs Woods from Oxford. She was a
writer, the daughter of a Dean, and the wife of the Head of
an Oxford college. Mrs Woods had just written a book, *A
Village Tragedy*, which Henry James praised highly. Her
next book was to deal, in part, with an artist's life in Paris;
she was therefore desirous of meeting some painters. Would
we come and meet her at dinner, and perhaps show her something of studio life? So we gaily concerted to take the en-
quiring lady to some innocent restaurant, where our friends
would dress up *à la Murger*, and play the fool generally.
However, when in fact we did meet Mrs Woods at Miss
Ruebell's, our hearts at once melted. Instead of a prim blue-
stocking we found a delicate, Shelley-like person, who talked
delightfully in a clear, silvery, incisive voice. I was placed
next to her at dinner and began a friendship which has proved
ever closer and richer with the years.

But to return to Whistler: I doubt whether the present
generation of young artists and writers admires its older contemporaries as we admired some of ours. Admired seems
too weak a word. To me Whistler was almost a legendary

figure, whom I never thought to meet in the flesh. I must
have felt very shy on this occasion. Mrs Whistler, an ample
and radiant figure, who was, I think, amused and pleased at
our obvious reverence for her husband (I say *our* reverence,
for Studd, Frazier and Howard Cushing had also been bidden
to meet 'the master') put me at once at my ease, asking us all
to come and see them when they were settled in their new
apartment in the rue du Bac. Was it possible I was really to
meet the great man again, and in his own house? They were
to be at home on Sundays, she said; but before the next
Sunday came round, early one morning there came a knock
at my door, and who should walk into my studio but Whistler
himself. I was quite unprepared for his visit, and somewhat
abashed, at which Whistler was pleased, I think, for he
laughed and walked lightly round, examined all I had hung
on the walls, rolled a cigarette and asked to see what I was
doing. My friends Studd and Frazier must have spoken
generously of my efforts to Whistler; there was a strong
element of curiosity in his nature—the reason, perhaps, of his
visit. The next day came a little note asking me to dine,
accompanied by a copy of one of his brown-paper pamphlets,
with an inscription signed with his butterfly.

He had found an enchanting apartment set far back in the
rue du Bac, a small, late-eighteenth century pavilion which,
as he usually did with his houses, he had completely transformed. The outer door, painted a beautiful green and white,
gave promise of what was within—a small and exquisite
interior: a sitting room simply furnished with a few pieces of
Empire furniture, and a dining room filled with his famous
blue and white china and beautiful old silver. There was a
Japanese bird-cage in the middle of the table, whereon he and
Mrs Whistler used to make lovely, trailing arrangements of
flowers in blue and white bowls and little tongue-shaped
dishes. There was a single picture on one of the dining room
walls, but none, I think, in the sitting room.

Outside was a good sized garden, into which, one day,
Whistler's favourite parrot flew. Neither coaxing nor food

would tempt it down; it finally died from starvation. Next door was a convent, from which came the frequent sound of the nuns chanting. Whistler liked old ways, and this added to the charm of his Paris retreat.

Keen-eyed Whistler! fixing one with his monocle, quick, curious, now genial, now suspicious. One walked delicately, but in an enchanted garden, with him. He found amusement, I think, in my inexperienced ways. I remember his joy when, during a dinner-party at his house, my white tie—I was only just learning to tie my own tie—came slowly undone. He wanted always to know what one was doing, whom one was seeing. There was a certain gaunt, wan, Botticelli-like model (she was a friend of Ary Renan) who sat to me a good deal, whom he pretended to believe me in love with. He liked to assume that I lived a Don Juan-like career—a fancy he had that was half embarrassing, half flattering to a foolish youth. But his chaff was tempered by a charming interest in our work, which he always treated with respect. For anyone he admitted to his friendship must needs be an artist—how could he be otherwise?

Whistler complained bitterly of his treatment in England. He never tired of disparaging England and all things English. His strictures were sometimes amusing; but at times a little tiresome. One afternoon the Whistlers took me to a party— at the American Ambassador's, I think—where a famous American dancer was to dance. On the way, Whistler said something about the British flag covering a union—of hypocrites. For her last dance the lady was arrayed in the American flag, and I whispered to Whistler that I was bound to admit that the Stars and Stripes at any rate concealed very little. Whistler enjoyed a jest of this kind; indeed, he allowed one a good deal of latitude, so long as one was 'accepted', and he often repeated the indiscretions of 'the vicar' with amusement. He used to produce derogatory press-cuttings from his pocket and read them aloud; meanwhile I would ask myself why he took notice of such trivialities. Was he not Whistler, the acknowledged master? I know now that great artists are as

84

fallible as small ones, that small things annoy them as much
as great ones do; but I had much less knowledge of human
nature then. And because I was dazzled by Whistler's brilliant wit, by his exquisite taste, and of course by the beauty
of his work, so I thought his powers beyond question, and
I was puzzled that anyone else should fail to think likewise.
He was so obviously a prince among men. There was something extraordinarily attractive, too, about his whole person.
He wore a short black coat, white waistcoat, white ducks and
pumps; a low collar and a slim black tie, carefully arranged
with one long end crossing his waistcoat. He had beautiful
hands, and there was a certain cleanness and finish about the
lines of his face, the careful arrangement of his hair, and of
his eyebrows. On Sunday afternoons, while talking to
his visitors he usually had a little copper plate in his hands,
on which he would scratch from time to time. But at this
time I think he did more lithographs than etchings. He was
experimenting with coloured lithographs, and it was at his
studio in the rue Notre Dame des Champs that he made the
beautiful drawings, on a special kind of transfer paper, from
his favourite model, Carmen.

In spite of his constant reference to the stupidity of the
English and the intelligence of the French, I doubt whether
Whistler's work was so well understood in Paris as it was in
London. It was rather the cosmopolitan painters—Boldini,
Gandara, Helleu, Tissot, Jacques Blanche—who knew and
understood him and his work. He was generally considered
a mere shadow of Velazquez and of Manet; something of a
poseur, in fact, as Wilde was in England.

CHAPTER VIII

OSCAR WILDE

A visit from Wilde I HAD heard of Wilde only vaguely as the original of du Maurier's Postlethwaite, as Bunthorne in Gilbert and Sullivan's *Patience*, the young man who walked down Picca-dilly with a poppy and a lily; and when one day Frazier burst into my studio to announce that Wilde was coming up the stairs, I expected to meet someone pale and slender. Great was my surprise at seeing a huge and rather fleshly figure, floridly dressed in a frock coat and a red waistcoat. I was not at all attracted by his appearance. He had elaborately-waved, long hair, parted in the middle, which made his forehead appear lower than it was, a finely shaped nose, but dark-coloured lips and uneven teeth, and his cheeks were full and touching his wide winged collar. His hands were fat and useless look-ing, and the more conspicuous from a large scarab ring he wore. But before he left I was charmed by his conversation, and his looks were forgotten. Whistler, whom I told of this visit, was pitiless in his comments. Soon after, I met Wilde again at Miss Ruebell's, and again found his talk enchanting. He held the whole table both during and after dinner.

Oscar Wilde talked of me as a sort of youthful prodigy; he was enthusiastic about my pastels. He introduced me to Robert Sherard, to Marcel Schwob, and to Rémy de Gour-mont, to a new circle of writers and poets. Studd, who had got to like Conder, distrusted Wilde. I, who was in some ways more innocent than most youths of my age, saw little to be afraid of in this new friendship. There was certainly something florid, almost vulgar, in his appearance; and his manners were emphasised. But he was not only an unique talker and story-teller—I have never heard anyone else tell stories as he did—but he had an extraordinarily illuminating intellect. His description of people, his appreciation of prose and verse, were a never-failing delight. He seemed to have read all books, and to have known all men and women. Tell me about so and so, Oscar, you would ask; and there would come a stream of entertaining stories, and a vivid and genial personal portrait. He was remarkably free from malice. Moreover, I had met no one who made me so aware of the possibilities latent in myself. He had a quality of sympathy and understanding which was more than mere flattery, and he seemed to see better than anyone else just what was one's aim; or rather he made one believe that what was latent perhaps in one's nature had been actually achieved. Affected in manner, yes; but it was an affectation which, so far as his conversation was concerned, allowed the fullest possible play to his brilliant faculties. If a man have great wit, he may be excused for adopting some mannerism for holding the attention of his company. In the clatter of general conversation the wisest or the wittiest remarks may pass unnoticed. Painters show their pictures, poets publish their poems, why should not a talker, when the mood is on him, make sure of being heard? Wilde talked as others painted or wrote; talking was his art. I have certainly never heard his equal; whether he was improvising or telling stories—his own or other people's—one was content that his talk should be a monologue. Whistler's jibe about Oscar's stealing is beside the point. His talk was richer and less egotistical than Whistler's, and he showed a genial enjoyment of his own conversation, which was one of his most attractive qualities. Granted that Whistler as an artist was far profounder than Wilde; that Oscar talked what he ought to have written; all the better for those who knew him as a talker. It is nonsense to say that he talked shallow paradox which dazzled young people; I still recall perfect sayings of his, as perfect now as on the day when he said them. Moreover, he took as much trouble to amuse us youngsters as if we had been the most brilliant audience. I remember that once, when he asked me to dinner, I took with me a pretty English model who was then sitting to me, a good-natured but rather untidy and commonplace girl. I understand now Oscar's amused expression when he saw us arrive together; but he was no less entertaining during the whole of the evening.

I was doing drawings of the two Coquelins at the time. Coquelin was anxious that Oscar Wilde should see him play the part of Petruchio in *The Taming of the Shrew*, so he sent me tickets. I invited Juliette, Picard's friend, who was a great admirer of Coquelin, to come with us. But before Shakespeare's play there was a curtain raiser, the scene of which represented a dinner party. During this piece Wilde amused himself by pretending that the translation of *The Taming of the Shrew* was all wrong, as if he mistook the foregoing piece for the Shakespeare. He next feigned annoyance that the actors should dare to take their meals on the stage. 'In England', he told Juliette, 'our actors are more correct; they have their dinner before the play begins. I am shocked at this want of manners—and really, at the Comédie Française!' Poor Juliette tried to explain that what we were seeing was not *The Taming of the Shrew* at all, and that the dinner was part of the play. At the end of this play we went behind, and I introduced Wilde to Coquelin. There was not much time:

'Enchanté de faire votre connaissance, Monsieur Wilde. Vous comprendrez combien je suis pressé en ce moment; mais venez donc me voir à la maison.' Wilde, who spoke a rather Ollendorfian French with a strong English accent, said:

'Je serai ravi, Monsieur Coquelin, quand est-ce que je vous trouverai chez vous?'

'Mais je suis toujours chez moi vers les 9 heures.'

'Vers les 9 heures,' said Wilde, 'bien, je viendrai un de ces soirs.'

88

'Mais, monsieur, c'est vers les 9 heures du matin que je veux dire.'

Wilde stepped back, looked at him as though with astonishment and admiration, and said:

'Oh, Monsieur Coquelin, vraiment vous êtes un homme remarquable. Je suis beaucoup plus bourgeois que vous. Je me couche toujours vers les 4 ou 5 heures. Jamais je ne pourrais rester debout jusqu'à cette heure-là! Vraiment vous êtes un homme remarquable.'

Coquelin stared blankly at Wilde, he quite failed to appreciate his Irish humour.

Off the stage Coquelin never behaved in the least like an artist. He collected paintings, but without judgment; he paid small prices for small works, and had an astute but small mind. He flattered grossly when he wanted anything, and, wishing to be considered a man of taste, he coveted the society of artists and connoisseurs. Both he and his brother Cadet showed the French bourgeois soul, loving and talking much of money; knowing, as Wilde put it, the price of everything and the value of nothing. But what splendid faces for comedy they had, and what rich, unctuous, powerful voices! Coquelin in *Les Précieuses Ridicules* was superb—one forgave him everything. I can see him now, seated in a great chair, his hands placed across his stomach. I can see his large humorous mouth and his cunning little eyes; and as Tartuffe he was inimitable.

To Friant he was a true friend; he genuinely admired the painter and respected the man. Indeed, I may perhaps have been unjust to him; for unlike many contemporary collectors, he did buy pictures he liked and could understand. After all, he was a bourgeois with bourgeois tastes. Friant and Dagnan-Bouveret were the painters he most appreciated. I met Dagnan at his flat more than once, a gentle, charming man. I went with Friant to Dagnan's studio, and liked a painting on which he was busy, of recruits who were leaving to join their regiment; fine, serious faces they had, and there was a swing in the composition. It showed a severer quality than was

usual with Dagnan's painting. Dagnan enjoyed a great reputation in England as well as in France. John Swan thought
him the greatest living painter, while Dagnan held Swan in
high regard. Their fame is now sadly diminished.

I made several drawings and pastels both of Coquelin *aîné*
and his younger brother, the first commissions I got. These
I made at the Comédie Française, where I enjoyed the stir
and bustle of the *foyer des artistes*, the glimpses of the actors
and actresses making up in their dressing rooms and the
excitement and confusion of the rehearsals. The seeming
miles of cupboards, in which hung the dresses for the whole
repertory of the theatre, astonished me. Duvent, Royer
and Vuillard also worked much for both the Coquelins,
for small sums, I think. But we were glad enough to be
earning, Vuillard especially, for he was then very poor.
Oscar Wilde also sat to me for his portrait, in a red waistcoat,
which he wore, doubtless, in imitation of Théophile Gautier.
The pastel I made was exhibited at the small exhibition I held
with Conder. I think it was rather more frank than he liked
—only its colour pleased him, the red waistcoat and gold
background. 'It is a lovely landscape, my dear Will; when
I sit to you again you must do a real portrait.' Nevertheless,
he acquired the pastel and used to take it about with him. It
was stolen from him a few years afterwards in Naples, and
has never been traced.

Wilde was much attracted by Conder's paintings on silk,
especially the fans. He was surprised that people were not
tumbling over one another to acquire these lovely things.
Conder, who was always hard-up, was anxious to sell his
work at any price, and Wilde said of him: 'Dear Conder!
With what exquisite subtlety he goes about persuading someone to give him a hundred francs for a fan, for which he was
fully prepared to pay three hundred!'

But Conder was leaving Paris for a while. He had been
more reckless than ever, and his health was suffering. A friend,
de Vallombreuse, had a villa outside Algiers, and pressed
Conder to stay with him there. Conder wrote from Mustapha:

'I suppose by this time you are at Bradford preparing for Christmas and such like "ploom pooding". Here one feels quite in Australia again, even the old remembered gum trees have been transplanted and summer reigns; they say its winter anyhow its spring. There is a long line of almond trees budding in the garden and a pearly sea behind underneath all rows of white bengal roses. Its a delightful place and quite equals one's expectation; the house is white inside and out and was once the abode of a Pasha and his thousand wives. Even in my room there is the inevitable chamber of the thousand and one nights where the favourite sleeps. I wish you were here dear boy, to enjoy all this with me—but—never the time and the place? You I'm sure would be happy in this grand park of flowers where one finds microscopic corners full of that "joie de la vie" one hears of in Paris. One's thirsting for novelty is satisfied for the nonce and one's only difficulty is to fight against that spirit of peace which means idleness. I have been nowhere but in the garden, but my next letter will have some news. My malady is much worse and yesterday I was nearly shipped into hospital, and the doctor said I only need rest and suspension of all treatment.

'This won't interest you much but it will excuse a short letter, and if you would hear more of Alger and myself you must write and tell me what has befallen you since last we met.

'I was thanks to my stupidity landed in Marseilles without my luggage. I haven't got it yet and am going in search today, though I rather dread the journey into Algiers about half an hour from here. Vallombreuse is very charming and has made me very comfortable. Write me soon like a good boy.'

CHAPTER IX

PARIS NIGHTS. DEGAS

Whistler and Wilde MEANWHILE Oscar Wilde was the lion of the season in Paris; he was invited everywhere. The newspapers were full of his doings and sayings; Madame Adam took him up, and asked numbers of people to meet him. I think the only contretemps at the time was Whistler's presence in Paris. Wilde felt his hostility keenly. Whistler used to chaff me mercilessly about him, and Wilde was touchy, thinking I was being prejudiced against him.

I went sometimes with Oscar Wilde to the Café d'Harcourt, on the Boulevard St Michel, in a corner of which Moréas reigned over a *cénacle* of noisy poets. Moréas, a pale Greek with long moustaches and blue-black hair, magnificently eloquent, propounded rich and complex theories on the art of poetry, theories which found an enthusiastic response from Stuart Merrill, his disciple Raymond de la Tailhade, and other poets of the École Romaine. At a certain period of the night Moréas would call, 'Raymond, l'Ode!' and Raymond would stand up and, above the din, cry 'Ode à Jean Moréas', and, when something like silence had been obtained, would recite a long laudation in verse before his complacent master and the rest of the company! The Rat Mort and the Café de la Place Blanche were temples of silence and order compared with the Café d'Harcourt. Men and women passed constantly among the tables, already packed to overflowing, throughout the night. The atmosphere was stifling, and thick with tobacco smoke, with the strong perfumes of the *grisettes* and the fumes of alcohol, and the noise was deafening. At times there would glide in among the crowded tables a sinister figure, often with a bouquet of flowers—stolen, of course—which he would place in front of some favoured poet. This was the notorious Bibi la Purée. Far into the night this company would remain, tirelessly discussing theories of verse, reciting poems and execrating their successful contemporaries, while the *soucoupes* piled up before them on the marble tables. One night I went with Sherard, Stuart Merrill and Oscar Wilde to a famous night-haunt of the Paris underworld, the Château Rouge, a sort of doss-house with a dangerous and unsavoury reputation. The sight of the sinister types lounging about the crowded rooms, or sleeping on benches, made me shudder. None of us liked it, while Sherard, to add to our discomfort, kept shouting that anyone who meddled with his friend Oscar Wilde would soon be sorry for himself. 'Sherard, you are defending us at the risk of our lives,' said Wilde; I think we were all relieved to be out in the fresh air again.

True, I was often low-spirited after late nights in such company. So then I would stay indoors and read Tolstoi and Balzac, and feel then that my home was not in the wild haunts which my friends preferred, but elsewhere. These men I was meeting were hardly the friends I would have chosen; I was happier with men like Lomont and Marcel Schwob, who, with open and enlightened minds yet had faith in something. Cynical negation depressed me; I needed the ardour of hope in mankind.

In my studio I felt safe. An artist is well occupied only when at work at his easel. Away from his easel he is more open to attack, perhaps more than other men. Reckless and versatile, he is at the same time thin-skinned. Wilde spoke truly when he wrote, 'He who lives more lives than one, more deaths than one must die.' Yet the restlessness of youth constantly tempted me away from the studio; I was avid of life, curious and venturesome; moreover, like the rest, I was bewitched by that fascinating, overpowering siren, Paris! And when I remembered the Slade, and my cautious companions there, I thought: with all their faults, what faith in the life of the mind these French painters and poets have!

One evening, sitting outside the Café de la Paix with Oscar Wilde, we were joined at our table by Caton Woodville, the war correspondent. He was something of a Münchhausen, and liked to boast of his exploits. He had recently been painting a picture for Queen Victoria—I forget what the subject was—in which the Queen herself was portrayed. When it was finished, he received a command to take it to Windsor. He described how Her Majesty entered the room, went up to the picture, examined it carefully in silence and then walked towards the door. As she opened the door she turned round and said coldly, 'We are redder than that, Mr Woodville,' and swept out.

I didn't care for the poets' cafés—they were too crowded and noisy; and though I could, on occasion, sit up most of the night, I was not a *noceur*. Wilde said of me that I was like those dreadful public-houses in London—punctually at midnight all the lights went out of my face.

I was too keen on my work to waste many nights among these wild poets. I didn't, at the time, take men like Moréas very seriously; indeed, I was surprised to discover, many years later, that Moréas was a poet of some distinction. Stuart Merrill was an American, educated in France, who wrote French verses; a charming fellow, intelligent, but, I fancy, rather idle and easy-going, who had associated himself with the symbolists. He was not very productive; and all he had published, one or two volumes, appeared in a precious form. All these poets admired Mallarmé and Verlaine; but Verlaine's company was not liked at this time; people said he was impossible. Mallarmé, on the contrary, was deeply respected by everyone, and no wonder; he had scholarship, great personal charm and a simple dignity, in fact, all the qualities which were lacking in poor Verlaine. He was always warm in his praise of Verlaine's genius. His Tuesday evenings were crowded; for while his poetry was obscure and rather diffi-

94

cult, his conversation was crystal-clear. The friendship between him and Whistler was close and affectionate; it was
delightful to see them together. Whistler's lithograph of
Mallarmé, printed as a frontispiece to a collected edition of
his poems, slight though it was, is an extraordinary physical
and spiritual likeness. I think Whistler cared for Mallarmé as
much as for anyone living.

Whistler was also friendly with Comte Robert de Montesquiou, the dandified author of *Les Chauves Souris*, who, it was
generally supposed, was Huysmans' model for *des Esseintes*.
Montesquiou too had a tortoise whose shell he inlaid with
jewels; the tortoise's retort on this outrage was direct and
emphatic—it died. Montesquiou was the kind of *précieux* who
alienated me; he was on too familiar terms with art, literature
and music. Being rich and a Count as well, he knew everyone
and went everywhere. He advertised the talents of Helleu and
Gandara, and blew a loud trumpet for Whistler. Whistler
painted a full-length portrait of him, not, I think, in the pale
mauve frock-coat with shirt, collar and tie to match, in which
I met him one day on his way to hear Weber's music, when
he told me that one should always listen to Weber in mauve!
He had the affectation of Wilde without Wilde's touch of
genius, and without his geniality and sense of fun.

To Paris came more than once Mr and Mrs Jack Gardiner.
Mrs Gardiner was already famous as a collector of pictures,
as a fastidious and somewhat eccentric woman, and for
her great necklace of black pearls. She was notorious as a
non-beauty, a fact she had the wit to recognise. Sargent had
painted a striking portrait of her, in a plain black dress, very
décolletée, and wearing her pearls. She was a warm supporter of Sargent throughout her life, but she fully recognised
Whistler's genius. Thinking she might be interested in my
work, Whistler asked me to meet Mrs Gardiner at dinner.
She was curious, too, about the bohemian corners of Paris,
and Whistler had advised her to have me act as her guide,
'un vieux qui a moult roulé en Palestine et aultres lieux,' he
used to say of me laughingly. So I took her to hear Yvette

at the Divan Japonais and Xanrof at the Chat Noir; and to
hear Bruant sing his songs at his cabaret. She herself entertained lavishly at her small and modest-looking hotel in the
rue de la Paix. I also took her to Conder's studio, where she
bought, I think, the first fan he ever painted. She was anxious
to acquire a Whistler. Why she thought this a perilous project
I had no idea; Whistler was surely not averse from selling his
pictures; but she thought that I might be useful and she took
me with her to the studio in the rue Notre Dame des Champs.
Whistler was in his most genial mood, and showed a number
of his canvases, among which was a lovely sea-piece with
sailing ships. Mrs Gardiner nudged me; I could see she was
eager to have it. 'Why don't you put it under your arm and
carry it off?' I whispered. She was always ready for any
unusual adventure, and she boldly told Whistler that she was
going to take the picture with her. Whistler laughed and did
nothing to stop her. She told us later that on her asking
Whistler how much she owed him for this beautiful work,
Whistler named £300 as the price. How absurdly small a
sum this seems to-day! When Studd paid £200 for one of
Monet's haystacks and the same price for a painting by
Picard, it was the talk of Paris.

Picard was a painter who belonged to our circle at the
Rat Mort. Juliette, his mistress, was one of the loveliest
women I have ever seen. Adored by us all, she had the
lightest grey-blue eyes in a perfect Botticellian face. She
wore her hair *en bandeaux*, then the fashion among artistic
ladies. She had a noble neck and figure, and an enchanting
swaying, lily-like grace. Picard was jealous—and vigilant,
and no wonder; I marvelled at the time that no one carried
her off. But it seemed she was loyal as she was beautiful. The
painting by Picard which Studd had acquired, and which
made something of a stir in the Salon, was a Leonardesque half-
length nude of Juliette. What has become of it now I don't
know; I have no recollection of seeing it in Studd's house at
Chelsea. Later, when Studd became uniquely devoted to
Whistler and his art, his taste changed considerably, and it

96

may well be that he no longer cared for his Picard. For Studd was soon to transfer his entire allegiance to Whistler. But Studd, who had come to live at Montmartre, was then greatly taken with Picard. Picard was keen to see the National Gallery, and some of the private collections in London, so Studd invited us both to stay for a week at his mother's house in Hyde Park Gardens; and thither we went from Paris. A perfect example of a Victorian house it was, the grandest I had ever been in. It had a splendour, a unity of a kind peculiar to the period; the cheerful chintzes, bordered wall-papers, the large flower-patterned carpets, the Sèvres and Rockingham china, the heavy Victorian silver, achieved the harmony of a brilliant nosegay. Studd was acquainted with many influential people, and was able to take Picard and myself to Holland House, to Bridgewater and Dorchester House, to the Leylands' to see Whistler's peacock room, to the Cuthbert Quilters' and to the Hendersons', who had recently acquired Burne-Jones' *Briar Rose* series. I remember that when we called at the Leylands' mansion in Prince's Gate, the bell was answered by a major-domo, with powdered hair, yellow livery with heavy knots across the shoulders and noble silk-clad calves, so impressive a figure, that Studd, in presenting the letter of introduction at the door, instinctively took off his hat. This task of introducing Picard to London gave both Studd and myself the chance of visiting collections we might not otherwise have seen.

Through Studd I got to know the Leslie Stephens at Hyde Park Gate. (George Duckworth I had previously met in Paris; Gerald was then at Cambridge.) Leslie Stephen filled me with awe. He came down to the family tea, which was held in the basement. George was cheerful and talkative, but his sister Stella, and Virginia and Vanessa his step-sisters, in plain black dresses with white lace collars and wrist bands, looking as though they had walked straight out of a canvas by Watts or Burne-Jones, rarely spoke. Beautiful as they were, they were not more beautiful than their mother.

Mrs Leslie Stephen was sister to Mrs Fisher, Herbert

Fisher's mother; she was grand-daughter to one of the Pattle sisters, who had been brought up with the Prinseps, among the dazzling circle surrounding Watts. Her rare distinction had inspired both Watts and Burne-Jones, and a striking portrait of her by Watts hung in the house. During one of my visits I had the temerity to ask her to sit to me for a drawing; with her gracious nature she could not say no. When the drawing was done she looked at it, then handed it in silence to her daughter. The others came up and looked over her shoulder; finally it reached Leslie Stephen. The consternation was general. I was already looked on with suspicion, for in those days Whistler, whose disciple I was known to be, was anathema in Burne-Jones' and Watts' circles. The alarm must have spread upstairs; for a message came down from old Mrs Jackson, Mrs Leslie Stephen's mother, and the drawing was taken up for her to see. A confirmed invalid, Mrs Jackson had not come down from her room for many years; but on seeing the drawing she rang for a stick, like the Baron calling for his boots, and prepared to give me a piece of her mind. I can still hear the thump of her stick as she came heavily downstairs; and the piece of her mind which she gave me was a solid one. I went away thoroughly awed, and well punished for my rashness. I had quite forgotten the drawing when, some 35 years later, while staying in Dresden with my friend von Hofmann, I came upon it in an old brown-paper sketch book, which I had given him once in Paris. Although it did but scant justice to Mrs Stephen's great charm and rare beauty, it was not quite so bad, perhaps, as they thought it.

Later I did more than one portrait of Leslie Stephen himself; and was to find the shy and silent daughters emerge, one as Virginia Woolf, the other, no less gifted, as Vanessa Bell.

One more memory of the Stephen household. Calling one day to see George Duckworth, I was shown straight into Leslie Stephen's study. I was aware of a gaunt, bent and melancholy figure, pacing up and down. He looked startled at seeing me, and I too was frightened at finding myself alone

and face to face with this shy and awe-inspiring figure.
Knowing vaguely that I was a painter, and feeling it incumbent on him to provide some form of entertainment, he walked slowly to his book-case and took out a book, one of Thackeray's manuscripts, which was full of absurd little thumb-nail sketches. Holding the book stiffly in front of me, Leslie Stephen began slowly turning over the leaves, stopping each time he came to a drawing. I tried desperately to say something intelligent, while he went on turning, turning, turning the pages, and looking sternly at me each time to mark the result. My tongue was dry, sweat poured down my forehead, hours seemed to pass, when at last we were both relieved from the dreadful situation by George Duckworth's entry.

Philip Burne-Jones was an intimate friend of the Stephen family. He was a boisterous visitor, full of fun, with whom the daughters were far less reserved. So they were to a lesser degree with Studd. Before he met Whistler, there was a genuinely naïve and primitive element in Studd's painting. He had an affection for the Breton peasants, and he found a house at Le Pouldu where he lived for months at a time. A Breton fisherman acted for many years as his servant-companion, going with him wherever he went. He made many studies of the men, women and children of Le Pouldu; I wish he had gone on working as he did then. The time was not yet when rather naïve work was understood. Had Studd continued to paint peasants with the very personal feeling he showed in his early work, he might well have made a distinctive place for himself. I doubt whether he was of a temperament to follow art for art's sake. His nature was more closely allied to Millet's and even to the early manner of Gauguin, than to Whistler's. But Whistler, who mesmerised us all at one time or another, won Studd's lasting devotion; indeed, so loyal he was, he looked on the defection from Whistler's influence of myself and others as a kind of *lèse-majesté*; and when later Whistler quarrelled with me, it caused a breach between Studd and myself.

99

The model I mentioned, who frequently sat to me, one day brought me two paintings by Puvis de Chavannes, which she wanted to sell. She had offered them to several French artists, but no one seemed to want them. She asked 600 francs for them both—what a chance! But my allowance was only 300 francs a month; I was already behind-hand with the colour merchant and framer, and 600 francs was for me a large sum. So I told Studd about the paintings, and fortunately he was able to buy them. These two paintings now hang in the National Gallery in London. Whistler used to tease me about this model. She had a small child. One night during dinner, Frazier, Studd and I were sitting near Mrs Whistler, who was asking about this child, when Whistler, who usually wanted to know what was going on if he heard sounds of laughter, broke in—'What, a child too! Well you know Parson! and how old is the young brat?' 'A child of eight,' I said. 'What! were there as many of you as that,' was Whistler's quick retort. In appearance this model recalled a phrase of Henry James': 'The wanton was not without a certain cadaverous beauty.' I made many pastel drawings of her, one or two of which were acquired by Studd. Another figured in an exhibition which Conder and I held together, of which I have spoken, and was reproduced, together with a drawing of Duvent, in *L'Art Français*, a periodical long defunct. These two drawings point to a certain economy and severity of treatment at this early stage of my career. I have been twitted with having been an amusing and brilliant artist, grown serious since; but the tendency of these drawings does not seem to me to differ much from that of my later work. This show of Conder's work and of mine was held at the little gallery of le père Thomas on the Boulevard Malesherbes. Thomas was a courageous but reckless dealer, one of the few who, at this time, risked their small capital on men in whom they believed. It was Lautrec who made our work known to him. Both Conder and I were very young and obscure; Conder was 23, and I was 19; yet with no chance of getting back his money the good Thomas

A MODEL AND CHARLES DUVENT (1891)

placed his gallery at our disposal. Conder showed paintings
of orchards, and drawings inspired by Omar Khayyam; I
showed pastels, chiefly portraits, including the one of Oscar
Wilde. The little show was favourably noticed in *Le Figaro*.
I remember this because we were told to leave cards on the
art critic!

It is memorable also for the visit of Camille Pissarro, who
came with his son Lucien, and for the warm encouragement
he gave me, and for the friendship I then began with them
both. Lucien's painting, his beautiful books and coloured
woodcuts, have brought me life-long pleasure. Both Conder
and I sold several things, the greater part to a Portuguese
collector, Azavedo, of whom I have never heard since. We
both burst out into frock-coats and stocks, *en mil huit cent
trente*, and in Conder's case, peg-top trousers. These last I
did not venture on, but they suited Conder's figure, and they
were then the wear in Montmartre.

Whistler used to say that I carried out what in others was
merely gesture; this of course was pure flattery. But with its
many faults, my work at this time was generously noticed by
older artists. It attracted the notice of Degas, who sent word,
oddly enough through a little model of his who came often
to our table at the Café de la Rochefoucauld, that I might, if
I cared, pay him a visit. Degas as well as Whistler! And but
two years before I was drawing casts at the Slade School and
longing to know one or two of the older students.

Although I was always somewhat excited when visiting
Whistler, his curiosity to know what I had been doing, whom
I had been seeing, his friendly chaff, would put me at ease.
With Degas, I was never quite comfortable. To begin with,
nervous people are apt, when speaking in a foreign tongue,
to say rather what comes into their heads, than to say what
they mean. Moreover, Degas' character was more austere
and uncompromising than Whistler's. Compared with Degas
Whistler seemed almost worldly in many respects. Indeed,
Degas was the only man of whom Whistler was a little afraid.
'Whistler, you behave as though you have no talent,' Degas

had said once to him; and again when Whistler, chin high, monocle in his eye, frock-coated, top-hatted, and carrying a tall cane, walked triumphantly into a restaurant where Degas was sitting: 'Whistler, you have forgotten your muff.' Again, about Whistler's flat-brimmed hat, which Whistler fancied, Degas said: 'Oui, il vous va très bien; mais ce n'est pas ça qui nous rendra l'Alsace et la Lorraine!'

Degas was famous, and feared, for his terrible *mots*. He was unsparing in his comments on men who failed in fidelity to the artistic conscience. Flattery, usefulness and subservience provided in some cases the key to intimacy with Whistler; with Degas integrity of character was a *sine qua non* of friendship. One thing he had in common with Whistler—a temperamental respect for the aristocratic tradition, the 'West Point' code of honour, a French West Point, which included anti-Republican and anti-semitic tendencies, which later made him a strong partisan of the Militarists and anti-Dreyfusards. He heartily disliked the cosmopolitanism which was ousting the narrower but more finely tempered French culture—destroying it indeed, so he thought; hence he wanted to save what he could of French art from the new-rich American collector, then already beginning to cast his efficient nets, baited with dollars, in Parisian waters. Degas was buying as many drawings by Ingres as he could; he had also acquired half a dozen of his paintings, and many drawings by Daumier and Delacroix. Daumier he placed high among the nineteenth-century painters; 'If Raphael', he said, 'returned to life and looked at Gerome's pictures, he would say "connu"; but if he saw a drawing by Daumier, "Tiens, c'est intéressant, ça, et d'une puissante main" he would say.' Degas owned several large slips of Manet's *Execution of Maximilian*, two of which are now in the National Gallery. A dealer bought the original painting, and, being unable to dispose of so large a canvas, cut it up and sold the fragments separately; most of these Degas was able to secure. He had, besides, two beautiful still-life paintings by Manet, one of a single pear, and one of a ham. He had thought him over-worldly:

'LA DANSEUSE', CARICATURE BY PUVIS DE
CHAVANNES

'Mais tu es aussi connu que Garibaldi; que veux-tu de plus?' *A retort*
Degas chaffed him once. Manet's answer came pat: 'Mon *from Manet*
vieux, alors tu es au-dessus du niveau de la mer.' He spoke
with particular admiration of Manet, regretting that he had
not appreciated him enough during his lifetime. Whistler
habitually belittled Manet's work, disliking to hear us praise
it. Like Whistler, Degas had no great opinion of Cézanne as
an artist.

Degas was a confirmed bachelor of simple habits. He
occupied two apartments, one above the other, in the rue
Victor Massé, over which a devoted old servant ruled and
guarded the painter against intruders. The walls of the lower
flat were hung with his beloved French masters, while upstairs he kept his own numerous works. With those whom
he had once admitted to his friendship he threw off much of
his reserve, and showed and discussed his treasures. I eagerly
listened to his affectionate tributes; he never tired of lingering
over the beauties of his Ingres drawings. He pressed me to
look out for unknown originals which, he believed, were in
England; for Ingres had employed a tout in Rome and in
this way got many commissions from English tourists, before
he became famous. I did, in fact, find that two of my friends,
the Misses Colthurst, owned such a drawing, done by Ingres
at Rome, of two ladies, their forebears. Miss Anne Colthurst, herself a gifted artist, had the drawing photographed,
and took it herself to Degas. She was warmly received, and
remained in friendly relations with Degas until the end of
his life.

Degas in appearance had something of Henley and something of Meredith, but was too heavy for Meredith, and too
finely featured for Henley. His raised brows and heavily-
lidded eyes gave him an aspect of aloofness; and in spite of
his baggy clothes, he looked the aristocrat that he was.

One or two things I saw at the rue Victor Massé remain
in my memory: a beautiful pastel of a woman lying on a
settee in a bright blue dress, a work which I have not seen
again, nor seen reproduced; a small wax model of a horse

leaping to one side, which he made use of in a well-known composition of jockeys riding. This was the most highly finished of Degas' *maquettes* which I saw at the rue Victor Massé. Until now I was unaware that Degas modelled. He owned some casts of an Indian dancing figure, a *nataraja* or an *apsara*, the first examples of Indian sculpture I had seen.

Degas was then making studies of laundresses ironing, and of women tubbing or at their toilets. Some of these were re-drawn again and again on tracing paper pinned over drawings already made; this practice allowed for correction and simpli-fication, and was common with artists in France. Degas rarely painted directly from nature. He spoke once of Monet's dependence in this respect: 'Je n'éprouve pas le besoin de perdre connaissance devant la nature,' he mocked.

Degas complained much of his eyesight. Young people to-day, who prefer the later work of Degas and of Renoir, hardly realise how much of its looser character was due to their failing sight. Degas, in the 'nineties, was still able to see fairly clearly; but towards the end of his life he was obliged to use the broadest materials, working on a large scale, hesitating, awkward, scarcely able to find his way over the canvas or paper.

He was by nature drawn to subtleties of character and to intricate forms and movements. He had the Parisian curiosity for life in its most objective forms. At one with the Impres-sionists in rejecting the artificial subject-matter of the Salon painters, he looked to everyday life for his subjects; but he differed from Manet and his other contemporaries, in the rhythmical poise of his figures and the perfecting of detail. He found, in the life of the stage and the intricate steps of the ballet, with its background of phantasy, an inexhaustible subject-matter, which allowed for the colour and movement of romantic art, yet provided the clear form dear to the classical spirit. He delighted in the strange plumage of the *filles d'opéra*, as they moved into the circle of the limelight or stood, their skirts standing out above their pink legs, chattering together in the wings. The starling-like flock of

young girls, obedient to the baton of the *maître de danse*,
Degas rendered with astonishing delicacy of observation.
He never forgot that he was once a pupil of Ingres. Indeed,
he described at length, on one of my first visits, his early
relations with Ingres; how fearfully he approached him,
showing his drawings and asking whether he might, in all
modesty, look forward to being, some day, an artist; Ingres
replying that it was too grave a thing, too serious a responsibility to be thought of; better devote himself to some other
pursuit. And how going again, and yet again, pleading that
he had reconsidered, from every point of view, his idea of
equipping himself to become a painter, that he realised his
temerity, but could not bring himself to abandon all his
hopes, Ingres finally relented, saying, 'C'est très grave,
ce que vous pensez faire, très grave; mais si enfin vous tenez
quand même à être un artiste, un bon artiste, eh bien, monsieur, faites des lignes, rien que des lignes.' One of Ingres' sayings which came back to Degas was 'Celui qui ne vit que
dans la contemplation de lui-même est un misérable'. Degas
had lately been at Montauban, Ingres' birthplace, where the
greater number of his studies are preserved. Degas was full
of his visit, and of the surpassing beauty of the drawings.

When I got back to England I was indignant at the general
misapprehension of Degas' character; for instance, he was
fiercely assailed by Sir William Richmond on account of
a picture—*L'Absinthe*—which had lately been shown in
London—a portrait of Desboutin, the etcher, sitting with a
woman at a table at the Nouvelle Athènes. Desboutin was,
as a matter of fact, a good, sober, bourgeois artist, a familiar
and picturesque figure in Montmartre. Degas himself lived
very austerely; no breath of scandal had ever touched him.
He once told us an amusing story of how, being constantly
twitted by his friends about his complete indifference to the
other sex, he felt he must make some demonstration of
gallantry. Finding that one of the little dancers who sat for
him was going to America, he thought this an opportunity
for the appropriate gesture. He booked a passage on the

boat following her's, reached New York, remained quietly on board, and returned to France. Impossible to do more, he said, than show himself capable of pursuing a lady all the way from Paris to New York!

Each time I knocked at the door in the rue Victor Massé my heart beat fast; would I be admitted? But the old lady had her orders; once accepted, one might come again. But I seldom went, afraid lest the acquaintance, so unlooked for, so intoxicating, might come to an end. Yet how I looked forward to seeing something of Degas at work, to hearing his comments on painters and paintings! Yet, as in other like cases, I was sometimes too acutely self-conscious and inwardly excited to enjoy myself. It was in retrospect that I most appreciated my visits. Admiration and detractions were equally exciting to hear; though it is not, to my present way of thinking, quite decent for young men to sit and listen complacently to attacks on others, when their own integrity has yet to be tested. I was, however, all eyes and ears at the rue Victor Massé, and my friends too were eager to hear me repeat Degas' latest *mot*. Truth to tell, I heard more of admiration than of abuse.

Degas liked Forain and his work; he was interested, too, in Lautrec's. To my surprise, he greatly disliked Rodin, who, in our eyes, was one of the Olympians. Among English artists, he rated Charles Keene highly. He was curious about Brangwyn's work, which he had noticed somewhere, perhaps at Bings'. Bing was the well-known dealer, who had spent many years in Japan. Through him collectors acquired their Japanese prints, paintings and lacquer. Bing and Hayashi knew more than anyone else about Japanese art. But now Bing had embarked on an ambitious project. His galleries were to become the centre of *l'art nouveau*, the French arts and crafts movement, and Brangwyn was to decorate one of his rooms, and Conder the other. Conder painted a set of panels on silk, which for long hung at Bings', but found no purchaser, until they were bought by Fritz Thaulow.

CARICATURE OF WHISTLER

Sargent and Helleu Degas held in little esteem. Helleu
was a rising star, an adroit draughtsman and an able pastellist.
An appreciation of fine breeding and of feminine fastidiousness, combined with a delicate sensuality, so refined as to
please rather than offend the sitters he chose for their beauty,
made him the chosen artist of certain great ladies—of Mme
de Montebello and of Mme de Greffuhle. He had married a
beautiful young girl with delicate features, slight and slim
fingered, of whom he made some of his best dry points and
drawings. She presided with modest grace in his flat, a flat
which he furnished with choice examples of eighteenth-
century taste. I remember his showing a new acquisition, a
bowl of finest porcelain, moulded, he declared, from the
breast of one of Louis' court favourites, perhaps from the
Du Barry's. But it was not only women with whom Helleu
was occupied; he was making studies of blue hydrangeas,
flowers as dear to him as they were to Comte Robert de
Montesquiou, and of the fountains of Versailles. Versailles
was his temple, and Watteau his household god; did not
Degas call Helleu himself *le Watteau à vapeur*? Yet physically
he looked more like a southern Frenchman than one from
the north, with his raven-blue hair, and his pale, finely-
chiselled features. I didn't care for Helleu, and he didn't like
me; he was polite because he met me at Whistler's. I felt
about him something of the *arriviste*. The very young are
suspicious of artists who frequent fashionable circles; in this
they are often unjust, for the refinements of life need inter-
preting also, and men with the talent and taste of Helleu and
Gandara are not often available. It is right that there should
be artists who cater for wealthy people with cultured tastes.
Watts in England is an example of an artist's relations with
such a world. But young men with gifted friends, who, may
be, live in neglect, are apt to be critical of those whom fortune
has favoured.

The so-called fashionable portrait painter is too often a
mere transcriber, whose intellect, on a level with that of his
sitters, is not likely to offend by seeing in them either dignity

107

Gandara   or character. Yet fashionable people it appears choose precisely those artists who are blind to the fineness of fashion.
Could anything be more fatal to the virtue of fashion, or
more vulgar or stupid, than the long rows of portraits an-
nually shown at the Salon or the Royal Academy? Helleu, at
any rate, could satisfy a discriminating taste; he had a sense
of the wit, distinction and subtleties of mode. His stick of
sanguine could at least give style and elegance to his portraits. Later on, as commissions poured in, he became
mannered, and gave a mechanical distinction of feature to all
his sitters.

Another painter, Antonio de la Gandara, whom I thought
a more serious artist than Helleu, was also much in request
as a portrait painter. He showed a painting of his wife
walking in a wood, an effect of *sous bois*, at the Salon, which
seemed to promise a new kind of beauty. I was likewise
attracted by his drawings, which for a time strongly influenced my own. Whistler, also, thought them interesting,
and he sat to Gandara. Whistler promised that I too should
make a drawing of him, both in Paris and, later, in London.

Both Helleu and Gandara were ardent supporters of
Whistler, and were often at the rue du Bac. While Helleu
collected eighteenth-century furniture, Gandara was an
amateur of the Empire period. His studio, with its grey
walls and lemon panelling, was furnished with a few severe
pieces of Empire furniture, which he introduced into his
portraits. He was painting the Princesse de Chimay, an
American lady, in a white Empire dress of the finest transparent muslin; beside Gandara, with his dark complexion
and coal-black hair and moustache, she looked dazzlingly
radiant; and later, when I saw the Goyas in Madrid, I thought
again of the two figures, one so fair, the other so dark, in
the pale grey studio.

DEGAS AND SICKERT

CHAPTER X

CONDER

Mrs Whistler sometimes gave us tea in her husband's studio; to this we greatly looked forward, for if Whistler was in a good mood he would bring out a canvas, and having shown one, others were sure to follow. It was exciting to see such a succession of his works, but the privileged occasion was not without its embarrassment; for Whistler's comments on his own work were so loving, so caressing, that to find superlative expressions of praise to cap his own became, as one canvas or panel after another was slipped into the frame on the easel, increasingly difficult and exhausting. But I was to see another side of Whistler's character. We had been dining at the Hôtel du Bon Lafontaine; after dinner Whistler proposed we should go to the studio. We walked to the rue Notre Dame des Champs. Climbing the stairs we found the studio in darkness. Whistler lighted a single candle. He had been gay enough during dinner, but now he became very quiet and intent, as though he forgot me. Turning a canvas that faced the wall, he examined it carefully up and down, with the candle held near it, and then did the like with some others, peering closely into each. There was something tragic, almost frightening, as I stood and waited, in watching Whistler; he looked suddenly old, as he held the candle with trembling hands, and stared at his work, while our shapes threw restless, fantastic shadows, all around us. As I followed him silently down the stairs I realised that even Whistler must often have felt his heart heavy with the sense

of failure. A letter to Fantin-Latour, published long after, in
which he regretted that, while still a student, he had not
learned to draw like Ingres, reminded me vividly of what
I had seen that night.

It is true that Whistler, while he had an inimitable sense
of drawing, was not, in the full sense of the word, a good
draughtsman. Yet so exquisite was his feeling for form, he
succeeded where less sensitive draughtsmen failed. And so
elusive was the mark at which he aimed, and so often, as he
thought, he failed to achieve it, his fastidiousness cost him
the destruction of a large part of his life's work.

There are two different approaches to painting: one is that
of surrendering oneself to life in order to interpret its vivid,
surprising, articulated forms, to get to grips with each aspect
of nature, to ravish from each individual object or person
something of life's vivacity and profundity, something that
shall stand for life as a whole. This was the way of Velazquez
and Hals and Chardin, which the realists and impressionists
followed. But there is another aspect of life in painting: there
is a finality of form, removed from momentary appearance.
This aspect has been supremely expressed in certain Italian
paintings, where form is seen as though carved from agate or
ivory, hard, resisting, everlasting, so that the figures dealt
with have something in common with images set in shrines,
through their very remoteness from life, images which evoke,
in those who worship before them, a comfort, a beauty, a
truth of which all men get an inkling at rare moments.

Now this agate-like quality of design and form which so
dignified painting, and which I missed in the realists, has
always moved me. Certain drawings have this quality; I was
dimly aware of it in some of Rossetti's early drawings,
especially in his pen-drawing of Miss Siddall at the South
Kensington Museum; later on I found it in other of his clear
and close-knit designs. This was at least Rossetti's aim, if not
the aim of the other Pre-Raphaelites, to achieve completeness
of conception rather than finish. Whistler, too, aimed at
something less accidental, something more foreseen, than his

French contemporaries, and he laboured to achieve a quality of material and surface which should suggest both the mystery and the permanence of life.

Strangely enough Cézanne, whom Whistler so much disliked, was haunted by a similar desire. Manet, Degas, Renoir and Monet were less disturbed by such dreams. Only Millet achieved the perfect fusion between movement and form, between what was passing and what was permanent. Perhaps it was the inkling I had of his underlying desire for something other than casual appearance that drew me so strongly to Whistler's work. Of all his portraits, I most liked the Rose Corder, which was shown, with several other paintings by Whistler, at the first Salon du Champ de Mars. There was a flavour of consciousness in the portraits of Carlyle and of Whistler's mother, and in that of Miss Alexander; but the Rose Corder portrait was a triumph of unaffected ease. Whistler said, when I was telling of my admiration for his painting of Rose Corder, that he had painted this portrait for Howell, and that to his surprise Howell had paid for it, had given him a hundred guineas. He was less surprised when he discovered that Howell had possessed himself of a quantity of his etchings; the hundred pounds was perhaps a sop to his conscience!

Both Whistler and Oscar Wilde told me innumerable stories of Howell. It was from Whistler I first heard the tale of the Chinese Cabinet, the subject of a pamphlet, *The Paddon Papers*, which was printed, but never published[1].

He also told about a clock that belonged to Swinburne, which Howell carried off for repairs, and which, needless to say, Swinburne never saw again. According to Whistler, Howell managed, in one way or another, to get into relations with people of importance: royalties, millionaires or cabinet ministers. He had got together a collection of foreign decorations, one of which, some Portuguese order, had actually

---

[1] I possess Whistler's own copy of this pamphlet with his corrections, which show that Whistler was not above tampering with the text if it suited his purpose.

been conferred on himself. One of the French Royal Princes
was to lecture on some remote part of the world—Paraguay,
I think it was—at the Royal Institution. Howell turned up
with the rosette of the Legion of Honour in his button-hole,
listened to the discourse, then rose and made a long and
flattering speech, substantiating from a long experience in
Paraguay the statements made. The Prince was delighted,
Howell was presented, and knew well how to make use of
his opportunity.

Whistler always asserted that Howell was still alive and
would turn up again in a new character; like Rossetti, he was
tickled by his brazen audacity, by his skill in escaping from
his many dilemmas. Howell could palm off whatever he
would on some client or another, and he had many and
marvellous ways of extracting money from wealthy people.
He was an adept at finding rare things, with which he supplied collectors. One day Howell had a visitor—I forget his
identity—who came to look over some recent purchases.
Among other objects he noticed a black china tea-pot and one
or two cups and saucers. He asked Howell what they were.
'Oh,' said Howell, 'they are things of no importance.' But
the collector was curious and returned again and again to the
subject. 'Well,' said Howell, 'they are not beautiful and they
aren't in your line; apart from their rarity they aren't worth
looking at. You probably know that when Kien Lung lost
his favourite wife, he ordered complete mourning—black
everywhere: black hangings, black carpets, even black cinders
on the paths round the Palace. You know, of course, that
black china was then no longer produced, so a special service
had to be made. Most of these pieces have disappeared, but
by an extraordinary bit of luck I happened to come across
this tea-pot and two cups—probably the only ones left of
the set.' The client's acquisitive passion was roused; he in-
quired the cost, which Howell for long refused to divulge.
To cut a long story short, the collector fell into the trap and
paid Howell a big price for his bargain. A year or two afterwards, prowling through Wardour Street he espied, in the

window of a china shop, two or three of the precious black cups and saucers. He felt a thrill of excitement, went in, bought a number of things, and then asked casually what the price of the cups and saucers would be. The dealer, evidently unaware of their value, mentioned a trivial figure. The amateur of china, hiding his elation, directed the dealer to send the other things along; he would take the black cups and saucers with him.

'Were you interested in black china, Sir?' asked the dealer. 'Perhaps you wouldn't mind coming in here'—taking him into a small room at the back of the shop, where every shelf was packed with this ware from floor to ceiling. 'You may not remember that —s put this line on the market; I bought a quantity, but it never took on, and most of it has been left on my hands. I shall be glad to let you have any quantity!'

Whistler also said that Howell had such influence over Miss Corder, by devious ways, he made her forge Pre-Raphaelite pictures, especially paintings and drawings by Rossetti, many of which he passed off as originals; 'Well, you know,' Whistler added, 'there isn't much difference.' But both he and Rossetti put up with Howell; he was worth more than what he got out of them.

Whistler was vague about geography. I got a *petit bleu* one day asking me to dine the same evening. On my arrival, Whistler explained that the Rathbones were passing through Paris—didn't I come from the same town as they did? Of course I would know them. Liverpool and Bradford are two different places, but the Rathbones were charming. Whistler reminded the old gentleman how, on a previous occasion, he had been excited at seeing the soup served on some particularly beautiful blue and white plates. 'Why, Whistler,' he had said, 'these must have the six marks,' so he turned his plate up and the soup flowed gracefully over the table.

Another time I was asked to dine at the rue du Bac, and there I found Howard Cushing, Mallarmé and Mme Mallarmé. Dinner was to be at eight. Mrs Whistler, whose French was not very facile, was a little agitated. Mallarmé, spoke delightful English, but his wife, I think, spoke none. We walked in the garden waiting for Whistler. Half past eight—nine o'clock—no Whistler, and Mrs Whistler getting more and more anxious. At a quarter past nine Whistler arrived, not in the least perturbed; nor did dinner seem the worse for being an hour and a half late. Whistler was very particular about food. While his house was being got ready, he stayed at a charming old hotel frequented, he said, 'you know by Cardinals and Archbishops'—the Hôtel du Bon Lafontaine, in the rue de Grenelle. The kitchen, of the old-fashioned bourgeois type, Whistler declared was equal to any in Paris. I recollect a wonderful dish of *langouste* prepared, he explained, according to a mediaeval recipe; and I remember that when the coffee came it was cold, at which Whistler was much upset.

One evening, at the rue du Bac, a man from Goupil's came, very worried, to ask Whistler's advice. Goupil's had been asked to clean Burne-Jones' *Love Among the Ruins*; they had foolishly treated it as an oil painting, and thereby had ruined it. What was to be done? Whistler had never forgiven Burne-Jones for giving evidence against him at the Ruskin trial. He shouted with derision at the disaster. 'Didn't I always say the man knew nothing about painting, what? They take his oils for water-colours, and his water-colours for oils.' Whistler never forgot and never forgave. His judgments on his contemporaries were as much dictated by his personal relations with artists as by his aesthetic standards. Hence his lavish praise of Albert Moore. Of past English painters he praised only Hogarth—the one English artist, he used to say, who knew his business. He deemed *The Shrimp Girl* a masterpiece. Turner he called 'that old amateur'.

Whistler never liked Conder, and didn't care for his work. I don't think he ever invited Conder to the rue du Bac. He probably thought him too involved with ladies at Montmartre, too fond of his absinthe; for though Whistler was not censorious, he shrank from contact with anything coarse

or ugly; he liked people to fit into the pleasant social frame
in which he lived. The gaiety that wine enhances, yes; but
not the excitement and depression of alcohol. Although he
was constantly railing against England, he really respected
the fine temper and polish of English society.

Poor Conder would have liked to cut a figure, to be a sort
of Lucien de Rubempré. He had an immense respect for
people he thought influential, believing that this or that man
could effect wonderful things in his favour, wanting to introduce me, so that my fortune too could be made. Through
the prism of Conder's dreamy imagination, the men and
women he met would assume rainbow colours; especially
the women. One often hears of the attraction of certain men
for women—how irresistible they are to the frailer members
of the other sex. I am no psychologist, but in the case of the
two or three men I have known whose charms were fatal, the
reason seemed plain; nothing succeeds like desire, with
unusual ability to satisfy it. Most sensitive men are only
attracted by certain affinities, but to Guy de Maupassant, it
was rumoured, any woman could appeal. I first heard from
Dr Charvot who was then constantly seeing him, that this
explained the sudden collapse of his powerful brain. Something of this dangerous power belonged to Conder; he was
often without a sou, but he was never without a lady. But
to Germaine he had been faithful longer than was usual with
him. For weeks they would be together, loving and quarrelling; and I was bewildered by adulation and complaints
from each in turn. They had parted, for ever, and in a few days
I would find them together again. Conder and she would go
off into the country, Conder to paint apple blossom or willow
trees; he had found a place near La Roche Guyon, a tiny
hamlet with the lovely name of Chantemesle. Chantemesle,
how like one of Conder's own pensive paintings! From
there he wrote me, while I was staying at Montigny:

'Here I have a charming house all to myself' with a little
flower garden (rather a *verger*) and a skiff of my own
which I have hired: I could almost say "*had*" with the

mystress that I rowed away myself to the train the same
morning. So this letter will not be sunny—forgive me—
written I confess from loneliness to one who if even from
analytical reasons will not be too unsympathetic.

'I do feel a little lonely; but it's a huggable loneliness
which made me even angry with a small moth who sat
himself on the corner of the last page—Ah, as I write he
has got too near my lamp. "Why," cries this moth, "were
lamps made that I should so easily get sore wings?"
I was delighted to get your letter and had just been
thinking about you. It came as a true friend and I filtered
away two vermouths on reading under the old towers at la
Roche Guyon. So you're at Montigny bored unto death
I imagine with this cursed weather—"rain beating against
the windows has a leaden effect on my literary composition".
Indeed this morning même we sat and watched it in a small
room and felt angry and how large and wide the world was;
"so we disputed and parted". We had jolly times she and I
but many discussions—I knew always that it would be so
and that I am not sufficiently sympathetic to stay long—but
rain—rain, Rothenstein, upsets anyone and women are hard
and will bore one. If we could only look—as I look at the
pink rose on the table and hear no stories of past glories then
all would be well. But these past glories send one's personal
vanity to dead water and this with rain makes wells and
storms. I will not bore you any more with the girl unless anything very charming in the way of reflection crops up; but
should it I must give way. My table is covered with wrecks
of moths—it makes me sad. I am so very humane this night.
So landscape does not attract you, William? I can quite
understand that in the abstract; but think of one thing—what
wonderful invention landscape is. How it employs one's
time—keeps still, has no exciting effect on the nerves—and
then—then you will do it as I do. Then after all perhaps it's
as interesting as doing people's faces. I know one thing
largely true: I believe that men seem small beside it; one has
only to trot one's model out to find this. Then think of the

soothing effect; don't you feel it in the evening? In this
wonderful city of insects and stillness I do—it makes one
feel devilish ridiculous sometimes with all the petty ambitions and jealousies that follow us through those big cities.

'Perhaps Omar or Browning don't seem small beside all
this; but then these people arrive at being perfect symbolists
using external things as an architect uses colour—only
beautiful colours mind you. I have achieved 3 or 4 small bad
toiles which are all carefully packed up as so much gold
above my head—more carefully packed than painted—one
might say from my brilliant example of this June. When the
lion loved, a painter became he and then perhaps a fisherman—and ended then in the Royal Academy perhaps, if
he fished sufficient imbecility out of his passion and so on.
I am stuck here fervently awaiting money in a letter, like an
American student; having given my lost one all my super-
fluous coin—the money nuisance. I have accepted giving my
unholy presence to Dujardin. "Chevalier du Passé" (with
an eyeglass perhaps) of to-morrow, and the night after a
dinner—so you see I ought to be in Paris—after these few
days the Lord knoweth where I shall be—perhaps come and
see you and dear Salle for a day or two. No, these round water
marks are not tears, only flies from the soda and milk I am
imbibing. It stays and stays and stays; I haven't cried since
my brother died 8 years ago—what a boast! Talking of
brothers, thank that brother of yours when you write. He is
a good fellow to think of me. I am glad you had a good time
in London—I am to dine with Lautrec soon if all be well.
And then we shall hear about it. What late hours I am keeping; when I was married I always went to bed at ten—ten
indeed! sometimes 8.30. But don't envy my feminine society.
I have no more of it. I have lots of hope of seeing you
again—you two or three know my best and worst, such is the
magnet of friendship—the worst is hard to swallow and true
friends don't spit at me.

Yours

CHARLES CONDER.'

How like Conder his letters were! with a vagueness, a wantonness, a wistfulness all their own. He tried hard to forget Germaine; but life at Chantemesle without her proved unendurable, and he soon followed her to Paris.

I was trying my hand at figure painting for the first time, at Montigny, and was absorbed in this new task. Hence, probably, my reference to not caring about landscape. When I got back to Paris, Germaine had left Conder again, and Conder was in the country. He wrote to me from Vétheuil:

à la Crosnière,

par Vétheuil.

S. & O.

My dear Will,

I don't know if this letter will find you in Paris or Montigny. I send it to the latter. I am no longer as you will see at Chantemesle, but about a mile thereabouts to the East on the outskirts of Vétheuil.

I am again a widower and finding the life solitary; took this house with Anquetin for the season. The house itself is large and we have some six acres of very delightful upland behind with chalk inland—before the house the road and the Seine. If you care to come we shall be glad to have you, if you can content yourself with a rough and tumble kind of existence. We have a cook, a friend of Anquetin's friend Templier, and ladies' society is not wanting as A. seems to have an immense stock of ladies in waiting; so the house is full of new people. Perhaps the life has not quite enough monotony for steady work, but one manages to do a little somehow. I hardly did a stroke when dear Germaine was with me, though I cannot say it was her fault; rather the spirit of unrest that took hold of me.

These August nights are very beautiful and last night we made a jolly party on the Seine—full moon—vain aspirations to paint it as always happens—resolves etc. for tomorrow, but the sun comes out of the fog at eight and we paint in green and yellow—poor moon.

Anquetin is a good fellow and we get along splendidly. If you see Germaine in Paris give her my love and say I'm not a bad fellow at bottom, if a little bit of a nuisance to most people—I haven't said a word in reply to your regrets—I fancy them a good thing as you have twenty years and lots more to come. I hope you will have new loves to waste in masses before the aspiration can be realised. Don't misjudge my sentiment—or think that I would take any standpoint—I tell you after all like most people who advise you what you know already—and we are better in the fight than out at our age. I am in hopes of seeing you in a few days; and bring something to amuse yourself and forget the bother of the studies that don't please....

Frazier's brother came down for a day or two on his bicycle some two weeks ago. Anquetin enjoys galloping a horse and many women—I too, but it's a rude affair to love and makes one woman enough—however.

I have a wonderful subject to paint in the mornings, some oak and willow trees, and a rosy bank that Apollo might have run down to find some live nymphs. Streeton sends his love to you and wants to know about a pastel you promised him. Innocent Streeton. Well goodbye, love and try to come down.

Yours—CHARLES CONDER.

But Conder couldn't keep long away from Germaine. Unfortunately, during the weeks at Vétheuil, the beautiful Germaine had become friendly with Dujardin. The friendship ripened, but the estrangement between Conder and the lady again proved impermanent and Dujardin found himself deserted. Relations became in consequence strained. One night, Conder and I were dining at the Taverne Anglaise, when suddenly Dujardin strode in, glowered at Conder, walked straight to our table and said: 'Bonsoir Rothenstein, je regrette de vous voir en si mauvaise compagnie.' Conder

119

flushed scarlet, rose, raised his arm and made a gesture of striking Dujardin. I held his arm; Dujardin retired and sat down at another table. Conder sent a waiter with his card and Dujardin, calling for writing materials, sent across a note to me: 'Mon cher Rothenstein, M. Conder m'a fait venir sa carte; je voudrais bien savoir si je dois me tenir chez moi demain et à quelle heure. Pardonnez-moi de recourir à votre intermédiaire pour le savoir, cela tout officieusement, d'ailleurs. Votre Édouard Dujardin.' What a business! Could this be serious? To Conder it was serious enough; I was inclined to treat it as a romantic gesture. However, after dinner we went up to the Café de la Rochefoucauld to talk the matter over with Lomont and other French friends. They certainly took it seriously. Lomont, in his grave way, said that he and I must at once communicate with Dujardin and arrange a meeting with two of his friends. For an affair of this nature black gloves and black clothes were *de rigueur*. In the morning black gloves were duly purchased, and later Lomont and I set out for Dujardin's flat. Dujardin, who was expecting us, at once introduced us to two gentlemen, also in black coats and gloves, and retired. The matter was discussed with the utmost solemnity. Lomont claimed that Conder, being the insulted party, had the choice of weapons; the other two gentlemen disagreed; it was Dujardin who was the aggrieved party—Conder had made a gesture of striking, technically he had struck a blow. This was not Lomont's opinion; no blow had actually been struck. Finally, after much argument, it was decided that Conder should have the choice of weapons. We had our instructions; Conder was no swordsman—we chose pistols. We prepared to retire. But before we left, Lomont, who knew the rules, pleaded for a reconciliation; so serious a culmination should at least be reconsidered; seeing that Dujardin had not been struck, 'Seriously, gentlemen, was there a sufficient cause for an encounter?' I forget the details of the final arrangement. We returned to the Café de la Rochefoucauld where Conder was sitting surrounded by friends, and when we gravely informed

him that the regrettable incident was to be considered at an
end, Conder was half relieved and half vexed. I blush to say,
serious as the matter was for Conder, to me it had a comic
side—too comic for discretion. I came on Dujardin's note
only the other day among a lot of papers, and was reminded
of my one and only experience as a potential second in an
affair of honour.

I was, at the time, painting Conder in his studio, in a long
overcoat and tall hat. It was the first and only painting
I showed at the Salon du Champ de Mars. Conder wished
me to make him look more *Daumieresque*, to stylise his coat
and give him a *fatale* and romantic appearance. He was a
born stylist; I was by nature a realist, and I already felt
dimly that style should be intrinsic in one's work, not a thing
imposed. I painted other and similar full-length figures, one
of a French literary *précieux*, Marcel Boulanger, in a frock-
coat and a black stock; also a self-portrait, acquired, with
a number of other canvases, by Conder's friend, de Vallombreuse, when I came to leave Paris.

Marcel Boulanger was one of the few among my French
friends who asked me to his home. He had a very small
library, that contained only the few books he held worth
reading—precious editions, beautifully bound; and while his
mother's friends sat down to their cards, he, with a few chosen
friends, mostly dandies like himself, would discuss the latest
writers and poets.

Another friend who introduced me to his family was
Maurice Faure. His father was the famous opera singer, who
had been a constant supporter of Manet. The Faures' house
was full of Manet's paintings; among them the picture,
Concert aux Tuileries, now in the National Gallery, and a
striking portrait of Faure in the rôle of Hamlet.

I was fairly well read in French nineteenth-century literature, and had several literary friends. Besides the Latin
Quarter poets, I used to meet Mallarmé, Rodenbach, Henri
de Régnier, André Gide, Camille Mauclair, Montesquiou,
Rémy de Gourmont and, most frequently, Edouard Dujardin

and Marcel Schwob. My zest for Zola was past; Balzac and Stendhal, Flaubert and Maupassant were my chosen writers; among poets, Baudelaire and Verlaine. Conder also adulated Verlaine. Marcel Boulanger introduced me to the writings of Barbey d'Aurevilly and Villiers de l'Isle-Adam, and *Les Diaboliques* and *Contes Cruels* became favourite stories of mine.

CHAPTER XI

LAST DAYS IN PARIS

At Whistler's I first met Joseph Pennell. I felt, the moment I met him, that he disliked me at sight. We were speaking of Mallarmé, and I happened to praise his poetry; Pennell sneered at me for affecting to understand what baffled other people. He was so rude that when he left, Whistler was apologetic, saying: 'Never mind, Parson; you know, I always had a taste for bad company.' After my return to England Pennell remained steadily hostile.

Walter Sickert also came to the rue du Bac. I took to him at once. He and Whistler were close friends, but Whistler seemed to have some grievance against him, fancied or real, and Sickert was quiet and a little constrained. I was to see much of him later, and to find him, not less, but more fascinating on closer acquaintance.

During this spring, Pearsall Smith brought a friend of his, Lord Basil Blackwood, to my studio, whose father, Lord Dufferin, was then Ambassador in Paris. He was staying at the Embassy and wished to see something other than official life, something of studio-life and Montmartre. And he wished me to draw his portrait. A charming person I thought him, and was pleased when he asked me to Balliol to stay with him there.

One day a young American came up to me at some party. He had a letter; he was told I knew everyone in Paris; would I introduce him to Whistler, and to some of the French writers? He was handsome, richly dressed, and spoke as

though he were a famous writer. I knew nothing of his
writing, but he was clearly a robust flower of American
muscular Christianity—healthy, wealthy, and, in America,
wise. His particular friend was Charles Dana Gibson, the
popular creator of the type of which Davis himself (it was
he) was a radiant example.

Richard Harding Davis had never met any artists like
Conder and me; he was respectful of our dazzling intellects;
but he regretted that we were not, like himself, noble and
virtuous. We puzzled him sadly; he even at times had doubts
in regard to himself; but these doubts, when in the morning
before his glass he brushed his rich, shining hair and shaved
his fresh, firm chin and called to mind the sums his short
stories brought him, proved fleeting as last night's dream.
I liked Davis; I was touched at his wanting to make me a
better and seemlier person, a sort of artistic boy-scout,
springing smartly to attention before embarking on the good,
wholesome work of art I was to achieve each day. He knew
Basil Blackwood, and encouraged my going to Oxford; to
mix with healthy young aristocrats would do me all the good
in the world; but when later he heard I was seeing Walter
Pater, he lost hope.

I also had a visit from a young journalist, Grant Richards,
secretary to W. T. Stead, who had managed for the first time
to come to Paris. Unlike Davis, he was frankly envious of
the life we led, of the company we kept, of our familiarity
with a world from which he was shut off. Some day he would
get away from the obnoxious Stead, a man with no feeling
for beauty, a kill-joy, a fusty-musty Puritan. To make up
for the dreary letters he must copy during the day, he read
with avidity the most venturesome books he could get. He
was full of *Dorian Gray*, which he admired more than I did
—he had never read *A Rebours*, and did not know how much
Wilde had taken from Huysmans. He was enthusiastic in
his appreciation of my drawings and paintings and Conder's
fans, and begged me, when I came to London, to stay in his
flat, which he shared with his cousin, young Grant Allen,

and with Frederick Whelen. How hospitable English people
seemed, I thought, compared with the French!

About the same time came D. S. MacColl, the protagonist of Whistler and Degas in England. He was visiting Paris. Meeting Conder, he at once fell in love with his painting, with which he never fell out of love. He knew Whistler, had dined with him at the rue du Bac, and afterwards called on him at his studio. Whistler came to the door, palette and brushes in hand and declared he was hard at work. MacColl ran his fingers across his brushes, which were dry and devoid of paint, and Whistler, laughing, let him in. Hearing I was going to Oxford, MacColl very kindly gave me letters to Frederick York Powell and Walter Pater.

I spent a pleasant week with Basil Blackwood at Balliol, and met many people, among them York Powell at Christ Church; on one occasion I scribbled some caricatures of Verlaine and Rodin and other people whom Powell knew, which seemed to amuse him. A day or two later he met John Lane, and showed him these scraps, suggesting that Lane, who was on the look-out for fresh talent, might get me to do a set of Oxford portraits. Lane wrote to me, and I saw him on my way through town. The upshot was, he agreed to publish 24 drawings of prominent Oxonians, for which he would pay me £120. This was an exciting commission; I was to begin work at the commencement of the autumn term. Returning to Paris I told Whistler of my good fortune. I thought of making pastel drawings; Whistler said 'Why not do lithographs? Go to Way, he will put you up to all the tricks.'

Incidentally, I did Whistler an ill turn before leaving Paris. Early in the year I had a *femme de ménage* who pilfered. A girl who sat to me recommended in her place a young brother who wanted a job. He proved a handy and presentable lad; he wore a green waistcoat with sleeves, and looked very smart. When I gave up my studio, Whistler asked me what was to become of Eugène, and decided to try him. He proved satisfactory, I heard, for a time; then he

125

vanished, together with some pieces of Whistler's old silver. He was caught, tried and imprisoned; but the silver was lost; he had melted it down.

When the time came to give up my studio, I wondered whether I was wise to leave Paris. I had dug myself in, as it were, into Paris life; my sympathies, too, were with French painting. I loved Paris and I had made many friends. My memories of London were not very happy ones; Whistler and Oscar Wilde had both extolled life in Paris, to the disadvantage of London. Conder thought I was making a great mistake, that I would soon have a name in Paris, whereas people in England wouldn't understand what I was aiming at. But Lane's commission was not one to be lightly refused. I was always ready for fresh experience.

Before I left I destroyed the most worthless among my drawings and canvases. My friends begged or bought a number of those they thought worth preserving; a good number were acquired by a friend, de Vallombreuse. Richard Harding Davis, too, bought some pastels. With the money I got I was able to pay my debts, owed chiefly to colour merchants and framers. Then I prepared to go off for a summer's painting to Montigny. Uncertain whether or not I would return to Paris, I gave up my studio. It was taken by Bernard Harrison, Frederick Harrison's second son, a landscape painter.

Before I left Paris I heard that Verlaine was in hospital, and more than usually miserable. Though Verlaine was universally admired as a poet, his habits proved too much even for his friends, as I mentioned before. Latin Quarter poets, who were not over particular, had helped him again and again, but he had become impossible. Still, it seemed hard that a man of his genius should be deserted by all, unaided and wretched. I loved his poetry, and knowing him to be ill I wrote and told him how much I cared for his poems. A message came—would I go to see him at the Hôpital Broussais?

Verlaine was pleased, I could see, at my visit. We spoke

about England, where he had been, and of his memories of
London and Brighton. His talk was amusing, with a child-
like kind of humour. He liked being in hospital; he was clean,
and, in addition, perfectly sober. He had a Silenus-like head;
his baldness made his forehead look higher than in fact it
was, and his small brown eyes with yellow lights and with
their corners turned up, looked queer. He was very pale.
His eyes had a half candid, half dissipated look, the effects
of drink and of white nights; but they also had at times an
engaging candour. Beneath were broad cheek bones, a short,
Socratic nose, heavy moustaches, and an untidy, straggling
beard, turning grey. One almost expected to find tall, pointed
ears under his thin locks.

He begged me to come and see him again, and I went back
to the hospital several times. He talked much of his illness,
and of his poverty, complaining bitterly of the miserable
sums Vanier paid for his poems—and of the trouble he had
to get paid. Lately he had been able to make a little money
by giving some conferences in Holland and Belgium; but
the money had all disappeared. Why not give some readings
of his poems in England? I suggested. I was sure he would
meet with a cordial reception. The idea of going to England
pleased him; he talked again of the days spent at Brighton,
where he had been a schoolmaster, and of visits to London
with Rimbaud. The doctors and nurses, he said, were all kind
to him; he had nothing to pay, and lived *à l'œil* like a fighting
cock. It was his leg that troubled him; but he would soon
be out, and then I must come and see him, and meet his friend
Eugénie. She was a good creature, he said, 'mais quelquefois
un peu rosse'.

I heard from him when he came out of hospital; would
I come and see him at the rue Descartes? I found him living
in a single room, poorly furnished, and not very clean. A short,
shapeless, coarse-featured woman with dark hair dressed
close over a low forehead, with the hoarse, throaty voice of
the *banlieue*—could this be she to whom Verlaine had written
so many passionately amorous verses, and to whom, despite

127

infidelities, he returned again and again? Eugénie treated me
with humiliating respect, not as an artist, but as a kind of
miché; she was on what she thought was her best behaviour.
Verlaine must have told her of English editions, or possible
conferences, which to her meant, *tout bonnement, la galette*.
On subsequent visits the Krantz resumed easier ways and a
more homely manner. She threw out hints that anything
coming to Verlaine should pass through her hands; she
whispered terrible things into my ears, as to what would
happen otherwise. Verlaine, with his shrewd and unashamed
frankness, taunted her with her greed. She continually
robbed him, he cried; he never had a sou, quoi! hadn't even
enough to buy himself a shirt and collars; as for drinking,
why he didn't want to drink, but still, *nom d'un nom*, sometimes one wanted to offer a glass to a friend. There would be
fearful *engueulades*, and then, like two cats in a yard, they
would walk away from each other, and Verlaine would
quietly resume his talk about literature, other poets, and
plans for new poems. There was a queer mixture of ribaldry
and delicacy in his talk, and something child-like and in-
gratiating in his manner.

Before returning to England, I spent the summer at
Montigny-sur-Loing, a charming little village between Moret
and Marlotte, where for a few francs weekly I hired an
untenanted house in which I could paint. I had brought
down a model to sit for me. There was a little shop at Montmartre where beautiful old dresses were to be had, for a few
francs, and I had purchased some dresses and some bonnets
as well of the 1830 period, and was eager my model should
wear them. So she decked herself out in this past finery, and
I did some paintings which were later shown at the New
English Art Club.

Montigny was only a few miles below Grez. I had been
there before, with my friend, von Hofmann, when we had
made the acquaintance of Armand Dayot, and of his charming daughter, Madeleine.

There were no other painters at Montigny; but Grez, a

VERLAINE AT L'HÔPITAL BROUSSAIS (1893)

mile or two away, was 'an artists' village', well known to
English and American painters on account of its association
with Robert Louis Stevenson. Ernest Parton, whom I met
at the inn there, had known Grez well in Stevenson's time—
wild days they were then, he said. I couldn't associate
Parton with anything wild; he was a meek and successful
painter of birch trees. Nobody wanted anything but birch
trees from him, he complained; having once made a success
with a painting of birch trees at the Royal Academy, he was
sentenced to paint these, and nothing but these, all his life.
At the inn too was Sarah Brown, the most famous model in
Paris; whenever she came to Julian's she was mobbed; the
whole school crushed and crowded into the studio where she
sat. In many ways the English are more generous than the
French, but the French are generously grateful for the gift
of beauty; a sympathetic trait, which plays its part in sup-
porting the self-respect of the class from which our models
came. Sarah was fair, and her figure, small bosomed, had
the creamy unity of a Titian. Perhaps the figures of our
models when they emerged from the clothes then worn, the
high shouldered bodices, with their wasp-cut waists, the rigid
corsets and long, bell-shaped skirts, seemed yet more nobly,
more radiantly classical by contrast. And contrariwise, after
seeing young girls looking like goddesses on the model
stand, how disillusioning to see them when they resume their
poor, trumpery finery; they seem shrunken to half their size.

Sarah Brown at Grez was very entertaining. She was *en
villégiature*, agreeably sentimental over trees and birds, the
flowers in the fields, envying the country wenches their innocent lives—O Maupassant!—but, after dinner and a glass
of *vin doux*, not sorry to have a *rapin* from Paris to chatter
with. The last time I saw Sarah was at the Bal des Quat'z
Arts, whither she had come, carried by four students in a
litter as Cleopatra, clad only in a golden net.

Another village near by was Marlotte, where a Montmartre
friend, Armand Point, had a rose-embowered cottage. Staying with him were two lady friends, both beautiful and

intelligent, whom he put into his pictures. Point, before Maurice Denis and in a less personal way, had studied the Italian primitives, and wanted to bring something of their poetry and simplicity into modern painting. He was one of the few French painters who knew the work of the English Pre-Raphaelites. He had a charming nature, and as an artist he had much in common with Howard Cushing, who was likewise a lover of the early Italians.

Cushing was staying at Moret, where I went to see him. I remember the occasion only too well. Moret was ten miles away, and I bicycled over. That morning I had read of an attack on a cyclist in the forest of Fontainbleau, near by. A cord had been drawn across the road at night-fall; the cyclist rode into it, was thrown from his machine, was set upon, robbed, and left dangerously injured. It was a *fait divers* which had little effect on me when I read it; but when I left Moret in the evening and was riding back in the dark through the forest, the incident suddenly came to my mind. There was no moon, and the road was deserted. Suddenly cold fear came upon me. Never did 10 miles seem so endless. Now and again as sinister sounds would come from the forest, my heart beat fast. Suddenly—what was that? my heart stood still, and a great white owl flew out into the night. I arrived at Montigny exhausted and covered with sweat.

CHAPTER XII

BEARDSLEY AND MAX

I N the autumn I prepared to migrate to Oxford. Basil Blackwood had asked me to stay with him at Balliol for a week or two, while I looked for rooms. York Powell offered to put me up later at Christ Church, and Mrs Woods had asked me to Trinity College. So there was plenty of time to look round before I settled in lodgings.

Migration to Oxford

Before going to Oxford, I spent some days with Grant Richards in London, making final arrangements with John Lane about the book I was to do, and trying stones and transfer papers at Way's printing office.

The firm of Thos. Way was an old-established business of lithographic printers. They were Whistler's pet printers. It was at their office in Wellington Street that he made his early experiments on stone and on transfer paper, sometimes using wash as well as point. He would come there often to work on his stones. The Ways had been associated with Whistler for many years. Old Way, besides owning a unique collection of Whistler's prints, had acquired many of his paintings. He was a cross-grained old man, with an uncertain temper, but where Whistler was concerned, a willing slave. I received a warm welcome from father and son; Tom Way, whom his father kept in rigid subservience, knew all the processes and tricks of the trade, and took endless trouble to help me with my first essays.

Grant Richards was still acting as secretary to Stead, a task he much disliked. He had literary and sartorial ambitions,

neither one nor the other received encouragement from Stead
nor indeed from Richards' own family. He, too, looked with
envy on my frock-coat; on my freedom and my reckless
ways. Meeting Stead in London, I sympathised with Richards.
Stead, journalist, mystic, reformer, rescuer of fallen women,
imperialist, and goodness knows what else, didn't impress
me. He had the typical nonconformist presence; the way his
hair grew suggested nonconformity, so did the rather obvious piercing eyes. A strong plain man, whose mission was
naturally wasted on me. Other of Richards' friends were more
to my taste, especially Le Gallienne, whose appearance was
fascinating. He looked like Botticelli's head of Lorenzo. I at
once itched to draw him, and spent a week-end with him
and his young wife at his house at Hanwell. A charming
person he was, every inch a poet, with long hair, wide collar,
and high ideals. He had recently published his *English
Poems*, which helped to revive the fashion for reading poetry
—a feather, truly, in his cap. He had attracted the notice of
Oscar Wilde by his poetic appearance as well as by his
verses; at the same time he had caught some of Oscar's
mannerisms, too. I remember his showing me a photograph
of Yeats, of whom I then knew nothing, of which he
nervously asked what I thought. He evidently thought much
of Yeats; but he was not displeased at my ignorance of who
he was. We parted swearing eternal friendship. I was to
make a drawing to appear in his next book, and would soon
return for the purpose. Each had flattered the other, as young
men on the threshold of life are eager to do.

I went with Richards to see *A Woman of No Importance*,
Oscar Wilde's new play which had taken the town by storm.
Oscar was delighted, as he had been on the success of his
first play, *Lady Windermere's Fan*. At last he had achieved
a popular success. In addition, he was making a great deal
of money. In Paris he had been rather apologetic about his
first play; as though to write a comedy were rather beneath
a poet. When I saw it I thought, on the contrary, here is the
genuine Wilde, making legitimate use of the artifice which

was, in fact, natural to him; like his wit, indeed, in which his
true genius lay. I know now that the money his plays brought
Wilde did neither him nor anyone else much good. He was
offended with me when I met him in London; he had heard
I took sides with Whistler against him, though there was no
need to listen to Whistler to hear disagreeable things about
Wilde; there were plenty of people who disliked and mis-
trusted him, I was finding out. I reassured him, and went to
see him and his wife at Tite Street, where I also met his two
charming boys, Vyvyan and Cyril. I liked Mrs Wilde. She
wasn't clever, but she had distinction and candour. With
brown hair framing her face, and a Liberty hat, she looked
like a drawing by Frank Miles, or (to name a better artist),
by Walter Crane. I knew little of the difficulties which were
beginning between Wilde and his wife; they seemed on
affectionate terms; he delighted in his children; only I felt
something wistful and a little sad about Mrs Wilde.

One of Mrs Wilde's intimate friends was Mrs Walter
Palmer, who was a close friend of George Meredith and of
his daughter, Mariette, afterwards Mrs Henry Sturgis. One
eventful evening, George Meredith came to a party at Mrs
Palmer's, at which I was present. What a noble head! I
thought, as he sat on a sofa, and how like one of his own
characters he talked. This was the only occasion on which
I met Mrs Wilde at a party with Oscar. I went down with
her to supper, and later, when she discovered me to be, like
herself, a whole-hearted Meredithian, she took me up to the
great man. He was still on his sofa, surrounded by a bevy
of fair ladies, and we joined the group and listened to his
scintillating talk.

I was anxious to meet Ricketts and Shannon, of whom
Wilde often spoke so admiringly; he had shown me the
drawings they did for his *House of Pomegranates*, and
Ricketts' lovely cover; and it surprised me to hear of these
gifted men, of whom we knew nothing in Paris; so I went
to the Vale one evening with Oscar. I fell at once under their
charm, and hoped, when settled in London, to see more of

them and their work. They spoke to me of Beardsley, who, earlier that year, had called on me in Paris. He had lately sprung into fame through an article by Pennell in a new periodical—*The Studio*. He had seemed interested in my paintings in Paris, and welcomed me warmly when I went to see him.

Holme, who owned *The Studio*, which had at once achieved a success with Pennell's opening article on Beardsley, wanted to have articles on others of the younger men and approached me about it. But I objected to Holme, for not paying his artists, though he paid his writers. We artists had so little chance of earning money, and it seemed only fair that we should be paid at least a small fee for our work, the more so since the illustrations were the essential feature of Holme's paper. Holme was willing to pay me for writing, and I wrote some Paris notes, and reviewed an Academy exhibition—very irreverently, I fear; but we finally quarrelled over the non-payment of reproductions. But I was unfair to Holme, for I learned later that his practice was the usual one.

Beardsley was living in Cambridge Terrace, Pimlico, with his mother and his sister Mabel. The walls of his rooms were distempered a violent orange, the doors and skirtings were painted black; a strange taste, I thought; but his taste was all for the bizarre and exotic. Later it became somewhat chastened. I had picked up a Japanese book in Paris, with pictures so outrageous that its possession was an embarrassment. It pleased Beardsley, however, so I gave it him. The next time I went to see him, he had taken out the most indecent prints from the book and hung them around his bedroom. Seeing he lived with his mother and sister, I was rather taken aback. He affected an extreme cynicism, however, which was startling at times; he *spoke* enormities; *mots* were the mode, and provided they were sufficiently witty, anything might be said. Didn't someone say of Aubrey that even his lungs were affected? It was a time when everyone, in the wake of Whistler, wanted to take out a patent for

brilliant sayings. Referring to my bad memory, Beardsley
remarked 'It doesn't matter what good things one says in
front of Billy, he's sure to forget them'.

Beardsley was an impassioned worker, and his hand was unerringly skilful. But for all his craftsmanship there was something hard and insensitive in his line, and narrow and small in his design, which affected me unsympathetically. He, too, remarkable boy as he was, had something harsh, too sharply defined in his nature—like something seen under an arc-lamp. His understanding was remarkable; his mind was agate-like, almost too polished, in its sparkling hardness; but there was that in his nature which made him an affectionate and generous friend. Max Beerbohm, in the sympathetic and discerning study he wrote on Beardsley after his death, said no one ever saw Beardsley at work. I could not quite understand this, as Beardsley pressed me, whenever I came to town, to make use of his workroom. Before going to Oxford and while I was mainly there, I was glad enough to have somewhere to work when in town. Beardsley seemed to get on perfectly well as he sat at one side of a large table, while I sat at the other. He was then beginning his *Salome* drawings.

He would indicate his preparatory design in pencil, defining his complicated patterns with only the vaguest pencil indication underneath, over which he drew with the pen with astonishing certainty. He would talk and work at the same time; for, like all gifted people, he had exceptional powers of concentration.

But one was always aware of the eager, feverish brilliance of the consumptive, in haste to absorb as much of life as he could in the brief space he instinctively knew was his sorrowful portion. Poor Aubrey! he was a tragic figure. It was as though the gods had said, 'Only four years more will be allowed you; but in those four years you shall experience what others take forty years to learn.' Knowledge he seemed to absorb through his pores. Always at his drawing desk, he still found time to read an astonishing variety of books.

He knew his Balzac from cover to cover, and explored the
courts and alleys of French and English seventeenth and
eighteenth century literature. Intensely musical, too, he
seemed to know the airs of all the operas. No wonder Oscar
thought him wonderful, and chose him at once as the one
artist to illustrate his *Salome*.

Since the first appearance of his work in *The Studio*,
Beardsley's drawings were constantly abused; none of the
illustrators of the day would say a word in his favour. Worse
still, they joined the howling crowd in crying for Beardsley
to be put in the stocks. Their stupidity, meanness and blind-
ness were even more abnormal than was Beardsley's genius.
A similar outcry arose over Max Beerbohm's first essays; in
fact, we were all to be lumped together as 'decadents'. On
the other hand, a few people hailed Beardsley as one of
the greatest draughtsmen who had ever appeared; such
exaggerated praise is scarcely less irritating than stupid
abuse.

While I worked at Beardsley's, I stayed with Grant
Richards, a hospitable person. Many people came to his
flat at Rossetti Mansions, among others, Lady Burton.
I was prejudiced against her, as I heard that she had lately
destroyed the unpublished manuscripts of her husband, Sir
Richard Burton; a wanton act, it seemed to me, and
since she spoke so adulatingly of him, the more to be
blamed.

An attractive character, who came often to Richards' flat,
was old Dr Bird, who had been Leigh Hunt's doctor and
was full of stories of Hunt and his circle. Later I became an
intimate friend of his sister, Miss Alice Bird. At her death
our last link with the people who had known Keats and
Shelley was severed.

When I had sufficiently practised drawing on stone at
Way's I proceeded to Oxford, to begin work on the portraits
for Lane. As I left school unusually early, I found, up at
Oxford, many old schoolmates, in their second and third
years. It was pleasant to meet Hammond, Meade, Dyson,

Walrond and other Bradfordians again. Many Bradford
scholarships were held at Queen's College. Hammond and
Meade were at St John's. At Balliol I met a very entertaining
set of men, none more so than Basil Blackwood. He had
great gifts, about which he was very modest; he would, I
thought, go far, if he cared, as a politician or diplomat, but
he lacked ambition; a little diffident—a little indolent perhaps.
He had a turn for drawing, and as B. T. B. did the amusing
pictures for Hilaire Belloc's *Bad Child's Book of Beasts*. Belloc
himself, although he had taken his degree, had come back to
Balliol for further reading. I was astonished at the copiousness and brilliance of his intellect, and of his talk. Half
French and half English, he seemed equally at home in the
life and literature of either country. I rather fancied myself
for my small knowledge of French literature, but before
Belloc's encyclopaedic mind I had need to be modest. He
had the sparkling energy of the Gallic temper; emphatic and
assertive, brimful of ideas, he was formidable in attack. The
man who stood up to him best was Hamilton Grant; his
quick wit would parry Belloc's vehement statements. Round
these three were gathered a number of attractive young men:
Claud Russell, Lord Alexander Thynne, Hubert Howard,
Lord Kerry, Oliver Borthwick, Geoffrey Cookson, Anthony
Henley and J. F. Kershaw. A sudden change, it was, from
Whistler, Oscar Wilde, Conder and Lautrec, to this bright,
fresh, youthful company. No doubt I tried to impress
them with my Parisian experiences, as a 'dog' who had led
the devil of a life, one who was on familiar terms with poets
and painters whose names rang musically in the ears of young
men of my age. I must have appeared a strange apparition in
Oxford, with my longish hair, and spectacles, and my un-
Oxonian ways and approach to things and people. Moreover,
I was supposed to be an Impressionist, a terrible reputation
to have at the time.

When I left Balliol, I went to stay with York Powell at
Christ Church. York Powell was one of the personalities of
Oxford, an historian, an Icelandic scholar, and an authority

on Roman Law and on boxing. He was a friend of William
Morris, Henley, Wilfrid Blunt, Meredith and Rodin. To my
surprise I found he had Rodin's bronze of *l'Homme au nez
cassé* in his rooms; also many Japanese prints, not so common
then as now. A burly, untidy man, with hearty and genial
manners and a jolly laugh, his tastes were as untidy as his
dress. His mind was a jungle of knowledge. It was strange
to find this boisterous, free-thinking man at Christ Church.
One of his intimate friends was William Hines, a socialist
chimney-sweep; Powell himself was suspected of socialist
leanings; had not Bernard Shaw been his guest at Christ
Church! But everyone respected his wide knowledge, and
his honest opinions, though I felt that Dodgson, the author
of *Alice*, then a student of Christ Church, was not very
cordial to Powell at the high table. Dodgson could scarcely
have approved of York Powell's opinions; he certainly did
not approve of mine. I found that Powell knew something
about most of the poets at the Café d'Harcourt, and had read
all Verlaine and Mallarmé. He had discovered, in a French
schoolmaster at Oxford, Charles Bonnier, an old friend of
Mallarmé. With York Powell I saw much of Bonnier, of
W. P. Ker and Ray Lankester. We started a Rabelais club
at Oxford, dining together once a month, when someone
would read a paper. W. P. Ker discovered the meaning of a
certain English phrase in Rabelais, which had for long puzzled
scholars. It was a good piece of Scotch, he found, and com-
municated his *trouvaille* to the club. I remember, too, Herbert
Fisher reading a paper, and trying vainly to hide his blushes,
as he intoned some very Pantagruelistic passage. W. P. Ker
had the gift of radiant silence. He fairly glowed over his
wine, and when he did speak it was to say something short
and pregnant. Ray Lankester, Herbert Greene, a don at
Magdalen, and York Powell had a hoard of Rabelaisian
stories, which they distributed generously.

MacColl had given me a letter to Walter Pater. Pater's
appearance was unexpected; neatly dressed; slightly stooping shoulders: a thick moustache, above rather heavy lips,

grey eyes a shade too close together, a little restless, even
evasive, under dark eyebrows. He had a habit, disquieting
to young people, of assuming ignorance on subjects about
which he was perfectly informed. He questioned me closely
about Mallarmé and Verlaine, Huysmans and de Goncourt,
and the younger French writers. Guarded in his talk, careful
of expressing his own opinions, he was adept at inviting indiscretions from his guests. I naturally wanted to hear his own
views on things and people, but young men cannot decently
ask older men what they think of their contemporaries.
He asked much about Whistler, for whom he had no great
admiration. I did try one day to get his opinion of Oscar
Wilde, who regarded Pater as his master. 'Oh Wilde, yes,
he always has a phrase.' I told this afterwards to Oscar,
who affected to be delighted. 'A perfect thing to have said
of one,' he murmured, *'he always has a phrase.'* Just as
certain intellectuals affect a passion for detective stories, so
Pater made a practice of entertaining the football and cricket-
playing undergraduates, while he rather ignored the young
precieux. He gave regular luncheon parties on Wednesdays;
each time I was invited, I met very tongue-tied, simple,
good-looking youths of the sporting fraternity. But Pater's
close companion, Bussell, was always of the party, to share
Pater's slightly malicious enjoyment.

York Powell was not only a generous host, but he took
endless trouble to guide me in the choice of likely subjects
for my book; and to persuade these subjects to sit. One of
my first sitters was old Sir Henry Acland, who had been the
intimate friend of Ruskin. I fear I at once shocked him by
beginning my drawing without pinning down my paper;
every artist for whom he had sat had always stretched or
pinned down his paper. It was my misfortune at this time
to draw many people who, like Sir Henry Acland, had in
their younger days sat for George Richmond. Richmond's
portraits were extremely capable, and showed a high finish,
which delighted his sitters. To make much less accomplished
drawings of these in their later years was in truth an

ungrateful task. Young eyes look unpitying on old age, knowing nought of its early splendour. Older artists can catch fleeting traces of youthful fire in the features of contemporaries whom they knew in their prime. Work premeditated is like a drop of water, seemingly clear; once undertaken, it is like the same drop of water seen through a magnifying glass, no longer pure, but swarming with life. So, all at once, my task was fertile with surprises and troubles. But with the hopefulness and cocksureness of youth, I foresaw them not, but plunged gaily into my task.

The first drawing I did of Sir Henry Acland was a feeble one, which both he and his daughter, quite properly, disliked. I should never have had it put down on the stone. Like many young men, I was conceited and thought that any objection to a drawing was a proof of its worth. I respected Sir Henry's taste for Ruskin's drawings, but his bias against anything new doubtless encouraged me to believe that his judgment of a contemporary drawing was worthless. I myself had misgivings about the drawing; and Sir Henry's opinion, whether worthless or not, was far-reaching, for there came a letter from Elkin Mathews telling me that the publication had failed largely on account of the antipathy of Sir Henry Acland and his friends to the portrait of Sir Henry in Part I, and the booksellers were rebelling against taking the second and future parts. After the first drawing appeared, Sir Henry Acland sent me a very courteous letter, with a view to my doing another:

June 18, 1893

Dear Mr Rothenstein,

I happened to mention to you my valued friend Mr George Richmond the Academician, last night. Should you care (though it is a delicate task for me to suggest it) to look at his sketch of a few years ago, I can show it you: both original and engraving. There is often with every artist a view of style and subject—and it is interesting often to compare the ideas. Then Mr Richmond sketched with deliberate care.

I have several of his drawings which I should be delighted to show you.

I am, dear Mr Rothenstein, faithfully yours,

H. M. ACLAND.

P.S. Mr Richmond's engraving is in my room where you can see it any time you pass.

I knew it was hopeless for me to attempt a drawing comparable with George Richmond's; alas, I did not sketch with deliberate care, but I was willing to try again; fortunately my second attempt was a little more adequate. Nothing would have pleased me more than to make a drawing worthy of Sir Henry's handsome presence; there was a character, a distinction about all the men and women connected with the Pre-Raphaelites; Sir Henry himself had the grand manner, tempered by a rare courtesy, of the older generation of Victorians. His house had the stately cosiness of the period, full as it was of prints, drawings, fossils, white peacocks, botanical plates and rosewood furniture. Among many paintings was Millais' portrait of Ruskin, standing by a waterfall. While at work on this portrait, Millais fell in love with Mrs Ruskin, to whom, as is well known, he was later married. Sir Henry Acland described how Ruskin later insisted that Millais should finish the portrait; it was a duty to Art. Millais came, Ruskin stood, and the work was completed, without a word having passed between them.

After Acland came Robinson Ellis, a great character, but not handsome like Acland. The eminent Catullus scholar wrote agonised letters to Joseph Wells and York Powell. To Powell he wrote: 'Rothenstein's "character sketch" of me seemed to me yesterday so remarkably hideous that I should be very unwilling to let it appear. He said he would show it to you, and I feel assured you would agree with me. Will you let him know unmistakably that it must not appear. I might be a Kalmuck Tartar or a Mongol of an unusually horrid type. Besides it would be very uncomfortable for the person

141

who appears in company of such a monster!' Both Powell
and Wells reassured him; then came the following letter:

Trinity College,
Oct. 20, 1893

Dear Sir,

Both Mr York Powell and Mr Wells of Wadham have
written to me about the sketch, stating that they have not
the same objections to it which I confess to feeling when you
showed it me. I suppose it may be that I for the first time
saw my true self, and comparing it with previous photographs, and with Mr J. Hood's picture, felt annoyed at coming
out so dreadfully ugly. For that, I think you cannot deny
it is, and in a great degree.

The last thing I should wish to do would be in any way
to injure you as an artist. But, odd as you may think it, I am
not convinced that many of my friends would like to recall
me from your sketch. This says nothing in detraction of your
powers as an artist: it only means that you took me at an
unfavourable moment and caught an expression which is not
very pleasing. Of your sincerity, again, I have not the least
doubt; but this sketch cannot in any way be said to *flatter*.

As you seem to think (which I can believe) that my with-
drawing from the series would injure you, I have only to say
that I am very willing to look at the picture again from 2.30
to 4 to-morrow; and in any case to make my peace with you.
It is, indeed, a compliment which I do not deserve to be
thought worthy of any sketch: and perhaps in its finished
state I may find it more presentable.

Yours very truly, ROBINSON ELLIS

Of course I was ready to try again, and Ellis was equally
willing to sit. The second attempt, as with the drawing of
Acland, was more satisfactory, both to my sitter and myself.
Meanwhile Robinson Ellis was made Regius Professor of
Latin; in reply to my congratulations he wrote from Bourne-
mouth: 'How kind of you to write congratulating me on my

election. I might not have disgusted you with my parti- *Burdon-*
cularity *in re* your sketch, and yet I am tolerably sure that your *Sanderson's*
later sketch will be more likely to please my friends than the *rabbits*
other; so I don't regret what I made you do; I hope the
series is selling pretty well: it takes some time before a good
thing is known, and Oxford criticisms are apt to be cold.
Many of your portraits will be far more pleasing, of course,
than mine: and these will make up for the defects of old
stagers like me. Please, when you come to Oxford, come
and dine in Hall with me, if on a Sunday in Corpus: if otherwise in Trinity.' Nevertheless, Ellis took a morbid delight in
praising, among my drawings of other people, the ugliest
ones—more especially because of the accurate likeness.

An eminent Victorian, to whom York Powell introduced
me, was Burdon-Sanderson, a remarkable-looking figure, tall
and gaunt, with features strangely like Dante's. He took me
round his garden, in which I noticed he kept rabbits. I was
rather touched at this somewhat gloomy, sardonic, old man
keeping pets. When I got back to Christ Church, I remarked
on this charming trait during dinner at the High Table,
upon which the whole company burst into laughter. Only
then I discovered that Burdon-Sanderson was a famous
vivisectionist!

I had no learning; my reading was restricted to novels,
and I knew little or nothing of the fame and achievement of
most of my sitters, among whom were James Murray, editor
of *The New English Dictionary*, Ingram Bywater, Arthur
Sidgwick, Margoliouth, and, of course, Max Müller. I was
particularly amused at my reception by Max Müller. Before
I drew him, he went upstairs and fetched an illustrated paper
with a tailor's advertisement showing him dressed in a very
smart frock-coat. This, he observed, was how he wished to
be drawn! It seems incredible; but unless I dreamt this it
was so. The drawing done, he took me downstairs to show
me a large cabinet of photographs, all of himself, and all
ready signed, with quotations from favourite poets inscribed
on each. He solemnly presented me with one. Was this too

143

a dream? And did I also dream of a life-size full-length photograph of the German Emperor hanging on the wall?

York Powell delighted in the stories I brought back from my sittings. The most unconventional don in Oxford, he had no great veneration for some of his colleagues.

I insisted, much against John Lane's wishes, on including a few portraits of undergraduates among those of the dons, arguing that, in a record of contemporary Oxford, undergraduates should have a place. So I drew C. B. Fry, the greatest all-round athlete of the time; W. A. L. Fletcher, the leading oarsman; Hilaire Belloc, and Max Beerbohm. I owed my introduction to Max Beerbohm to Viscount St Cyres, a Merton man who had taken his degree and was now a 'Reader' at Christ Church. A baby face, with heavily lidded, very light grey eyes shaded by remarkably thick and long lashes, a broad forehead, and sleek black hair parted in the middle and coming to a queer curling point at the neck; a quiet and finished manner; rather tall, carefully dressed; slender fingered, with an assurance and experience unusual in one of his years—I was at once drawn to Max Beerbohm and lost no time in responding to an invitation to breakfast. He was living in a tiny house at the far end of Merton Street— a house scarcely bigger than a Punch and Judy show. His room, blue-papered, was hung with Pellegrini prints from *Vanity Fair*. Beside these, there were some amusing caricatures which, he said modestly, were his own. 'But they are brilliant', I said, and he seemed pleased at my liking them.

We met frequently. Though we were the same age, and in some ways I had more experience of life than he, his seemed to have crystallised into a more finished form than my own. So had his manners, which were perfect. He was delightfully appreciative of anything he was told, seizing the inner meaning of any rough observation of men and of things, which at once acquired point and polish in contact with his understanding mind. Outside Merton only few undergraduates knew him; all who did know him, admired him.

WALTER PATER (1894)

His caricatures were sometimes to be seen in Shrimpton's *A companion*
window in the Broad; and in time, through these, he acquired *volume*
some reputation outside his own small circle; for he was
fastidious in the choice of his friends. My Balliol friends
scoffed when I spoke of him as the most brilliant man in
Oxford.

Max Beerbohm was, of course, amused and interested in
my career as a portraitist at Oxford; he sympathised with
my difficulties, but could not resist poking fun at my adventures among the dons. I had shown him Miss Acland's
letter, in which she objects to her father's portrait. One
morning he wrote to me:

Dear Will,

I waited a long time for you by the breakfast table: why
did you not come? I had accepted your invitation—what
kept you? Tell me. By the way, I should have told you
before. John Lane has consented to publish a series of caricatures of Oxford Celebrities by me: they are to appear con-
currently with yours in order to make the running. In case
any ill feeling should arise between us on this account, I am
sending you the proofs of the first number. Very satisfactory,
I think. Do not think harshly of John Lane for publishing
these things without consulting you—there is a taint of
treachery in the veins of every publisher in the Row and,
after all, though our two styles may have something in
common, and we have chosen the same subjects, I am sure
there is room for both of us.

Yours, MAX.

P.S. I have sent a copy of Sir Henry's picture to Miss
Acland, she has just acknowledged it; such a nice graceful
note of thanks. She says it will be one of her chief treasures.

Little did he think when he penned this note how many
portraits he himself was destined to create and, early in his
career at least, not without similar criticism.

Max played no games, belonged to no college society,
never went to the Union, scarcely even to lectures. While

aware of everything that went on in Oxford, he himself kept aloof; going nowhere, he seemed to know about everyone; unusual wisdom and sound judgment he disguised under the harlequin cloak of his wit. He always declared he had read nothing—only *The Four Georges* and Lear's *Book of Nonsense*—and, later, Oscar Wilde's *Intentions*, which he thought were beautifully written.

Wilde came regularly to Oxford during the year I spent there. He and Beerbohm Tree were friends, so Max knew him already. Max the man appreciated to the full Oscar's prose and his talk; he thought him, in his way, a perfect writer; but nothing escaped the clear pitiless grey eye of Max the caricaturist, and Oscar Wilde winced under the stinging discharge of Max's pencil. Pater, Max knew only by sight; he attempted more than once to caricature him, but couldn't hit on a formula. I tried to show him where he had gone wrong, offering to fetch the lithograph I had recently made of Pater; 'No thanks, dear Will; I never work from photographs,' was Max's reply.

There came sometimes to visit Max, Reginald Turner, who had recently gone down from Oxford, one of the wittiest men, I thought, I had ever met, and one of the friendliest. He was then, and has ever remained, one of Max's closest friends; each was at his best when with the other; their talk was perfect duologue.

At Wadham, as at Balliol, there was a brilliant group of men—C. B. Fry, F. E. Smith, John Simon and F. W. Hirst. Of these I rather think C. B. Fry had then the widest reputation in Oxford. Extremely handsome, a triple blue, a good scholar, with a frank, unassuming nature, small wonder he was a popular hero. After him F. E. Smith played second fiddle. Smith had a brilliant but uneasy mind, a gifted tongue and obvious ambition. I saw much of him and of Fry during my year at Oxford; the only time I got intoxicated at Oxford was when dining with F. E. Smith at some annual function at Wadham. He had failed to warn me of the potent effect of the warm spiced ale.

MAX BEERBOHM AT OXFORD (1893)

Now not being a member of the University, I saw more of university life than most undergraduates. I used to say that I was a member of no College, but the belly of all. For, associating with both dons and undergraduates, I met with generous entertainment. At Exeter were Malcolm Seton and O'Flaherty—a brilliant but eccentric Irishman; at Christ Church, Lord Beauchamp (the single undergraduate I knew who had a whole house, Micklam Hall, for his lodging) and John Walter; at Magdalen Lord Balcarres and Lord Alfred Douglas, Douglas an erratic but most attractive person, defiant of public opinion, generous, irresponsible and extravagant. He was very good looking, blue-eyed and fair, but although a good athlete, he had rather a drooping figure. I made pastels of him, and of other undergraduate friends; one of Lord Beauchamp, and another of Anthony Henley, in whose rooms hung an engraving of an early Henley painted by Lely, which might have been done from him; they were as like as two peas. Another drawing I made was of Arthur Colefax, then a science don at Magdalen. Later, when he was married, his wife heard of the drawing and was anxious to have it; but with many others it had long since disappeared. Still, my pencil had not, and I often wondered why a lost drawing was so precious that it might not be drawn again. But most persons covet a picture which somebody else has already acquired; and maybe no new drawing would have had the value of an earlier one. I also drew Trelawney Backhouse, an eccentric undergraduate of Merton. He would entertain Max and myself, and in the middle of dinner would make some excuse, and leave us for the rest of the evening. He worshipped Ellen Terry; once he engaged a whole row of stalls, which he filled with undergraduate friends. He collected jewels, and later, in London, he would bring priceless emeralds to show me. Then he disappeared. Years after I heard he was living in China, when, with J. O. P. Bland, he produced a masterpiece, a book on the Empress Dowager.

147

CHAPTER XIII

EDMOND DE GONCOURT
AND VERLAINE

A lecture tour
for Verlaine I HAD to go up to London from time to time to take my drawings to Way, and there, meeting Arthur Symons, I told him of Verlaine's readiness to give some readings in England. He too had heard from Verlaine, and was warmly in favour of the project. He promised to make all the arrangements, and to look after Verlaine while he was in London; and York Powell offered to arrange for a lecture at Oxford.

Verlaine wrote from more than one address. He had been giving conferences in Holland, at Lunéville and other places; he was still obliged to return to the hospital from time to time for treatment: 'Excusez mon cher ami que je n'ai pas répondu plus tôt à votre bonne lettre. Mais ma maladie, grippe, influenza, engueulade ou le diable! m'a repris de plus belle et mis littéralement sur le flanc.' He complained that he hadn't yet been paid for his Dutch lectures. 'Mon intention est de parler de la Poésie Française en ce moment du siècle (1880–93) avec beaucoup de citations dont plusieurs de moi,' he writes of his coming conference in London; and again: 'Avez-vous quelques vues sur les projets de conférence à Londres et ailleurs, s'il y a lieu? Renseignez-moi, je vous prie. Je compte sortir bientôt, mais vous recevrez de moi quelques mots auparavant. En attendant jusqu'à nouvel ordre—15 jours 20 francs à peu près. M. Lane m'a donné 4 livres pour 2 pièces de vers. C'est très honnête. J'attends encore des nouvelles, à bientôt, des nôtres. Tout à vous,

P. V.' A few days later he is back in hospital: 'Veuillez m'indiquer les heures de départ et d'arrivée. Dois-je passer par Londres? Et quand aura lieu la conférence? Les prix des trains et bateaux—les bénéfices approximatifs à Oxford et Londres.' He wasn't long detained by the doctors, and reached London safely. Here he stayed with Symons at Fountain Court. He gave two readings in the Hall of Barnard's Inn, which were well attended. I heard from both Arthur Symons and John Lane about the lecture. Lane wrote: 'Verlaine was a great success last night. He, so I learn, leaves Paddington to-morrow morn: for you. He called at the Bodley Head this afternoon—but I was out. Meredith sent a message to me that he would like to have Verlaine down to his place for a day, and this morn: he wired in reply to me that he would be delighted to have him on Sunday night if I would take him down, but Verlaine is not feeling very well and he is not sure how long he will remain. Perhaps you will consult York Powell about it, and anyhow I am free to take him down on Sunday. Will you write to me and let me know the joint wishes of Verlaine, Powell and yourself on the subject. Let me know on Friday per letter or wire so that I may let Meredith know finally.'

What prevented the visit to Meredith I don't remember. From Symons I had an equally reassuring letter:

My dear Rothenstein,

I hope you duly received my telegram, and Verlaine after it. Please write and tell me how things have gone, and if the lecture was a success; also if Verlaine goes on to Manchester or not. And I want you to remember to get from him, before he goes, my copies of 'Sagesse' and 'Amour' that he borrowed from me, and please remind him to write his name in them, as he said he would. As you see, I am already far away, within sight and sound of the loveliest sea in the world, and in my native county, which I have not visited for years and years.

I bought the P. M. B. on my way down. Your portrait is excellent, one of the very best I have seen.

Verlaine's visit, to me, has been most delightful, and I think we ought all to congratulate ourselves on ourselves for having brought him over, and on our luck in getting him. I hope he will get a decent amount of money in Oxford: the London sum will be, I think, about £30.

Yours very sincerely,
ARTHUR SYMONS

Symons put Verlaine into the train at Paddington. I met him at Oxford station. A strange figure he looked on the platform, as he limped along in a long great-coat, a scarf round his neck, his foot in a cloth shoe. I took him at once to Christ Church, where Powell had a room for him.

Verlaine gave his lecture in a room at the back of Blackwell's shop, and read a number of his own poems. As a conference it was a poor affair; he spoke indistinctly in a low, toneless voice; he had brought nothing with him, and he knew but few of his poems by heart; fortunately, York Powell and I between us provided the books, from which he read. There was only a sprinkling of persons present; probably few people in Oxford knew much about the poet or his poetry; but Verlaine was tickled with the idea of having lectured before what he believed was an audience of doctors and scholars of the Ancient University of Oxford.

Verlaine was delighted with Oxford—with the beauty of the colleges, with the peace of the quads and gardens. He showed no sign of wanting to leave; he was gay and talkative, and wished to be taken everywhere; but York Powell, admirer of Verlaine though he was, was in terror lest the poet should get drunk while staying at Christ Church. What would the Dean, what would Dodgson, say? So far, nothing untoward had happened; but after two or three days, Powell suggested that I should give poor Verlaine a hint that guest-rooms were only to be occupied for a short period at a time. This was not easy, for Verlaine, in spite of a certain childish-

ness, was yet shrewd enough, and surmised that York Powell
was nervous; but he by no means wished to leave Oxford.
He needed a good deal of gentle persuasion before he was
put into the train again for London.

Before returning to Paris he lectured at Salford. Meanwhile I had a letter from Eugénie Krantz, warning me of the
machinations of 'another person', and begging me, if I heard
from Euphemia, not to let her know anything of the poet's
movements. I gathered that, on his return, there were dreadful complications between the three of them. Whatever happened, it was evident that the money he took back with him
quickly disappeared. He had returned with £80 in his pocket,
a fortune for poor Verlaine in those days.

This year at Oxford was one of the happiest of my life.
After the hectic life of Paris, the sense of order, of a settled
social system, was good for my undisciplined spirit. I enjoyed, too, the constant sight of splendid youth thronging
the streets, going down to the river, or to the playing fields,
in flannels and shorts, or strolling, two by two, in and out of
the sheltered quads and gardens. In buildings and gardens—
in gardens most of all—the evidence of man's careful and
loving husbandry lingers, when so much else of the past has
been destroyed. Lawns and flower-beds are rather art for
art's sake, while the fruit garden, with its beautiful and ancient
lore of grafting and pleaching, its espaliered trees, its long
ruddy walls, built to trap the sun, its formal rows of bushes,
prove that use is no bar to beauty. Knowing little of the
great English country-houses, the buildings and gardens at
Oxford gave me a new sense of what harmonious beauty lies
for ever latent in the nature of man.

A favourite spot was the Botanical Gardens, just below
Magdalen Bridge. Then there was the Thames itself, with
beautiful places within reach—Godstow, Abingdon and
Dorchester. And what could be lovelier than the Cher? So
long as I live, the memory of its overhanging trees, sparkling
by day, grand and solemn by night, will remain with me.
The quiet, graceful and efficient figures handling the punting

151

poles, the pleasant voices, the sound of the water, of boats scraping as they touched the banks—a stream of youth indeed, whose beauty is beyond compare.

I said that Max took no exercise; I did him an injustice; he shared a canoe with a Merton friend, L. M. Messell, and did sometimes strike the water of the Cher with his paddle. Perhaps it was merely a gesture; at least it was made in the Cher. Further afield I never knew him to go. He boasted once that he had never worn cap nor gown; I swore I would see him in both before he left Oxford; for he spoke of going down without taking his degree. I managed to get hold of a Proctor's notice, had it copied by a London printer, and sent out the copies to Max and a dozen others; they were to present themselves before the Proctor at Balliol College, at 9 o'clock on a certain morning. I took care to be at Balliol betimes, and saw them all arrive in trouble and uncertainty *and*, Max among them, in cap and gown. Then I watched them disappear up the Proctor's staircase. At Christ Church in the evening I found the other Proctor furious over the hoax. I told York Powell about it privately; he was fearful lest my crime be found out, staying as I was with him at the House. He tried to be solemn about it, but I think he was secretly amused. But not a word must I breathe to anyone about the unpardonably wicked thing I had done.

Mrs Woods and her husband, the President of Trinity, took as much trouble as York Powell did to bring me into touch with possible sitters. The Lodge at Trinity, built by Thomas Jackson, had little of a scholastic atmosphere; under Mrs Woods' care, who loved flowers and arranged them beautifully, its rooms had a radiance all their own; and Mrs Woods' many gifts brought her a wide circle of friends. While staying at Trinity Lodge I first met Robert Bridges and his wife, whose friendship I was fortunate enough to win, Dr Gore, and Henry Daniel, the Viking-like Head of Worcester College. Mrs Daniel, too, lent charm to her beautiful house, bright and gay with old English needlework. Henry Daniel, besides being Provost of Worcester, had a private printing-press, one of the earliest then in use. During my Oxford year Walter Pater's *Child in the House* was being printed, I think for some charitable object. Was it in this connection too that a memorable performance of *Alice in Wonderland* was given in the gardens of Worcester, in which Rosina Philippi and Nigel Playfair appeared? Also the two flaxen-haired Daniel children, Ruth and Rachel? A charming sight it was, this play in Worcester Gardens.

My lithograph portraits appeared in monthly parts. They had, I gathered, but a limited circulation at Oxford; but to my delight Whistler subscribed for the publication. He wrote from Paris that 'your own drawings of the Dons and Captains we are immensely pleased with. They are better and better. Bravo!' In answer to a letter I had written to him, he asked: 'why this untimely confession, my dear Parson?' He had no doubt that I had been giving him away and that everything was as bad as could be, but that no one knew anything about it. He was glad to find, however, that there was something of the redoubtable boulevardier left in the new undergraduate. I must come back and 'breakfast in the only garden bijou in Paris'. I was glad of Whistler's encouragement, but Conder didn't care for the Oxford drawings; I scarcely expected him to: and he thought I was making a mistake in leaving Paris. He wrote to me from the rue de Navarin:

'Thank you very much for the *Oxford Characters*. I am very pleased to have it and wish you every success in the affair. As you may suppose I don't like the drawings as much as those you showed me in your studio. Paris has been as gay as usual and it has been the usual bother to get to bed before the small hours. I cannot say I respect as much as I would like this bad habit of keeping late hours, and which as I get older only seems to increase—it looses expression a good deal from habit and perhaps one is better away from the alluring odour of the cocotte and her doubtful presents.

'However from the fact that the object itself loses flavour, we ourselves *lasse* and find it less dangerous.

153

'I have seen very few of your friends lately and done hardly any visits—when the time comes round for them one feels tired, and it's almost as good fun to watch the trees outside my studio. You will perhaps remember how we saw them last year and I can assure you that this autumn has been almost finer in my garden. I say mine, for it *is* almost and I regret nothing so much as leaving my studio on account of it. I hope all the same you find as much pleasure in Oxford as I do in Paris, and I am sure that it is not on account of one's friends that the place is so very charming for one to live in.

'I would like to see Oxford some day very much, and have already heard so much of its old courts and gracious trees. I think I might perhaps be able to render you service just now if you cared to send me some sketches, for one or two might be well placed with a picture merchant that I know here and is likely to sell some of my own.

'*Ne vous emballez pas trop pour l'Angleterre.* You would have done as well here and have had more help and sympathy. I can't understand the English enough for them to understand me—can you? I am to sell a picture to the State, I hear from a man that called yesterday and was on the last delegation. He says I only lost by two votes; think what it would be to get one's living by painting in one's own way. I only ask for one thing, to be independent of all these worries that make us so dependent on others. I think things will be better for us in a few years and you will do well to keep yourself in people's memory here in Paris. I look back at England with hardly any pleasure.

'When you have time your letters will always give me pleasure. Ask Lane to give me a book cover to do and you will be a very good boy.'

But Lane evidently did not ask Conder for a book cover, since a few weeks later he writes again:

My dear William

Thanks very much for the *Oxford Characters*. I liked it very much and after such a dedication would be too afraid

to give offence in chiding as I did the first. I believe anyhow that you will do even better when the stone gets warmer— *Bussell and*
I was delighted with the Xmas card and wish you the same. *Pater*
No particular news. Frazier has brought some good things
from the South—quite *à la Manet*. Howard Cushing and
divers other people enquired after you—the bronzed Rinky
also—

Your brother has bought a fan; I hope you will see it.
I fancy it's one of the best. I hope you will try and be good
and unselfish this new year and *won't* get into too many
scrapes and don't forget Lane about the picture book cover
for me.

With love—

CHARLES CONDER

I always enjoyed Conder's letters. They were vague and
suggestive like his talk—like his painting, too. I wondered
what people in Oxford would have thought of him.

I wanted to include a portrait of Pater in the Oxford set,
but he was morbidly self-conscious about his appearance.
He had been drawn as a youth by Simeon Solomon, and was
reluctant, later in life, to be shown as he was. Still, he seemed
interested in the drawings I was doing and, hesitatingly,
suggested I should try Bussell first. Bussell sat and Pater
approved of the result. Perhaps Bussell added his persuasion
to mine; at any rate he said that Pater was no longer averse
to sitting. A drawing was duly made, and sent away to be
put down on the stone. When the proofs came I showed one
to Pater. He said little, but was obviously displeased; according to Bussell he was more than displeased, he was upset.
He had taken the print into Bussell's room, laying it on the
table without comment. They then went together for their
usual walk; but not a word was spoken. On their return, as
Pater left Bussell at his door, he broke silence. 'Bussell, do
I look like a Barbary ape?' Then came a tactful letter from
Pater:

155

My dear Rothenstein,

I thought your drawing of me a clever likeness, but I doubt very much whether my sister, whom I have told about it, will like it; in which case I should rather not have it published. I therefore write at once to save you needless trouble about it. Put off the reproduction of the drawing till you come to Oxford again, and then let her see it. I thought your likeness of Bussell most excellent, and shall value it. It presents just the look I have so often seen in him, and have not seen in his photographs. I should have liked to be coupled with him, and am very sorry not to be. I think, however, you ought to publish him at once, with some other companion; and I will send you four or five lines for him soon.

With sincere thanks for the trouble you have taken about me, I remain,

Very truly yours,

WALTER PATER

Pater duly sent me the note on Bussell—the last words, I believe, he was destined to write for publication. Some time afterwards I heard from Tom Way, the printer: 'We have just had a visit from Mr Lane before your note came. He came expressly to say that no more proofs were to be pulled from the Pater. I understand Pater has used great stress as to what he will do if it is published. It is very small for these people to go on so, I think.'

I usually found that each of my sitters thought twenty-three of the twenty-four drawings excellent likenesses; the twenty-fourth was his own. Had I paid too much attention to my sitters' feelings, few of my portraits would ever have seen the light. Any record sincerely made from life has a certain value; this fact, I felt, was my justification.

But imperfect as my portraits were, I know my case was a common one. Wasn't it Sargent who said that a portrait is a painting in which there is something wrong with the mouth? Even the great Sir Joshua Reynolds had a large

number of rejected portraits on his hands—300, I read somewhere. I remember Neville Lytton telling me, when I was
speaking with particular admiration of Watts' beautiful portrait of his mother, that though they had a chance of acquiring
it at the time it was painted, it was rejected by his mother's
family; and many years later, when Lady Lytton was an old
lady, she paid a visit to Little Holland House, and seeing the
portrait again was moved to tears at the thought that she
had once been so beautiful as she appeared in the painting.
But Watts would not now let the portrait leave his studio.

Alas! before the Oxford book was finished, Pater died;
and when my portrait was finally included in the volume his
friends were glad, as so few records of Pater existed. Besides
the early drawing by Simeon Solomon, there was only a not
very satisfactory photograph.

Lionel Johnson, whom Elkin Mathews had asked me to
draw for a forthcoming book of his verses, wrote me a
charming note, in which he refers to the overcoming of Miss
Pater's prejudice against the portrait:

20 Fitzroy Street,
Oct. 24, 1894

My dear Rothenstein,

Too great an honour! or shall I say, premature? I should
be charmed to sit to you at any time, when you want an
excellent model for nothing: but a portrait in my book would
be too great a vanity, even for me. Wait till the Laureateship
is mine, or—don't be insulted—the P.R.A. is yours. I am
explaining to Mathews, that the very portrait itself would
blush: which is undesirable for a lithograph by you. Only
Academicians' portraits ought to blush. Seriously, in a first
volume of verse, it would be a little absurd: greatly as I
should appreciate the honour of immortality from your
hands. You must give it me later.

Delighted to hear that the Pater lithograph is to appear.
I am just back from Oxford, where I have been going through
all Pater's MSS.

Yours ever,
LIONEL JOHNSON

157

When the summer term ended I went over to spend some weeks in Paris. William Heinemann, who was preparing an English edition of the de Goncourts' *Journal*, was also going to Paris, and he proposed I should make a portrait of Edmond de Goncourt to be reproduced in the book. I jumped at the chance, not only of drawing him, but, as I hoped, of seeing his treasures.

De Goncourt made no difficulties about sitting, and I lost no time in paying my respects to the great man, who, through his, and his brother's, influence on the modern novel had become almost an historical figure, and who with his brother had done so much to draw attention to the importance of the eighteenth-century painters in France. I had read more than one volume of the famous *Journal*, and knew something of the house at Neuilly. Ushered in and shown up a staircase hung with fascinating-looking prints and drawings, I at once received a suggestion of good things to come. I was shown into Edmond's study, lined with books, where was the white-haired veteran I had long admired from afar—a big, powerful head, wax-like in its pallor, with two great velvety eyes looking out. His clothes were of an old-fashioned French cut; he wore a handkerchief carefully knotted about his neck, as in the Bracquemond portrait. Studiedly reticent at first, before I left he had become much more genial. He appeared surprised at my youth. When I returned to the house for a first sitting, he was much interested at my drawing directly on to the stone. I was the first person he had seen to work in this way since Gavarni died. He talked much of Gavarni, with whom he and his brother Jules had been long and intimately associated. When later I mentioned Daumier, he became bitter at once. 'Ah, fashion,' he said, 'how stupid she is. Gavarni had a hundred times Daumier's talent,' and then, in the same breath, he assailed Villiers de l'Isle-Adam and Barbey d'Aurevilly; 'Oui, c'est la mode aujourd'hui d'admirer tous les morts qui, vivants, n'avaient pas le sou.' When he came to look at my drawing, he did not approve of the hair; to show me how he would like it,

EDMOND DE GONCOURT (1894)

he went to the glass, and with his old trembling fingers
carefully untidied it.

That Whistler was a great artist he was unwilling to hear.
'Il m'ennuie, c'est un farceur.' With Degas he was annoyed,
because Degas had told him that modern writers got their
inspiration from painters. He had replied that in *Manette
Salaman,* before Degas had begun to paint in his present
manner, he and his brother had written that ballet girls and
laundresses were subjects made to an artist's hand. 'Degas
is too clever,' he said, 'and is sometimes scored off. For
instance the other day, at Alphonse Daudet's, he remarked
that our writing was twaddle, that the only man of real talent
among us was le père Dumas. To which Daudet: "Yes, my
dear Degas, and the only modern artist of genius was Horace
Vernet."'

I made two lithographs of Edmond de Goncourt during
the short time I stayed in Paris. He liked talking about
painting and drawing, and showing his treasures. He had
marvellous eighteenth-century drawings and Japanese prints;
many of these last were pretentiously framed. I wondered at
his valuing his drawings by Boucher as highly as his Watteaus,
of which he had some admirable examples. But what books
and manuscripts he possessed! He showed me the original
account books of the Pompadour, giving the prices she paid,
among other things, for furniture and *bibelots*. I was astonished how costly these were, when new. What admirable
faith these people had in their own contemporaries! De
Goncourt too had not altogether lost this faith. He knew
little of any but French culture; like Degas he was intensely
conservative and nationalist. But his taste was very uncertain; round a room at the top of his house he had glass-
topped tables where he kept presentation copies of books from
his friends bound in vellum, with their authors' portraits
painted on the covers; Zola by Raffaelli, Montesquiou by
Gandara, Rodenbach by Alfred Stevens, Daudet, and another
by Carrière, a charming one and the only drawing which
appeared to me suited to a book cover, by Forain, and many

others in more dubious taste and badly painted. How strange
that the sensitive biographer of Outamaro, of the Pompadour and *Les Femmes au 18me Siècle* should indulge in such
doubtful fancies! He said, when I last saw him, that he was
undecided about his next Japanese monograph—whether it
should be on Horonobu or on the better-known Hokusai.
He was anxious I should draw Mme Daudet, as well as
Saint-Victor, Zola and Daudet; also the Princesse Mathilde.
I wrote to the Princess, who didn't reply, perhaps because
I began my letter 'Chère Madame'. I had little experience of
writing to Royal Princesses. De Goncourt seemed very
devoted to Alphonse Daudet, and to his wife. He said
I must draw them both; he would write and tell them so.
He also gave me a letter to Zola.

Daudet received me cordially. Of course he would sit
since his dear friend Edmond de Goncourt wished it. He
was exciting to draw; very pale, almost glistening white,
with long black hair and beard just beginning to turn grey.
He looked terribly ill. His hands were white and bloodless.
Very sensitive hands they were, closed on a black ebony
stick, his support when walking. I had read Daudet's *Tartarin* at school; it was almost a classic, as well known to boys
as Mark Twain's *Tramp Abroad*. Other books I read later;
but Daudet was now less in favour among the élite. I think
he knew this, for he complained loudly of the newer writers,
much as the older men do to-day. 'Ah, vous autres jeunes
gens d'aujourd'hui, you came into the world with all your
teeth fully grown—you are so bitter, so unkind. Men of my
generation sympathise with old and young. I try to find
good in all.' He was anxious to get Whistler to paint his
daughter. When my drawing was done, he was so flattering
about it, he made me uneasy. 'How old was I? Wonderful;
what a future before me! I must show it to Mme Daudet;
n'est-ce pas que c'est moi craché?' Mme Daudet was flattering too, but with a shade of ennui. She must have tired
at times of Daudet's meridional superlatives. True he had
great charm; but there was something in him that didn't ring

true, that was slightly embarrassing; perhaps one felt he was too well aware of his fascination.

For Edmond de Goncourt he expressed unbounded admiration. He asked much about Meredith's position in England. Lord Dufferin, he said, often came to him in the evenings to read to him. He had just translated, *viva voce, Modern Love*. I asked him if he found it difficult to follow; he said, no, he understood everything perfectly. As Lord Dufferin was not reputed a perfect French scholar, and as *Modern Love* is difficult to read, even for English people, this was surprising. I had just been reading *Un Caractère*, by Léon Hennique. Daudet was delighted to hear his friend Hennique praised; he agreed that he was an exquisite writer. Speaking of Verlaine, he told me that Verlaine had once tried to stab him at dinner just after the publication of one of his books.

I met their son, Léon, several times at the Daudets. I thought him very clever, but too cocksure. He told his father that he had made up his mind, that his opinions were finally settled, on every aspect of life. He had inherited the meridional temperament of his father, with his tendency to exaggerated praise and blame. His mentality was clearer cut, but he lacked his father's charm and grace. His wife, Jeanne, a granddaughter of Victor Hugo, was a handsome blonde, rather like Saskia. I went to lunch with them at their luxurious flat, where they lived in more state than the older Daudets. He gave me two of his books, which I have not re-read; but lately I came across a book of his reminiscences, dealing with this particular time, which was brilliant I thought; his prose portraits are sharp and convincing. The book recalled very clearly this period of my life in Paris.

The last time I saw Daudet was at one of de Goncourt's evenings. Mark Twain was expected. No one knew anything about Mark Twain; strange! they talked of him as though he were a sort of Edgar Allan Poe. I told them as best I could what his books were like. Meanwhile people stood about listening to de Goncourt and Daudet. While

161

they were discussing Mark Twain, the names of George
Moore and Oscar Wilde were mentioned, coupled, for some
unknown reason, together. Oscar Wilde they took more
seriously as a writer than I expected. I was amused that
Edmond, with his indiscreet *Journal*, should complain of
George Moore that he dined at their tables and took notes on
his cuff. Finally, Mark Twain didn't arrive.

I was rather embarrassed one day when de Goncourt told
me he had lately made a great discovery: the life of a cour-
tesan written by an obscure English author in the seventeenth
century—a wonderful book, the precursor of the modern
realist novel. He then began to describe *Moll Flanders*. I did
not like to tell him that this was a kind of classic in England,
well known to everyone who knew Defoe's work.

The ignorance of French writers and painters of all but
their own art and literature, used to surprise me. De Goncourt had heard vaguely of Swinburne and Rossetti, and I
told him about the beauty of Rossetti's early work, and of
Swinburne's poetry. That Edmond de Goncourt would
write down any scraps of my chatter, I had never imagined.
He asked me many questions about England—about the
Pre-Raphaelites especially. I suppose I told him the little
I knew, and mostly through Whistler's stories; what young
man wouldn't do his best to be informing with an old man
of de Goncourt's eminence? Whistler had given me very
funny accounts of the Rossetti household at Cheyne Walk,
and I must have been indiscreet enough to repeat them. Two
years later, when the last volume of the *Journal* appeared,
I received a rude shock.

De Goncourt gave me a letter to Zola, whose portrait was
to appear in the English edition of the de Goncourts' *Journal*.
I was rather taken aback by Zola's house in the rue de Rome.
I had scarcely expected to find the author of *L'Œuvre* and
L'Assommoir in such luxurious surroundings. His study was
filled with expensive-looking antiques, rich carpets and
hangings, bronzes and caskets—no armour I think, but it
was the kind of room in which one expected to find suits of

PAUL VERLAINE (1894)

armour. On the wall hung his portrait by Manet, in Manet's
early dark manner. Zola's personality did not impress me;
he was not at all amiable, in fact rather sulky. I suspected
that there was little love lost between him and Daudet and
de Goncourt. Perhaps it was because I had come from
Edmond de Goncourt that Zola was not very cordial. Lately
I read that in the famous *Journal*, which was to have been
published 30 years after Edmond's death, the references to
Zola are so libellous that even now it cannot be published.
I felt at the time that there was something ungenerous about
de Goncourt and Daudet—that they were both rather
jealous, perhaps, of the phenomenal success of Zola's work,
not only in France, but throughout Europe.

Zola wore a kind of monk's habit; he was writing his book
on Lourdes, and getting himself into the right frame of mind;
though not knowing this at the time, such a costume on Zola
was rather startling. He was not in a mood for talking. I had
my drawing to make, and as this was the only occasion on
which I met him, my impression of his character was of course
superficial.

I had not forgotten Verlaine. Verlaine's room looked more
forlorn still after Zola's palatial *hôtel*; and he was, as usual,
dans la dèche. 'Mon cher ami,' he wrote, 'Je compte sur vous
pour mercredi…voudrez-vous et pouvez-vous contribuer *un
peu* aux frais de nos frugales orgies pour ce déjeuner-là, et
m'apporter le Figaro avec son supplément. Quand même,
venez surtout, n'est-ce pas?…'

Verlaine was not well enough to come out to meals, so of
course, since he often asked me to join him and Eugénie at
lunch or dinner, I usually procured some addition to their
larder from the restaurant below. But Verlaine must indeed
have been poor to have asked for the *Figaro*; and lately he
had been in hospital again, this time at the Hôpital St Louis,
where he had had to pay for his keep. 'Mon cher ami,' he
had written me, 'Que devenez-vous? Moi toujours ici.
Mieux, mais lent à redresser, ce pied qui n'en veut pas finir!
et 6 francs par jour! etc. etc. aussi serais-je bien reconnaissant

163

à vous si pourriez auprès du Fortnightly activer l'avance ou le solde qui me ferait tant de bien. N'est-ce pas, veuillez vous en occuper vite. Symons est à Paris. Il est venu me voir 2 fois déjà, dans mon ermitage, où je suis très bien d'ailleurs: tout seul dans ma chambre. Droit de fumer et de recevoir tous les jours. Bonne nourriture. Mais ce n'est pas la liberté. Quand viendrait-elle, enfin sérieuse, pour moi? Définitive? Vu hier Mallarmé (qui attend des nouvelles d'York Powell). Moi aussi et du livre—et de Lane.'[1]

Then again complaints about the *Fortnightly*: 'J'ai tant besoin de cette galette! Il y a aussi des vers dans l'Athenaeum dont j'attends de vagues argents. Pour ce, voir Gosse, à qui j'ai écrit sans avoir de réponse.'

'J'ai tant besoin de cette galette'—not he alone, for his needs were few; but Eugénie was greedy, and there was someone else, too. For, soon after, I heard from him again: 'J'ai une rechute de mon mal, que je soigne sérieusement et qui m'a rendu incapable de beaucoup écrire. Je n'ai pu, en raison de cette rechute, me rendre en Belgique et moins encore en Suisse. J'ai déménagé et même divorcé. Ecrivez moi rue St Jacques 187 et veuillez m'envoyer 2 ou 3 exemplaires du Pall Mall Budget, où est mon portrait par vous. *Surtout n'envoyez rien rue Broca.*'

The last sentence is significant. When I saw him again he said he had got rid of 'cette harlot'. But soon after the Krantz was sharing his new room in the rue St Jacques; and Verlaine wrote: 'Notre ménage est dans la joie. Nous allons avoir des petits—canaris! et nous nous sommes enrichis d'un aquarium avec deux cyprins dedans.'

Before I left Paris I heard from Beerbohm:

My dear Will,

2 *Chandos Square,*
Broadstairs

I made my entry into Broadstairs quite quietly last Sunday.

[1] John Lane was to publish a selection of Verlaine's poetry, with an introduction by York Powell, and a portrait, but the book never appeared.

I find it a most extraordinary place—a few yards in circumference and with a population of several hundred thousands. In front of our house there is a huge stretch of greenish, stagnant water which makes everything damp and must, I am sure, be very bad for those who live near to it. Everyone refers to it with mysterious brevity as the C. I am rather afraid of the C. And oh, the population! You, dear Will, with your love of Beauty that is second only to your love of vulgarity would revel in the female part of it. Such lots of pretty, common girls walking up and down—all brown with the sun and dressed like sailors—casting vulgar glances from heavenly eyes and bubbling out Cockney jargon from perfect lips. You would revel in them but I confess they do not attract me: apart from the fact that I have an ideal, I don't think the lower orders ought to be attractive—it brings Beauty into disrepute. Never have I seen such a shady looking set of men in any place at any season: most of them look like thieves and the rest like receivers of stolen goods, and altogether I do not think Broadstairs is a nice place— Are you in Paris? How charming—I am sending this to your publishers who know, probably, your address. By the way, did you remember when you saw that poor fly in the amber of modernity, John Lane, to speak of my caricatures? Do write to me and tell me of anything that you are doing or of anyone you have seen....

Photography—what a safeguard it is against infidelity. If Ulysses had had a photograph of Penelope by Elliot and Fry in his portmanteau, the cave of Calypso might have lost an habitué....

Yours ever,
MAX

Have you entered any Studio yet? I would recommend you to draw from the life: nothing like it.

CHAPTER XIV

CHELSEA IN THE 'NINETIES

Return to
London

ON my return from Paris I set about looking for a studio staying at Morley's Hotel in Trafalgar Square. Morley's Hotel, an old-fashioned family hotel on the site of which the offices of the Dominion of South Africa now stand, is associated in my memory with a visit from Max Beerbohm, when he tried on my frock-coat, a style of garment to which he was strange. It amuses me to think of Max the exquisite examining himself in the glass, clothed in a garment of mine.

While I was looking for rooms, Jacomb-Hood, who was going abroad, offered me the use of his house in Tite Street, a comfortable house with a good studio, of which Godwin was the architect, as he was of many of the houses in Tite Street, among them Whistler's White House. Another house in Tite Street was occupied by Oscar and Mrs Wilde. These houses were very characteristic of the 'eighties, the period of Walter Crane and of Libertys. Whistler was contemptuous of Oscar Wilde living in one of a row of houses. In Paris Whistler had described this row, drawing it to show the monotonous repetition of each house, only differentiated by its number, and putting a large 16 on Oscar's house. I noticed then how childishly Whistler drew when drawing out of his head.

I was glad of a studio, having just received a first commission for a painting, through Claud Schuster, whose friend, Basil Williams, wanted a portrait of his sister. In Tite Street I also painted a group of friends—Wilson Steer, Charles

Furse, Walter Sickert, D. S. MacColl and Max Beerbohm.
I wish I had carried out more groups of the kind; but it is
difficult to get busy men to sit. A few years later I began
another canvas of Sargent, Steer and Tonks, which was never
finished.

Whistler had said 'of course you will settle in Chelsea'.
The men who counted most for me lived there—Sickert,
Steer, Ricketts and Shannon. The name itself, soft and creamy,
suggested the eighteenth century, Whistler's early etchings,
Cremorne, old courts and rag-shops. I was at first disappointed with the long King's Road, a shabbier Oxford
Street, with its straggling, dirty, stucco mid-century houses
and shops. But the river-side along Cheyne Row was
beautiful; what noble houses! and there were Lindsay Row
and Cheyne Row and Paradise Walk, and the Physic Gardens
and the Vale.

The Vale was then really a vale, with wild gardens and
houses hidden among trees. Oscar Wilde had taken me to
the Vale to see Ricketts and Shannon before I came to live
in Chelsea, when I was charmed by these men, and by their
simple dwelling, with its primrose walls, apple-green skirting
and shelves, the rooms hung with Shannon's lithographs, a
fan-shaped water-colour by Whistler, and drawings by
Hokusai—their first treasures, to be followed by so many
others. Walter Sickert too lived in the Vale, in a house belonging to William de Morgan, with a studio full of Mrs de
Morgan's paintings. For this reason perhaps Sickert preferred painting elsewhere. He had a small room where he
worked, at the end—the shabby end—of the Chelsea Em-
bankment, west of Beaufort Street. Needless to say, this
room was in one of the few ugly houses to be found along
Cheyne Walk. His taste for the dingy lodging-house atmosphere was as new to me as was Ricketts' and Shannon's
Florentine aura. I had known many poor studios in Paris,
but Walter Sickert's genius for discovering the dreariest
house and most forbidding rooms in which to work was a
source of wonder and amusement to me. He himself was so

fastidious in his person, in his manners, in the choice of his clothes; was he affecting a kind of dandyism *à rebours?* For Sickert was a finished man of the world. He was a famous wit; he spoke perfect French and German, very good Italian, and was deeply read in the literature of each. He knew his classical authors, and could himself use a pen in a masterly manner. As a talker he could hold his own with either Whistler or Wilde. Further, he seemed to be on easy and familiar terms with the chief social, intellectual and political figures of the time; yet he preferred the exhausted air of the music-hall, the sanded floor of the public-house, and the ways and talk of cockney girls who sat to him, to the comfort of the clubs, or the sparkling conversation (for so I imagined it) of the drawing rooms of Mayfair and Park Lane. An aristocrat by nature, he had cultivated a strange taste for life below stairs. High lights below Steers, I used to say, in reference to this predilection, and to his habit of painting in low tones. Every man to his taste, I thought; but had I a tittle of your charm, your finished manners, your wit and good looks, I should not be painting in a dusty room in the squalidest corner of Chelsea. Nor, for that matter, should I be laboriously matching the dingy tones of women lying on unwashed sheets, upon cast-iron bedsteads. And there were other things in Walter's pictures that puzzled me. He himself told how Menpes, looking at one of his canvases, praising it to the skies—'lovely colour, my dear Walter, beautiful tone, exquisite drawing, but—could you—not that it isn't perfect as it is—could you manage just to coax,—the *one* eye is capital—to coax that other eye into the face?' And Walter would go off into a peal of laughter. What stories he told of Whistler, of the days before I knew him, when Sickert, Menpes, Roussel and the Greaves brothers formed an artistic bodyguard round 'The Master'! Some of the master's mannerisms Sickert had caught; yet he seemed to me, in his own way, to be as unique a personality, and as rare a wit, as Whistler himself. He was an *enfant de la balle*, for his father had been a distinguished painter, a member of the sound old

168

Munich school, a painter of the rank of his friend Scholderer,
and of Fantin-Latour. But Walter had for a time turned to
the stage, and had played with Irving and Ellen Terry.
A propos of Miss Terry, he told me how, when a youngster,
on the occasion of a first night or some special performance,
wishing to pay honour to the great actress, he had drawn on
his slender resources to purchase a bouquet of roses, and
wishing to make sure that at the appropriate moment this
should reach her, he loaded the end of the bouquet with lead.
The roses, thrown from the gallery, fell with a violent thud
on the hollow stage, narrowly missing Irving, surprised and
indignant at this outrage. A loud ha! ha! rang through the
house. Whistler had observed the scene. If my memory does
not play me false, this was the occasion which led to the close
association between him and Sickert.

How far Whistler was aware of Sickert's or of Greaves'
genius is problematical; I am inclined to believe he did not
wish to recognise it; at any rate, he made every use of their
devotion; but he saw to it that the limelight should be
focused on himself; he deemed a farthing dip good enough
for his disciples.

When Whistler came to London he still made use of
Sickert's studio. Indeed, one day, seeing a half-finished
canvas on the easel, he began working on it, and getting interested, he finished the canvas, carried it off, and I believe,
sold it as a work of his own. But a coolness was already
beginning between them at this time, while Sickert was as-
serting himself more and more as an independent painter.
Besides, 'Jimmy' was not the only recipient of his admiration
—Whistler shared this with Degas and with Fantin-Latour;
but chiefly with Degas.

Night after night Sickert would go to the Bedford or
Sadler's Wells, to watch the light effects on stage and boxes,
on pit and gallery, making tiny studies on scraps of paper
with enduring patience and with such fruitful results. Incidentally he memorised the songs, storing his mind with the
pregnant nonsense of music-hall doggerel and tunes. I envied

him his memory, I, who had a talent for forgetting; and much else; indeed all save his poverty, which, seeing the quality of his gifts, was to me inexplicable.

Steer and Sickert, though not so closely allied as Ricketts and Shannon, were often associated together as leaders of the English Impressionists. There was also a similar contrast between the two—Steer had affinities with Shannon, Sickert with Ricketts. An instinctive artist, with a faultless sense of colour, Steer had the conservative instincts and prejudices of the middle-class Englishman. Had he been a politician, he would have voted against the Reform Bill, against the abolition of the army purchase system, against the entry of Jews and Roman Catholics into the House of Commons. Why change? he would have said; change only means bother, and England is all right as she is. The first literary criticism I heard from him was that he didn't see why anyone need write poetry now; wasn't Byron good enough? He preferred painting to poetry, of course; but here his insularity broke down. He placed Monet and Degas beside Turner and Constable, and he particularly relished French eighteenth-century engravings. He respected Whistler's painting; but he couldn't understand why, if a man could paint like Whistler, he should want to write letters and make things uncomfortable. Steer was all for a quiet life. He was in constant dread of colds; they were certainly disturbing. So even in the height of summer he wore a heavy overcoat, and a yachting cap, and his footwear resembled a policeman's. His studio was filled with pictures; he had scarcely sold anything, he said, for seven years. They were mostly paintings of yachts and the sea, and of girls paddling, girls with long, slender legs, like Sheraton tables. He was fond of painting pretty girls; he liked them young, and had a shrewd eye for any who would make good models. His habits were simple. He was extremely matter of fact; in life, for him, there was little romance. Without a brush in his hands, he was indifferent to most things save dry feet and freedom from draughts. If he had any passion it was for Chelsea figures. I used to say that

he had the best bad taste of anyone I knew. A revolutionary
painter, he hated change. He was content to meet the same
people every day. He liked, too, to hear the same jokes; with
a little gossip, a naughty story or two, the evenings passed
pleasantly. Sickert and George Moore, Tonks and Harrison,
MacColl, Frederick Brown, Sargent and myself formed his
regular circle. He was very modest about his achievements.
He used to say, when we praised his work, that if he got a
kind of quality it was because he couldn't draw or paint with
any certainty, as Sargent could, for instance; he could only
get something done by muddling about and repainting. In
Steer there was a stolid unimaginativeness, combined with
an intuitive rightness of judgment, peculiar to a certain type
of Englishman. For English he was to the core; neither
Scotch, Irish nor Welsh. He was like a piece of Staffordshire
ware in a collection of Sèvres china—a little absurd, a little
crude, but there is something ampler and saner and more
poetical in this rather naïve English piece, than in the refinement and finish of the more expensive ware. His painting,
like himself, was unintellectual, but intuitively right. I thought
him easily the most interesting of the English realistic painters,
though in the early 'nineties his painting seemed to me a little
loose. But then loose painting was admired. MacColl was its
prophet, and for him the looser the nearer to excellence.

MacColl was the Ruskin of the Impressionists, and like
Ruskin, he was a sensitive draughtsman. Ruskin believed
art to depend largely on the moral character of the artist,
and of his age; while MacColl cared more for Whistler's
doctrine of art for beauty's sake—a doctrine much older
than Whistler; it was also Fichte's and Keats' and Baudelaire's. MacColl's independence and his high intellectual
gifts gained him a foremost place among the critical writers
of the 'nineties, and he became a power in the land. His
belief was in the survival of the commencement; woe to anyone who, like myself, strove to carry painting and drawing
beyond this. Whistler and Degas among the older, and
Conder and Steer among the younger men, were MacColl's

171

idols. He was then the art critic of *The Spectator*, writing with courage and a gallant style, carrying fire and the sword into the Academic camp. To Conder and Steer, his first loves, he had remained constantly faithful. From his judgments I have often differed, but his integrity and high chivalrous character I have ever admired.

Sargent who, like Jacomb-Hood, was abroad, had lent his studio to Charles Furse, a few doors from Jacomb-Hood's house. I had met Furse in Paris, where we had been to the Louvre together, and made friends. He proved a helpful and most hospitable neighbour; he liked people to come in while he was painting, to discuss his work, and to make suggestions; and while he was painting his talk boiled over into politics, military tactics and literature. So his studio was usually full of generals, admirals, distinguished and admiring ladies, painters and poets; while he strode up and down, working away with huge brushes and boisterous energy. At his studio I first met Laurence Binyon—Furse flung at us, 'Binyon! Rothenstein! don't you know one another? Two decadents!' It is amusing to think of the scholarly Binyon being classed as a decadent. For Furse, with his high spirits and genial faith in his artistic and social security, behaved like a kind of elder brother to us all, though he was but four years my senior, and was considerably younger than Sickert and Steer. Yet he had a generous respect for the gifts of others. He knew that, in spite of his larger range, he lacked the refinements of colour and line which came naturally to some of his friends. He was loud in his praise of Steer, and took a generous view of my work. He tried hard, when he was commissioned to decorate some spandrils for the Town Hall at Liverpool, to get me associated with the undertaking. Though the Academy was always ready to welcome him, he showed his smaller work at the New English Art Club, where it was invariably singled out for praise. In those far-off days *The Times* gave a few lines only to these exhibitions; the young were kept in their places, and very poor places they were.

But Furse from the first was marked out for success. Had he lived, he would have been President of the Royal Academy. Even in those days symptoms of the disease which too early attacked and defeated him were already showing themselves. Yet who, knowing Furse, would have suspected that he had this grim and tenacious enemy to fight?— heavily built and square-shouldered, he looked so robust, in his knickerbockers and tweeds, with big biceps and full calves. There was a suggestion of Rembrandt in his massive head, with its small, humorous eyes; and he wore a short moustache and tuft under his lip. Pugnacious, argumentative, ever trailing a coat, he was the joy of his friends, of whom no man had more. Like his friend Henley, he was impatient of weakness and affectation; perhaps, like Henley too, he sometimes mistook sensitive discernment for these. Sargent he admired above all living painters; indeed, he often declared him to be the greatest of all portrait painters of any age.

But in those early Chelsea days I was especially attracted by Ricketts and Shannon—they were so different from any artists I had met hitherto. Everything about them was refined and austere. Ricketts, with his pale, delicate features, fair hair and pointed gold-red beard, looked like a Clouet drawing. Half French, he had the quick mind and the rapid speech of a southerner. He was a fascinating talker. His knowledge of pictures and galleries astonished me; he had been nowhere except to the Louvre, yet he seemed to know everything, to have been everywhere. And he knew the names of rare flowers, of shells and of precious stones.

Shannon was as quiet and inarticulate as Ricketts was restless and eloquent. He had a ruddy boyish face, like a countryman's, with blue eyes and fair lashes; he reminded me of the shepherd in Rossetti's *Found*. Oscar Wilde said Ricketts was like an orchid, and Shannon like a marigold. Ricketts, in giving his opinions, always said 'we'. The partnership seemed perfect; there was never a sign of difference or discord; each set off the other, in looks as in mind.

173

They knew few people, and prided themselves on going nowhere: their few intimates came to see them, usually on Friday evenings. Oscar Wilde often came to the Vale; he was devoted to both, and at his best in their company; and but for Beardsley's *Salome*, they alone illustrated his books. I wondered whether he knew how gross, how soiled by the world, he appeared, sitting in one of the white scrubbed kitchen chairs next to Ricketts and Shannon and Sturge Moore. And sometimes Sickert came over; he too at his best, irresistibly witty and captivating in his talk, and appreciative of both our hosts. Indeed, no better talk was to be heard than round their table. We all admired Shannon's lithographs, which seemed to me the loveliest things being done at the time. Both he and Ricketts were then busy cutting woodblocks for their edition of *Daphnis and Chloe*, working late into the night, and rising late in the day. Bending over their blocks they looked like figures from a missal. I had never come into touch with the Morris movement, and this craftsman side was new to me. I was therefore the more impressed by their skill and patience. From them I heard countless stories of Rossetti, of Burne-Jones, Holman Hunt, Millais and Madox Brown; in fact, at the time, I thought they would carry on the Pre-Raphaelite tradition. But their admiration for the Pre-Raphaelites was tempered, on Shannon's part by admiration for Watts and Puvis, on Ricketts' part by his predilection for Delacroix and Gustav Moreau—Moreau, of whom Degas remarked 'celui qui peint des lions avec des chaînes de montre'. I revered these two men, for their simple and austere ways, their fine taste and fine manners. They seemed to stand apart from other artists of the time; and I was proud of their friendship, so rarely given, and of the encouragement they gave to my work.

Shannon was reserved and quietly appreciative, while Ricketts had a passion for influencing others. There is no word to describe this fatal desire, this *Einflusslust*. I believe all consciously exerted influence to be a bad thing. Certain people, certain books and pictures, fertilise a man's spirit; but

CHARLES RICKETTS (1894)

this can only be at a given moment, when the mind is *à point*, prepared to receive the seed. At such a time, when we are putting out feelers in certain directions, the conviction we need may come from others. Such influence is natural and healthy; but that which is forced on us cannot be properly assimilated. Twice-cooked food is notoriously indigestible; equally so are twice-chewed ideas. Indeed, good examples imitated may be as fruitless as bad ones. The tendency to study works of art too enthusiastically, to reflect the appearance of mastery rather than to enter, like the spirit of the Chinese artist in the legend, the heart of nature herself, is perhaps a weakness of English painters.

I felt that Conder, in his own dreamy way, did respond to the visual harmonies and the pulsating vitality of nature; while Ricketts and Shannon depended over much on conscious artistry. Art does not generate art. Lilies and columbines and golden grain grow from the rough earth; indeed, so do weeds; but who fears to sow though charlock springs up in the sprouting corn? Nor may an artist neglect to keep the soil clean—the soil from which his seed draws its life, lest the weeds of mannerism spring up. These weeds, too, wear brave colours—scarlet, yellow and blue, and the critic will often prefer the weed to the priceless ear.

But Ricketts was a strong believer in tradition. He held that painters should learn their art by copying; that, through copying, the old masters had acquired all their knowledge. The most faithful of his disciples was Sturge Moore, who in his poetry and in his wood-cuts strove for a conscious beauty of form and content. Sturge Moore was one of the contributors to *The Dial*, the lovely quarto which Ricketts and Shannon produced at their own expense and risk, a work which had a powerful influence on contemporary drawing, engraving and printing, both in England and abroad. Another disciple was John Gray, for whose *Silverpoints* Ricketts had designed one of his exquisite bindings. John Gray was then a fastidious young poet and something of a dandy. He also wrote plays with André Raffalovitch, a wealthy friend of

Ricketts. Then Gray became a Roman Catholic, and he has since devoted himself and his fine poetic and artistic gifts to the Church, making his home in Edinburgh.

Reginald Savage, who had been a fellow-student with Ricketts and Shannon at Lambeth, was also a familiar at the Vale. Later came Roger Fry and Charles Holmes. Fry at this time was living with Robert Trevelyan in Beaufort Street. There was then little to indicate the road he took later. He was still very much as he was when he first came to Paris —shy, rather afraid of life, painting in the manner of the early English water-colour painters. He, too, sat at Ricketts' feet, though he was never admitted to the inner circle of the faithful, to which Sturge Moore and the others belonged. Fry was an admirable writer, and was beginning to follow in MacColl's footsteps as an art critic. He was then, and for many years afterwards, a staunch supporter of my work, both in private and in the press.

Charles Holmes too did etchings and drawings in his spare time, much encouraged by Shannon and Ricketts; and he was a resourceful writer on art. But Ricketts' masterful personality dominated all who came into contact with him. The more intellectual draughtsmen, including Beardsley and Laurence Housman, looked to him as their leader. He was in fact the artistic Warwick of the age.

After spending some weeks in Jacomb-Hood's house, I found a studio with a couple of rooms in Glebe Place. Glebe Place, a turning just off the King's Road parallel with Oakley Street, was full of studios. Later Conder also rented a studio in Glebe Place—a studio belonging to Miss Isabel Ford. Miss Ford was a follower of Watts and Burne-Jones, and it was amusing to hear her views on Conder's work and habits, and likewise Conder's opinion of her.

James Guthrie lived round the corner in a fascinating house built by Philip Webb, facing Cheyne Row. I liked Guthrie, the most gifted of the Glasgow artists, I thought; I used to say of the Glasgow school, so much admired in Munich and Dresden, that their reputation was 'made in

Germany'. Guthrie's fine intellect and breeding showed in the quality of his paint; he was a pleasant neighbour and I missed him when he left to settle in Edinburgh, where he became the distinguished President of the Royal Scottish Academy.

Derwent Wood also had a studio nearby. He too had studied under Legros at the Slade School, later acting as his assistant. One would not have suspected this from his work, though he was easily the most scholarly and accomplished of the academic sculptors. He was a brilliant linguist with a quick incisive mind, at times, perhaps, a little too quick, and inclined to be quarrelsome. He had a very fine head, putting one in mind of a contemporary of Rouget de Lisle; he was, I believe, partly French. Tweed lived close by, and so did Dermod O'Brien and Henry Tonks. My studio had previously been occupied, for a short time, by Walter Sickert. An old settee I picked up, a bed and a few chairs, an enormous painting table with a glass top which I bought from Sickert for a pound, an easel or two, and my studio was furnished, except for the Daumier lithographs I hung, of which only Sickert and Steer took notice. I was at once given a commission by Lady Pearson (Weetman Pearson had lately been made a Baronet). She asked me to paint her daughter Trudie, and I rashly accepted. Trudie, with her fine auburn hair, blue eyes, and rose and cream complexion, was a fitter subject for Watts or Millais; it was mistaken kindness on Lady Pearson's part to invite me to interpret this delicate English beauty. Of course I failed; and being young and vain, I wouldn't admit my failure. I would go my own way, and so, for a time, to my loss endangered a precious friendship.

One of my first sitters was Jan Toorop, the Dutch symbolist. He had a magnificent head. The son of a Dutch administrator and a Javanese princess, he had the physical glamour of a portrait by Titian or Tintoretto. I painted a one-sitting study—a small canvas later acquired by the Tate Gallery. In those days, indeed, I did each part of my painting in a single sitting; not because of any theory I had, but for the reason that I didn't know how to repaint. I sometimes

regret that later the habit of repainting grew upon me. To
paint a head or any part of a figure at a sitting makes one
concentrate on the day's task; repainting calls for a similar
exercise of will, for it needs the completion of each part
attempted; but there is a tendency to put off the final effort
till another day. I remember Sickert saying that, with
Whistler, repainting was like trying to say the Lord's Prayer
in a shorter time than was possible—as though one would
at first get as far as 'Thy will be...' at the next time would
manage 'on earth as...' and so on; but never have the time
to get through the whole prayer.

After my visit to Spain, and a careful study of Goya's
painting, I had my canvases prepared with a red colour
similar to that used by Goya. I found this an admirable
ground for painting *à premier coup*. An unprimed canvas,
sized, also serves for this. In later years I have been, perhaps,
too little inclined to experiment with grounds and mediums.
Thin paint, although easier to handle than solid paint, is
inclined to sink and darken, while stiffer material, though not
allowing the same subtlety of modelling and tenderness of
pigment, gives a certain radiance, more of the reflecting
surface of things; and, without oil or turpentine, paint keeps
its freshness and purity.

For some time, however, I remained under Whistler's influence. To Whistler any roughness of pigment was ab-
horrent; he habitually scraped down his canvases after each
day's painting. But he was careful to place his model far
back in the studio, well out of the range of direct light, so
that he need not render the full power of colour and light.
He was doubtless wise to limit himself in this way; but like
others in need of defence, he thought the best way of defending himself was to attack; so he was unjust, at least when
I knew him, to many of the French painters, who loved sunlight and full colour. He himself, in his younger days, came
under Courbet's influence, and his Piano picture, solidly
painted, rich in colour and quality, remains one of his most
satisfying works.

CHAPTER XV

THE BODLEY HEAD

BESIDES Toorop, I painted a portrait of Albert Toft, the first painting to find a place in a public gallery, and next, a small full-length of Conder. I gave this to Conder. It is now, I regret, in the Davis collection in the Luxembourg Gallery; for it is irretrievably spoiled. Conder, having allowed it to get covered with dust and dirt, coming home late one night, began to clean it with turpentine, and so removed much of the surface, before Sir Edmund Davis acquired it. I also painted Conder, reflected in a mirror, a canvas called *Porphyria's Lover*. For the woman's figure a beautiful girl, Miss Marion Gray, sat; she was sent to me by Oscar Wilde, and I did many drawings from her. One of these Beardsley carried off; and later, much against my will, reproduced it in *The Savoy*. It was too slight a drawing for publication.

A portrait spoiled

Another portrait I painted was of Cunninghame Graham in fencing dress. My meeting with Graham came about in an unusual way. Beardsley and I were at the first night of Shaw's *Arms and the Man*, for which Beardsley had drawn a poster. We were both ardent admirers of Bernard Shaw, and followed the play intently. We laughed so frequently and heartily that we attracted the notice of an elderly lady who was sitting near. In the interval she came up to us, saying that our enthusiasm had given her so much pleasure, that she would like to make our acquaintance; she introduced herself as Mrs Bontine—'Robert Cunninghame Graham's mother',

she added, and 'my son is a great friend of Mr Shaw'. She
hoped we would come to see her, and at her house in Chester
Square I met Robert, of whom she was so frankly, so justly,
proud.

I had heard of Graham only vaguely as a Socialist who, at
the time of the Trafalgar Square riots, a year before I came
to London, had been imprisoned with John Burns; and as a
thorn in the side of the House of Commons. I remember
writing home that I had met a Socialist, as though that were
a remarkable thing. How odd that seems to-day, when half
the people one knows claim to be Socialists!

Graham was one of the most picturesque and picaresque
figures of the day, and extremely entertaining. He had a
witty and caustic tongue, told the best Scotch stories I had
ever heard, wrote, fenced and rode a frisky horse with a long
tail, all in an equally gallant manner. I liked to see him
putting his fingers through his long, thick, golden-red hair,
making it stand high above his fine, narrow, aristocratic forehead. Twirling his moustaches, and holding his handsome
person proudly erect, he would stride into the room with the
swagger of a gaucho, and the elegance of a swordsman.

He insisted on taking me, graceless as I was, to Angelo's,
then in St James' Street, that I too might learn to fence.
Whether I acquired any grace from the lessons I doubt; but
I enjoyed the strenuous exercise, and the Regency atmosphere
of Angelo's; while Max and Beardsley, who used sometimes
to join me there, looked on, fascinated by the survival of this
classic establishment; now, alas, a memory only!

I often think now how Beardsley must have envied us,
who were so robust and full of life. He must have known
how slender were his own chances of living; yet he showed
no sign. The two earliest letters he wrote me, in 1893, both
refer to illness, and to difficulties with Lane, which I shared.

I had never got on well with John Lane, but when, during
the Wilde scandal, he dropped Beardsley, my scant respect
for the man was still further diminished. I rather wondered
that Lane managed to keep so many of his authors, Lionel

180

R. B. CUNNINGHAME GRAHAM (1895)

Johnson, Lord de Tabley, John Davidson, William Watson
and others. For John Davidson I had a great respect; I
liked his *Fleet Street Eclogues* and his *Ballad of a Nun*, and
Beardsley particularly admired his play *Mr Smith, a Tragedy*.
Perhaps we attributed qualities to Davidson which he did
not possess; since Davidson cared not at all for the baroque
fantasy which pleased Aubrey so much in his play. He was
a serious-minded, straight-hitting Scot—the last man, I had
thought, who would put an end to his life. But I never knew
what a struggle he had. Though there was a vogue for minor
poetry, there was also one for limited editions, so poets themselves got little or nothing for their pains. For some reason
I coupled Davidson with William Watson, perhaps because
I often met them together at the Hogarth Club when Lane
was entertaining his authors, and I wanted to draw them
together. Davidson was willing, but William Watson preferred to sit alone. Looking at my drawing of Davidson,
Max remarked on the subtle way in which I had managed his
toupee; greatly to my surprise, for I had not noticed, to Max's
amusement, that he wore one. How much more observant
was Max than I! He told me that Davidson was far from
wishing to look younger than in fact he was, but having to
depend on journalism for a living, he feared a bald head
would prejudice his chances.

Lane certainly produced his books extremely well, and he
had the courage to publish unknown or unpopular authors.
He was above all the poets' publisher, and he managed to
monopolise Beardsley. Beardsley wrote to me while I was at
Oxford: 'Very many thanks for the beautiful Book of Love.
It was so charming of you to remember it. I am looking
forward to seeing your Verlaine in the Pall Mall Budget.
I hope they will reproduce it properly. I have a hellish
amount of work to get through during the next 20 days or
so, and am wretchedly ill at the same time. However I intend
to visit you at Oxford unless those two words have already
become synonymous. Have you had a satisfactory explanation with Jean de Bodley? Or are you ready to join the

newly formed anti-Lane society? I suppose you saw Max's
latest caricatures. The George Moore I thought simply incomparable. It is some time since I was at Vigo Street, so
I have not had an opportunity of seeing his sketches of ourselves, or your own of Verlaine.'

And again later: 'Thanks very much for your letter. I am
sure you must have had a very funny time with Jean Lane
[who by the way is behaving (*I think*) very treacherously
both to you and myself]. Am so glad you have got such a
charming model. I have been very ill since you left—rather
severe attacks of blood spitting and abominable bilious attack
to finish me off. This is my first day up for some time. The
Salome drawings have created a veritable fronde with George
Moore at the head of the frondeurs. I have made definite
arrangements about "Masques". Max Beerbohm is going to
write the occasional verse. Will you be stopping in London
at all before you go on to Oxford? Hope I shall see something of you soon. Impossible for me to come over to Paris
so soon. For one thing I should be funky of the sea in my
present condition. I would like a dressing gown if you could
get a nice one. Let me have a line if you see one. Don't
trouble about anything else. I should like a nice long one,
full and ample. I have just found a shop where very jolly
contemporary engravings from Watteau can be got quite
cheaply. Cochin & Co. Pennell has just returned, but is off
again to Chicago. He is very enthusiastic about your Oxford
lithographs.'

Beardsley was one of the first, and one of the few, to
appraise Max's caricatures at their true value. He was equally
quick to appreciate his writing, and a warm friendship sprang
up between the two. Nor was Max slow to see the beauty
of Beardsley's work; indeed, his caricatures at this time bear
witness to his sympathy with Aubrey's style. Max wrote,
soon after leaving Oxford:

'Whilst I write I am coming of age: I was born twenty one
years ago today and am ever so sorry that I cannot possibly
come and live with you in Scarborough as you so charmingly

The Three Musicians

Along the path that skirts the wood
The three musicians wend their way,
Pleased with their thoughts, each other's mood,
Franz Himmel's latest roundelay,
The morning's work, a new-found theme, their breakfast and
        the summer day.

One's a soprano lightly frocked
In cool white muslin that just shows
Her brown silk stockings gaily clocked,
Plump arms and elbows tipped with rose,
And frills of petticoats and things, and outlines as the warm
        wind blows.

Beside her a slim gracious boy
Hastens to mend her loosened shoe,
And dies her favour to enjoy,
And dies for nickname 'reveille'
At Paris and St Petersburg, Vienna and St James' Hall.

The charming cantatrice reclines
And rests a moment where she sees
The château's roofs that softly shine
Amid the dusky summer trees
And fans herself, half shuts her eyes and smooths
        the frock about her
            knees.

The pianist is at her feet
And weighs his chance with his chance.
His fears soon melt in noonday heat.
The Tourist gives a furious glance,
And his guide looks grave, moves on, and
        offers up a prayer for France.

Aubrey Beardsley —

ask me. I have to go into the country tomorrow for a week
to stay with relations and cannot possibly put them off. Why
do I write on this odd paper? because it was wrapped up with
two very lovely drawings by Aubrey Beardsley which J. Lane
has just given me. They lie before me as I write: I am
enamoured of them. So is John Lane: he said: "How lucky
I am to have got hold of this young Beardsley: look at the
technique of his drawings! What workmanship! *He never
goes over the edges!*" He never said anything of the kind
but the criticism is suggestive for you, dear Will? And
characteristic of Art's middleman, the Publisher—for of such
is the Chamber of Horrors. How brilliant I am! I forget
whether you like Salome or not. Salome is the play of which
the drawings are illustrative? I have just been reading it
again—and like it immensely—there is much, I think in it
that is beautiful, much lovely writing—I almost wonder
Oscar doesn't dramatise it.'

'I almost wonder Oscar doesn't dramatise it'! Max had
uncanny premonitions; soon came the news that the censor
wouldn't sanction the performance of *Salome*. Wilde was
very angry. Sarah Bernhardt had offered to play the part of
Salome; but the censor was obdurate; no objection was
raised to the publication of the play in book form, yet its
presentation on the stage was forbidden. Wilde wrote from
Bad-Homburg:

'The Gaulois, the Echo de Paris, and the Pall Mall have
all had interviews. I hardly know what new thing there is
to say. The licenser of plays is nominally the Lord Cham-
berlain, but really a common-place official—in the present
case, a Mr Pigott—who panders to the vulgarity and hy-
pocrisy of the English people, by licensing every low farce
and vulgar melodrama—he even allows the stage to be used
for the purpose of the caricaturing of the personalities of
artists—and at the same moment that he prohibits Salome,
he licensed a burlesque on "Lady Windermere's Fan" in
which an actor dressed up like me, and imitated my voice
and manner!!!

'The curious thing is this: all the arts are free in England except the actor's art; it is held by the censor that the stage degrades and that actors desecrate fine subjects—so the censor prohibits not the publication of Salome but its production: yet, not one actor has protested against this insult to the stage—not even Irving who is always prating about the art of the actor.—All the dramatic critics, except Archer of The World, agree with the censor that there should be a censorship over actors and acting—! This shows how bad our stage must be, and also shows how Philistine the journalists are.'

He complains here of Irving, but he had previously praised Irving to me for habitually choosing bad plays; thus showing, he said, that Irving realised the true importance of the actor. 'Remember, my dear Will, that good plays can be read; only the actor's genius makes a bad play bearable.'

Wilde admired, though he didn't really like, Beardsley's *Salome* illustrations; he thought them too Japanese, as indeed they were. His play was Byzantine. When he gave me a copy on its first publication in its violet paper cover, he knew at once that it put me in mind of Flaubert. He admitted he had not been able to resist the theft. 'Remember,' he said with amusing unction, 'Dans la littérature il faut toujours tuer son pere.' But I didn't think he had killed Flaubert; nor did he, I believe.

I fancy Beardsley was relieved to get his *Salome* drawings done. The inspiration of Morris and Burne-Jones was waning fast, and the eighteenth-century illustrators were taking the place of the Japanese print. Conder, and also Sickert I think, influenced Beardsley just at this time. I have some hesitation in suggesting that paintings of mine—the *Souvenir of Scarborough*, for instance, and the studies of the girl in an 1830 bonnet exhibited at the New English Art Club, were not without their effect on Beardsley's outlook. Ross told me that in his introduction to *Volpone*, after Beardsley's death, he had written of Beardsley's debt to Conder and myself, but Smithers obliged him to take it out. This is not for a moment to take away from the originality of Beardsley's con-ceptions; but this change from the Japanese to the eighteenth century was as marked as that from Morris to the Japanese.

I remember Conder and myself chaffing Beardsley about the influence of Morris and Burne-Jones on his work, and Beardsley saying that while Burne-Jones was too remote from life he was inimitable as a designer. 'Imitable Aubrey!' I agreed, 'imitable surely?' a jest that delighted Aubrey.

There was truth in Beardsley's statement, and in my jest. Burne-Jones was indeed one of the great English designers, but it was not the true Burne-Jones who was imitable. For his design was a child of the imagination, which had led him into an enchanted land, hidden behind high, rocky moun-tains, where Knights and Princesses rode through dark forests and wandered dreaming by moated granges, or looked out from towers of brass, and about whose shores mermaidens swam and centaurs stamped their hairy hoofs. But wasn't all this long since discovered by Mantegna, and Piero di Cosimo and Botticelli? you may ask; and what of our music-hall and girls on sofas? had we, or Manet and Degas, seen them first?

Beardsley was too intelligent not to recognise the stature of an artist like Burne-Jones. He knew well that a little master was all he, or any of us, could aspire to be; we were too interested in every aspect of the visible world, had still too much faith in what life had to offer us, to understand the wistful vision of a painter who too loved the visible world, the great hills, the valleys through which flowed rivers re-flecting earth and sky, and fields bright with flowers; but one whom the sordidness of life saddened and bewildered.

Beardsley and I began writing a dialogue together, to no end, I think, but our own amusement. Some years afterwards I came upon a page or two, and gave them to Robert Ross, who fancied them. Beardsley was a brilliant writer. He read me the original manuscript of *Under the Hill*, afterwards printed in an expurgated form in *The Savoy*. He wrote with astonishing ease and command of language. When he moved to Chester Terrace, he would often come round in the morning to my studio, hastily dressed and without a collar. One day he began scribbling some verses about three musicians; afterwards he sent me the whole poem.

He was a tireless worker. His work done, Aubrey loved to get into evening clothes and drive into the town. So did Max and I. I used to infuriate the older members of the Chelsea Club by passing in front of the windows wearing white gloves and evening clothes. Nor did my conversation annoy them less; for the Chelsea Club was a kind of miniature Arts Club, frequented by cautious candidates for the Academic fold, whose opinions it was a temptation, too rarely resisted, to outrage. No doubt I made myself thoroughly objectionable, and deserved to be unpopular; but I was supposed to be clever, and being irrepressible was indulgently accepted as an *enfant terrible* by most of the older men.

When Swan was elected a full Academician, the Chelsea Club gave him a dinner. Swan was a good fellow, and in his way a real artist, but his speech was a little pompous; it suggested we had only to do as he did and we too would live to become Academicians. So when he sat down I stood up and begged to be allowed to couple the name of another distinguished Academician with Swan's, that of Leader! Steer, Tonks, Frederick Brown, Russell and Sargent were regular members of the Chelsea Club, and we formed a group apart. Maitland and Roussel, both 'followers' of Whistler, used the Club as well; so did Stirling Lee and Holloway, an old landscape painter, of whom Whistler painted a small full-length. Roussel was a Frenchman, intelligent, witty and a little *méchant*. He was a fastidious painter and etcher, but a poor draughtsman; but not so poor a one as another of Whistler's henchmen, Mortimer Menpes. When Menpes shall go to Heaven, I used to say, he will be tried *in camera*! Roussel told me that while on his way to dine with Whistler, he had met Pellegrini and asked him to come along. 'Dine with Vistlaire! Oh no! One *salade*, one sardine, 'arf a crown for a cab! Oh no!' But Beardsley's sudden leap into fame upset

JOHN DAVIDSON (1894)

etchers and illustrators, of whom there were many, and Robert Ross
roused their hostility, not against him alone, but against anyone bold enough to defend him.

One of Beardsley's most ardent supporters was Robert
Ross. He was a general favourite. Although not himself a
creative person, he had, in those days especially, a genius for
friendship. No man had a wider circle of friends than he. He
had a delightful nature, was an admirable story-teller, and a
wit; above all he was able to get the best out of those he
admired. Oscar Wilde was never wittier than when at Ross's
parties; the same was true of Aubrey Beardsley and Max
Beerbohm. Ross was a member of the Hogarth Club. On one
occasion he had been entertaining a party, one of which was
Oscar Wilde. After dinner we adjourned to the Hogarth
Club. As we entered the room, an old member of the Club,
ostentatiously staring at Wilde, rose from his chair and made
for the door. One or two other members also got up. Everyone felt uncomfortable. Wilde, aware of what was happening,
strode up to the member who was about to leave, and haughtily
exclaimed: 'How dare you insult a member of your own club.
I am Mr Ross's guest, an insult to me is an insult to him.
I insist upon your apologising to Mr Ross.' The member
addressed had nothing to do but to pretend very lamely that
no insult had been intended, and he and the others returned to
their seats. I thought this showed great pluck on Oscar's part.

But Wilde could scarcely complain if sinister rumours
were beginning to circulate. In Beardsley there was no such
perversity; and Beardsley, now that we look back on his few
years of hectic, hurried life, is a touching and lovable figure.
But at the time, with his butterfly ties, his too smart clothes
with their hard, padded shoulders, his face—as Oscar said—
'like a silver hatchet' under his spreading chestnut hair,
parted in the middle and arranged low over his forehead, his
staccato voice and jumpy, restless manners, he appeared a
portent of change—symbolic of the movement which was
associated—and was to end—with the last years of the
century.

Meanwhile Lane feverishly reaped the harvest of decadence. He started *The Yellow Book*, the first number of
which included most of the names now associated with the
'nineties. Oscar Wilde, Aubrey Beardsley, William Watson,
John Davidson, Crackanthorpe, Le Gallienne, Lionel Johnson and Lord de Tabley were Lane's strong men. Lord de
Tabley had wandered in among the younger poets much as
Brabazon became associated with the New English painters.
Both belonged to an older generation; neither had been recognised by their contemporaries; both were delighted to
find themselves, in their old age, honoured and admired by
us youngsters. Both had the courtly demeanour of the great
world; in their presence our speech and manners became
gentler, and Lane cooed like a dove. The deference paid to
us younger painters by Brabazon was almost embarrassing.
A cultured country gentleman, whose passion for painting in
water-colours (he carried his paint box with him wherever
he went) was held to be an amiable trait, he had been quietly
filling portfolios with lovely drawings for 60 years. One
night, dining with a friend, Sargent noticed some drawings
on the wall, and was told they were Brabazon's. He at once
recognised their unique qualities; and Brabazon at the age of
80 found himself suddenly accepted as a master of his craft,
elected a member of the New English Art Club, and enjoying
the esteem of a younger generation. He was an honoured
visitor at Glebe Place, where he often came, delighting to
talk of painters and painting, of Goya especially, whose work
he had studied closely. I had written something about Goya
in *The Saturday Review*, and Brabazon wrote, encouraging
me to write more.

> *September 23*
> *Oaklands*
> *Battle*
> *Sussex*

Dear Mr Rothenstein,

I must write a few words to you to say how *grateful* I am
for yr. 2 articles in the Saturday Review. I have preached

188

H. B. BRABAZON (1895)

Goya 'to the winds' for years & no one ever seemed to
know anything about him and to care still less. I wd. so
wish if you wd. give the world an elaborate critique on *all*
his works. The splendid portraits in private collections in
Madrid reminding one sometimes of Gainsborough—so
delicate and so delicious in tone. He cd. be brutal enough
as you well know in some moods—

 thanking you again for yr splendid notices

Believe me
Yrs Most truly
H. B. BRABAZON.

CHAPTER XVI

JOHN SARGENT

SARGENT I met soon after I had settled in Chelsea. He had liked a canvas of mine, of a peasant girl painted at Montigny, and Jacomb-Hood brought him to see me. I had, of course, seen his paintings at the Royal Academy and at the Salon, and admired their brilliant virtuosity; though I didn't think of him as inhabiting the same mansion as Whistler and Degas, Monet and Renoir. But on meeting Sargent I was at once aware of something large and dignified in his nature, something imposing in his person and manner, which set him apart and commanded respect. Reticent, yet cordial, there could be none of the easy familiarity with Sargent, which existed between Steer, Sickert, Tonks, Furse and myself, although there was nothing superior about him. Like Henry James, he had the English correctness of most Europeanised Americans, which brought a certain *je ne sais quoi* of self-consciousness into his relations with his friends. We all acknowledged his immense accomplishment as a painter to be far beyond anything of which we were capable. But the disparity between his gifts and our own we were inclined to discount, by thinking that we had qualities that somehow placed us among the essential artists, while he, in spite of his great gifts, remained outside the charmed circle. I was used to hearing both Whistler and Degas speak disparagingly of Sargent's work; even Helleu, Boldini and Gandara regarded him more as a brilliant executant than as an artist of high rank. One must bear in mind, too, that there were a number of extremely efficient painters among the older generation, who were also outside the small circle of men whom we looked on as the 'twice born': Sargent's master, Carolus Duran, and Tissot, Duez, Gervex, Roll, Bonnat, Boldini, were all men of great executive ability, able to carry out any subject which attracted them. It was not then the fashion, nor is it now, to admire Carolus; but few modern portraits can rival, or even approach, his *Lady with the Glove*, in the Luxembourg Gallery. It seems as though the pursuit of a certain kind of artistry has lowered the standard of painting throughout Europe. Manet, Degas and Fantin-Latour had, together with their artistic qualities, an equipment and knowledge equal to those of the best academic painters. This was not the case with Whistler, whose vision and impeccable taste replaced what he lacked of constructive power and virtuosity; and none of us, neither Steer nor Sickert nor Conder, had at his disposal the equipment which our older contemporaries carried with comfort and ease. Nor was it only in France that the older painters were able to do difficult things. Who among those who looked to Watts and the Pre-Raphaelites for inspiration could achieve such a work as his *Wounded Hawk*, one of Watts' earliest pieces? And who could approach, in conception or execution, paintings like Watts' *Waggoner and Horses*, or Madox Brown's *Work*, or *Farewell to England*? Ricketts and Shannon were in the same relation to the Pre-Raphaelites as Sickert, Steer and Conder to the Impressionists. We all trusted vaguely to our 'artistic' qualities to bring us up to the mountain top; the critics too flouted us, not for our incompetence, but for our supposed eccentricity: MacColl, the best among them, himself preferred suggestion to thoroughness, charm of colour to solid construction. So far has this insensibility to incompetence gone, that critics, nay even some artists themselves, actually regard this as a sign of genius, and have come to believe that impotence is the sign of creative ability; a strange paradox! Prophetic, in truth, was Hans Andersen's story of the King and his golden clothes.

191

Sargent must have given me some advice about portrait painting, for I find in a letter from him the following:

'I have been in Paris for a week, and am only just re-turned—I left Abbey in Paris—Hôtel de Lille et d'Albion, rue St Honoré—on his way south. Do come in any day—if you will take pot luck at lunch at 1 o'clock. Hood told me that he had told you certain views of mine about the danger of going in for portraits. I hope you did not think me impertinent.

Yours sincerely,
JOHN SARGENT.'

I have now forgotten what Hood said, but I am sure it was excellent advice. Sargent at once saw that I was insufficiently trained; he thought he could help me, and proposed I should join him to paint a nude in his studio. I was glad enough of the chance to see Sargent at work, and to benefit by his counsel; but although the nude I painted was thoroughly bad, and Sargent's was a marvel of constructive skill, I tried to believe, despite this clear evidence, that there was something vaguely superior in my temperamental equipment. Sargent's reticence prevented his telling me how bad my painting was, and I was too stupid and conceited to see that here was a chance of acquiring the constructive practice I lacked, and above all, a scientific method of work.

Sargent, when he painted the size of life, placed his canvas on a level with the model, walked back until canvas and sitter were equal before his eye, and was thus able to estimate the construction and values of his representation. He drew with his brush, beginning with the shadows, and gradually evolving his figure from the background by means of large, loose volumes of shadow, half tones and light, regardless of features or refinements of form, finally bringing the masses of light and shade closer together, and thus assembling the figure. He painted with large brushes and a full palette, using oil and turpentine freely as a medium. When he repainted, he would smudge and efface the part he wished to

JOHN SARGENT (1897)

reconstruct, and begin again from a shapeless mass. He
never used what was underneath. I had acquired the habit of
standing near to my canvas, some way from the model. If
one paints sight-size there is method in this practice too; but
often my figure was larger than sight-size, and I struggled in
consequence with difficulties which, had I followed Sargent's
example, I must have avoided. There is a common and mistaken belief that we *instinctively* feel the right way of doing
things. The contrary is true. Take any instrument—the
common scythe, or the woodman's axe; when at first we are
shown the correct way of handling these, it seems unnatural
and awkward. Efficient use of either has to be painfully
acquired. So with brush and pencil: they, too, are tools, and
must be correctly handled; and the placing of the canvas near
to, or at a given distance from, the subject, so that the sitter
and image can be compared together, is an essential factor of
representative painting. Painters often deplore the loss of
tradition, and speak with regret of the days when artists
ground their own colours; but knowledge of the visual
methods of the older painters, rather than of their technical
practices, seems to me of equal, if not of greater importance.
The methods of Velazquez and Hals were not unlike Sargent's; but how Titian, Rubens and Rembrandt painted is
unknown to us; for while they were masters of rhythmical
construction, they were able to reproduce, in their studies,
the subtle details of eyes and lips, of hands and finger nails,
with no loss of breadth. How they achieved an appearance
of unity, as seen from a distance, combined with the clear,
satisfying rendering of features visible only when close to
the model, is a mystery to painters. Sargent had made admirable copies after both Velazquez and Hals, and had closely
studied their methods. He could indicate hands and heads
and figures with surprising felicity; but he too often failed
to reveal the solidity and radiance of form.

But we are apt to forget that each one of us can use only
those gifts, great or small, which the gods have given him.
It is the use we make of our gifts, not the character of the

gifts themselves, which merit praise, or else blame. And no man made fuller or more honourable use of his talents than Sargent.

Yet I never felt quite comfortable in front of his paintings or drawings. I admired, and respected, but I never loved. Again and again, feeling my own inability acutely, I have said to myself, 'Sargent would have achieved triumphantly where you have fumbled and failed,' and have blamed myself for having criticised a man of such evident stature; but I could never overcome a certain hesitation in paying full tribute to Sargent's paintings, a hesitation which stood in the way of full intimacy.

I felt that something essential was lacking in Sargent. He was like a hungry man with a superb digestion, who need not be too particular what he eats. Sargent's unappeased appetite for work allowed him to paint everything and anything without selection, anywhere, at any time. It was this uncritical hunger for mere painting which distinguished him from the French and English painters whom he rivalled, and often surpassed, in facility. He accepted any problem set him with equal zest; it was for him to solve it successfully. He never relied solely on his facility, but gave all his energies to each task.

I was touched by Sargent's generous enthusiasm for Manet and Monet, for Rodin and Whistler; for, as I said, I had heard Degas and Whistler speak disparagingly of Sargent, as a skilful portrait painter who differed little from the better Salon painters then in fashion. He was allowed to be Carolus Duran's most capable disciple, but not a markedly personal artist. With the exception of Rodin, I never heard anyone in Paris acknowledge the worth of Sargent's performance.

Even Helleu, his closest friend, whose work Sargent adulated, regarded him with a patronising eye—a worthy painter, a dear good fellow; scarcely an artist.

On the other hand, at the Royal Academy where, having settled in England, he exhibited regularly, Sargent appeared as a daring innovator. Although he had as many commissions as he could execute, they came chiefly from Americans. In London his warmest admirers were the wealthy Jews. But it would be a mistake to suppose that Sargent preferred the aristocratic to the Jewish type, that he painted Jews because they happened to be his chief clients. On the contrary, he admired, and thoroughly enjoyed painting, the energetic features of the men, and the exotic beauty of the women of Semitic race. He urged me to paint Jews, as being at once the most interesting models and the most reliable patrons. The more conservative English were at first shy of facing the cold light of Sargent's studio; the absurd legend that he brought out the worst side of his sitters' characters also helped to keep people away.

There was neither flattery nor satire in his portraits; his problem was to make his work visually convincing. Not for him any short cuts; his integrity was unquestionable. And yet in his brilliant rendering of the men and women who sat to him, he seemed to miss something of the mystery of life. I remember how this sense of the dramatic element of good portraiture came on me when looking one day at photographs of Titian's and Giorgione's portraits of young men, so proud in their bearing, and from whom death, I suddenly felt, was never far off. But what relation have Sargent's men and women to the drama of life and death? Sargent rarely succeeded in removing his figures from the model stand, from the Louis XV or Louis XVI chair or settee dear to the new rich; from pearl necklaces and glittering medals, and Worth dresses of velvet and satin. Looking, too, at his out-of-door work, so accidental in composition, at those sparkling paintings of flickering sunlight over mountains and plains, over trees and buildings, I felt as though they had sprung up before him by a sort of magic: feverish, transitory apparitions with no past and no future, that would fade away after he had folded up his easel and painting stool.

But this was, after all, the real Sargent; for the qualities I missed in his painting were qualities he did not particularly

195

admire in others. It was not the gravity of Velazquez and Hals that he cared for so much as their perfection of handling. Similarly with his admiration for Manet; it was for Manet's brilliance of execution that he preferred him to austerer painters like Fantin-Latour and Legros. Cézanne's work he altogether disliked. Oddly enough, when later I was painting Jews in the East End, he thought I was aiming at too abstract a representation, and wanted me to paint scenes in Petticoat Lane, or the interiors of tailors' shops, as showing the more intimate side of Jewish life. Yet it was just this lack of intimacy that I missed in his portraits. But then Sargent himself had little of this intimacy in his own life. His studio was that of a cultivated cosmopolitan, filled with French, Italian and Spanish furniture and bric-à-brac; he could scarcely be expected to paint people in the middle-class interiors in which Degas, Fantin-Latour and Cézanne saw their sitters.

But herein Sargent was true, and wisely true, to himself. On the other hand, when he gave up portrait painting to devote himself solely to his Boston decorations, he showed unworldliness and a touching desire to escape from the slavery of the model-stand; but his shortcomings were at once revealed. The American element in his nature asserted itself; he approached the scene of the Divine Comedy not with the great Mantuan, not with the noble Giotto, nor yet with the passionate El Greco, but with Edwin Abbey by his side. Truth to tell, Sargent's taste and judgment in painting were very unexpected. He was a keen admirer not only of Hals and Velazquez, but also of El Greco and of Tiepolo; and, what was more strange, of the early work of Rossetti. He was an ardent musician. When I was painting with him, he always improvised on the piano while the model was resting. He had many musical friends, chief among them Fauré, whom he invited to England to stay with him, taking endless trouble to introduce him to musical people in London, inviting them to his studio to hear Fauré play his own compositions.

Like Steer and myself, he was a keen chess-player, and he often asked us round to his mother's flat for a game in the evenings. He adored his mother, while her pride in him was touching to see—a quiet undemonstrative pride, as became a lady of old Bostonian lineage.

Perhaps Sargent's closest friends were Laurence Harrison, and his wife, 'Alma Strettell', the translator of Roumanian folk-songs, and also of Émile Verhaeren. I had known them both in Paris, and valued Harrison's judgment and his work more than that of most artists. It was difficult to induce him to show his canvases, for Harrison belittled himself, and was over modest; but some of his interiors and sea-pieces reached the level of Steer at his best, I thought.

Harrison was a man of unusually fine taste, taste apparent throughout his beautiful house in Cheyne Walk. Besides Sargent, Steer, Tonks, George Moore and MacColl met constantly round his table.

Those were days of vital friendships in art, when our faith and trust in one another were as yet undimmed.

CHAPTER XVII

NEW FRIENDSHIPS

An exhibition
*with Shannon*I HAD not been long in Chelsea when I made friends with a cultured picture-dealer named van Wisselingh. At his gallery in Brook Street I found paintings and drawings by Daumier, then little known in London, by Delacroix, Courbet, Millet and Mathew Maris. He generously offered me the use of his gallery; I talked the matter over at the Vale, and Shannon agreed to join me in a small exhibition of prints and drawings. Shannon's work was then little known, but his contributions to *The Dial*, and his delicate illustrations to Oscar Wilde's *House of Pomegranates*, had impressed a few discerning people; at the exhibition we held at Brook Street his sanguine and silver-point drawings, exquisitely mounted and framed, and a selection of his lithographs, created immediate interest, and established him as a refined and able draughtsman. His prints and drawings found many purchasers.

I too, on this occasion, sold some of my drawings, including a pastel of a beautiful girl whom I had met at the Vale, whom Shannon had drawn more than once. At the Vale she was called Amaryllis; she looked like a 'Rossetti', had rich auburn hair, and a heart of gold. Shortly afterwards I heard that the purchaser of this pastel had bought my painting of Conder as well, at the New English Art Club, and Francis Bate, then, and for long afterwards, acting as honorary secretary to the club, wrote that the purchaser wished to make my acquaintance. His name was Llewellyn

Hacon, a bachelor, a conveyancer by profession; I met him first at his club, and found him a typical clubman; a man of the world, well read and informed on a variety of subjects, with that special knowledge of the secrets of notables, past and present, which men of his character possess. His friends were mostly clubmen like himself: good-living, easy-going, slightly cynical, prosperous men. Hacon, stout, ruddy and clean-shaved, looked the picture of a seventeenth-century country gentleman; he might have walked out of one of Congreve's or Wycherley's comedies. The character was new to me; he on his part was amused at meeting an artist, an enthusiastic youngster, eager for experience, full of illusions as to the importance of his work. For Hacon had rather lost his own zest for life, was neglecting his practice, and allowing his fine intellect to get slack; and I think this fresh interest in art, and the new acquaintances it brought him, revived his spirits and renewed his attachment to life.

He proposed I should paint his portrait; he would take a house in the Isle of Wight, hire a yacht to do some 'mud-dodging', and any other work I might do there he would take off my hands. This all seemed too good to be true; but true, at least for a time, it was. A house was hired at Yarmouth, where Hacon's butler and a manservant looked after us.

Hacon seemed to enjoy sitting; and there was the yacht, with a skipper and a couple of handy men, in which we sailed round the island. I enjoyed the sight of the proud yachts, leaning over at dangerous angles as they cut through the waters of the Solent, and the sensation of steering the sensitive and responsive organism that I discovered a yacht to be.

Hacon's portrait finished, we returned to town, where I introduced him to Conder, and to Ricketts and Shannon. Hacon had generously offered to finance me—taking so many pictures and drawings each year. With a yearly allowance of £100 from my father, and with the confidence of youth, I declined. But knowing Ricketts to be eager to design type and to embark on book production, I urged

Hacon to finance this promising adventure instead. This he
was ready to do, and again a new interest came into his life.

Hacon had hung my pastel of 'Ryllis in his rooms in St
James' Place, and was anxious to meet her. She had come,
at my invitation, for a day's yachting, and there and then
Hacon had fallen in love with her. They were married soon
after, and as Ricketts was leaving the Vale, Hacon took over
the lease, and the Vale became under its gracious and radiant
mistress a still more hospitable and cherished haven.

The Hacons kept open house: Max Beerbohm, Conder,
Ricketts and Shannon, Laurence Binyon, Harry Reece and
I met constantly round their table. Binyon spoke rarely;
indeed, sometimes I thought his silence meant disapproval,
until I found it was not so, that behind a shy and diffident
manner was a rich, humorous and most human nature. In
Binyon I found a life-long friend, one who was quick to
perceive and to welcome unusual talent in others, who re-
joiced in what was new and vital in literature and painting,
and yet loved, and retained, a fine taste for scholarship and
lofty language. His *London Visions* had just appeared: he
was a true poet, I thought. Binyon was urging me to write
on Goya; he shared my admiration for Goya's etchings, and
I wrote a small book for a series which Binyon edited. I was
a source of trouble to poor Binyon, no doubt, for I find
many letters on the subject passing between us. Binyon,
who was already in the Print Room, was one of the few
scholars who consulted us artists—rare modesty, which I have
seldom met with in the expert. Sidney Colvin would sometimes show drawings about which he was doubtful; but he
would never pay one the compliment of asking directly and
openly for an opinion. He waited for an opinion to be
offered, and no doubt considered it, among others. I do not
believe an experienced draughtsman with two drawings, an
original and a copy before him, would mistake one for the
other. On my return from Spain I remember I found a wash
lithograph among the Goya drawings at the British Museum,
which Colvin for long refused to believe was other than an

original drawing. Finally an expert lithographer examined it with a glass and pronounced it a print hitherto unknown.

Ricketts and Shannon moved to Beaufort Street, where they prepared title-pages, engraved wood-blocks and designed type for the forthcoming books of the Vale Press. A little shop was found behind Regent Street for which Shannon painted a lovely swinging sign, and Charles Holmes, being now free, was induced to look after the new venture.

Among the early publications was a little paper-covered set of three lithographs I had made of Verlaine, and I was proud to see my name in the finely-printed catalogue of the Vale Press; and I never regretted having assisted, in a modest way, the birth of the beautiful books which issued from the fertile brain of Charles Ricketts.

Through my recent exhibition with Shannon, I gained other valuable friendships: those of Mrs J. R. Green, of Elizabeth Robins, of Lawrence Hodson, and of the Michael Fields. Mrs Green showed me endless kindness, and her house in Kensington Square, where many of the more adventurous characters and thinkers of the time met together, became, after the Beerbohms', the most friendly and familiar to me in London.

Mrs Green knew I had rather a struggle to keep going, and was constantly trying to get me commissions, asking me frequently to dinner parties at her house in Kensington Square, where I met many attractive people: Stopford Brooke, Mrs Henry Myers, J. J. Jusserand, John O'Leary, Miss Mary Kingsley and Mrs Hugh Bell and her daughter, Gertrude. Gertrude Bell was one of the few young people to be found at Mrs Green's parties. She was exceptionally intelligent, but she gave little idea of the powerful personality which was growing within her.

A dominating figure at Kensington Square was Miss Mary Kingsley. She had recently come from Central Africa, and stories of her courage and resource as a traveller were on everyone's lips. I was rather taken back to find her, striking talker though she was, almost aitchless. I gathered that she had been brought up in the country by an old nurse, whose accent she caught, and had never been able to throw it off. I am amused to find Mrs Green writing:

'Will you come to supper here on Sunday the 18th? The Sidney Webbs are to be here. He practically disposes of the County Council soul and purse in art; she is a very original personality.'

This is the only time I have known Sidney Webb's name to be associated with art! À propos of some lady, Mrs Green writes again:

'I fear you have lost another actress; but I am told Esther Waters proves that Mr George Moore has found a soul. Will that set the world's crazy balance straight again?'

No book would do this last; but *Esther Waters* was an event of importance nevertheless.

At Mrs Green's I formed a friendship with Arthur Strong. A great scholar (he looked strikingly like Erasmus); he had lately been made Librarian to the Duke of Devonshire. Though an orientalist, he knew as much about works of art as Ricketts and Berenson. Why he should have taken a fancy to me was a puzzle; but experts don't always like experts— my ignorance perhaps was refreshing.

I mentioned the 'Michael Fields'. These were two ladies, an aunt and a niece, Miss Bradley and Miss Cooper, who wrote under this name. Highly praised, on the appearance of their first volume of poems, by Robert Browning, they had naturally looked forward to the encouragement and sympathy of their contemporaries. But book after book appeared and, save by a few, remained unnoticed. Happily they were not discouraged, and though disappointed at the obtuseness of the critics, they devoted themselves to perfecting their gifts. Proud and aloof, they tended their minds as precious vessels prepared to receive all they held lovely, both in the physical and the spiritual world. They were the feminine affinities to Ricketts and Shannon with whose work they had fallen in love. All four seemed made to understand and appreciate one another. I lost no time in taking 'Michael

Field' to the Vale, and a friendship was formed which lasted to the end of their lives. For a time the interest of these ladies in me was eclipsed. But closer relations were resumed, which in my case, too, were to prove enduring.

It was Mrs Costelloe, Logan Pearsall Smith's sister (afterwards Mrs Bernhard Berenson) to whom I owed this precious friendship. Mrs Costelloe was then living close to the Pearsall Smiths at Friday's Hill, where I spent the greater part of the summer of 1894, painting a portrait of her sister, Miss Alys Pearsall Smith. Friday's Hill was a hospitable house, which saw much, and some oddly varied, company. Logan and his sisters held enlightened views; each had his or her circle of friends. Old Mrs Pearsall Smith was a Quaker of strict and narrow principles, rigidly held. Her children, while respecting her faith, talked freely before her, and encouraged their friends to do likewise; and as they brought to the house anyone they thought interesting, whatever his or her views might be, there were lively discussions.

It was my first country-house visit, and the ways of a large household were new and attractive. Mrs Costelloe took me under her wing. I was devoted to her two young children, Ray and Karin; their mother was writing a story book for them, for which I made drawings. Meanwhile I worked regularly on my portrait.

There were pleasant visits to neighbouring houses, to the Frederick Harrisons', to the Rollo Russells', to the Tennysons' and to Mrs Rogerson's, where I would meet my *National Observer* friends; George Street, George Steevens and Charles Whibley were constant visitors. Lady Henry Somerset and Miss Willard paid a visit to Friday's Hill, and overawed me by the ethical and social ideals they preached. I was a very moderate drinker, but not an abstainer; and I knew that my life would not bear the scrutiny of Miss Willard's searching eyes. But I had Logan and Mrs Costelloe, thank Heaven! to support me. Logan was all for adventures, of the spirit at least. A Puritan himself, he enjoyed the indiscretions of others, and his broad intellectual sympathies were at the service of all his friends. Among these was Zangwill, who visited Friday's Hill just after I left. I heard from Logan:

'Zangwill was here—it was the last of our parties for the summer. Have you seen Mrs Woods' book? I wonder what it will be like? Zangwill's novel, "The Master" is finished—everybody is writing about artists—you people are in great demand as models. I am going to start a literary "Carlo-rossi", a night class for lady novelists—will you pose—you used to so well!

'If the star I follow wanders to the London skies I will come and see your Early-Victorian ladies and your co-operated nude.'

Zangwill had won fame with his *Children of the Ghetto*; but *The Master*, his next book, was a disappointment. It was, as Logan wrote, about artists; but no novelist, not even Henry James, has to my mind done a convincing study of a painter or sculptor. We posed right enough; but as happens in a night-class, the drawings were never well enough constructed.

The following letter from Logan is characteristic of the period:

Aug 18 '93
Friday's Hill,
Haslemere.

Dear Rothenstein,

I was very sorry to hear that you had been ill—I hope you will be all right soon.

I got back here a day or two ago, after a delightful visit. It was a charming and shabby old park, with a quaint ugly house, and as soon as I arrived I felt myself back in 1830. A footman ran out across the lawn to let my trap in; Lady Jane received me, and we walked out in the twilight, into a long and ancient terrace, with over-arching elms down the green perspective of which I saw advancing several maidens and young men. There were flower baskets and little woolly dogs—and of course I saw at once that they were walking

out of the English novel to welcome me. Indeed the whole
time I was between the covers of the old fashioned novel; in
the still hot afternoons I would sit talking to Lady Jane; a
little way off the squire was surveying his acres and whistling
to his dogs, while from the river that lapsed away below the
terrace there came echoes of talk and laughter, and then we
would see a boat splashing up slowly, in which a young lady
in pink was being rowed by a charming young man in white.
Their talk was about the Prince Consort, I make sure, and
Landseer's wonderful pictures of animals and Canova's sculpture, which he said was what one must admire. But Lady
Jane and I were more serious; fixing her eye on the horizon,
she told me of the deplorable changes that were coming over
the country side; old families gone away. Their places taken
by dreadful *nouveaux riches*; the peasantry losing their reverence for the squires; the farmers aping gentlemen, & even
maids in the best houses wearing hats with flowers in them
instead of bonnets. Lady Jane was short and thin and strenuous, she had a fine even aristocratic profile and always wore
a creaking silk dress with a train. We found that we had many
sympathies in common, and we both deplored the dreadful
spread of Atheism and Socialism, and all their evil conse-
quences; old places ceasing to be kept up as they used to be;
men of place and position marrying Americans, of whose
antecedents Heaven only knows what they are.

Then we agreed too about the horrid tone of modern
French literature, which, as we put it, always left a bad taste
in the mouth—and as for the pictures, well, it was hardly
decent so much as to mention them.

Poor Lady Jane! She showed me her needlework, & a
polar bear on an iceberg that she had painted on a screen. . . .

Friday's Hill lifts its slopes up in the sunshine and it is very
hot and quiet. We called on Mrs C— yesterday. I don't
think I liked her very much; she talked of her novels and
publishers, as one would talk of things made and sold by the
yard, and when I tried to throw in a joke or compliment, she
would only pause for a moment, fix me with a cold eye, and

then continue. If you knew with what impatience I expect the favour of your reply, I assure myself your charity would oblige you to set at quiet the mind of

Yrs L. PEARSALL SMITH.

This ending is out of an old book. Is it not charming?

In London other friendships were forming, with the Vernon Lushingtons, the Phillimores and others. Furse at this time was engaged to Miss Eleanor Butcher. She and her sisters, Mrs Crawley and Mrs (afterwards Lady) Prothero, were three enchanting ladies, spirited, enlightened and vivacious talkers. I soon ceased to regret Paris. While I lived in France, I believed life to be freer and more quickening than elsewhere. But I soon came to think, in spite of Whistler's jibes (he asked me if it was true that I was to become a naturalised English artist), that English social life was the flower of European civilisation. I was not thinking of the aristocracy, of whom I knew little, but of the people I was meeting, of their considerateness and hospitality, their easy manners, freedom from prejudice and good feeling towards one another, combined with a reticence which was far removed from narrow-mindedness. There were so many people who seemed not only incapable of mean actions, but of harbouring mean thoughts. Such natures as Eleanor Butcher's made life seem more worth living; to have her friendship, and that of others like her, was, I felt, a privilege. Alas! she who so loved life was to lose it soon. Nor was her sister, Mrs Crawley, destined to survive her for long.

Two other ladies of great charm and character, whose friendship I likewise valued, were Ida and Una Taylor. People who have never known the quality of the Victorian atmosphere may be excused an ill-informed attitude towards it. Sir Henry Taylor had been associated with the most eminent men of his time, and the daughters were a mine of information about the Gladstonian period. They were both ardent Home-Rulers. John Redmond was one of their intimates. And the example of finely-bred women caring less for their private privileges than for public causes, was not then so familiar to me as it afterwards became. No wonder many delightful people came to their little house in Montpelier Square. There I first met Watts. He was then a very old man, very gentle, obviously delicate in health, but of serene and dignified aspect. He wore a black velvet skull-cap and a fine cambric shirt, with delicate wristbands setting off beautiful, old, veined hands. When I spoke with admiration of one of his latest exhibited pictures—a great oak tree strangled by ivy—he said hesitatingly that he had something in his mind at the time which inspired it, though he scarcely liked to speak of this to me—the undisciplined art of the day slowly sapping the life of a centuries-old artistic inheritance. In the presence of a man of Watts' character and achievement, I realised how trivial our painting must appear in his eyes; and how misguided our lives. Watts and the Pre-Raphaelites are now held in small esteem; but they are still with us, to be assailed. How many of us now painting will survive to meet with similar treatment by a succeeding generation?

Watts' didactic comment had some point: compared with the giants then still alive, Watts and Whistler, Burne-Jones and Ruskin, William Morris, Meredith, Hardy and Swinburne, we were little men. Consider the achievements of these men, and their relation to the great social and aesthetic movements of their time. A generation which knew these veterans was reluctant to accept Oscar Wilde, Sickert, Beardsley, George Moore and Crackanthorpe as their successors.

While Sickert, Steer and Beardsley represented the 'new' art, Le Gallienne's name then stood for the 'new' poetry, as Hubert Crackanthorpe's stood for the 'new' short story. Although Kipling had shown how brilliantly an Englishman could handle this form of writing, the younger short story writers looked to France—to Maupassant especially—not only for their style, but also for their subject matter. Crackanthorpe, basing his stories on Guy de Maupassant, was thought to be a daring, an immoral innovator. Poor Crackanthorpe! His life was as short as one of his stories. Far from being daring, he was rather timid; he belonged to a good, solid family, lived a quiet life in a workman's flat in Chelsea, and was devoted to his wife. It was rather she who was free from prejudice. Forty years ago a man felt it more of a disgrace when his wife took the reins into her own hands and drove away with another man on the box seat, than he would do to-day. But when poor Crackanthorpe put an end to his life, it was said to be the judgment of God for adoring French idols. There was Frederick Wedmore too, a thin nature, he seemed to me, and a querulous. But some held Wedmore to be a master of English prose, and of the short story. I thought him a master of prosiness, and though he praised my drawings in his articles, and had me make his portrait, he wearied me. Nor did Henry Harland, another writer of short stories, impress me. Such very minor writers were so many of these men, yet their pretences were not small. There was one writer, however, who stood apart from the aesthetic school, and who, if he looked abroad, looked rather to Norway than to France. This was Bernard Shaw.

Bernard Shaw I had met soon after I settled in Chelsea. He was then chiefly known as a journalist, at this time writing musical criticism for *The World*, and as a Fabian closely associated with Sidney Webb. Already he had ardent admirers, and ardent detractors. Roger Fry likened him to Christ. I couldn't see the resemblance; but I admired Shaw for one thing especially—he did not wait until he was famous to behave like a great man. In fact, he had early singled himself out from among his fellows as a remarkable character. He had all the ease and assurance, the endearing right-headedness and wrong-headedness, the over-weening outspokenness, that English society recognises so generously, now that the whole world has acclaimed him. But he worked long and hard to be accepted in the position he so candidly assumed. He declared that he missed no opportunity of

GEORGE BERNARD SHAW (1895)

attending meetings and speaking in opposition to other
speakers, no matter how little he knew of their subjects.
Thus, by these mental gymnastics, he fortified his natural
gift of speech, and his mental alertness. De Goncourt said that
the artist was *libertin d'esprit et chaste de corps.* Shaw was a
wild man in public, violent, aggressive and paradoxical; in
private he was the instinctive gentleman, ever on the side of
the oppressed and unpopular, tender-hearted and generous,
though he had little enough in those days to be generous
with. He lived with his mother and sister in a flat in Fitzroy
Square, fending, I imagine, for them as well as for himself.
Although he assumed antagonism to art for art's sake, and
was more associated with Morris and Fabian ideas than with
those of Whistler, he was very friendly with all of us, and
lent his support to the more adventurous activities of the
younger artists and writers.

Not much older than Steer and Sickert, Shaw was considerably older than Beardsley, Max and myself. He was one of
Max's firmest supporters, and one of the first to realise
Beardsley's genius. To me he was genially encouraging; he
was one of my earliest sitters, and I may claim to have been
a staunch defender of Shaw at a time when people generally
regarded him as little more than a crank or a charlatan. I have
been amused at the belated acknowledgment of Shaw's
genius by men who, in the days of which I am writing, would
not allow a word in his defence. It is not the rats who desert
a sinking ship, but those who so sleekly invade the home-
coming one, I object to so much.

No man has shown less resentment at contempt and hostility than Shaw. He held his head high, and kept his temper
and poured out his wit. Every gallant cause has had his
support. Ideas were ever to him what the fox is to the
hunter—to be pursued thorough bush, thorough briar, over
hill, down dale, for the joy of the chase. I always felt that
Shaw was more interested in the platonic or theoretical aspect
of things, and of people, than in things and people themselves. In my opinion he doesn't see people or things as they

are; neither comeliness nor plainness is evident to his eyes; his eyes and ears are attentive to his own vision, to the sound of his own voice. If his vision is not often the artist's, and if his talk is more like the boxer's use of a punch-ball, who hits this way and that, to left and to right, upwards and down, than his bout with a living opponent, it keeps him, as the boxer is kept, in wonderful fettle. No step was lighter, eye fresher, nor tongue freer nor cleaner than Shaw's. No decadence in him; he was a figure apart, brilliant, genial, wholesome, a great wit, a gallant foe and a staunch friend, a Swift without bitterness, sharer and castigator of the follies of mankind, whose cap though of Jaeger was worn as gaily as motley. I loved Shaw; he again was of those I could not imagine harbouring mean or ignoble thoughts; a true knight without fear and without reproach. Yet many men deemed him a cad, a vulgarian, a dangerous charlatan, while he went his way, head high, body alert, ready to spring at the sight of wrong, injustice or stupidity. His attacks on the first might have been overlooked; on the third they were unforgivable—the fellow was not only a busy-body but impertinent.

Shaw introduced me to Janet Achurch, the English interpreter of Ibsen, whose photograph had impressed me so in Conder's studio. She was somewhat more matronly than she appeared in his Australian days, but was an admirable actress. I saw her as Nora in *The Doll's House*. We were all mesmerised by Ibsen in those days. Max wrote, many years later:

In days of yore the Drama throve within our stormbound coasts,
The Independent Theatre gave performances of 'Ghosts',
Death and disease, disaster
And darkness, were our joy.
The fun flew fast and faster,
When Ibsen was our master,
And Grein was a bright Dutch boy, my boys,
(chorus) and Grein was a bright Dutch boy.

'Death and disease, disaster.' Shaw and Barrie were soon to drive these off the stage. Meanwhile they flourished

vigorously at the Independent Theatre, to the satisfaction
of Shaw's young 'iron brows' of both sexes. *Ghosts* was
privately performed; Elizabeth Robins staged *Little Eyolf*.
I wrote home after the first night: 'I went to the performance
of Little Eyolf and amused myself as much with the audience
as with the play....I was in Mrs (J. R.) Green's box part of
the time, with Mrs, now of course Lady Poynter. Mrs Pat
came up after the first act. Mrs Woods was there in a box
with Lady Burne-Jones and Forbes-Robertson—Pinero came
up to me and was very flattering about my Grafton portrait.
...Miss Robins is probably going to take a theatre in the
autumn and has asked me to be her art adviser, to manage
the scenes, lighting, etc. and have the scenery painted under
my direction.'

Gordon Craig must have trembled in his shoes.

In another letter home I wrote: 'I went to the first night
of *Gossip*, a bad play, but Mrs Langtry looked wondrous
well and handsome. Zangwill's play has been refused by all
the London managers—it must be very bad for that.'

But much as I enjoyed these plays, I enjoyed no less what
Shaw wrote about them each week. Shaw had recently left
The World to become dramatic critic of *The Saturday
Review*, then owned by Frank Harris. Harris had had an adventurous career, he began life as a cow-boy, like Cunninghame Graham. Later he married a wealthy wife, wrote
brilliant short stories, became a personality in London and
gained influence through his ownership of *The Fortnightly
Review*. He was a daring and enlightened Editor. After the
Fortnightly he acquired *The Saturday Review* and gathered
round him a dazzling group of writers: besides Bernard Shaw,
there were D: S. MacColl, Churton Collins, Cunninghame
Graham, J. F. Runciman and Max Beerbohm. Harris was
a good talker, though as a talker he played what Wilde
called 'the Rugby game'. He had a rich, deep voice, which
rose and swelled like an organ as he charged into the conversation. With ample means, he was able to become a
patron of art and literature. Alas! our patrons in those days

Forty years back were not reliable supports. Young men complain to-day of their hardships, often with reason. The time between leaving the art school and setting up for oneself is a hard one, but at least there are many people to-day on the look-out for promising work. Forty years ago patrons were rare. We were poorly paid for our pictures; Steer complained that he had sold nothing for years, and though Sickert sold more, he got insignificant sums for his canvases. Sickert believed in selling at any price; he approved of the French system by which a dealer buys a number of works from the artist; even though this meant a trifling sum for a single work, by selling a quantity an artist was enabled at least to live. English dealers sold only on commission; so that until something was bought the artist got nothing. I remember Sickert telling how, when he was unusually hard up, he took a trunkful of his canvases over to Paris. To impress the dealers, he took a room in a good hotel, which, before he had disposed of something, he could ill afford. He was long in finding a purchaser, and directly he had been paid he had to settle his bill. Once he had money in his pocket he felt bound to leave his clean comfortable room in the excellent hotel and take the cheapest room he could find in a third-rate *maison meublée!* Steer had private means, and could afford to wait; I lived by my drawings; so did Shannon, who in fact had not yet begun to paint.

Arnold Dolmetsch, among others, was hard put to it to earn a living. In spite of an unmusical soul, I used to go to Dolmetsch's concerts at his little house in Bayley Street, off Tottenham Court Road, to watch him, his wife and daughter, playing on their lovely instruments. I did some lithographs of Dolmetsch playing the virginals, the lute and the viola d'amore. He had just made an exquisite clavicord, with a keyboard painted by Helen Coombe. Runciman brought Frank Harris to see it; Harris seemed really moved by its beauty. He boomed and bellowed enthusiasm, wanted at once to possess it, and hearing it had been specially commissioned, he insisted that Dolmetsch should make a similar

FRANK HARRIS (1895).

instrument for himself. When some months afterwards the clavicord was completed, Harris' enthusiasm had cooled; for a moment he wanted to get out of his bargain; then, in his impulsive, free-handed way, Harris gave the lovely instrument to Runciman. It was through Horne, I think, that George Moore met Dolmetsch; and from Dolmetsch he got the information he needed for the 'musical' parts of *Evelyn Innes*.

To me, too, Harris talked as though he were going to be a marvellous patron. He sat for his portrait which, needless to say, he rejected—since, as he said, I had made him appear a truculent rascal. However, he bought three of my pastels: one of Shaw wearing a broad-brimmed hat, one of Alphonse Daudet, and another of Verlaine.

Harris liked the look of my studio at Glebe Place, and he asked me down to Kingston, where he was then living, with a view to my re-arranging the interior there. He drove a very spirited horse every day to *The Saturday Review* office in Southampton Street, and as he was usually tired and nervous after his day's work, he was glad to surrender the reins to me, whenever I went down to Kingston. I thoroughly enjoyed the excitement of driving through the traffic, and, once out of London, the peace of the lovely Kingston Vale.

These were Harris' days of prosperity, when he entertained lavishly, usually at the Café Royal. I remember especially a dinner he gave there at which Oscar Wilde, Max Beerbohm, Aubrey Beardsley, Robbie Ross and myself were present. Harris on this occasion monopolised the conversation; even Wilde found it difficult to get a word in. He told us an endless story, obviously inspired by the *Étui de Nacre*, while Oscar grew more and more restive; when at last it came to an end, Max said, 'Now Frank, Anatole France would have spoiled that story.' But Harris wasn't thin-skinned; he proceeded to tell us of all the great houses he frequented. This was more than Oscar could bear—'Yes, dear Frank,' he exclaimed, 'we believe you; you have dined in every house in London, *once*'—the only time I heard him say an unkind thing.

Another time, I was lunching with Max at the Café Royal, when Harris was sitting near with a lady friend. As we passed his table he called out, twisting his moustaches, 'You're getting older Will, I'm getting younger.' 'Well, Harris,' I replied, 'we can both do with it.'

If Harris' rather truculent manner drew repartee, he had a geniality, a boisterous vigour, which won the loyalty of *The Saturday* circle. And Harris had a love for literature and audacious critical insight. His book on Shakespeare showed a true writer's penetration; *Elder Conklin* contains one of the best English short stories. But his itch to shock, to rummage in the rubbish heaps of men's lives, prejudiced people against him. He wished us to believe himself the recipient of the most intimate confidences from Carlyle and others—astonishing confidences made to himself alone. Of his conquests among ladies, the more said about them, he thought, the better.

We all live in glass houses; and stones, which lie everywhere, are easily picked up. Yet not a few could tell tales of Harris' bounty.

CHAPTER XVIII

A JOURNEY TO MOROCCO

Chance to see Spain

WHILE I was painting Cunninghame Graham he was planning a journey to Morocco and pressed me to go with him. As an inducement, he proposed returning through Spain. When, three years before, Friant offered to take me to Spain, I had fallen ill; but this time I was well, and I had just sold my painting of *Porphyria*; so everything favoured my seeing the Prado, and seeing the world, under exceptional guidance.

We went on a P. & O. boat from London to Gibraltar, making one of the roughest journeys on record. All our boats were carried away, and our cabins were swamped. Graham, a wretched sailor, was ill most of the time, but between whiles was amusing and cheerful. A handsome youth had introduced himself to me on board, a student from the Slade School, Gerard Chowne, who was going to Gibraltar with his mother. I managed to join him on deck sometimes, watching the great seas. After such weather it was a relief to lie in quiet water outside Gibraltar, where we anchored till morning. The Rock looked magnificent under the stars, mysterious and grand in the solemn simplicity which night throws over the world. I was up by daylight, for this was my first taste of true foreign travel. With Chowne I explored the Rock thoroughly, delighting in the steep streets and the Spanish-looking houses in the rocky slopes, and the clinging bushes and trees. We hired horses; Chowne could ride, I couldn't; but I managed to stick on my Rosinante,

215

bumping ungracefully, yet enjoying a first sight of the austere
brown landscape of Spain, of a village with its empty bull-
ring, and of Spanish peasants.

From Gibraltar we took ship to Tangier, at which place,
there being no harbour, we were met by a flotilla of small
craft, manned by Moors, into one of which we jumped;
our luggage was thrown in after us, and we were rapidly
rowed ashore. On the crowded quay sat a white-robed Cadi,
with his attendants, at the customs; he let us pass with a
grunt when Graham said something in Spanish, or perhaps
in Arabic, of which he knew a few words.

Tangier, in those days, was a truly Eastern city, and
Morocco was still an undeveloped, unruly country, and perhaps the least explored of any near Europe. The market place
looked like an illustration to the *Arabian Nights*; so did
many of the streets, especially by night. We stayed at a hostel
with the unromantic name of the New York Hotel, just outside the town. From here the sweep of the town was very
fine; I began a painting, but Graham was anxious to get to
Wazan, if possible to Fez, though for foreigners, he said, to
reach Fez was not easy. The reason was simple: if a European
were robbed, or murdered, the Sultan levied a heavy fine on
the district; irresponsible travellers were therefore not popular
with the Sultan's subjects. With the help, however, of Walter
Harris, the well-informed *Times* correspondent, and of Bibi
Carlton, an adventurous Levantine Englishman whose name
was known throughout Morocco, we got permission to travel
in the interior. Walter Harris lent us tents and everything
else we needed, and with Carlton arranged our itinerary. We
were supposed to take guards with us, but Graham would
not. We set out with a cook, three other servants, four mules,
and two donkeys to carry our baggage, which included two
large sacks of Moorish silver; Graham had a horse for himself,
whilst I had a serviceable pony. I was nothing of a horseman,
and some of the ground over which we travelled was fairly
rough; but after a day or two I got used to the saddle. We
were not heavily armed; Graham carried a large revolver;

I had a shot-gun and a toy revolver. I fancied myself, riding with a gun slung over my shoulder; and when I discovered that my pony was so trained that I might safely shoot from the saddle, I felt like a Byronic corsair.

We followed the coast till we came to an old Moorish fortress, where an old chief whom Harris knew had been living, so the old man told us himself, for 48 years. He wanted to know if England was still at war in the Crimea, and whether there was any war going on in Spain. He had heard that guns were so formidable now, he feared his little place might be blown up one of these days. He gave us some delicious bread to eat, baked between two hot stones, and we passed out of the old man's sight, and came next to a small, squalid Moorish town full of Jews in black caps and gabardines.

Our first stopping place was Howara, a small village beside a vast lagoon. Our men were wonderfully quick in unpacking the mules, and in less than half an hour we were seated on gorgeous rugs in a large, airy tent, drinking green tea, impatiently awaiting dinner. Never had I eaten with such appetite, and so little niceness. Directly afterwards we lay down on our mattresses and at once fell asleep. We were wakened at dawn; tent and baggage were packed, and we mounted our horses and were soon far ahead of the mules.

We rode miles without meeting a soul, seeing nothing but foot-prints here and there in the sand; then there would come a procession of laden mules and men with long guns, either walking or riding; or else a messenger, with his bag of letters, would run by at a steady trot. They run thus for days, Graham said, eating only a few dried dates.

At midday we reached Arzila; thence on to Sid-bu-Mereisch, a saint's tomb on the coast at the foot of magnificent hills. We were all weary after a long day's ride, and were soon stretched on our carpets. A party of villagers arrived and built a great fire and acted as watchmen through the night; there were marauders about, our men told us, and they were afraid for our horses. Our two tents at the foot of the great hill, the sacred tomb, surrounded by wild olive trees, with the flickering light of our fire on its walls, looked beautiful in the night.

The next day we reached El Arash, or Leratsche, as the Spaniards call it, an imposing place, with its square walls and mediaeval fortress, built by the Portuguese four hundred years before.

From El Arash we pushed on to Alcazar, a small but interesting Moorish town, with its streets hung with matting from roof to roof, from which ivy and creepers grew—quite the filthiest place I had ever been in.

At dawn came a Moor to our camp, who saluted, and said that his master, the British Consul, begged we would do him the honour of entering his house. The Consul turned out to be a Levantine Jew, and since Englishmen rarely came here, his duties lay lightly upon him. Now, however, we found his household in a state of feverish activity. We had not yet breakfasted, and when, after a great deal of talk, a bottle of brandy and tumblers were brought in by our host, Graham did his best to explain, I am sure in the politest Spanish, that while our host, who so well understood English ways, was kindness itself, we were both accustomed to drink our tumblers of brandy later on in the day, being men of eccentric habits. Leah, his wife, and Rebecca and Rachel his daughters, with their henna-haired handmaidens, observed the scene through the half-open door.

At the next town lived the Governor of the district, to whom Bibi Carlton had announced our coming. We were invited at once to his residence, a typical Moorish building with a cool courtyard, and fountain. The Cadi, a handsome, white-bearded old man, received us courteously and with great dignity. A repast had been prepared—great bowls of rice and saffron, and chicken. This we ate with our fingers, sitting on the ground; and when green tea, with violets and mint leaves, had been brought, Graham paid the habitual compliments on the beauty of the apartment and the excellence of the repast. In reply the Cadi shook his head sadly and said: 'This is my prison.' The unfortunate man, we heard later, had been Governor of Fez, when the Sultan had allowed him to extort what he would from the people, biding his time. When the treasury was full, the Cadi was seized, dragged with a rope round his neck through the streets and thrown into prison. There he stayed, chained and manacled, until he had declared where his wealth was hidden. Once possessed of the spoil, the blessed Descendant of the Prophet, as a sign of great mercy, gave him the governorship of this small town, perhaps, who knows, to pounce again when the hour should be ripe. Thus justice was done, wealth kept in check, extortion punished, and the Sultan's coffers replenished.

I saw more than one Moorish prison, all pitiful dens. It seemed incredible that such places should still exist. The first prison I saw was half underground, with a barred window opening on to the street. At this opening filthy and miserable-looking men, ragged, verminous and half-starved, clamoured piteously for food. It was terrible to see human beings in such a state—one gave what one could, and hurried away in shame and horror. Some no doubt had committed crimes; but among them were many who were imprisoned, or so we were told, on no other ground than that of suspected wealth, whose whereabouts nevertheless they would not reveal. So harsh were the Sultan's laws, that a traffic existed to sell European nationality to the wretched Moors. But sometimes, it was whispered, the newly-acquired nationality was sold back to the Sultan again, and thus a rascally traffic was doubly enriched.

Knowing the present state of Morocco under the French, it is difficult to realise how wild and disorderly a country it was forty years ago. At every village where we stopped for the night, the villagers turned out to guard us, lighting big fires round which they sat till daylight. This they did, not out of love for strangers, but for the reason already mentioned, that if a traveller were robbed or suffered injury of any kind, the whole district was heavily fined. But while they acted thus, they wished, we could see, to get rid of us quickly. We rewarded the villagers with a sheep or two, which we bought; these they roasted whole in true biblical fashion. In fact the whole Moroccan scene put me in mind of the Dalziel illustrated Bible, familiar to us as children.

We rode through beautiful country, passing many of the Sultan's orange gardens. Sometimes we would meet a party of mounted Moors, dignified-looking men with their long guns slung over their shoulders, their feet in short, heavy stirrups, looking with their hooded bernous very like the figures in Delacroix' paintings. As a rule they rode silently by, too proud to show curiosity, to stare or look back; but once, outside a small town, we met with fierce and threatening looks from several parties of Arabs. I felt nervous; even Graham looked anxious. We found out afterwards that we had passed too near to a tomb that was held in great veneration, and this, seeing we were infidels, they resented.

This winter of 1894 the rainfall was exceptionally heavy, and we were more than once held up by rivers so swollen that to cross them was, for a time, impracticable. There were no bridges, but usually we swam the fords, while we sat uneasily balanced on our animals' backs. Only occasionally were there ferries. One day, when a party of Jews came down to a ferry to cross, there was a long and excited dispute with the boatmen before the price was settled. But once in mid-stream the Moors threatened to throw the Jews into the water unless they doubled the price agreed on. The poor Jews were treated like dogs.

Finally we reached a river where there was neither ford nor ferry; the current was so swollen and swift that to cross on horseback was unsafe. Parties of Moors were encamped along the banks, waiting patiently for the flood to subside. The Moors proved friendly enough, and to pass away the time gave exhibitions of riding and marksmanship, with their queer, long Moorish guns. Graham won their respect by lifting one of these guns over his head by the muzzle end, and then slowly lowering the gun and his arm in one line, till

A RECOLLECTION:
OSCAR WILDE, CHARLES CONDER, MAX BEERBOHM AND THE WRITER
AT THE CAFÉ ROYAL, BY MAX

both were at right angles to his body—no mean feat. They were interested in Graham's revolver; for firearms a Moor would sell his soul; Graham, to impress them, had me throw oranges into the air, at which he shot. Not one of them did he hit, nor did it strike the innocent Moors that anyone aiming at a mark could fail to hit it. They grunted their approval each time Graham's revolver went off, but they never thought of examining the oranges! I think Graham was amused, as I was, at their simplicity. But praise is sweet, even when undeserved, and Graham enjoyed the prestige he got.

But we had not the placid patience of the Moors; with the Spanish journey before us, we renounced the idea of reaching Wazan, since the swollen river showed no sign of abating, and turned towards Tangier.

But I had thoroughly enjoyed our journey inland, and was now quite at home on a horse. No one walked in Tangier. Our servants were always at hand with our mounts, and we rode into the town, or along the seashore, with others we knew who were visiting Tangier: Mrs Alec Tweedie, the Duke of Fryas, Cecil Hunt the painter, Walter Harris and Bibi Carlton.

One day, while I was riding after a pig-sticking party outside the town, being somewhat late and hurried, my pony slipped on the rough stone cobbles, and threw me on to my head. The mentality of the Moor is a simple one. As I lay stunned and unconscious, the onlookers took me for dead, and sent word of my death to Graham, who was naturally upset. He had urged me to come out to Morocco, and now he must write to my parents and dispose of my corpse. Happily I recovered my senses, and was able to find my friends; and though I saw no pigs, I enjoyed riding about in the scrub, little the worse for my fall. Graham reminded me that the test of a horseman was not how he stuck to his mount, but how he fell off.

One starry night, riding with Graham along the seashore, we passed Bibi Carlton. We stopped and talked, but Carlton was clearly constrained; he was probably gun-running, Graham said. For Bibi had to live somehow; he was one on whom women loved to look; and though himself no liege of the Sultan, he was the father of many of the Sultan's subjects. A rough, wild soul was Bibi's, recking nothing of the romance of the life he led. Careless of hardship and danger, illiterate, unpolished, yet with something simple and endearing, which won one's respect and affection, he possessed as well a profound knowledge of the ways of the Moor.

Walter Harris, too, was brave and adventurous, and had travelled all over the country. He was of that small distinguished company of Englishmen who, while remaining as English in their manners and ways as though they had never left home, combined a love of courage and adventure with an innate understanding of, and sympathy for an alien people. But he was also a man of the world. Walking with me one rainy day, he drew my attention to a hole in his umbrella. 'A curious thing,' he said, 'I once stayed at a house where the Prince of Wales was staying, when his cigar fell into my umbrella and burnt that hole.' Walter Harris had treasured that umbrella, it seemed, ever since. Harris lived outside the town, in a typical Moorish house, full of treasures. He and Carlton were known to every Moor in the land. Bibi Carlton knew their most hidden ways; Harris was more in touch with their political difficulties.

Harris and Graham would sit for hours talking politics, and exchanging experiences; Harris rather dry and precise, Graham half cynic, half romantic, knowing men's foibles, while forgiving them easily, aware of his own shortcomings as a son of Adam, but thanking God that Adam was not all Scotsman, but part Spaniard, like himself.

When at last the weather allowed of our crossing to Spain I, too, was glad of Graham's ancestry. For, arrived at Cadiz, Graham made friends with the first man he met, a dentist, who proved an admirable guide, and took us at once to the tobacco factory, where I made sketches of black-eyed girls, with flowers in their hair and shawls over their shoulders,

and with thickly powdered faces. Incidentally I noticed,
when we left the factory, that people turned round and
smiled—I wondered why; until Graham observed that my
shoulders were white with powder, from the faces of the girls
who had pressed round me while I was drawing.

From Cadiz we went on to Cordova. Without knowing it
we had chosen a fortunate time. The day we arrived the
peasants were pouring into the town from the villages round,
riding in on their mules, their women behind them. The
squares and the streets as well were crowded with folk in
old-fashioned Spanish costumes, most of them dating from
the eighteenth century. Whether this was a local fête day or
some special occasion, I don't remember. In the evening the
streets were lively with masqueraders, who made one think
of Guardi and Longhi; later I saw how perfectly Goya had
rendered the soul of the Spanish people.

No description could give an idea of the magnificence of
the Great Mosque of Cordova, with its forest of pillars, its
lovely proportions and exquisite carving, its courts and
fountains, and even its beggars outside, who might have
walked straight out of pictures by Velazquez or Ribera—
ragged, sunburnt, veritable princes in rags, whose mien conferred honour on all who gave them alms.

At Seville we saw more evidence of the splendour of the
old Moorish civilisation than we had found in Morocco.
There Graham had many friends, who took us to places
where the toreadors and matadors meet, where we saw their
chulas dancing, not in the regulation mantilla and bright
swinging skirt, such as Carmencita wore, but in shabby old
gowns, ill-made and ill-fitting. They looked heavy and dull
to my eyes as they sat round the room, but the moment they
rose to begin their dance, they shed their ennui in a flash
and their dress was forgotten; never had I seen such dancing,
beginning slowly and gracefully, getting more and more impassioned, while the men shouted and took off hats and even
coats in their excitement, and flung them at the feet of the
dancers.

Sargent had told me at all costs to go to Toledo to see the great El Grecos there, but unfortunately the violent storms that had swept over Spain early that year had broken down the railway and we were unable to get to Toledo, to our great disappointment.

Sargent told me also of Goya's decorations: had I seen the El Grecos at Toledo I should have thought less of these. But Goya's art was of the kind to dazzle a young painter. The two *Majas* at the Academy of San Fernando, the great painting of the *Dos de Mayo*, which had so marked an influence on Manet, the designs for the tapestries, the cupola and the wall paintings of the church of San Antonio—a church, I wrote at the time, more like a boudoir than like a shrine—the many portraits at the Prado: the range of Goya's genius astonished me. In fact the only picture I copied in the Prado was Goya's little painting of a mounted picador. At the Academy of San Fernando I acquired a copy of Goya's *Los Desastres de la Guerra*, which I thought, and still think, to be one of the greatest series of etchings ever made.

It seems strange that these were unknown during Goya's life. For political reasons it would have been difficult for him to publish these etchings. No doubt the French would have objected. No one has ever done such daring pictures of war. The plates are conceived, and needled, with a terrible, a haunting energy, and they record, for all time, an artist's indignant protest against the savagery of war. They are perhaps the finest figure compositions produced since Rembrandt, only equalled by the four lithographs he did in his old age at Marseilles.

Passing the window of a print shop in Madrid, a print of an 1830 Spanish dancer caught my eye: under it was written her name—Aurora la Cujini. The name took Graham's fancy, and later he wrote an attractive 'imaginary portrait' suggested by this print.

I was sorry to leave Madrid, and to be leaving Spain; but now my money was spent, and therefore I had to return to England at once.

Arriving in Paris one morning soon after, and buying a newspaper, the first thing therein that caught my eye was a large headline—something about Oscar Wilde. This was the first I knew of the libel action that Wilde had brought against the Marquis of Queensberry, which was to end in Wilde's imprisonment. When I got back to London this matter was naturally the one topic of conversation.

A friend of mine went more than once to the court while the case was going on. He told me that Carson, who had been with Wilde at Trinity College, Dublin, and had always disliked him, cross-examined Wilde with almost indecent brutality. Oscar Wilde, he said, was magnificent in his replies. Before his libel action came up for trial, many people hoped he would leave the country, as he did for a time, and spent a few weeks in Algeria. But wisely or unwisely, who shall say? he preferred to face the charges made against him. When his Counsel, Sir Edward Clarke, threw up the case, what followed was inevitable. Though one had felt there was something insecure in his prosperity and fame, the end was no less tragic. Naturally the meanest people threw the largest stones. People who had been glad to know Oscar while he was successful, hastened to deny him when he was down. John Lane withdrew his books from circulation; George Alexander removed his name from the play bills of *The Importance of Being Earnest*; the bailiffs took possession of his house; all his books, papers and effects were sold. I went to Tite Street on the day of the sale with the intention of buying some small thing (my voyage to Spain and Morocco had emptied my pocket) which I might sell later to benefit Wilde. The house was filled with a jostling crowd, most of whom had come out of curiosity; the rest were dealers, chiefly local people, come to pick up bargains. And bargains there certainly were. Bundles of letters and masses of manuscripts, books, pictures and prints and bric-à-brac went for almost nothing. I bought a painting by Monticelli for eight pounds, which later I was able to sell to Colnaghi to help Wilde.

CHAPTER XIX

SWINBURNE AND THEODORE WATTS

A new annual SOON after my return from Spain I found that Ricketts and Shannon were planning a new annual, *The Pageant*, of which Shannon was to be the artistic and Gleeson White the literary editor. The annual was to be published by Henry and Co., a firm in which J. T. Grein was a partner. Ricketts was to design the cover and to look after the lay-out; and besides all the great swells, several of us younger men, Conder, Max Beerbohm and myself, were to contribute.

Shannon asked me to write to Whistler to induce him to give us a lithograph, and to Verlaine for a poem; Verlaine, he suggested, might write on Whistler's *Symphony in White*; I was to find out whether this would appeal to Whistler. Whistler, in his reply, wrote of his not being 'prepared for this apotheosis at the hands of a great poet', 'but that a literary combination as between Editor and Bard has brought about a culmination of recognition that I might otherwise have gone from you without ever personally achieving'. Shannon was to have carte blanche in the matter of a lithograph and I was to convey to Verlaine Whistler's high sense of the distinction proposed—'In the mean time, your reverence, adieu.' But the poem was never written, why, I cannot now recollect. It was on Rossetti's *Monna Rosa* that Verlaine finally wrote. I sent Verlaine a photograph of the *Monna Rosa*, and a description of the painting. Incidentally, in my letter to Verlaine, I made a slip which the poet repeated. In Rossetti's painting there was a Chinese

ALGERNON CHARLES SWINBURNE (1895)

hawthorn jar which I said was Japanese; an awful error to be guilty of, which cost me a sleepless night. 'Cher ami, reçu votre lettre et la photo. Voici vers,' he wrote in sending the poem, 'je les crois appropriés, ad hoc, and the right lines of the right thing. Si vous pouvez me les faire payer tout de suite, quelle reconnaissance! Car je dois déménager le 8 8bre. Quelle scie! ne sais où irons....Ah, tâchez donc, si possible, d'achever mes affaires pour le 3me article (conférences) au Fortnightly, travail corrigé, non payé. Je finirai par me fâcher. Il est des juges à Londres! Mais préférerais "money"...Courtney, naughty boy! Harris très gentil,' etc. I could never straighten out this trouble over the *Fortnightly* contributions. Verlaine was paid 100 francs for *The Pageant* poem, and in acknowledging it he again refers to some money owing. 'Je vous remercie d'avoir pensé à moi pour les vers à faire et l'argent à gagner. Me conseillez-vous d'écrire une lettre à cheval à qui de droit au Fortnightly Review, où on me doit 250 francs ou d'attaquer devant les tribunaux anglais?' Frank Harris assured me that Verlaine had been paid, and well paid, for his contributions.

I had also spoken to Robert Bridges about the venture, and he wrote to me later and promised to contribute.

My dear Rothenstein,

I had forgotten all about the Pageant. What you told me at Oxford interested me very much, and made me wish to help in any way that I could—and I am of course extremely gratified by your wish to associate my small talents.

There are real difficulties in the way of making such a magazine artistically satisfactory. The unavoidable expenses require a pretty wide sale, and it may be necessary for the Editor at any moment to play the fool to that end. The new reproductive processes have much lessened that difficulty, but I should like, before joining the company to have some sort of prospectus or scheme from the Editor, by way of assurance, e.g. that he is not coming out at the Kelmscott

Press in 'Troy type'. That would be a Pageant indeed. Then
if he is getting his first number together, he could tell me
whether a poem of 50 or 60 lines would be too long. I have
one of that length which I should like to send.

Is the Editorial Department a committee? or have you a
thoroughly uncompromising tyrant who is prepared to go
through with the bankruptcy business? Are you going to
include music? If so I should wish to know who is your
musical Editor.

Awaiting further intelligence
I am yours very truly,
ROBERT BRIDGES

Shannon asked Conder for one of his beautiful paintings
on silk, and he wanted me to do a portrait. He heard that
Maeterlinck was coming over to London, and proposed I
should draw him. Maeterlinck was the new hope of the
theatre. I had seen the first performances of *Les Aveugles* and
L'Intruse at a small theatre in Paris three or four years before
—they had seemed strange and novel. I admired the plays no
less when they were published. Other plays followed, and
Maeterlinck became a European figure. Texeira de Mattos
and Alfred Sutro introduced me to Maeterlinck at a reception
which J. T. Grein gave in his honour, and a sitting was
settled. The day he was to come to the studio I waited in
vain. How often this has happened! He wrote to excuse
himself some days later, after his return to Belgium.

Cher Monsieur—

Je suis absolument désolé de ce qui est arrivé. J'étais si
fatigué, si malade, mercredi, que Mr Sutro, dont j'étais l'hôte,
m'avait engagé à me [illegible] au feu, et à me mettre au lit,
disant qu'il se chargerait de tout, qu'il vous aurait prévenu,
m'aurait excusé, etc. J'étais donc presque tranquille, et voilà
que rien n'a été fait! Vous avez dû me maudire bien juste-
ment, et je ne sais si j'ai le droit de demander pardon.

J'ai vu hier, à Bruxelles, Camille Mauclair, qui m'a dit de vous tant de bien que cela vient encore augmenter ma confusion et mon regret.

Essayez de me pardonner un peu.

First meeting with Miss Kingsley

M. MAETERLINCK

At the reception to Maeterlinck I was introduced to a beautiful young actress, Miss Alice Kingsley (Miss Knewstub in private life), who was then playing Miss Ansell's part with Miss Irene Vanbrugh, and with Toole, in *Walker, London*. I used to wait for Miss Kingsley at the stage door, to drive her home to Tufnell Park, where she lived; walking back the four or five miles to Chelsea. Admiring Miss Kingsley as I did, I was prepared to think her a gifted actress. But the stage was then one of the few careers open to women. Miss Kingsley's father, Walter John Knewstub, spent his evenings at the Working Men's College, where Rossetti and Ruskin taught. Knewstub was so fired by Rossetti's teaching and example, that he left the Royal Academy school, where he was then studying, to become Dante Gabriel's pupil. Knewstub later became Rossetti's assistant, laying in the first stages, and painting duplicates of many of his paintings, both in oil and water-colour, which Rossetti himself signed and disposed of. Then Knewstub discovered a lady of rare beauty, who sat to him, and to Rossetti also. When Knewstub and she got married, the allowance he was getting from his family ceased, and Knewstub had to produce work for immediate sale. For a time he joined Madox Brown at Manchester, helping him with his mural decorations; but he found it more and more difficult to provide for an increasing family. Miss Kingsley, his eldest daughter, set to work at an early age to help, and when she went on the stage was able to send her two sisters to school. She was still giving as much as she could spare from her salary to help things at home. But I knew nothing of these difficulties at the time. Miss Kingsley herself might have walked out of a canvas by Rossetti. But when Bernard Shaw, in a review of a play in which Miss

229

Kingsley had a part, wrote that she was perhaps better known through my drawings than for her gifts as an actress, her father was furious. Only when four years later Mr Knewstub became my father-in-law, was I forgiven.

Miss Kingsley introduced me to the Rossetti household at St Edmund's Terrace, and I became warmly attached to the family. William Rossetti was the only one of the Pre-Raphaelites who was sympathetic towards the work of the younger writers and painters. He even thought that we youngsters were better draughtsmen and more skilful painters than was his brother. This, of course, was absurd; Rossetti's early drawings are among the great drawings of the world, and none of us could approach their quality of closely knit design. When talking with me, William Rossetti would constantly say: 'I am so glad to hear this from you. That was Gabriel's opinion too.' This was heartening and flattering, yet it made one feel humble and ashamed. But I was eager to hear all he could tell me about his brother, and of the old Pre-Raphaelite days. His house was full of paintings and drawings by Dante Gabriel and Ford Madox Brown. There was a portrait of himself painted by Legros, and he had countless small drawings by his brother put away in drawers, which he would bring out from time to time. He was formerly a Civil-Servant, but had now retired. While he was still in Government service, his children produced an anarchist paper, *The Torch*, to which he contributed, and his house was a centre for anarchists and refugees from every corner of Europe. When he reached the age limit of service, his children hung out a red flag in celebration of their father's retirement.

If William Rossetti had a sweet and modest nature, he was by no means the 'fool for a brother' that Morris proclaimed him to be; on the contrary, he was an admirable critic of literature and art; he had kept his faith in the power of art bright and clean; and his outlook on life was broad and humane. He didn't like the clatter the younger generation made in the press, and in the social world, so he lived in

retirement. But to any who went to see him, he gave himself
generously.

With Miss Kingsley, at Theodore Watts' invitation, I paid my first visit to The Pines, Putney. Watts was a little, round, rosy, wrinkled man, with a moustache like a walrus, and a polished dewlap. He was dressed in a sort of grey flannel frock-coat, which I suppose he had hurriedly donned, since a shabbier coat lay on the sofa. As we came in, he rose to greet us. He was very welcoming. I was naturally interested to see the interior of The Pines. The room we were in had a fine large window looking on to a long, narrow garden, surrounded by ivy-grown walls. In the middle of the garden stood a small plaster statue, near which was an ugly iron and cane seat, painted yellow. Round the walls hung large drawings by Rossetti, mostly studies for the *Pandora*, stippled in chalk, and a splendid drawing of Mrs Morris, lying back, her hair spread luxuriantly about her head, her hands held up before her. There was also a drawing, in coloured chalk, of Watts himself. Besides these there was a portrait of Rossetti by Ford Madox Brown, obviously like, but a little thin and somewhat dirty in colour; and an admirable self-portrait by Brown against a gold background; and there were several heads, charmingly painted, by Knewstub—Miss Kingsley's father; and a lovely little watercolour by Miss Siddall.

'Ah, I hear you know Whistler. Dear Jimmy,' said Swinburne's companion; 'how clever he is, indeed the most brilliant of men. I have known him intimately these 20 years. What genius! Latterly, owing to his quarrelsome nature—though I myself have had no difference with him—still, owing to his misunderstanding with my friend, I have ceased to see him. But what a talker! Is he doing well now? Some say yes, some no. Surely he was in the wrong over Sir William Eden. George Moore I am rather prejudiced against; but of course I don't know him, and I have not read his books. But I trust Jimmy always for being in the wrong, he loves a quarrel.'

I gently told Watts some of the facts of the Eden business. 'Yes, yes,' he broke in, 'but how foolish of Whistler, to challenge Moore. And so you have drawn Pater! A curious man, whom I never quite understand. Swinburne of course invented him—took him round to see Rossetti, who disliked him extremely. Yes, a wonderful prose writer, a better one than Swinburne, to my mind. But will his work last? Baudelaire started *l'art pour l'art* in France, then Swinburne trotted her round here, dropping her very soon, seeing there was nothing, after all, in her. Then Pater took the theory up—beautiful prose, yes, beautiful prose, but surely a little late; and will it last? The *coup de grâce* was given to the movement by that harlequin Wilde.' Watts was not very kind to men who had had a youth since his own; he ended every criticism by saying 'but will the movement last?' He even wanted to know if *The Yellow Book* would last. He seemed to think Beardsley represented all that was living in modern art. It was pleasant to hear him praise Théophile Gautier 'up to the skies'. I wanted, of course, to hear him speak of his contemporaries; he who had been intimate with Dante Gabriel Rossetti and was one of the last links which joined us to the most remarkable band of men of the century. Before we left, he told me he had made Swinburne, with great difficulty, promise to sit to me—'A rare thing for the poet to be gracious on that point; we both dislike sitting,' he added, with a glance at his own portrait drawn 25 years earlier by Rossetti.

I was amused at Watts, but did not take to him. He had a great reputation as a critic and as an authority on poetry. I remember, by the way, Oscar Wilde saying: 'I have suddenly realised why Watts is an authority on the sonnet; the sonnet of course is made of six and eight.' Watts was, by profession, a solicitor! He seemed to me absurdly vain, but he must have had great qualities to win the trust and friendship of Swinburne, and of Rossetti before him; and though I would not have called him a great talker, he was certainly an entertaining one. There was a good deal of malice in his talk—not unattractive to one of my age.

Watts told me one thing that Whistler had never mentioned. In complaining of Whistler's attack on Swinburne in *The Gentle Art*, he said Whistler had pressed him to get Swinburne to write something about the *Ten O'Clock*; a review by the Bard, it appeared, would be a very good thing. Swinburne had needed a good deal of persuading, but at last had consented; hence the resentment of both Swinburne and Watts at Whistler's subsequent onslaught. But Swinburne, for his part I think, missed the point and beauty of the *Ten O'Clock*. Obviously from a man of Whistler's character one would expect something in the nature of a testament, and no doubt he was deeply hurt at Swinburne's failure to appreciate his exquisite ultimatum. Of course, if Watts' statement was true, and it was at Whistler's repeated request that Swinburne had reviewed his pamphlet, one can sympathise with Swinburne's feelings at being held up to ridicule. But not even Swinburne himself, with all the magic and power of his pen, has written such noble prose, nor so perfect, as Whistler's *Ten O'Clock*. I marvel often that no portion of it has so far appeared in any anthology. Whistler's writing, so biblical in some of its aspects, so finely chased, so elfish in others, seems to me to have a unique place in English literature.

After I had drawn Swinburne, Watts asked me to make a portrait of himself, and was very tiresome when sitting. He said that while drawing him Rossetti would consult his opinion, as I ought to do, and be guided by him. He was plainly afraid of a too realistic portrait, and his want of faith in my interpretation prevented my finishing the two drawings I began.

I found, among some notes which I made in 1895, the following account of Swinburne:

August 10th, 1895.

Go to The Pines, Putney. Swinburne gets up as I enter, rather like Lionel Johnson in figure, the same *chétif* body, narrow shoulders and nervous twitch of the hands, which,

233

however, are strong and fine. A much fresher face than I would have imagined from hearsay, a fine nose, a tiny glazed green eye, and a curiously clear auburn moustache and a beard of a splendid red. How young he looks! notwithstanding his years. He was so nervous, that of course I was embarrassed, and Watts being there we both talked at him, keeping our eyes off one another. Occasionally I would glance at his profile, less impressive, less 'like' than his full face. When at last the sitting began, no sitter ever gave me so much trouble. For besides always changing his pose, he is so deaf, that he could not hear me; and after sitting a short time, a nervous restlessness seized on him, which held him the whole time. I felt a beast sitting there torturing him. Nor did I feel that I could do anything worthy of him. When he saw the drawing he was kind enough to say 'It must be like, for I see all my family in it.' While I was drawing he recited a burlesque of Nichols, *The Flea*, he called it, and he talked a good deal of recent criticism—a number of newspaper cuttings were strewn over a couch near the window. He speaks with the accent of an Oxford don, and with a certain gaiety, with gracious and rather old-fashioned manners. He behaves charmingly to old Watts. He had on a new suit of clothes, as though specially for a portrait, which seemed to cause him as much discomfort as sitting still. He was like a schoolboy let out of school when I said I would not bother him any longer. He then showed me a number of his treasures—odd views of different scenes, an early Burne-Jones drawing, photographs of people, including a fine one of Rossetti. Watts suggested I should make a drawing of this for Swinburne, but Swinburne asked me if I could make one from a rather poor engraving of George Dyer, Charles Lamb's friend, one of his heroes. And this of course I promised to do. Swinburne talked violently against the French, saying he had lost all interest in them, since France had become a Republic, as they are always ready to fly at our throats and would crush us at any moment, if they could. He praised Baudelaire as a poet, and said he liked Meredith

—as a man—the same thing that Leslie Stephen said of Browning one day at Hyde Park Gate.

On my way home I went to the Vale, and showed the drawing to Ricketts and Shannon. To my surprise they were immensely pleased with it. They want to reproduce it at once in *The Pageant.*

I made a second drawing of Swinburne, and he afterwards, when I lunched at The Pines, very charmingly asked me to make a small painting of him for his mother. I was proud and delighted, of course, and a first sitting was arranged. But how indiscretions come home to roost! An entirely un-expected thing was to come in the way. I happened to notice a review of the last volume of Edmond de Goncourt's *Journal.* Being curious to read it, since it dealt with the years I had spent in Paris, I got the book, and there, to my horror, was a reference to me, together with an account of the Rossetti household I had light-heartedly given. For de Goncourt, I remembered, had asked me to tell him anything I could of the Pre-Raphaelites, of whom little was known in France. To me, people like Rossetti and Swinburne were immortals of whom one talked as one might speak of Keats or Shelley. But how easy and pleasant it is to repeat what one hears! I had never imagined that tales told an old man by a youngster would one day be printed. I was very upset. The best thing, it seemed, was to draw Watts' attention to the passage before someone else should do this, and to make a clean breast of the matter. I was to lunch at The Pines to discuss the portrait I spoke of, so when the day arrived and before going upstairs where Swinburne awaited us both, I showed the menacing passage to Watts in the hope that he was human enough to understand my dismay. Watts at once closed the door, read the paragraph, and said: 'This is the kind of thing that gets into the newspapers.' He then suggested that I had better not lunch with Swinburne—I should have my lunch brought down to Watts' room! There was nothing to do but to leave the house. Dining that night with York Powell,

235

I told him of this; he was indignant, especially that Watts should stand in the way of the painting which Swinburne wished me to do. I never saw Watts again; nor Swinburne either, to my great regret. Later my wife continued to see them from time to time.

I was away at the time of Swinburne's death. My wife, when she heard he was ill, at once went up to The Pines, found him critically ill, and Watts-Dunton[1] in bed with influenza. On her next visit she was to find the poet on his bier. 'He looked magnificent,' she wrote. 'So truly grand, lying there with his beautiful head on the pillow and a long, long sheet down the bed past his feet.' Her one burning wish was to preserve something of this grandeur for others to see. A death mask, she felt, should be made. Watts-Dunton was still in bed, but she told his wife that she would go at once and get Epstein to come and do what was necessary. Epstein at once acquiesced; but on reaching home, my wife found a telegram from Watts-Dunton, asking her not to arrange for a death mask. It appears that Watts-Dunton, who was a great respecter of reputations, disliked the idea of employing Epstein, then little known, but, on his doctor's suggestion, had approached Drury instead, who made a cast of Swinburne's head. I never understood precisely what happened, but Mrs Watts-Dunton told us that when asked for the mask, Drury looked confused, and said that somehow the mould had got lost. This was some time later; he had moved meanwhile, when the mould was mislaid; at any rate, it was never found. After Watts-Dunton's death, his wife came to see us, when my wife recalled how she had wanted Epstein to make a death mask; a pity it was, she added, that no record of the kind was now in existence. By this time Epstein had made a great name, and when Mrs Watts-Dunton heard that her husband had rejected his services, she almost cried with vexation.

[1] Watts had assumed the name of Watts-Dunton in 1896.

CHAPTER XX

GEORGE MOORE AND OTHERS

WHILE for Sickert the music-hall was a workshop, for the rest of us it was a pleasant dissipation. The Empire Promenade was the orthodox place to go to. I remember meeting Le Gallienne there, just after he published his *Religion of a Literary Man.* He was a little self-conscious at being found in this equivocal haunt, and explained he had rather be lying on his back in an orchard, looking up at the sky through blossoming trees. 'I know, I know, dear Dick,' I said; 'that accounts for your oddly foreshortened view of God.' *The Religion of a Literary Man* infuriated Henley and Whibley, and the young men of *The National Observer.* Le Gallienne was their pet aversion. Later, their *bête noire* was Stephen Phillips, when Le Gallienne had gone to the States.

At the Empire, or the Tivoli, or the Oxford, one would surely meet Arthur Symons, Ernest Dowson, Herbert Horne, Selwyn Image, Beardsley, or Max. Poor Dowson was a tragic figure. While we others amused ourselves, playing with fireworks, Dowson meant deliberately to hurt himself. While for Beardsley, perversities were largely an attitude he adopted *pour épater les bourgeois.* I doubt if Dowson wanted to live; he was consumed by a weary hopelessness, and he drank, I thought, to be rid of an aspect of life too forlorn to be faced. He was deeply in love with a waitress at a little restaurant in Glasshouse Street, a decent, rather plain, commonplace girl, a Dulcinea in fact, quite unable to understand Dowson's adoration, his morbid moods or his poetry.

237

Dowson had a beautiful nature, too tender for the rough-and-
tumble of the market place, and he punished and lacerated himself, as it were, through excess. He and others used to meet after
theatre hours at The Crown, a public-house in Charing Cross
Road. To The Crown came regularly, besides those previously
mentioned, Stewart Headlam, Texeira de Mattos, Norreys
Connell, Edgar Jepson, Lionel Johnson, Oscar Wilde,
George Moore and Charles Conder. We generally met in a
little room, away from the bar, where we could talk. Hot
port was the favourite drink. At 12.30, 'Time, gentlemen,
please!' was called, and we continued conversing outside.
Sometimes I would prevail on Dowson, who lived far away
in Limehouse, to spend the night with me at Chelsea. There
was a cabman's shelter near Hyde Park Corner where one
could get supper of a kind, hot tea or coffee and thick bread
and butter. Dowson liked the warmth of the place and the
rough company. It was not always easy to get him away
when he was very drunk, nor past some poor street walker
who would seize his arm, and try to inveigle him to her
lodging.

Arrived at my studio, he would usually refuse the spare
bed, and insist instead on lying under an old-fashioned piano
which stood in the sitting room. Yet I never knew either
Dowson or Lionel Johnson, however intoxicated, lose their
gentle good manners. While Dowson was homeless, miserable and unkempt, Johnson appeared to lead the life of a
scholar. He lived in pleasant rooms that were lined with
books, near Lincoln's Inn. In person he was scrupulously
neat and his habits were quiet and studious. No one, not
seeing him constantly, would have suspected his weakness;
for a long time, indeed, I was unaware of it. His speech was
the typical Oxford don's; a Roman Catholic, a follower of
Newman, he had the polished manners and dialectic of an
Oratorian. Stewart Headlam and Selwyn Image, likewise
distinguished by their scholarly habits and the charm of their
manners, had the good luck to be sober, as most of us had
who frequented The Crown.

238

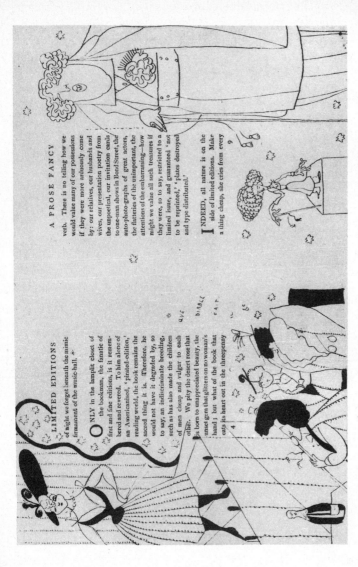

LIMITED EDITIONS

ONLY in the lamplit closet of the bookman, the fanatic of first and fine editions, is it remembered and revered. To him alone of an Americanised, 'pirated-edition,' reading world, the book remains the sacred thing it is. Therefore, he would not have it degraded by, so to say, an indiscriminate breeding, such as has also made the children of men cheap and vulgar to each other. We pity the desert rose that is born to unappreciated beauty, the unset gem that glitters on no woman's hand; but what of the book that eats its heart out in the threepenny

A PROSE FANCY

verb. There is no telling how we would value many of our possessions if they were more arduously come by: our relatives, our husbands and wives, our presentation poetry from the unpoetical, our invitation cards to one-man shows in Bond Street, the auto-photo-graphs of great actors, the flatteries of the uninportant, the attentions of the embarrassing—how might we value all such treasures if they were, so to say, restricted to a limited issue, and guaranteed 'not to be reprinted,' 'plates destroyed and type distributed.'

INDEED, all nature is on the side of limited editions. Make a thing cheap, she cries from every

RICHARD LE GALLIENNE AT A MUSIC HALL, AND THE SAME BESIDE OSCAR WILDE, BY MAX

At The Crown Arthur Symons would give us ecstatic accounts of his latest acquaintance in the Corps de Ballet. As people are sometimes vain about their smart friends or their intimacy with the great, so Arthur Symons was elated at knowing, however distantly, any of the dancers at The Empire or The Alhambra. A disciple of Baudelaire, Verlaine and Laforgue, he was even now deeply read in the French decadent poets and symbolists. I used to say of him that he began every day with bad intentions, and broke them every night.

Herbert Horne, editor of *The Hobby Horse*, a finely printed and somewhat precious magazine (a forerunner of Ricketts' and Shannon's *Dial*) was an architect, a minor poet, a decorator of books, a critic of art and literature, an ardent collector, and a student of the Caroline poets. In fact Horne, with his pale face, his hard red lips and spare features, wanted only a wig to have sat for his favourite poet, Rochester. With Mackmurdo, he designed the Savoy Hotel. He spent much time prowling about the old print shops, picking up old masters' drawings and early English water-colours. He was a secretive and economical collector, who rarely paid much for what he bought; as in those days one needn't, when drawings and water-colours of every kind were to be picked up cheaply in the London print shops. High prices were then unknown. One of Rossetti's finest drawings, a study of Fanny's head, for *Found*, now in the Fairfax-Murray Collection at Birmingham, was going begging for five pounds.

Parsons' in the Brompton Road was the great hunting ground for drawings. Parsons went to sales and bought up all the parcels of old prints and drawings to be had, and collectors came regularly to look through his portfolios. Happily for the rest of us, these collectors were not always quick to recognise good things, or certain of their own judgment. Five shillings was Parsons' usual price for a drawing. He always pretended to examine the drawings picked out, though he didn't know one from another. I found two drawings by Rembrandt there, at five shillings each, and under Sir Charles Robinson's nose! Many now important collections were largely made from Parsons' portfolios.

Herbert Horne, Arthur Symons and George Moore were then very friendly. Herbert Horne lived in the Temple, at King's Bench Walk, where Moore, too, had a flat, though he left it about this time to take a larger one in Victoria Street. Then Horne came to live in Chelsea, whence he later migrated to Florence, to write his great biography of Botticelli, to which he gave up years of intensive research. Did not Reginald Turner say of him: 'Dear Herbert Horne! poring over Botticelli's washing bills—and always a shirt missing!' I had no idea that Horne was so wealthy. He bought and restored a Trecento Palace of the Burgess type, filled it with his collection of drawings, paintings, furniture, cutlery, pottery, etc., and finally bequeathed it to the city of his adoption. The 'Musée Horne', locally pronounced 'Orne, is now one of the most popular but not least delightful sights of Florence.

George Moore, it was often supposed, was associated with the decadents in literature, yet he had nothing in common with such, save an admiration for French literature and painting. In art his sympathies were with the New English Art Club. He had written one of the few remarkable books on modern painting which showed appreciation of the aims of Manet, Whistler, and the so-called Impressionists. He had known Manet personally—had indeed been painted by him. He would sometimes clinch an argument, when driven into a corner, by saying: 'But I have known Manet'! Moore amused and puzzled me. I had heard much about him from Dujardin; Conder admired his *Drama in Muslin*. I had seen his *Confessions of a Young Man* on the bookstalls in Holywell Street; it was supposed to be a very naughty book. But I had read nothing of Moore's until Steer lent me *Modern Painters*. Moore was respected as a writer, while as a man he was regarded with affectionate amusement by his friends. The Moore of to-day, the author of some of the best books of our time, the master of English prose narrative, was then unsuspected, save by a few.

GEORGE MOORE (1895)

Although he was many years my senior, his character did not command unmixed respect from a youngster. There was no reticence in Moore, but a Rousseau-like candour, naked and unashamed. He had no pretence of dignity—that mantle Moore, even in his later years, has never assumed—but he had humility, the humility of the artist, mixed with an ingenuous egoism, which gave him a unique personality. His pastime was talking—'O Rothenstein, I am so glad you have come, I can only think when I am talking.' And talk he would, unceasingly, sometimes so admirably, that I would leave him with the affection that great intelligence invariably arouses in me; at other times he could be frankly silly. He would insist on his absence of moral and social sense, sometimes amusingly, at other times in a wearisome way, and often, too, with an indiscretion that made me wonder how much was naïvety and how much *méchanceté*. He talked as he wrote, with a stress on his gallantries that was quite unconvincing. Were it otherwise, he would have compromised half the women he knew. But no one could have a subtler appreciation of his own absurdities than has Moore himself. What a discerning self-portrait he draws in *Salve, Ave* and *Vale!* and what a remarkable trilogy indeed!

He had one thing in common with Steer—as Steer was possessed by his brush, so was Moore by his pen. With a pen in his hand, Moore's intelligence was uncanny; without it his hands looked limp and purposeless, his brows were lifted in vacant expectancy, his eyes without depth, his lips loose under the pale moustache. It was as though Moore's pen supplied rectitude, tact and delicacy—virtues which were sometimes discarded when his pen was laid down.

Moore wanted me to make a drawing of him for his next book: 'I think I have arranged for Scott to give you a fiver for the right to reproduce the drawing. In that case you will, I suppose, give me the drawing,' he wrote; but for some reason, now forgotten, the drawing was not used, and remained on my hands. Moore said of this drawing rather fatuously—'Now of whom do you think it reminds me?'

241

I could think of no one like Moore. 'Don't you see a likeness to de Goncourt?' he said. I couldn't conceive of two
men more unlike.

He talked with enthusiasm of Pater's prose, but he ridi-
culed Newman: 'They call him a great stylist, but his style is
execrable.' And he took up the *Apologia*, and began to
read—'Did you ever hear anything more ridiculous? But
the English don't know what style is.' Then he talked of
Héloise's letters to Abelard. He had just read them; 'Last
night, I dined with Mrs Craigie, and I talked about these
letters; no woman has ever written *me* such letters, I said;
could they be genuine?' Moore's candour stood his writing
in good stead. He felt that what occurred within himself
was unique, and analysing his emotions with patient minuteness he discovered what was true for others as well. I was
finding so many painters to be decent men, but dishonour-
able artists. Moore's artistic probity was blameless. There
was an innocence about Moore, too, that was comical—and
endearing.

He had lately been staying with Sir William Eden at
Windlestone. During his visit Eden drove over to the funeral
of one of his neighbours; 'I thought I would join him, for
the sake of the drive,' said Moore, 'And when we got to the
church, as I was wearing a rather loud check country-suit,
Eden said it wouldn't do at all for me to come into the
church, dressed as I was. But I got tired of waiting, so I
strolled in, and sat by Eden; and, would you believe it? he
was quite annoyed with me afterwards.'

But what he most liked was to talk about painting. Having
known Manet and Degas, not to speak of Walter Sickert and
Steer, he was familiar with the opinions of painters. But why
should a writer wish to see like a painter? and to talk like one,
too? Moore had attuned his mind and eye to one kind of
painting; to great dramatic or imaginative art he was insensitive. I had rather he talked about literature. But to
Steer and Tonks, who then preferred eighteenth-century and
nineteenth-century painting to that of the earlier schools,

Moore's opinions were always acceptable. Not that Steer
minded much what Moore said; so long as Moore didn't
worry him with anything unexpected, and was happy talking,
Steer would sit and listen, at his ease, his hands folded across
his stomach, his feet closely drawn up under his chair.

Tonks was to become closely associated with Moore. He
had been a surgeon, but disliked operations, so he sat under
Frederick Brown at Westminster. Finally he had the courage
to give up his surgical work and to exchange a certain for an
uncertain livelihood. He joined Dermod O'Brien and shared
a house with him in Cheyne Row. He much relished the
minor Pre-Raphaelites—especially Windus, Boyd Houghton,
Pinwell and Frederick Walker, and the illustrators of the
'sixties. I was amused at this tall, angular student with a
grim face lined like Dante's, drawing and painting pretty
girls, dressed as they appeared in the vignettes of the 'sixties.
His drawings were rather thin and tentative; but Tonks was
modest and determined; and, like Moore, he was to do remarkable work later.

Moore found in Steer and Tonks his most sympathetic
listeners; in neither was there any intellectual nonsense; like
Moore they laughed at my strange taste for Giotto and
Millet, and the rather austere subjects that appealed to me
didn't attract Steer and Tonks. Nevertheless, close ties of
sympathy and affection united us, and we met constantly, at
one another's studios, or at the Chelsea or the Hogarth Clubs,
and often at Moore's flat in Victoria Street. I was teased
about my penchant for Ricketts and Shannon; Moore especially railed against them; Sickert alone supported me.
You never knew what Sickert would like or would not like.
He did like Beardsley and admired his drawings, and the
feeling was mutual. One of Beardsley's rare oil paintings
(now at the Tate) is a portrait of Sickert. Moore couldn't
abide Sargent; he was abusive whenever his name was mentioned. It was one of his rare differences with Steer and
Tonks. But he couldn't let Sargent be. He was like a puppy
worrying a rag doll.

In 1895 Charles Furse's health broke down. He was sent off by the doctors to South Africa; he might work there, they said, but not in England. And work there he did; at the same time his health rapidly improved. He knew that by remaining in the dry South African climate he could keep well, and at the same time paint Rhodes and the military and civil officials, and the wealthy financiers. But he couldn't bear to be away from the centre of things, and he unwisely returned to England in the year following. He set to work at once; his studio was soon full of canvases in various stages of completion. We were all glad to have him among us again, though his health made us anxious. But he was as boisterous and courageous as ever, and appeared to have no misgivings. Sargent was painting Coventry Patmore and Ian Hamilton and Graham Robertson about now, three of his best portraits of men. He still came sometimes to lunch at the Chelsea Club, but complained that he couldn't get enough to eat there. So he often went to the Hans Crescent Hotel, where, from a table d'hôte luncheon of several courses, he could assuage his Gargantuan appetite.

When Lane dropped Beardsley after the Wilde scandal, Beardsley at once found a patron in Smithers. Smithers was a bizarre and improbable figure—a rough Yorkshireman with a strong local accent and uncertain *h*'s, the last man, one had thought, to be a Latin scholar and a disciple of M. le Marquis de Sade. Smithers had a bookshop in Bond Street, where he dealt in fine editions and in erotic art and letters. He was also an adventurous publisher, the publisher of *The Savoy*, and the first to issue a book of Max Beerbohm's caricatures. He commissioned Conder to illustrate *La Fille aux Yeux d'Or*. This was Conder's favourite story. The subject appealed to him strongly, as did certain parts of *Mademoiselle de Maupin*. Smithers wanted me to make a set of etchings for Voltaire's *La Pucelle*. I prepared a number of drawings and worked on some plates—one of the drawings was published in the first number of *The Savoy*—but I disliked Smithers and his ways, and I withdrew from the contract. I thought Smithers had an evil influence on Beardsley, taking him to various night haunts, keeping him up late into the night, which was bad, too, for Beardsley's health.

Smithers took as much work as he could from Beardsley. It is known that when Beardsley was dying he was filled with remorse at having been persuaded to supply Smithers with so many erotic drawings; he told me so when I last saw him in Paris, and how anxious he was that none of these should survive.

I fancy that things in the end went ill with Smithers. What finally happened to him I could not discover. I afterwards tried to trace a portrait of Beardsley I made, which Smithers took in exchange for a complete set of Balzac's works, but without success.

In Smithers, Conder found a boon companion who encouraged his worst excesses, excesses which brought on an attack of delirium tremens, which thoroughly frightened Conder. I sat up with him sometimes, for most of the night; he was in terror of being left alone.

During this time, poor Oscar Wilde was in prison; we heard of him from time to time from Ross and from Ricketts, who visited him there, and told us of his shame and misery. Ross' devotion to Wilde, then and thereafter, won general admiration; and this, when the strong repugnance to Wilde is taken into account, was a remarkable tribute to Ross' character.

Smithers, Symons, Beardsley, Dowson and Conder used often to run over to Dieppe. Dieppe, with its harbour and quays, its beautiful churches and dignified streets, had for long attracted artists. Like so many continental places, it kept much of its original character. It was one of Sickert's favourite haunts; Thaulow had settled down with his family at Dieppe, and Jacques Blanche had a villa and spent most of the summer there. I remember Beardsley, Conder and Dowson starting off from The Crown one night, wandering about London, and taking the early boat-train to Dieppe

without any luggage—Beardsley and Dowson coming back
a few days later looking the worse for wear. Conder stayed
on. He made great friends with Thaulow and with Jacques
Blanche. Thaulow, indeed, used to buy his pictures and
commission him to paint silk hangings, dresses for his wife,
and all sorts of odds and ends. Conder wrote and begged me
to join him:

> 2 *Rue de l' Oranger*
> *Dieppe*
> *Seine Inf*^{re}
> 14 *Aug.* 95

My dear Will

I will send you over the picture soon that you want for
Miss K. I do wish you'd come over; there could be no
difficulty in Dieppe as far as I can see where one can do
absolutely what one likes. The sea air has done me a world
of good. Then Smithers is often here and sometimes as you
may imagine my arguments are only weak from the want of
backing up. For one can hardly expect sympathy from men
who think so differently about many matters to ourselves.
You can draw your own conclusions; still Smithers is a good
chap. I want to talk to you very much and can't well come
over to London—but for the present if you can't do so—
remember that even the unity of two might upset a kingdom
(or a crown). I lay so much stress on this because Smithers
tells me you wanted to do the 'Fêtes Galantes' and had asked
if you could; so it might be with some irritation that you
heard of my doing it. You yourself suggested it to me and
I acted quite innocently; if it would give you any pleasure
to do it, I wish I could get out of it now, there are lots of
other things that one could do—même trop. There is a lot
one might do for Smithers; it would be doing both ourselves
and himself good, but at present I have found him hard to
convince on the value of quality and limited editions. It's
darned difficult to write these things, but you follow, I know,
and then I miss you very much Willy Rothenstein and you
would simply love Dieppe. I have rooms opposite the church,

an enormous gothic one—and a picture; saint at the door with geraniums on his head in garland. There has been a whole new existence here a little spoilt perhaps sometimes—for one loves to tell these things to someone who will understand.

The whole front of the sea is simply magnificent and reminds one of one's comprehension of some past time in our own century—it's lovely to see the *famille bourgeoise* again and finer still to see de Mérode, the dancer at the opera and a dozen such. If you come over from Saturday to Monday its *worth while* and I will get you a room. I am sure you would not spend more than 10 francs a day unless you want to. So try and manage.

Smithers has made Aubrey Beardsley editor of the new publication; I suppose you know that. The first part of the 'Fêtes Galantes' is to come out in it—amusant, n'est-ce pas— I might tell all about this place here but the sea air leaves one rather idle; one likes to believe oneself hand and glove with all sorts of poignant emotions but this sea is like some drug that makes one satisfied with the desire. Life is so beautiful that one thinks it must end soon; and ambition only comes in and interferes and makes one want to do, for example— pictures of *next* spring illustrated with portraits. It is very likely I shall settle here, I like the place so well and fancy the winter months will be encouragingly dull and good for work—I can't appeal to you now as a reasonable man, I know, but still the idea seems good.

Blanche is here and is doing a really good picture of Thaulow and his family. He has asked me to do him a picture, so that I am quite pleased.

I saw de Mérode bathing this morning and wished I was King David, so pretty she was, and didn't get too wet; I stayed near her to stave off cramps and drowning, but she could only say, the darling, that J'ai peur ici des trous. My dear naughty naughty Will, how we would laugh here if you would only come—Arthur Symons has taken rooms in this house and he has just written a poem as to the Dieppe sea being like absinthe—original, n'est-ce pas?

Ah dieu seigneur how I hate most men and like all women (pretty ones).

The distance from my room to the church is eight yards; between is a stall of a fair and a pretty girl who plays Jeanne d'Arc. And is burnt and all some fifty times a day. But the church is glorious and all the priests when they have their best clothes on look like silk canary birds.

Write me soon and come as soon as possible if only for a day; I want to talk to you. See Bevan and get my bill please, He might sell those pictures of Azavedo it would be the devil to pay.

Yours affectionately,
CHARLES CONDER

Another time, after he had gone over to Dieppe on the spur of the moment, with little or no luggage: 'I got tired of the Café Royal and the Gourmets and fancied a ragout in Dieppe to be near Vetheuil—"ces choses sentimental arrivent". Dowson came over too; we had some friends here and left today. I want you both to see that I have some things sent over as I brought insufficient linen and no paints etc. left the beautiful shawl behind, you might both go together and pack up these things. There are a pair of brown trousers I want in one of my drawers and all the collars and shirts etc you can find....I find it cheap here. Try a week and bring a plate over to do.' The plate refers, I think, to the Voltaire etchings Smithers had commissioned me to make. Conder writes again: 'Blanche asks me to apologise for changing his mind about the picture he was to have sent to London; now he decides not to send it but to keep it for another year. When are we going to see you? I fancied always that you were coming, and hope you will manage it still. How is your work getting on—have you finished *La Pucelle* yet? I am hoping to see them soon. Beardsley it seems wrote to you yesterday about Blanche's picture and now he would like you to choose a frame etc., but the picture can't be varnished. Blanche hopes you will not have already taken any trouble

and is quite *désolé*. He is going to exhibit it at the Salon first.
I think it will be one of the successes this year and wish you
could see it. Send over my portrait please to exhibit in the
Champ de Mars. It will be well placed and will be much
better placed than in London. You must not get into tempers
with my ancient self but come over to Dieppe and you shall
meet all the youth and beauty of the decayed aristocracy of
France. I have nearly finished *La Fille aux Yeux d'Or*, but
can't get *La Femme aux Cheveux d'Or* out of my head and
so quelquefois je m'ennuie. You had better come and live
over in Paris this year, I see clearly that I shall make my
fortune. At the present moment I hav'nt a sou. I am writing
you a short letter for there is no time. Dieppe is perfectly
beautiful and although the race people are gone—"still many
a garden by the river blows" in all acceptations of the word.
There is a spare room in the house I live in. Send me a line
as soon as possible.' The portrait to which he refers was one
I painted of him in riding dress, which is now, to my
regret, in the Davis Collection at the Luxembourg Gallery
in Paris.

Meanwhile Conder continued working in Dieppe, and
was constantly pressing me to join him; one of his drawings for *La Fille aux Yeux d'Or* was reproduced in *The
Savoy*, the new quarterly, to which he refers in his next
letter:

'Will you tell me when I may expect to see you here. At
present Symons and Beardsley and X are here but I hope
they do not intend to remain. In fact I am almost sure they
will be leaving tomorrow; X—who is too awful for words
but very good hearted. He has decked himself out in a whole
suit of French summer clothing from the *Belle Jardinière*, and
although it suits his particular style very well one is not
exactly proud of his companionship.

'Blanche has many friends here and is most desirous of
making your acquaintance; he has introduced me to some of
his friends, charming ladies who would be most interested
to meet you. The Crown descended on us last Saturday,

augmented by two whores from the east, and did a great deal to shatter that pillar of respectability, myself. If you see a man wandering about Chelsea with an enormous wedding cake in the shape of a Bombay temple you will know that he is my uncle looking for me and I hope you will remember to be very kind to him.

'There has been a great deal of excitement about the new quarterly here and discussion. Beardsley is very pompous about it all. I wish you would come and stay with me in Paris this winter, but you might not mention that I am leaving London at present. The scheme is very interesting but I have no time to explain it to you now. I feel singularly happy to-day and am dodging X—. Excuse this very foolish letter and do come over soon. I should so much like to see you.'

The Savoy, the now famous quarterly, which Arthur Symons and Beardsley were then editing for Smithers, created a stir. It contained some of the best drawings Beardsley ever did, as well as 'Under the Hill', and 'The Three Musicians', and articles by Henry James and Bernard Shaw. I was amused to come across the following letter from Beardsley from Dieppe:

Dear Billy,

Do forgive me for behaving so rudely. I had meant to get back to town on Sunday, but missed the boat and so stopped on here indefinitely.

Really Dieppe is quite sweet. It is the first time I have ever enjoyed a holiday. *Petits Chevaux* and everything most pretty and amusing. I shall leave at the end of the week. What about Gyp? Symons has written to Meredith to ask if he would sit to you for a portrait. Personally I think Gyp is much more desirable. Do bother Smithers about it. He comes over here on Friday en route to Paris, I fancy. How is the furnishing progressing?

Yours,

AUBREY

The idea of Gyp being preferable to Meredith tickled my
fancy.

I did go over and join Conder, and met Blanche and Thaulow. Thaulow was then at the height of his fame. A huge Norwegian, bearded, genial, a great trencherman, he dispensed hospitality to all and sundry. He was devoted to Conder, as was Mme Thaulow—a familiar figure through Blanche's portrait of the Thaulow family. She too was a Norwegian giantess. I used to go bicycling with her on a tandem bicycle; she, dressed in bloomers, on the front seat, taking charge of the machine, making me feel smaller than ever, behind her handsome, redoubtable figure.

Sickert was in Dieppe when I first went over, and he and I were full of irreverent jests. Blanche for a long time could not make me out; I was always joking and laughing; though Sickert had told him, he said, that I was a very serious artist. Blanche was an admirer, and a warm supporter, of Sickert, buying his pictures, and praising his work to his French friends; but he used to complain that Walter was sometimes *difficile*. Blanche was painting a portrait of Sickert during my visit to Dieppe. I remember one morning, while Blanche was at work on this portrait of Sickert, he told me how difficult he found it to keep the transparency of his colours. I asked him had he ever tried glazing, but of this he knew nothing. Now it happens that Blanche lately gave this portrait of Sickert to my son, and I find, after thirty years, that the flesh tones have that very transparency Blanche despaired of obtaining; delicate greys, too, have appeared, with which his palette had little or no concern. There is no doubt that white becomes transparent with time, and that much of the quality we admire in old paintings comes with age. Cézanne's paintings, which Conder and I often saw at Vollard's, looked different then, more opaque and cruder in colour than they appear to-day. The same thing applies to Monet's and Pissarro's paintings, and to Gauguin's as well; these once looked startlingly different from older paintings, now they take their place harmoniously beside them. I have heard

The permanence of paint Ricketts condemn the opaque paint which the Impressionists used, on the ground that its vitality was fleeting, and its quality too. But Ricketts is wrong; the great Impressionist pictures have become mellower with time, and thereby, like other good paintings, have acquired an added beauty and a mystery of handling, have gained, not lost, since they were painted. Paint alone is a permanent material; what is fatal to pictures is the impermanence of so many painters.

CHAPTER XXI

THE LAST OF VERLAINE

Looking up Legros

ON returning to London, I thought it right to pay my respects to my old Professor. I found him living in a dullish house in Brook Green. Whether from want of success or ambition, or through indolence, he had for some time produced little work. There was a discouraging atmosphere about him; nor by his own household was he treated with due respect, I thought; perhaps, now he had retired from the Slade, he had contributed little towards the household expenses.

Though I had never been a favourite of Legros' during my year at the Slade School, my visits seemed to raise his spirits. He was glad of someone to talk to; and I was eager to hear him speak of his early days, and to listen to his account of Delacroix and Ingres, of Baudelaire and Meryon, of Rossetti, Watts and Alfred Stevens. As a young man he had joined the crowd of students who followed Ingres round the Louvre. Once Ingres, he said, out of the corner of his eye, caught sight of Delacroix crossing one of the galleries. Turning quickly away and raising his head, he sniffed the air, 'Hu, hu, ça sent le soufre ici.' He told me an amusing story of his first meeting with Delacroix, at the house of a financier whose delight it was to entertain the young lions of art and literature. They came with flowing locks, flowing neckwear, fancy waistcoats, velvet coats, peg-topped trousers, *habits râpés*, in fact every kind of sartorial extravagance. Suddenly there entered a figure attired in a quiet but extremely correct

253

frock-coat, wearing canary-coloured gloves. 'Quel poseur!' Legros heard from the outraged *rapins*. It was Eugène Delacroix.

Legros was a vivid and copious talker. Had anyone written down his many stories, they would have made an interesting record; but in these there were significant lacunae. He had obstinate prejudices, and although he had been closely associated with the men who exhibited together at the Salon des Refusés, from most of them he had become estranged. For Courbet he still retained a certain respect; of Manet and Whistler he would never speak; nor would he hear anything good of the Impressionist painters. He had quarrelled with Fantin-Latour, and I observed a coolness when I spoke admiringly of Puvis de Chavannes. But when he spoke of the old masters, his views were markedly broad, and he had a profound knowledge of all the great schools of painting; indeed, I have never met anyone with a more catholic taste. Every school, and every artist, won his enthusiasm in turn, and he pored over the drawings in the Print Room of the British Museum, of Giotto, Mantegna, Signorelli, Michael Angelo, Leonardo, Raphael, Rembrandt, Poussin, Claude and Ingres, and even delighted in the eighteenth-century draughtsmen, enjoying the *espièglerie* and the deftness of Fragonard, as he enjoyed the beauty of Watteau. He seemed to have had differences with many of his old pupils; Strang he never saw, though Strang never ceased to speak in high terms of Legros' work. Only with Holroyd had he kept up close relations.

Because I spoke French and admired his own work, he could not see too much of me. He would often come to my studio, where sometimes his visits were inconvenient; for Legros was a little selfish, and would expect me to stop work and go with him to the Print Room or to the National Gallery. When I had a nude model, he would be glad to join me (models I gathered were frowned on at home). In his painting room at Brook Green, a dull room looking on to a backyard, hung the *Femmes en Prière*, which I had seen at the first exhibition of the New Gallery. No one had wanted to buy it, he said, and he had not in fact sold any pictures for a long time. The price was, I thought, absurdly modest—£200. I approached some influential people, and an appeal was sent out. Watts at once sent £50. Lord Carlisle saw Burne-Jones and other old friends of Legros, the money was quickly subscribed, and Holroyd was delighted to have *Les Femmes en Prière* for the new Tate Gallery.

Legros was charmed by Ricketts and Shannon, delighting in Ricketts' knowledge, and greatly admiring Shannon's painting. They treated Legros with marked consideration and, largely through their influence, a new interest was shown in his prints and drawings.

I introduced Arthur Strong, then Librarian to the House of Lords and to the Duke of Devonshire, to Legros; he and Strong were delighted with one another. Strong took Legros to Chatsworth, to see the great collection by old masters there; and Legros made a gold-point drawing of the Duke. Later Strong got Legros to carry out a stone fountain for the Duke of Portland, which was executed by Lantéri under Legros' immediate direction. Lantéri had succeeded Dalou as Professor of Sculpture at South Kensington. I went to see him there once or twice with Legros, little thinking that some day I should be in charge of the school. 'South Kensington' was in the 'nineties rather a term of reproach. Crane was later to try his hand at reforming the place, but after little more than a year he gave up the attempt—his difficulties with the Science and Art Department tried him too severely. The Department was full of Anglo-Indian officials, he said; I suppose he referred to Donnelly, with whom I first came in touch when an exhibition of lithographs was being arranged at South Kensington, when Shannon and I were members of the committee. This was in 1898—the year when Crane was appointed.

But to return to Legros. In addition to the fountain for the Duke of Portland, Legros was asked to carry out some important decorations for the City celebration of Queen

Victoria's Jubilee. Things at last began to go well with Legros. He sold his collection of drawings to Edmund Davis, and was able, for the first time, to put aside capital.

Legros told me that he had taken Swinburne's French poems to show Baudelaire. Baudelaire, while he recognised Swinburne's genius, declared that none but a Frenchman could write true French verse; yet when Swinburne sent him an appreciation in French of his *Fleurs du Mal,* he held this to be the most discerning study of his poetry. He sent it to his mother, and expressed his thanks in the warmest terms; but he inadvertently put the letter to Swinburne into a drawer, where it lay until after his death. But messages did pass between the two poets, for I find Arthur Symons writing to me: 'I saw an interesting Baudelaire relic to-night. I was dining at The Pines and Swinburne showed me his copy of the essay on Wagner's *Tannhäuser,* with an inscription in pencil "To Mr Algernon Charles Swinburne, en bon souvenir", and some more signed "C. B."'

Legros was an enthusiastic admirer of Alfred Stevens. He inspired MacColl to appeal for the completion of the Wellington Memorial in St Paul's, from which the horse, an essential part of Stevens' design, was omitted. It seems extraordinary to-day that the ecclesiastical authorities refused to sanction the effigy of a horse in a cathedral building. The mutilation of his original model had in fact broken Stevens' heart. He seems to have been shamefully treated while working on the Wellington Memorial. According to Legros, Stevens, having spent the sum due to him before the memorial was finished, was refused access to his work by the cathedral authorities; whereupon the clay began to dry and crack. Stevens had to climb over the scaffolding and burgle, so to say, his own work, in order to save it. Legros was also instrumental in getting a plaque placed on the house in which Stevens was born. He told me how, meeting Stevens, he, Legros, had expressed his admiration of Stevens' work, and had said that he thought that Stevens was easily the greatest

J. K. HUYSMANS (1895)

living artist. Stevens, Legros added, had accepted this tribute with a modest but dignified awareness of its truth.

Some of Legros' animus against the Royal Academy was due to the Academy's refusal to elect Stevens to the associateship, which, according to Legros, they objected to do for the reason that Stevens was living with a lady to whom he was not legally married. We went one day to see the house on Haverstock Hill where they had lived. It contained paintings and carvings from his hand, now, I fear, destroyed.

Another house which many of us hoped might be preserved was Sir James Thornhill's in Dean Street, Soho, the walls of which were covered with enchanting paintings by Thornhill, assisted by Ricci and Hogarth. We made a strong appeal in the matter, which was disregarded. I felt then, as often since, that to spend large sums of money on paintings and objects of art to be added to the already crowded galleries and museums, and to neglect native art, or worse still, to allow it to be destroyed, as in the case of these two houses, is questionable policy. If we fail to acquire a painting by some great master, at least it will be preserved elsewhere, and not be lost; while such a treasure house as that of Thornhill has gone for ever. It irks me to think of it.

Legros had hinted more than once that we might go together to see Burne-Jones, but had done nothing further. Then, one day in Regent Street, whom should we meet but the illustrious artist himself. Legros introduced me, and suggested our going to the Café Royal, nearby, for a talk. Burne-Jones gaily assented; and it amused me to sit in this place with these two grave artists; Burne-Jones saying that of course Rothenstein would order an absinthe. His face was no less spiritual than it appeared in Watts' fine portrait, and in photographs I had seen. I was at once aware of his playful humour and charm. He and Legros had not met for a long time, and were pleased, I could see, to have encountered each other. I did later go to his house at North End Lane, a delightful place, surrounded by a large garden, its interior rich and simple at the same time, full of things Italian, of

257

Morris furniture, and of his own pictures and studies. To
enter his house was to go, as it were, from the open into the
depth of a shady grove. There was something both rich and
remote therein, which has struck me again and again, something of which the Victorians alone had the secret. He had,
in addition to his studio at North End, another studio behind
St Paul's School, where he was then at work on *Arthur
in Avalon*, an immense canvas. Out of love with modern
life, Burne-Jones was projecting into this picture his last
wistful vision of a world fashioned after the desire of his
heart. My friends, with the exception of Ricketts and Shannon, cared nothing for Burne-Jones. I, too, was aware of
certain weaknesses; but no man who can draw and design so
nobly and thereby impress his vision on the world is to be
swept aside. Not that his reputation suffered from the dis-
paragement of Whistler and the younger men; his name at
this time stood for beauty itself. I thought him a great and
enviable figure, for like Watts he had lived a life of incessant
labour, had held aloof from the market place, yet had gained
the homage of the greatest minds of his day.

I had the privilege of visiting him two or three times,
when his studio was full of graceful, aesthetic young women.
Mrs Patrick Campbell, then at the height of her fame, was
evidently a familiar; she had lately achieved sudden and
dazzling recognition as Paula Tanqueray in Pinero's play.
Very beautiful she was, with a rich beauty; her dark eyes,
full lips, and heavy black hair, making her face look strangely
pale. I met Mrs Campbell again at the Elchos at Stanway
(one of the loveliest houses in England, I thought), where
I drew her in pastel. The drawing was quite unworthy; but,
in her high-handed way, she insisted on keeping it, and
carried it up to her room. It was only by threatening to
make her pay a gigantic sum for the drawing that I got it
back and destroyed it. She had a beautiful daughter, Stella;
Stella, and Cynthia, Lady Elcho's daughter, a lovely pair of
children, ran wild together like hares on the mountains, when
they were not making sticky toffee in the playroom barn.

Besides Burne-Jones and Watts, Holman Hunt was still busy painting in the 'nineties, as were Arthur Hughes and Frederick Shields; and there was Frederick Sandys, with whom Beardsley and I often sat at the Café Royal, a favourite haunt of Sandys'.

Holman Hunt was an impressive looking person, tall and bearded, like the Head of an Oxford college. I was preparing a new set of portrait drawings, and was keen to make one of Hunt. I had asked him whether he would give me some sittings, and he had consented. At his request I brought some of my drawings to show him. Of these he was very critical, pointing out inequalities in the features. All the time I felt a certain embarrassment on his part, and when I timidly reminded him why I had come, he explained that he had thought that I was a photographer, and did not realise I had meant to draw him. I was very much shocked. My belief was he had made enquiries and was told that I was an Impressionist. I knew that Holman Hunt was naturally a truthful man, and I felt ashamed that I had put him in a dilemma which prompted this deception.

Holman Hunt had a queerly literal mind; yet he was rarely inspired by the life about him. He would search the Bible for a subject, and when he had found one, he would turn to nature to aid him to paint it. Then he painted each object he needed with equal minuteness, figures, clothes and ornaments, tables, chairs, hills, trees, grass, flowers, as though each separate thing had been brought him to copy. What could be more literal than to introduce in his *Shadow of the Cross* the actual crown and ornaments supposed to have been offered to Jesus by the Kings of the East, as though Christ would have kept these in his carpenter's workshop! His *Hireling Shepherd* is a more convincing work; here we can easily believe the young woman is ready to dally with the handsome, red-haired rustic, while the sheep stray in the ripe corn. *The Hireling Shepherd*, indeed, remains one of the great English pictures.

The painter of this picture was a bigger man altogether

than the gentle Arthur Hughes or the finicking, fanatical
Frederick Shields. Hughes, with his kindly, fresh-coloured
face and white beard, was a benevolent survivor from the
past; from his own past, too, for he had done nothing to
equal his early painting. Shields was for long engaged in
decorating Herbert Horne's Chapel of Ease, near Marble
Arch. I met Shields sometimes with Charles Rowley, who
deemed him a great painter. Rowley was a Manchester
picture-framer, who had sought out Morris in his youth, and,
through Morris, had got to know Rossetti and Madox Brown.
He ran a Brotherhood at Ancoats, a Manchester slum, and
busied himself with the Manchester art school and art gallery.
But he had one thing, above all, to his credit: through
Rowley's insistence the decorations in the Town Hall,
illustrating the history of Manchester, were entrusted to
Madox Brown. A Belgian firm of decorators was to have
taken the work at £5 a foot, but the astute Rowley informed
the committee that an English painter he knew of would do
the work for the same terms! In this haphazard way, these
mural decorations, the most important, perhaps, in the
country, were given to Ford Madox Brown.

The date 1066, the first every English child learns, is a
momentous one, for many reasons, in English history, one
of these being that William the Conqueror, planning unity,
was the first to weaken our local culture. It is true that long
after that date great churches were built and decorated; but
the decision to make London the centre of power was taken
in the Conqueror's time, and has been kept to this day. If
London has gained thereby, other parts of the country have
lost. In Madox Brown's pictures, Manchester's citizens can
at least read the story of their city. Art students there might
well begin by copying them, as the Florentines copied the
Masaccios in the Brancacci Chapel. Thus a local school might
grow up, and local artists be of service to their native town.

Rowley asked me to talk about this at the Ancoats settle-
ment in Manchester, where I read a paper, after which a
young artist, Francis Dodd, came and introduced himself

to me. My subject had stirred him, he said, and he poured
out his enthusiasms and his troubles. No one cared for the
things he loved, or took any notice of what he was doing.
I went to see him; he shared a studio with another Manchester painter, Miss Dacre. His work was most promising,
especially his pastels of Manchester people and street-scenes.
Nevertheless, he could scarce earn a living. But when a few
years later he settled in London, he did not have long to wait
for success.

Rowley understood nothing of Dodd's outlook. Like so
many of Morris' disciples, he was blind to the beauty that
is everywhere, even in Manchester. In his eyes Manchester
was all ugliness, ugliness which could be redeemed only by
Morris tapestries and Burne-Jones windows. I was all for
encouraging local talent, believing that in this way local
schools of painting might grow up here and there to arouse
men's interest in their everyday life and surroundings. To
my mind artists alone understand the intrinsic beauties of
line and design, and of colour; to try to educate 'the people'
to a sense of beauty merely by showing them beautiful things,
is, I hold, fruitless. At Oxford I had seen how little the dons
had learned from the buildings and works of art among
which they lived. Whenever a portrait was to be added to a
college Hall, they invariably chose the painter in vogue; Holl
or Herkomer, Herkomer or Holl, was the verdict every time a
distinguished Oxonian was to be painted. I don't remember
seeing in an Oxford college Hall a portrait either by Watts
or by Whistler. The theory, so dear to educationalists, that
living among beautiful things gives to men an enlightened
understanding of living beauty, has again and again proved
false. This conviction grew upon me as time went on, and
it was at Manchester that I first tried, in my lecture, to put it
in words.

I spent most of the summer of 1895 in France, painting
landscapes and visiting old friends and old haunts in Paris.
Whenever I was in Paris, I spent much time with my
friends at Montmartre—Lautrec, Anquetin, Friant, Picard,

Royer, Duvent. Friant's kindness to me as a youngster I could never forget.

During this visit in 1895 I made a drawing of Huysmans, whom I had met before, at one of Edmond de Goncourt's parties at the Grenier. Huysmans, a small, shrunken, nervous man, with a parchment skin—looking rather like a *fonction-naire*, I thought, with his bourgeois collar and tie, and provincial clothes—was then at work on *La Cathédrale*. He had become absorbed by Catholicism—so absorbed, indeed, that he was soon to retire from the world. He smoked cigarettes one after the other, rolling them incessantly between his quick, slender fingers, yellow with nicotine. He asked about George Moore, who was writing about nuns, he had heard, but wondered—for he said that when he last met Moore, Moore didn't know a Poor Clare from a Sister of Charity.

Going to see Degas, I took some drawings with me, as he had asked to see them. I found a visitor with him, and as Degas looked at my drawings, this stranger glanced at them too. Before he left, he turned to me and asked me to come and see him. 'M. Fantin-Latour,' said Degas, in explanation. Fantin-Latour, of course! I thought his face seemed familiar. I should have known him through his self-portraits.

I found Fantin in a modest studio, in the rue des Beaux Arts. The studio walls were covered with canvases, mostly unframed; these were flower and still-life studies, small nudes, interiors, several self-portraits at different ages, many studies and copies after the old masters, including a superb copy of the *Marriage at Cana* by Paul Veronese, and two large paintings— the *Hommage à Delacroix* and a portrait of two ladies—his wife and sister-in-law, I found out later.

Fantin lived quietly with his wife, seeing scarcely anyone, occupied with his painting, or pottering over prints and drawings, or else going to the Louvre, where he had passed so much of his life, copying. Everything about him was simple and unpretentious: a few commonplace chairs, a sofa, a small table, and many shabby, ample portfolios ranged

against the walls. Here was just such a studio as Daumier
drew and painted. And Fantin himself, stout, baggily
dressed, with list slippers on his feet and a green shade over
his eyes, looked like one of Daumier's artists. His talk was
quiet and unpretentious; there were no fireworks nor sharp
wit, as with Whistler or Degas, yet what he said was wise
and to the point. I wish I had made notes of his talk; it
would have been worth while; for he probably knew more
about methods of painting than any other artist living. And
he had been associated with, and had painted, the most gifted
men of his time, Manet and Baudelaire—and how many
others! In spite of his remarkable portrait compositions, one
of which, hanging in the Luxembourg, had long been
familiar—no one, he said, ever asked him to paint a portrait.
But for his friend, Mrs Edwin Edwards, he had scarcely been
able to continue painting; through Mrs Edwards he sold
many of his flower pieces to English collectors, and this
made him feel very friendly towards England. He had a high
opinion of Millais—of his earlier work especially. Fantin had
been one of the pioneers of modern painting, but though he
knew his own paintings were out of fashion, I never heard
him complain. When Degas and others acquired his *Hommage
à Delacroix*, and offered it to the Louvre, Fantin was quietly
pleased. He knew the world and its vanities too well to be
elated.

What pleased me most was that Fantin, being a middle-
class Frenchman, painted middle-class life. He was of the
company of Chardin, Daumier and Cézanne. In the portraits he painted there were no Coromandel screens or
Louis XV settees; they were of ordinary men and women
sitting in the rooms where they lived. So in his still-life
paintings, the bottles of wine, the bread, fruit and knives on
the rough linen table cloths, were usual on any French
bourgeois table.

Fantin's studio always gave me a sense of rest and security;
and his active encouragement of my own efforts (he actually offered to sit to me, although he said he had never before

been model to anyone save himself) was generous and heartening.

I always went to see Verlaine as often as I could. He was obviously far from well, and looked terribly yellow. He was still living with Eugénie Krantz in a single room—a little tidier, I think, than when I last saw them. One day I arrived to find he had gilded all the chairs with cheap bronze paint, and was childishly delighted with the effect. 'That is how a poet should live,' he said, 'with golden furniture,' and he laughed, half childishly, half cynically. No one ever seemed to visit him; at least I never met any of his old associates there. Only Cazals was faithful still. As usual Verlaine was in need of money. He complained, whenever Eugénie was out of the room, that she still robbed him of everything. I had been doing my best to get people in London to publish his poems. Heinemann was very good, taking several for *The New Review*, and paying for them generously. Frank Harris, too, had published some of his poems in *The Fortnightly Review*. Verlaine complained that these were not always paid for, but this Harris emphatically denied.

In a few days, Verlaine told me, he would be fifty years old. I said we must celebrate the occasion; but the state of Verlaine's leg did not allow of his going out. I spoke to Eugénie and arranged for a little birthday party in Verlaine's room. She was to get food sent up from a neighbouring restaurant. Ray Lankester, who was on a visit to Paris, wanted to meet Verlaine, and I suggested his coming to the birthday party. We arrived punctually, Ray Lankester carrying a large bouquet of flowers in which a choice bottle of wine was concealed. Eugénie was as amiable as she knew how, though her standard of charm was not a high one; she had an uncomfortable way of fawning on people whom she thought might be useful. The flowers plus the wine pleased Verlaine's fancy; he was in the best of spirits during lunch. But the next time I saw him he was depressed and full of misgivings, 'Restez sage,' he said to me, 'take warning from me,' and as he leaned out of the window and

looked down on the people in the street below, he envied
them, saying they were happy; they could still walk. He
spoke feelingly of François Coppée and Mallarmé, as the two
friends who had always been true to him.

I found saying goodbye a painful business. I did not
expect to see him again, and when I spoke with enforced
cheerfulness of coming to see him when I returned to Paris,
I felt that he too knew what was in my mind. The day after
I left he sent me a note with a poem, *Anniversaire*, describing
our birthday party. I was touched at his writing and dedi-
cating a poem to me, the more so since I had promised to
make him a drawing of the interior of Barnard's Inn (a
drawing he had asked for more than once) to remind him of
his last visit to London, a promise I was not able to carry out.

My forebodings were only too true. A few weeks afterwards I got a letter from Eugénie Krantz to tell me Verlaine
was dead. She added that he had kept a reproduction of one
of my drawings hung over the bed on which he died. I wrote
to enquire for further details, and received the following
characteristic letter, the last, I think, I had from Eugénie.

'Monsieur, j'ai eu beaucoup de chagrin de ne pas savoir
votre addresse et celles de vos amis, car je vous aurai (sic)
écris plutôt pour vous apprendre la mort de ce pauvre
Monsieur Paul Verlaine.

'Je vous remercie de vous occuper de moi.

'Vous me demandez si l'on doit à Monsieur Paul Verlaine
en Angleterre; oui monsieur on lui doit encore 250 francs
que je serais bien heureuse d'avoir car je suis resté sans un
sou. Adieu monsieur Will Rothenstein veuillez accepter
l'assurance de ma cordialeté sympathic (sic)

EUGÉNIE KRANTZ'

Ugly and sordid as much of Verlaine's life had been, there
was something deeply endearing in his nature, something
childlike and natural, which touched one's heart. His figure
remains, after 35 years, one of the most vivid among those
that my memory evokes from a shadowy past.

CHAPTER XXII

A TIFF WITH WHISTLER

WHISTLER was still living in Paris, but he often came over to London, staying at Garland's Hotel. He went occasionally to the Chelsea Club. There, one evening, I found Whistler dining with Pennell. Whistler made me sit down next him, saying, 'My dear Parson, I can't play second fiddle to anyone, so I could not reply to your amusing letters.' He was very charming and lively, but Pennell was sulkily hostile. Talking of *Trilby*, which had lately been published, Whistler said that Du Maurier's manuscript had actually been sent to him, that he might delete anything he considered offensive to himself. He was in London, he said, about lithographs and law.

Whistler had taken a great fancy to Macmonnies; and he talked much in praise of Forain. He was to paint Alphonse Daudet's little girl; and he spoke about one of the Boston decorations, which he had been asked to undertake, as he wished. Speaking of Edmond de Goncourt, he said: 'The man who keeps a journal always ends in the dock.'

When Whistler was talking of someone to whom he had given letters of introduction, Pennell said pointedly, 'They all start that way, whether they have them or not.' I was angry, and I assured Pennell I had been received in London with open arms, because people knew I was not one of his friends. Whistler laughed and calmed Pennell down.

I didn't really dislike Pennell; but he showed such hostility to me that I was forced into an aggressive attitude

266

towards him. He was an uncritical worshipper of Whistler, resentful of sharing Whistler's friendship with people who showed independence. In his life of Whistler, a life which is full of interesting matter, and which gives a very vivid presentment of the man, he speaks with small respect of those whom he calls 'the followers'; yet what was he himself but one of the most sycophantic of these? He says truly that Whistler was not really so quarrelsome as people thought, or as Whistler himself would have them believe. It was people like Pennell who played on Whistler's vanity, and prejudiced him against certain people. Pennell, for instance, was interested in the International Exhibition; therefore the people connected with the International Exhibition must be shown in the most agreeable light.

No one adored Whistler more than myself, but the gross flattery offered him by men who could keep his friendship only by compromising their own dignity, revolted me. After the decline of the Grosvenor Gallery, the most important independent movement in England was obviously that of the New English Art Club. Pennell goes out of his way to speak maliciously of everyone connected with the Club. No artists were more stalwart supporters of Whistler than Walter Sickert, Wilson Steer, Henry Tonks, William Nicholson (who by the way was never a member of the New English Art Club) and Charles Conder. One of his strongest champions in the press was D. S. MacColl; yet Pennell suggests that MacColl was only a luke-warm supporter of Whistler, for no other reason than that Whistler had once or twice exhibited at the New English Art Club. This is a gross libel on MacColl's attitude to Whistler's art throughout his career as a critic. Sickert, during many years of his life, was Whistler's most intimate and ardent friend. Steer, whose nature was never demonstrative, had the highest opinion of Whistler's work. But Whistler required from his friends not only loyalty and admiration, but exclusive loyalty and admiration. This was asking too much of high-spirited youth, for the generosity of youth is unlimited. Whistler could absorb all the devotion and admiration, even flattery, which were given him; but like most people he would not look too closely into the work of his admirers. He was unlikely to be over critical so long as he had their homage; but the Pennells did scant justice to Whistler's fine critical acumen, in taking so seriously his pleasant ways with his worshippers; for Whistler knew perfectly well who were artists to be reckoned with, and who were not.

Max Beerbohm used to tease me about my admiration for Whistler. He wrote from Folkestone, where he was staying with an old Oxford friend:

> *West Cliff Hotel,*
> *Folkestone.*
> *Saturday.*

My dear Will,

Here I am, as you see by the royal devices under which I write, ensconced at merry Folkestone. Firminger is with me by the way and I find him a very nice camarade de voyage—very sympathetic and so forth.

It is at present in the off-season, and how charming in its contrast to London with her streets packed with faces and her pavements covered with feet! And how nice to be in a town where the season is just about to commence: charming in its expectant emptiness and not unreminiscent of Hardy's sweet distinction between the light—the twilight—of dawn and of sunset: 'The degree of light is equal exactly, it may be, at both times: but at dawn the bright element is active and the shadow passive and quiescent': so here in the middle of July there is none of the dreadful depression of spirits which falls as one watches the boats and the trains full of departing figures and the emptying streets and the houses as they grow blank. Good God, I write as though I have developed a sense of beauty or sentiment or something equally inappropriate to a modern (or modd'n) letter. Are' you working? Are you, in my charming phrase, staining the hair of a camel in gaudy chemicals and wiping them off on a bit of coarse canvas? Or have you given up that kind of thing? Talking of painters, by the way, I was taken to see a man—a nouveau riche named Crofter—the other day: he shewed me some chalk sketches by Whistler—nude women drawn in rough and short strokes—which I really found rather charming. I began to think that perhaps you were right in your idolatry and that the man really does possess a touch of genius.

My admiration for Whistler has never changed. He was without doubt one of the remarkable artists of the nineteenth century, and one of its great personalities. His faults were obvious; among them was his habit of judging people in relation to himself. But his character was a whole and rounded one, and one accepted it, and still accepts it, as unique and legitimate—legitimate for the reason that he made of his life an unity. When he attacked this man or that, it was largely because he stood in the way of his own reflection. His life was to be, as it were, a perfect self-portrait. The Pennells were blind to Whistler's human fallibility, blind to qualities outside Whistler's compass. One of the most touching letters Whistler wrote was a letter to Fantin-Latour in which he regrets that he couldn't draw with the precision of Ingres. Absurd modesty! say the Pennells, Whistler drew much better!

Besides Whistler, various Paris friends came over to London, among them Anquetin, Lautrec and Stuart Merrill. Poor Stuart Merrill! How bored he was in London! He did not stay long, but went off to Brighton, from where he wrote:

'J'ai beaucoup regretté de ne t'avoir pas vu une dernière fois avant ton départ de Londres. J'ai un projet intéressant à t'exposer: il est vrai que j'invente au moins dix projets par heure.

'Je m'embête ici, malgré un Empire et un Alhambra, où je m'abrutis consciencieusement chaque nuit. La Mer fait un brouhaha ridicule, le vent souffle toujours, et les gens ont les binettes de croquemorts.

'Et puis zut! Ma plume écrit mal et je te dis au revoir. Je serai sans doute de retour à Londres mardi ou mercredi, puis je filerai vers mon cher Paris.

'J'aurai donc peut-être la chance de te revoir.

A bientôt, ton STUART MERRILL'

What the project was I never discovered. Anquetin, too, had some plan. He had come to London 'pour la representation de Henri VIII de Saint-Saens', but was recalled suddenly to Paris for the sale of one of his big decorations. 'Je suis désolé du contretemps qui me prive d'un travail que j'aurais eu plaisir à enlever en votre compagnie.'

Sir William Eden was another amateur, besides Brabazon, who used to send to the New English Art Club. His water-colours were much inferior to Brabazon's, yet he was not without some talent, and since he was a patron of Steer and Sickert and other members of the New English Art Club, the jury was perhaps indulgent in judging his work. Eden had treated Whistler very meanly over a portrait of his wife. A quarrel ensued which assumed, as did all his quarrels, too much importance in Whistler's life. For a time everything centred round it, and it resulted in the well-known *Baronet & the Butterfly*. Hearing that a drawing by Eden had been accepted by the jury of the New English Art Club, Whistler went down to the Chelsea Club and said disagreeable things about me, for I was one of the jury; and all he said was of course repeated, probably with additions, when I next went into the Club. I was rather upset at what I was told, and a little annoyed that Whistler should discuss my affairs before the gossips and fossils of a club which, incidentally, was my club as well as his; he knew too there were many there who were glad to hear anything against the New English element. I was rash enough to write complaining of this to Whistler. Of course, I was no match for him. He pounced on me at once.

'I have ever admired your neat hand with the foil,' I wrote, 'but when in the other hand you brandish a scythe, with

intent to lop off my legs when my eyes are on your button
—*no!*' He promptly retorted: 'That is it Rothenstein. You keep your eye on the button, *I'll* do the rest!' And in subsequent letters he remarks on my having 'the toad in the belly'. I had a genuine enough grievance; but my letters were foolish, and I deserved these sound raps on my knuckles. Having administered them, Whistler seems to have relented; for I find friendly letters following.

CHAPTER XXIII

THE BEERBOHMS AND GORDON CRAIG

Max 'en famille' THE Beerbohms were then living at 19 Hyde Park Place, one of a row of late eighteenth, or early nineteenth-century houses, which has since been pulled down. Their home became the most familiar to me of all London houses, and the drawing room upstairs, with its bright chintz curtains and chintz-covered chairs, its little tables littered with silver nicknacks, its oval portraits of Max's grandparents in eighteenth-century dress—I marvelled that anyone's grandparents could have flourished so long ago—was the most familiar room. In a low chair on the right of the fireplace sat the charming little old lady herself, Mrs Beerbohm, in a black dress with a white shawl across her shoulders and a white lace cap on her head. With her hair done *en bandeaux* she looked like a miniature Queen Victoria; but perhaps the great Queen herself was as small—I rather think she was. Mrs Beerbohm was wrapped up in her children; but Max was the apple of her eye; and because of my own admiration for Max, I was treated almost as a member of the family.

Herbert Tree was of course already famous, but the family almost deified Max, and his every wish was household law. Always, on going to see Max, whose room was at the top of the house, I stopped on my way to chat for a while with his mother; I should have felt it a kind of *lèse-majesté* to pass her drawing room door without going in to pay my respects; and, needless to say, though we spoke of many things, it was to Max that the conversation always turned. She was anxious about his future, but my firm faith in his star brought her comfort. Criticism of Max's early essays and caricatures was by no means friendly—they shared something of the unpopularity of Beardsley's drawings. Herbert Tree was disquieted a good deal about the caricatures; he recognised their wit, but listened too readily to friends who told him that Max could not draw. Whenever we met, he urged me to press upon Max the need for correctness. In vain I explained that Max's manner of drawing was adapted to his needs; that it was, in fact, for its purpose, excellent drawing.

Tree, though he had an open and, on occasions, an adventurous mind, was surrounded, like most actor-managers, by flatterers, but he was too intelligent to be deceived. He was well aware of the value of the people about him, and he won the devotion of those who could serve him best. Tree had a sure sense of theatrical effect. His artistic adviser was Comyns Carr, who was in close touch with Burne-Jones and his circle. Indeed, Carr knew many artists, for with Charles Hallé he ran the New Gallery, and every year perambulated the London studios, selecting and rejecting pictures. I was inclined to scoff at an amateur, as indeed Carr was, taking himself seriously as a judge, and a jury as well.

I couldn't admire Tree as I did his brother, though in the eyes of the world Tree, and not Max, was the man. Nor was I ever quite at my ease with Tree, perhaps because he was not his natural self with me. Even at the Beerbohms and at his house in Sloane Street, I felt an element of constraint in the atmosphere. But at his supper parties at Sloane Street Mrs Tree's wit made a pleasant diversion. I often escaped from the distinguished company below to draw soldiers and policemen for little Viola upstairs.

I did one or two portraits of Tree at the Haymarket Theatre; but he was always surrounded by people, and I found it a hopeless task. However, one day he sent a hansom to fetch me to Jack Straw's Castle, where he was staying

with Mrs Tree, and where I made a pastel of him in peace.
Alone with his friends, he could be delightful.

Since the Morocco adventure I kept up my riding: 'What's
this I hear about m'rocking horses, Parson?' Whistler asked
me. I found a tradesman close by Glebe Place, who was in
the Yeomanry and wanted his horse exercised; so I rode
regularly in Battersea Park in the early mornings. Sometimes
Sargent, who had been ordered to ride for his health, would
join me, but he was a poor horseman and was never at ease
in the saddle. He used to say of himself that he looked, and
felt, like the proverbial sack of potatoes.

Tree, too, used to ride in the Row; but at times was too
busy, when he very kindly offered me the use of his mount;
but there must have been some misunderstanding when I
called at the stable, for Mrs Tree, whose wit always delighted
me, wrote: 'Dear Mr Rothenstein, I am in great dismay and
distress to hear that the horse which I fondly hoped was
grazing peacefully under your easel (not that you let grass
grow there) had been rudely denied you. I am furious with
the livery stable people, and you must be furious with me.
Could you come with me and hear them apologise, or do
you alas no longer want that head-eating horse? Oh, what
praises have I not heard of your work in the Grafton.
I congratulate you so much. You won't forget that I am to
sit? Yours very sincerely, Maud Beerbohm Tree.'

The Beerbohms invariably took me with them to the first
nights at the Haymarket, and later at Her Majesty's Theatre.
It was exciting to see the house full of famous men and
reigning beauties. Max knew them all by sight, and through
him I became familiar with the appearance of many of the
great social figures of the time. But I was never quite happy
at these first nights, for fear things should not go well; for
naturally Tree's success meant much to the Beerbohms.
Nor could I always admire the elaborate scenery and dresses
as much as I wished; and Tree was less successful in some of
his parts than in others.

After one of these first nights, while I was abroad, Max

wrote: 'Such a brilliant first night at the Haymarket on Wednesday. The stalls were simply infested with politicians, whilst peeresses-in-their-own-right were hustled into tiny boxes over the chandeliers. Zola was to have come, but, being travel worn, did not and went instead to the Alhambra. Oscar was also at the Alhambra, dancing attendance upon Zola's attendants. A propos of him, did I tell you that I saw a good deal of his brother Willie at Broadstairs?'

Max had a second brother, Julius, who had all the Beerbohm charm, and was more easy to get on with than Herbert. He thoroughly approved of Max's writing and drawing, and the warm appreciation of Robert Ross, Walter Sickert and Aubrey Beardsley was an added source of comfort to the family.

Only once did I fall into disgrace with Mrs Beerbohm. The occasion came about in this way. Max and I being one night at the Café Royal, we were joined by Gordon Craig. Craig had a book with him, in which he asked me to make a drawing. I did a little caricature of Max in pen and ink. Craig was then bringing out his charming *Page* at irregular intervals, and he asked Max to give him a caricature of myself, and proposed reproducing the two together. My little drawing seemed to me very harmless; Max's of me was particularly brutal. When *The Page* appeared, however, and Mrs Beerbohm saw my drawing, she was quite angry. I could not help being amused at her sensitiveness about a little *charge* of her son, when she, dear lady, was so indignant with people who complained of Max's incisive satire.

Maybe it was the drabness of ordinary life that made the music-halls so attractive. And not only the music-halls, but the theatres as well, and the fair and the roundabouts. There was also the Punch and Judy show, still, in those early days, a going concern. The old show was brightly painted, and the performance completer and more traditional than later ones I have seen. Punch and Judy have fallen on evil days. The few shows that are still to be seen in London are poor, shabby affairs. I was always attracted by the figure of Punch—a crude but virile precursor of Falstaff—more grossly comedic,

275

Punch and Judy as befits a popular figure appealing to an illiterate crowd. But what a gorgeous figure and what a drama! I used to feel its plot, so exciting, so full and direct in the characterisation, so rapid in movement, might serve as a model for contemporary playwrights.

Having hired a particularly good Punch and Judy show, I asked Bernard Shaw, William Archer, and other friends interested in the theatre to come to my studio for the performance. There was also a little ambulant marionette theatre which was set up in the London streets; this also I induced to come to Glebe Place, and made a number of careful pastel studies of some of the figures and scenes, which amused Gordon Craig.

Gordon Craig himself I had met, with Jimmy Pryde, in an auction room in the Strand, where cheap pictures were being sold; what a handsome person I thought, brimful of ideas, and apt to do and say unexpected things. He had lately been acting small parts with Irving; but for the moment he was free. Inspired by Pryde and Nicholson, whose romantic drawings gave Craig many hints about stage figures and scenes, he was doing wood-cuts in his spare time. How good an actor he was I don't know. I saw him once act as Hamlet, somewhere in Islington, and never had I seen such a touching and beautiful figure. I made him sit for a painting in his Hamlet dress, a small full-length, which was never finished; for he came, or stayed away, as the spirit moved him. He and Max Beerbohm are the two friends who, in my eyes, have altered least. Teddy has now as much enthusiasm for the theatre as then; and the same old fire.

William Nicholson had married Pryde's sister, and was living at Bushey. He or Pryde—I forget which—took me over to see Herkomer in his Rhine-Bayreuth-Bavarian castle. There was no lady combing her golden locks; but I met the courteous Hubert, who, save in name, bore no resemblance to a robber baron. Otherwise the Rhine-Bayreuth atmosphere was evident throughout, and I was not sorry that I had escaped a Bushey education.

GORDON CRAIG AS HAMLET

Pryde's passion in those days was to dress up as Pierrot; Ellen Terry
indeed, he had much of Pierrot's character. Nicholson deserved the fame and success he achieved with his London types, and his wood-block portraits; but Pryde had to wait a long time before Fortune took note of him.

Through Craig I had the privilege of meeting his dear mother. Ellen Terry took me to her heart at once. Was I not Teddy's friend? Craig was then without an engagement. The place that Whistler and Degas had for me among painters, Irving had in Craig's eyes. Unfortunately, Irving could not always provide work for Teddy; but Craig did not remain idle, and busied himself with writing and did book-plates, and made illustrations for *The Page*— a magazine of which, so far as I could see, he was the sole editor and art editor, and all the contributors and illustrators himself.

Clearly Craig's gifts were too varied to allow of his acting and nothing more; perhaps, too, his genius stood in the way of his talents. Ideas poured from his brain; but ideas are not easily coined into guineas, and while his mother adored him, she was often worried about him. My unshaken belief in his daimon naturally delighted Miss Terry, and won me her lasting affection and friendship. When in 1898 Ellen Terry took a theatre and gave Gordon Craig a free hand, he triumphantly justified this faith. I had never before, nor have I since, seen anything more completely satisfying than the scenery, dresses and dramatic grouping of Ibsen's *Vikings* and of Shakespeare's *Much Ado About Nothing*, which Craig produced for his mother.

Craig was keen to produce a play by Henley. He wrote from Thames Ditton:

My dear Will,

I have heard from Signor Henley. His *first* desire is that a good company should perform his play.

Natürlich!!

Now can you learn from Miss Kingsley if she is serious

when she says she may be able to find people with money
to start a provincial company.

Henley is probably tired of actors who visit him only to
mention his plays as *likely* plays—or graceful plays and
suchlike rot. So I will not go visit him till I can speak
definitely about this tour.

My idea is not to get 20 of the best actors in London to
play: that would turn the play into a variety entertainment
consisting of 20 turns. Recruits (and let them see to it that
they possess large noses) with enthusiasm, under a cold-
blooded deliberate gent like myself can get a better result.

So discover if your nice friend Miss Kingsley is serious
and means business.

I don't want this to fall to the ground.

Yours ever,

CORPORAL GORDON

My son gets more like the King of Rome every day. The
new baby has not arrived yet.

I have just read Shelley's *Cenci*. It's sent me mad.

The play never came off, but the baby arrived; and soon
after Craig wrote of the christening, 'There is always a great
ceremony. He or she is held by the nurse—the servants hold
wax candles, a priest is sent for and then I read in a loud
voice Polonius' advice to his son. The infant is touched even
to shedding tears!' and the letter was signed 'Gordon *Cenci*
Craig!'

CHAPTER XXIV

SOLFERINO'S

I HAD been wise to have passed a summer now and then *Yorkshire—*
painting in Yorkshire. The subjects to be found there are *and France*
bleak but have a beauty of their own, and for me, no subjects
had a stronger appeal. I went home to Bradford frequently,
but for week-ends only, and when each summer came, France
called to me. I liked French people and French ways; but
I knew little of France beyond the Seine country between
Rouen and Paris. One evening at the Gourmets I met
Sparling, then Miss May Morris' husband. Sparling told me
about the Burgundy country and how Morris thought that the
churches there were among the most beautiful in France. So
I went by train, as he advised me to do, to La Roche, and from
there I cycled through the Côte d'Or. It was lovely country
indeed, and Morris was right about the churches. There were
then few tourists in this country; the inns were cheap and
good, the wine was admirable, the innkeepers hospitable.
Here, it seemed, was *la vieille France,* a land of big-bearded,
genial men and sturdy, efficient, kindly women. How wonderful everything was! How enchanting to be an artist, and
young! When I saw Vézelay at the top of a lofty hill, about
which vineyards and orchards basked in the brilliant sunshine, I thought there was no place more lovely in all the
world. I had seen no building abroad so grand as the great
Basilica, a universe in stone! within which there were neither
stalls, confessionals nor seats. In England what cathedrals
and churches I knew were railed in; the ground on which

they stood was kept neat and tidy like a London square; no matter what surroundings they had, their precincts invariably kept them apart, like precious exhibits. Here in France the churches grew, as it were, from the ground; one felt that the church was the mother-roof, with the humbler roofs nestling around, like a hen with her brood of chicks. For this reason the French churches are more paintable than our own, though it is clear from the paintings of Turner, Girtin and Prout that early in the nineteenth century English churches were at no disadvantage in this respect.

Miss Kingsley and her sister, Miss Christina Knewstub, joined me in France just now. I remember how, on being shown over a monastery at Flavigny, I was so touched by the beauty of the interior and the sense of peace and security it induced, that the monk who was with me hoped that perhaps I was on the verge of conversion. He led me at last to his plain, white-washed room, where he bade me sit down, and then and there he tried to prevail on me to remain. All without was vanity, he said; only with them, and with others like them, could there be peace. I was moved, but a little uncomfortable. I was a painter, I explained, and to me the world was appealingly beautiful: in any case, I needed time for reflection. The Benedictine sighed, and conducted me to the door of the monastery where, with her bright gold hair, Miss Kingsley was waiting. I hardly think he expected to see me again. No, I didn't want to retire from the world. Indeed, I didn't want to leave Vézelay. The inn there was primitive, but the landlord was a character. He neglected his kitchen; his passion was for hunting. When he went off with his friends, gun on shoulder, game-bag by his side, laced gaiters on his legs, he looked superb. One day he beckoned me and took me into the cellar beneath the inn. So dark it was, I could see nothing at first; then with a shock I discovered the place was full of live birds, partridges and pheasants, which perforce had to tread daintily in perpetual twilight. Where he got them, or why he kept them in darkness, I never knew. I often returned to that part of France, and with every visit my pleasure increased.

The following Easter I went walking with my friend Woodford Sallitt in Yorkshire. Here there was none of the opulence of Burgundy, but the austerity of the farms and houses, the stark lines of the moorsides, the grim churches on whose hard roofs no lichens settled, brought back many youthful memories. We walked through Malham Cove and Gordale Scar—there could be no grander landscape I thought—and through Middleham and Middleton on to Richmond, a splendid place in which to paint, with its castle and its church. But after the houses in France, those in the little Yorkshire towns looked very small. Morris used to say, so Miss Morris had told me, that the French built houses for men, the English for rats. How true this was I now saw for myself. From Richmond we went on to Barnard Castle, ending our tour at High Force and returning through Ingleton and Kettlewell. I marvelled how Turner, after travelling through this country, had been able to paint, from the slightest notes, great and convincing pictures of places so briefly seen; so exact was his memory. The ease with which we to-day can refer to documents discourages the cultivation of memory. I remember reading in Balzac's *Maison du Chat qui Pelote* of the artist who, looking through a window, was so impressed with the scene he beheld, that he was able to reproduce it exactly. I thought this fantastic then; but now I believe it might well have been true.

In 1896 A. E. Housman's *Shropshire Lad* was published. It had an immediate success—perhaps success is not the right word, for rarely has a work of genius been at once accepted at its true value. But people who had sneered at minor poetry were silenced. Here was fine poetry, and a poet taking his place quietly as an immortal, as a great fiddler goes to his seat in the orchestra. There was no legend about Housman. No one seemed to know anything about him, save that he was Laurence Housman's brother.

Francis Thompson, too, had brought a new note of

281

sincerity into poetry, refreshing to people who were becoming
a little weary of Caroline pastiche and of the Anglo-French
accent, in poems of music-hall and prostitute. But we heard
strange stories of Thompson himself; he was a sort of De
Quincey; a mysterious figure who, once in a while, visited
a publisher's office to leave a roll of poems, and was then
lost again in the nameless London crowd. He had no home;
the arches under the London bridges were said to shelter him
at night. Then one heard that the Meynells had run him to
earth, and were helping him whenever they could, but he was
shy and elusive, and preferred his secret life, with its sordidness and poverty, to the life of the world. Not that the
Meynells were worldly. Mrs Meynell and her children were
very poetical beings; at their home in Palace Gate, there were
no carpets on the floor, but bare boards; they lived simply,
and at their plain but well furnished table room was joyfully
made for young painters and poets, and these were always
set at their ease. I liked Thompson, and respected him for
his independence. He was attractive looking, too, with his
fair beard and sad, rather brooding face.

Then Yeats: he was greatly admired by poets; but there
was too much of what Robert Bridges called Rosicrucianism
in his work at this time. Yeats impressed me. True, he had
an artificial manner, and when he was surrounded by female
admirers his sublimity came near to the ridiculous at times;
but he was a true poet, and behind the solemn mask of the
mystic there was a rare imagination and, what was less often
suspected, shrewd wisdom. Yeats, like Shaw, was a man of
great courage, who championed losing causes and men who
were unfairly assailed. Moreover, he maintained the dignity
of literature, and even in the midst of his lady admirers he
was a really fine talker.

Yeats occupied a couple of rooms in Euston Buildings,
where every week he held forth on fairies and magic, the
cabala, and the philosopher's stone. Sometimes, at these
gatherings, Miss Florence Farr would croon to the accom-
paniment of a single-stringed instrument which Yeats had

invented. Yeats suspected me of irreverence; but what
amused me more than his Rosicrucianism was his friendship
with George Moore. He was the Pied Piper who played
Moore into Dublin and the Irish mountains.

Stephen Phillips as well was a rising star. I asked Yeats
and Phillips to lunch at Glebe Place. Yeats was in one of his
best moods, and he and Phillips sat and talked for hour after
hour until I, who had a dinner engagement, had to break up
the party. In Phillips there was little of Yeats' nonsense,
and but little of Yeats' poetic sense; but he had admirers,
and his popularity made Yeats curious to meet him. Poor
Phillips! there was always something pathetic about him.
I suspected that, at heart, he didn't think himself a great poet;
but he accepted his luck at being taken for one by Sidney
Colvin, and his publishers, and many literary ladies. Max,
with his usual prescience, when someone asked him how long
Le Gallienne meant to stay in America, remarked 'He is
waiting for Stephen Phillips to blow over.' And blow over
poor Phillips did; but while he was draped in the mantle of
success, we were all a little unkind and ribald. I remember
that when Binyon had dedicated a book of poems 'To Joy',
I said to Max that Phillips' next volume would be dedicated
to 'Hope Brothers'.

Talking to Yeats one day I said: 'Yeats, you must write
a poem about a man who was too lazy to make a perfect
sonnet, so he raised a revolution instead.' An inconsequent
remark, with nothing of prophecy in my mind. But Yeats
put me in mind of it many years after when he was staying
with us in Gloucestershire, at the time of the Irish Rising of
1915, largely engineered by poets.

One morning I got a note from Max telling me of an
important change in his life: 'I am so sorry about to-morrow
—and I hope you won't be stranded. I have to go to see the
Saturdayers to-morrow morning—also G. B. S., from whom
I had a note this evening asking me to take over his business
now—his foot prevents him from going to any theatre, and
he is to be moved out of London as soon as possible. So

I have to go on the streets of journalism this week. An intellectual prostitute. I hope you won't pass me by and refuse to draw me for the *Juniorum*. Any other day will do for me—after Friday.' This was the result of Shaw's last article in *The Saturday Review* ending 'The younger generation is knocking at the door; and as I open it there steps sprightly in the incomparable Max. I am off duty for ever and am going to sleep.' What a charming tribute from the incomparable Shaw! A week later came a note from Max 'To-day, for the first time in my life, I had a printer's devil waiting for genius to correct its proof—very distinguished.'

This appointment suited Max perfectly. His tastes were modest: a few hansom cabs and telegrams; dinner now and then at Solferino's; coffee at the Café Royal. Since he lived with his mother, his expenses were light; so these Saturday articles gave him ample pocket-money. Every Thursday he shut himself up and wrote his weekly review; the rest of the week he was free to work or play.

I loved his room, distempered, as at Oxford, a sky-blue colour, and hung with caricatures by Pellegrini. He rarely left it. For Max took no exercise; he kept well without it. True he would emerge in the evenings to dine at Solferino's or to visit a music-hall, to hear Chevalier or Eugene Stratton or Cissie Loftus. He was fascinated by Cissie Loftus; she was the English counterpart of Yvette Guilbert.

'If I were not afraid', he wrote, 'my people might keep it out of the newspapers, I should commit suicide to-morrow —really I am rather miserable—I know what disappointment is.

'In my unregenerate days, I was far too much of an egoist to seek for any pleasure save in the contemplation of myself: taking myself as the standard of perfection, I always found myself quite perfect and never was disappointed. But now I have become a tuist and all is changed.

'Yesterday I woke dimly in the morning, murmuring to myself "To-night Don Juan is produced and from my stall I shall see my love in the white kirtle of a Haidee." I break-

VEZELAY CATHEDRAL

fast—and open the paper and find a dastardly postponement till Saturday next "owing to an accident to one of the principal performers". Heigho—I suppose there is such a thing as Saturday next—do you think so, Will?

'What was the accident? To whom had it happened? I went down to the Gaiety to ask and found that it was not, as I had almost hoped, the Lady Cecilia who had broken her heart for me—but only Mr Robert Pateman who had sprained his ankle. To Solferino's I went in solitary wretchedness and tried to forget the gates under a crown of vine leaves—but they only deepened the shadow upon my brow....'

Solferino's was a restaurant in Rupert Street where Max and I often dined. It was frequented by the staff of *The National Observer* and *The Pall Mall*—Harry Cust, Ivan Müller, Charles Whibley, George Street—the Henley Regatta, Max called the company. Henley sometimes joined them; Sickert too, and, on rare occasions, Whistler. It was quiet and the cooking was excellent; further, the manager was willing to give credit, though his trustfulness proved his ruin.

Harry Cust and Ivan Müller ran *The Pall Mall Gazette*; Whibley was Henley's chief henchman on *The National Observer*.

Charles Whibley was a great talker; he held his opinions obstinately, and the opinion of others he belaboured heartily, *pour s'encourager lui-même*, one might say. So far as I could see he stood in fear of two men only: Henley and Whistler. Henley, with whom I became friendly at the same time, was a kind of literary Drake, half admiral, half pirate, under whom Whibley and others served loyally. I didn't mind Henley's forceful opinions; nor, whenever I disagreed with these, did Henley mind either; but with most of his friends his word was law, and anyone who disputed his word was a heretic.

Henley himself was a blithe and lovable person, who, although crippled, enjoyed a full life. He was the literary counterpart of Charles Furse: both suffered from grave physical disabilities, both idolised physical strength and the virtues of men of action, both disapproved of 'decadents'. Indeed, anyone whom either Henley or Furse disliked was reckoned a decadent, whether or not; and I defended the Pre-Raphaelites and spoke up for Le Gallienne and Shannon and Wilde whenever Henley attacked them.

Ruskin's attack on Whistler was partly the cause of the sharp division between Impressionists and Pre-Raphaelites. It is well known that both Dante Gabriel and William Rossetti disapproved of Ruskin's attack and refused to support it. But Whistler, as I mentioned earlier, never forgave Burne-Jones for giving evidence against him; and it was rash to say a word in defence of either Burne-Jones or Ruskin in Whistler circles. But if mental freedom is dear to me, I can never be patient with the current opinions of the moment held by the élite. Whistlerites, Ruskinites, Cézannites bore me equally; hence I have not been popular with the critics nor with those who 'know about art'. I recollect once at the Gosses' sitting next to an aesthetic young woman who, in answer to some remark I made, said freezingly, 'I am afraid I like only beautiful things.' When the ladies retired I much amused my neighbour by observing how I would like to have slapped her Botticelli—she who liked only beautiful things! Well, there are many Botticellis I should like to slap. Among Muslims it is ill-bred to enquire of another's wife; I wish it were considered ill-bred at casual meetings with artists to invite their opinions on other artists; in fact, I don't know which I dislike the more, to hear an artist vulgarly abused or stupidly praised. How bored I got with the current discussions on Beardsley and Sargent! One never hears an *original* stupid remark—such originality would be only too welcome—but it is always the same stupidity one hears. I am sure that Solomon said to his cunning craftsmen, 'I don't pretend to know anything about art, but I know what I like,' and that Plato used the same words to Pheidias.

Now Ruskin I have always admired. His opinions never

seem to matter; indeed, only weaklings aspire to be right; but to his knowledge of art Ruskin added the wisdom and taste of a noble nature; after which, to be right is of minor importance. He had the prophet's vision, and his mind was an organ whence glorious music came. Henley was not a Ruskin; yet he was a stimulating, genial person, and the men who gathered round him had character and talent. Among these, besides Whibley, I particularly liked George Street. He was very polished, very urbane; yet his judgment of men and manners and events was incisive; there was no one whose opinion I valued more. Street was the author of one of the most amusing books of the early 'nineties, *The Autobiography of a Boy*. He had been at Charterhouse with Max, but they never met at school. They met one night at Solferino's. Street, like Max, was something of a dandy. Each aspired to be more coldly aloof than the other; but finally warmth crept into the party, and there and then a close friendship began between Max and Street. Street was a writer of fastidious prose. I have often wondered why his stories have not been republished.

Besides Solferino's we discovered a little restaurant in Lisle Street, *Aux Gourmets*, frequented by French workmen and clerks from Soho. It was cheap, and it soon became a meeting place for artists and scribes. Among them was Robert Steele, a learned mediaevalist, and a disciple of William Morris. I had earlier wanted to draw William Morris, and had asked Shaw to take me to one of his evenings. Shaw replied: 'No use; he's not to be drawn. It might be done with a kodak, taking the same precautions as you would if you were garotting him; but I know my man too well to suggest a sitting.' Steele doubted that Shaw was right; but alas, I knew better, for Morris had not even looked with a friendly eye on Ricketts and Shannon—neither on them nor their work. But at this time William Morris was very ill; despite his robust appearance and his immense energy, his health was broken and his life was to end prematurely. His daughter, May, often came to the Gourmets, and later, after

Morris' death, at her house in Hammersmith Terrace I was asked to meet Mrs Morris, an almost legendary figure to me. It was as though I were asked to meet Laura, or la Simonetta, or Vittoria Colonna. She had retained much of the beauty which Rossetti has immortalised; her hair, now grey, seemed as full and as rich as in his paintings. Memorable was one afternoon at Hammersmith Terrace when a visitor, bringing a copy of the Kelmscott Chaucer, begged Mrs Morris to write in it. Mrs Morris took the great book on her knees, and as with quill pen in hand she inscribed her name on the title-page, she looked like a splendid Sybil from the Sistine Chapel. I had heard and read of her moving, a noble figure, among the great people about her husband and Rossetti—noble but silent. I found her serene indeed, but interested in a thousand things; an admirable talker, wholly without self-consciousness, always gracious, and in her person beautifully dignified. Miss Morris' house was full of her father's prints, wall-papers and hangings; there hung Rossetti's painting of her mother, and many more photographs of her in her younger days. In Mrs Morris' presence I seemed to be living in a dream. Women married to famous men are over-shadowed by their husbands; but when they survive their husbands, there comes sometimes a later flowering, previously, perhaps, held in check.

I made a silverpoint of Miss Morris, but she preferred Charles Shannon's drawings to mine, and wanted her mother to sit to him. Mrs Morris, to my surprise, cared less than her daughter for Shannon's work; Steele told someone that my 'concrete' mind amused her more than did Shannon's poetical one; that she would not have been averse to sitting had I asked her to do so. What an honour this would have been! though after Rossetti's immortal drawings I should not have dared to ask her.

I got into trouble over Watts' fine portrait of William Morris. Frank Harris rashly asked me to edit a Christmas supplement of *The Saturday Review*. *The Pageant* had shown me the way, and I readily accepted the task. This number,

COVER OF THE 'SATURDAY' SUPPLEMENT

now very rare, is memorable in that it contained the first A fan by Conder
reproduction of a fan by Conder. Conder took great pains
to do a design that would reproduce satisfactorily:

'You were very good to think of me and I am very pleased
to do it. I am having more difficulty than I expected as I find
it difficult to keep the fan simple and at the same time give
it delicacy. I abandoned one that I was doing in sanguine and
green and now I am doing one in blue and black and I think
that will perhaps suit me better. I am sure to be sending it in
a day or two and hope that will not be behind time....I have
done a fair amount of work since I came up and have done
two marines which I hope will turn out pretty well. In the
fan I am doing for you I have used three or four shades of
the same colour and hope that's all right. I wish a fan I did
before getting your letter would have suited as it is certainly
one of my best, but it is painted in so many colours, and I fear
depends much on its colour for the effect.'

I had also asked Max to make one or two caricatures; but
when he sent them I had to reject the first ones, and evidently
made suggestions for others. Max writes: 'I have had a
glimpse at Bill Watson—though I remember him rather
faintly. I send you my Rowton also—you *must* have heard
of Rowton—Disraeli's secretary and friend and executor and
always all over the place. After all, even if he weren't at all
known outside the aristocracy you, as an Editor, should
remember that the aristocracy is a class to be catered for
too—There are said to be 10,000 of them—However—just
as you like—And I hope you will like the other caricatures.
Also that F. H. won't think they will give offence. Do take
a high hand with him....What about my writing something
for the thing? You see, I don't know what sort of writing
they want—essay, fairy story?'

To this I at once replied that nothing would please me
better than to have some of his writing, and in another letter
he wrote: 'Also I will do some kind of skit—possibly
parodies of various writers writing on the subject of Xmas—
"Seasonable Tributes" levied by Max Beerbohm? or some-

thing of the sort—What do you think? Mrs Meynell on "Holly"—Arthur Symons on "Xmas Eve in Piccadilly"—Henry James never mentioning Xmas by name and so forth—Rather amusing if acceptable. Yours, Max.'

This is remarkable in that it refers to what was the first inception of *The Christmas Garland*. It took us some time to agree about the subjects for Max's drawing. Finally he wrote to me:

My dear Will,

I wrote to Alfred Austin under an assumed name, asking to let me interview him for the *English Illustrated*. This morning comes an exquisite letter saying that 'The Poet Laureate greatly regretted that owing to his rules' etc. Isn't it rather marvellous of him to call himself these names—to a stranger? I can't think of anyone else. Can you? Isn't Labby a draw? My article on Scott is to be in the next *Saturday*. I am awaiting a proof.

Yours, MAX.

My sister, Constance, has heard from Mrs Campbell—She says she is 'afraid Mr Rothenstein did not succeed in his drawing, *but perhaps when he has got it in his studio he will be able to touch it up*'. My italics.

An idea! Wilson Barrett in The Sign of the X. Will go and see him in it and copy the drapery in the British Museum. He would really be a draw.

And he *was* a draw. The caricature was admirable, and duly appeared in the Christmas number.

Besides the cover, which I designed, several of my own drawings appeared in *The Saturday Supplement*. One of them was the portrait of Herbert Tree, which I had made at Jack Straw's Castle. Another was a drawing of Mrs Craigie. Here again the old difficulty occurred, Mrs Craigie writing: 'My father has seen the proof of your sketch, and while he thinks it admirable work, he does not consider it a satisfactory portrait. He is most unwilling that it should appear An editor's in the Saturday. If there were time I would gladly give you worries another sitting; but as it is, I fear I must ask you to cancel the sketch.'

Again I could not, of course, allow anyone to dictate to me whether or not a drawing should be exhibited or printed, for my own conscience would not allow me to publish a drawing I thought inefficient. So the drawing of Mrs Craigie appeared, with that of Tree, in the *Supplement*.

Hollyer was paid a fee for the right to reproduce his photograph of Watts' portrait of William Morris. But I was told that Watts was annoyed at its publication, and I therefore wrote to him to explain that we had Hollyer's sanction. Watts at once replied:

Limnerslease, Guildford
Dec. 24, 1896

Dear Sir,

I am very sorry for any annoyance my protest in the matter of the reproduction of Mr Morris's portrait has caused you. I promised at the urgent request of Mrs Morris that the portrait should not be reproduced, she wished it for a biography in which she is especially interested. So I have since then refused all applications.

I see by the letters from Mr Hollyer which you enclose and which I send back—that the permission was given long before Mr Morris's death, so of course I shall let Mrs Morris know that there can be no blame to anybody.

Very truly yours,
G. F. WATTS

I had an unfortunate experience with Heinemann. I met a Freiherr von Bodenhausen, a cultured German who, with Graf Kessler, was editing a quarterly based on Ricketts' and Shannon's *Dial*: Bodenhausen proposed to include my lithograph of Zola in an early number. Young artists incline to think their present work better than that done two or three years before; so I preferred to make a fresh drawing. Bodenhausen suggested a drawing of Walter Crane, whereupon Heinemann, hearing the Zola lithograph was not to be used, wrote me a Whistlerian letter, complaining that I had 'picked his pocket in a café'. This was unexpected and upsetting. It hadn't occurred to me that Heinemann had sold the print of Zola to Bodenhausen. But I couldn't forget that Heinemann was one of my earliest patrons, and some years afterwards I wrote to assure him that I had acted innocently in the matter; he responded as I expected, and pleasant relations were resumed.

I liked Walter Crane, and all his family. Besides Mrs Crane there were three charming children. At meals everyone sat on one side of a long table, like people in early Italian paintings. The Crane's house in Holland Street was very 'eightyish'; every available place in it was filled with china, pewter and brass, Indian idols, carved figures, plaster casts, model-ships, mummy-cases, soapstone carvings, and other curiosities, while the walls were crowded with blue Nankin plates, Japanese prints and fans, Italian engravings, Morris designs, early portraits of Crane's wife and children, landscape and decorative paintings by Crane himself. Crane's mind was similarly furnished. He was illustrator, painter, designer, craftsman and sculptor by turn; he poured out designs for books, tapestries, stained glass, wall-papers, damasks and cotton fabrics. His mind, perhaps like his house, was too full to be kept dusted and tidy; but he had unusually broad sympathies, and while he followed in the footsteps of Morris and Burne-Jones, he was free from prejudice—his spirit kept open house. I thought my friends unfair to his work. I liked his early portraits, and admired the ease and ability with which he painted landscapes and figures. His skill was extraordinary; he could do anything he wanted, or anyone else wanted. But most of all I admired his children's books. Nowhere is the peculiar character of the mid-Victorian aesthetic movement better interpreted than in these picture-books; and no one has drawn lovelier pictures of childhood and youth than Crane in his song-books. One of my earliest loves was for a lady in *King Luckieboys Party*; but she had formidable rivals in *Mrs Mundi*.

What delightful interiors he invented! and how easily and gracefully his figures moved, indoors and out of doors! Crane drew out of his well-stocked head; he used no models; Mrs Crane disapproved of models. She didn't disapprove of animals, however, and she kept a monkey, and other pets. Crane drew animals extremely well—observe the figures in *The little pigs who went to market* and the mice in *The Fairy Ship*.

As a maker of books Crane was a little master, as great a little master, in my eyes, as Beardsley was, while his range was wider, saner and more human. Like Morris, Crane was a Socialist; and Socialism meant to him, as it did to Morris, a seemlier life for the people; in a Socialist world, men as well as women would be becomingly dressed. Crane would have loved to wear knee breeches and buckled shoes, with the velvet coat and flowing yellow silk tie he did in fact wear. He held no very revolutionary views, his was a friendly, an affectionate mind, and his dreams were of a better-dressed and more beautiful proletariat, their labour interchanged with pageantry, and with dancing and singing to pipe and tabor. Well, there is something to be said on behalf of his dream. If we haven't as yet adopted pastoral dress, I have seen, during the last 40 years, ragged, barefooted boys and sluttish untidy girls vanish from the London pavements; and with dirt and rags, drunkenness, too, disappeared.

293

CHAPTER XXV

ENGLISH PORTRAITS

The National Portrait Gallery I WAS careless about getting or keeping proofs of my Oxford lithographs. When the book was published I could find only half a dozen of the original impressions. One of these was of Pater, and after his death I thought it might be of interest to the National Portrait Gallery, and someone spoke to Cust about it. Cust's reply was characteristic of the time: 'If Rothenstein wants to have a drawing in a gallery, he had better offer one to the Print Room.' Colvin, as a matter of fact, did ask Shannon and myself for some prints—a compliment at that time, when living artists were rarely represented in national collections. But it wouldn't have done me any good, or the National Portrait Gallery any harm, had Cust accepted a proof of Pater's portrait—the only one pulled, apart from the prints which subsequently appeared in the Oxford book. The National Portrait Gallery has now a more enlightened policy; and no one would imagine a young artist suffering from swelled head because he had a single print among its collection.

Pennell reviewed the Oxford book in *The Daily Chronicle* when it came out in 1896, heading his review 'Oxford Caricatures'. Beardsley had written me that Pennell was enthusiastic about the Oxford set; but there was little sign of this in his review. There was talk of a Cambridge set, and MacColl wrote of a plot to get me to Manchester and Liverpool, his brother-in-law, Oliver Elton, being the chief plotter. But nothing came of it, and the following year I proposed to

ROBERT BRIDGES (1897)

Grant Richards, lately become a publisher, to produce a set of drawings which should make a wider appeal.

I began working on these at once, at first drawing people I already knew, at the same time getting introductions to others whom so far I had not met.

My friends were generous in providing the text to accompany the portraits. As I asked people to sit for drawings alone, I clearly could not expose them to unflattering criticism as well; nor indeed to sugary praise. More than once I had to reject text which showed a touch of malice or more than a touch of flattery. My friends made many suggestions as to who my subjects should be.

Henley wished me to include George Wyndham. 'Dear Will Rothenstein,' he wrote, 'George Wyndham will sit to you *chez vous* with pleasure, and he will try to rope in A. J. B. (Mr Balfour). I did not give him your address, so you must write him to 35 Park Lane. Send me a proof of W. E. H. as soon as you can get one pulled.' In any case, he said, Wyndham wanted a drawing. I wrote to Wyndham while he was abroad, and he arranged to sit to me on his return. Unfortunately my list had been made out, and most of the portraits were already done; and I could not find room for George Wyndham. I was a little hurt when, having told Henley of my difficulty, I heard nothing further from Wyndham. He had a charming and gallant character, and it would have been a pleasure to have had him as a sitter.

Robert Bridges was keen that I should include his friend, Canon Dixon. Again I had to explain that the portraits were all arranged. Canon Dixon came to sit notwithstanding— an interesting man, with a long nose and a beard like a goat's, who in early days had been intimately associated with the Pre-Raphaelites.

Robert Bridges also introduced me to Hubert Parry, one of the most attractive men I have ever met. I recall him coming to lunch at my studio when Miss Terry was there. It was Miss Terry's 50th birthday and Hubert Parry said that he too was just turned fifty. They were both in high spirits.

Miss Terry wanted Parry to admire a portrait I had painted
of her son, when he confessed that he himself had never sat
to any artist. She insisted on my making a lithograph of him
which, at Robin Legge's urgent request, was published in
The Musician, of which Legge was editor. I hope it was not
this lithograph that killed the paper, for the number in which
it appeared was the last.

Lady Granby[1] sent me some charming letters about my
drawings. She herself, I thought, did far more gracious
portraits. She tried to get Cecil Rhodes to sit to me while
he was in London, and spoke to Miss Rhodes on the subject.
But Rhodes was much beset, and he left soon afterwards.
I made a drawing of Lady Granby for the *English Portraits*.
From a worldly point of view this was a mistake, for alas, her
interest in me thereafter diminished. I was not surprised that
the drawing failed to please her—I never pretended to be
able to draw beautiful women.

But some of her friends liked it—among them Henley,
who said of course I must include it. Asked if he would
write the text to go with the portrait, he replied:

'I fear I cannot. I know her ladyship only as a friend. Of
her [illegible] and position in society *rien de rien*. I wrote
to Miss Cust to ask her, and she says they are too intimate.
Now I have asked George Wyndham. I will let you know
his views. Come and see Bruce[2] and tell him about Legros.
I very nearly made him buy a landscape when he was still in
town. He has some gorgeous pictures, Corot, Rousseau,
Diaz, Monticelli and especially Jacobus Maris. He won't
affect either Whistler or Degas, either Manet or Monet, so
beware.

Yours ever,
W. E. H.'

Henley was devoted to Rodin, and was one of Legros'

[1] Violet, Duchess of Rutland.
[2] Hamilton Bruce, a well-known collector of pictures.

loyal supporters; he did his best to get people to buy their work. Rodin had made a fine bust of him, of which he was rightly proud. Henley had shocking health, but was uncomplainingly brave. 'I have been severely ill,' he wrote, 'Have taken nothing solid for close on three weeks, and am trying to gather strength enough to crawl into the country.' Again: 'At last a breathing space between Burns (done) and Byron (à commencer) a few days only. What is left of this week in fact—if health holds.'

I used to take prints and drawings to show Henley, who couldn't easily get about, and whose interest in anything to do with art was unfailing. 'I will tell you what to bring when I name a day,' he wrote. 'Anything Regency which you can find in any case and always; perhaps some Horonobu —enfin. Where did Max Beerbohm get his George?' Where, indeed, but from Thackeray's *Four Georges*, and his own head?

Henley was unusually kind over his own portrait I did; so indeed was his wife. Robert Bridges, too, wrote in generous praise. Bridges took much trouble over arranging the Dixon sittings.

'Dixon did not at all like your portrait of me, and I am surprised at his offering himself, but I know that he would like to be in the series—this sort of way of getting into it is of course impossible—except with——. You had better tell him that you have no power to put him in—and then see if he still wishes to sit. He would be good to do—some trouble with the mouth I expect.

'There are of course two sides to everything. I maintain that the devils that were sent into the swine had a school of art there—seeing strange sights.'

A week later he wrote:

Yattendon
Nov. 6, 97

My dear Rothenstein,

I am sure that the Canon would give the sum you mention, which seems to me very moderate, and I am nearly sure that he wants some sort of portrait of himself for his friends. So that if he shd. like the portrait that you have done of me I shall be able to suggest to him that he shd. 'approach' you.

I am glad that you have brought off a sitting from Parry. It is strange that an artist of 50 years shd. still keep his boyish expression, and show so little of his work.

I was at Oxford 2 days ago and saw Warren. What he told me of the 'notice' which is to appear with my portrait rather alarmed me. I am sorry, but can't help it. I explicitly instructed the writer *not* to say anything about my work. It seems that he has gone lengths. Still he said it was a good bit of writing—and I hope to survive its excesses.

I shall be anxious to see it.

Can you tell me if Swinburne is in town? I don't know his address, and I want to see him. If you can help me, I shd. be much obliged.

Oxford was looking magically beautiful in the low sunlight—and at the Botanical Gardens the blue and pink exotic water-lillies were making an unusual show. I rode home over the downs on my bicycle. It was lovely.

Last night we had a fine Guy Fawkes bonfire with a clear flame 11 feet high and G. F. in the middle of it.

Dixon had kindly offered to write the text for the Bridges' portrait, but it seems finally to have been done by Herbert Warren. When Shaw was to send me some lines on Ellen Terry, he wrote: 'On the occasion of the production of *The Silver Key* at the Haymarket three months or so ago, I wrote a lot about Ellen Terry, which ought to do exactly (part of it) for what you want. Will you look at it and see whether it will do; for I feel incapable of writing another word about her; she's a frightfully difficult subject. How soon do you want the stuff anyhow?' With Miss Terry I was no more successful than with Lady Granby; but she was ever partial to me on account of my friendship with Gordon Craig. Who could help loving him? He was so full of life, brimful of ideas, of charm, wit and talent. He was a delightful letter-writer—

W. E. HENLEY (1897)

one of the best—and he had his mother's good looks and irresistible ways.

I tried to draw Irving; the first attempt was a dismal failure. 'I know Sir Henry must be difficult (wrote Miss Terry), but you have given him a *very* grim visage—and his wig fits him not at all! I like the profile however.' But I had another try, a little, but not much, more successful. Pinero, always a conscientious worker, was unable to write the note to accompany the drawing. He answered:

My dear Rothenstein,

Alas, you approach me at a most unfortunate moment. I am hard driven by work, in danger of finding myself seriously behind time, and altogether incapable of thinking of anything but the task to which I am bound. I have not the knack of 'dashing things off', or I would send you what you ask for; everything with me must be well considered and most carefully done—a sure mark of a poor intellect.

It is a great regret to me to have to make you this reply, because I feel the fullest sympathy with you in your work, and hold (of course) Sir Henry Irving in true admiration and affection....

I was much concerned to read of the affront—so I considered it—offered you in Sloane Square, and had prepared myself to take measures this morning. Now your second note has reached me, and I am glad to find that all is well. I am delighted with the kind things you write about the little play.

Believe me,
Yours always truly,
ARTHUR W. PINERO

In great haste.

The 'affront' must refer to some difficulty at the Box Office of the Court Theatre; I can think of nothing else. I fancy the play referred to was *Trelawny of the Wells*.

Pinero was among those I drew for the *English Portraits*;

Max wrote the note on Pinero to go with this drawing. Then came a letter:

*Berkeley Hotel,
Bognor
Sussex*

My dear Will,

I sent you a post-card to your former address. Didn't you get it? Also, the Pinero thing was all right, and I have returned corrected proof, and will give you the MS. safely when you come back to London. Thanks for your entertaining letters. I am glad you are enjoying yourself there. I am having a quiet, but good, time. I don't quite know when I leave—it depends on Murray Carson with whom I am to write a play. Walter Sickert came down here for a day or two and made vague notes for a new caricature of me—which he has since finished and which has been taken by *Vanity Fair*. I don't know when it is to appear—soon, I hope. *You* have not appeared in *Vanity Fair*, my lad! I have been staying with the Harmsworths in Kent—Harmsworth wants to be painted by you. Furse, greatly improved, came down to make arrangements for painting Mrs Harmsworth—and there was much talk of north-lights to be cut in the roof and a white silk dress to be made and a small staircase to be built for Mrs Harmsworth to stand on—the Harmsworths are very charming people—he quite amazing and interesting—Furse seems to regard you with cordial toleration. Harmsworth has a firm belief in young men— that being, I suppose, the reason he asked me whether you charged much. I said your price for full-lengths ranged from £5 to £15—was I right?

The weather over here is rather ghastly....I don't think there's any other news—I have had a great '*succès*' with an attack on Hall Caine in the Daily Mail. I hear that Oscar is under surveillance by the French police—I am afraid he may be playing the fool.

I tell everybody you are on a sketching-tour in Burgundy.

Yours
MAX

300

The 'Pinero thing', like Max's price for a full-length portrait was not *quite* all right. Max could not resist a fling at Pinero. Pinero objected to the text and proposed that William Archer should write in place of Max. 'He, at least writes like a gentleman.'

There was a great party given at the Grafton Galleries by a hundred distinguished women, each of whom was to invite six guests. Nicholson, Max Beerbohm, Jimmy Pryde, Teddy Craig and I were guests of Miss Terry—a great honour I felt this to be. Miss Ailsa Craig came too, wearing as a cloak part of Irving's *Richelieu* dress. Tall and slim, she looked beautiful walking up the steps into the gallery. She came instead of her mother. 'I wonder did I apologise to you for being too ill to meet you at the Grafton Galleries? I should have done so—probably didn't!' I sent Miss Terry a basket of white currants afterwards, a tiny offering. 'I wonder did Ted go to see you yesterday? or did he write and tell you how ill and incapable I have been?' Yes, Teddie had written one of his charming notes.

On the rails leading to Ditton.

I saw my mother 5 minutes after I left you to-day. She is distressed. She cannot come to sit to-morrow, but swears to do so before Wednesday next. Write at once and get her to fix a day. If you knew how dead she feels—her voice nearly all gone and despair in her heart. But of course you understand. She says she got your white currants—which she delights in each year when young. This year yours arrived before she knew they were up and about. Heavens, you've nearly killed me to-day by your strides—not in your art—unless that is ever on the pavement. France—Joy—Burgundy!

Yes   I must come as Chicot to my sun douche—

Ever yours, G. C.

Craig wanted Max and myself to do something for *The Page*:

Dear Will,

You assaulted me, but I forgive you. On that night as Max struck me with his spear and you filled my ears with the vinegar of your laughter and your friends had no pity, I still prayed 'Father, forgive them they know no(t) what the devil they are doing'. I then instructed the cabman. But really—you are thoughtless to take me for a gallant.

I am no gallant and you no gentleman to be noisy at me when with a lady!!

To repair this blunder which is worse than ten thousand crimes send me something to cut for The Page. Some easy considered bit.

Won't Max write a note of *congratulations* (?) to the Queen on her birthday—for the Page. A few lines just to amuse the drooping loyalty of the subscribers.

I do pity them all so!!

Send me one of the Verlaine portraits (lithos) if you can. I should much care to have one.

Post me to *Lyceum Theatre*. The letters always forwarded.

Ever yours affectionately, E. C.

In addition to my painting, these portraits absorbed all my spare time. The first parts of the *English Portraits* were beginning to appear; I was to deliver all the drawings before the end of the year.

Hardy I had met at the Gosses' earlier in the year. He had been to the studio once or twice, and I had made several attempts at a portrait. He took a kindly interest in the new series, and suggested someone, though, I thought, with hesitation, who might be included—Lady Jeune; also, more hopefully, George Gissing. He had lately published *Jude the Obscure*, and was so upset at its reception, that he declared he would never write another novel. The feeling about his picture of Oxford was so strong, he scarcely liked going to the Athenaeum. He described one day how, while he was sitting quietly reading, unobserved as he hoped, he was suddenly aware of the menacing figure of a Bishop striding

302

towards him; now he was in for it, he thought; happily the
Bishop passed him by; but he was always in fear of being
assailed. In future, he said, he would limit himself to writing
verse. I cared deeply for his poems, truth to tell even more
for his poems than for his novels, though this was a taste
then shared by few people; and I thought the simple drawing made by Hardy himself for the *Wessex Poems* dramatic
and moving.

Hardy resented the constant charge of pessimism made
against him; he tried to depict man's life, its beauty and
ugliness, its generosity and meanness. Far from darkening
the picture, had he told the truth about village life, no one
would have stood it, he said. I loved a thing he told about
young trees when first planted—how, the instant their roots
came in contact with the ground, they begin to sigh.

He remarked on the expression of the eyes in the drawing
I made—he knew the look, he said, for he was often taken
for a detective. He had a small dark bilberry eye which he
cocked at you unexpectedly. He was so quiet and unassuming, he somehow put me in mind of a dew-pond on
the Downs.

I took Hardy's advice and approached George Gissing.
I had heard of Gissing from Frederick Harrison, whose sons
Gissing had tutored soon after he left Manchester University.
I liked him very much—a wistful, sensitive nature, a little
saddened, I thought, and perhaps a little lacking in vitality,
but with a tender sense of beauty. He had just come back
from Italy, full of enthusiasm for the loveliness of the Italian
scene; but had met with unexpected sorrow at home, on
hearing that one of his friends, with whom he had spent some
of his happiest hours, had recently come to a tragic end.
A man of rare culture, he said of his friend, with strong
puritanical inhibitions; yet he had certain inclinations against
which he had struggled in vain all his life. On account of
these, and feeling he could fight them no longer, he had
suddenly shot himself. Gissing, much more than Hardy,
seemed obsessed by the melancholy side of life. He was

naturally a man of fastidious tastes, but had never had enough
material success to satisfy them. I met him again while I was
staying with Sickert at a hotel in Newhaven. Gissing came
in looking lonely and depressed. Sickert and I were in our
usual outrageous spirits; and I like to think that we enlivened
Gissing for one long evening, and sent him off next day in
a more cheerful mood.

I asked Mr Hardy whether he would write a few lines on
George Gissing, since he had suggested him as one of the
subjects for the *English Portraits*. He wrote in reply: 'Strange
as it may seem, I have not the requisite knowledge either.
But I think I can help you to some one who could supply
the lines. I send herewith an excellent little "appreciation" of
Mr Gissing's work by Henry James—and I think if you
were to ask him he would shape some of the passages into
what you require; or allow you to do it yourself. He could
do it in a few minutes if willing; and certainly nobody else
could do it so well.'

I doubted Henry James doing anything in a few minutes.
I forget whom I got to write on Gissing; of Henry James
(who at this time wore a beard) I made two drawings. Then
came Sargent.

While I was drawing Sargent he couldn't bear to remain
idle; he puffed and fumed, and directly I had done, he insisted on my sitting to him. He made a drawing on transfer
paper, which was laid down on the stone by Goulding, six
proofs only being pulled. One of these Sargent gave to
Helleu, who asked for it, one went to the Print Room of the
British Museum, and two he gave to me. I asked Henry
James to write a few lines for the Sargent portrait, and had
the following very Jamesian reply:

Bath Hotel, Bournemouth
July 13, 1897

Dear William Rothenstein,

I am afraid I am condemned, in answer to your note, to
inflict on your artistic sense more than one shock; therefore

HENRY JAMES (1897)

let the outrage of this ponderous machinery deaden you a little at the start perhaps to what may follow. I am sorry to say, crudely speaking, that I don't find myself able to promise you anything in the nature of a text for your characterisation of Sargent. Why should not it, this characterisation, be complete in itself? I am sure nothing will be wanting to it. At any rate, the case as it stands with me is fairly simple and expressible: I have written so much and so hyperbolically and so often upon that great man that I scarce feel I have another word to say in public. I must reserve my ecstacies for conversation, at the peril of finding myself convivially silent in the face of future examples. Only the other day, or the other month ago, I sounded the silver trump in an American periodical—I mean on the occasion of his Academy picture. You painters are accustomed to such thunders of applause that the whole preparation for you in these matters is, I know, different. Yet I have thundered myself. After this, how shall I dare to say yes to your still more flattering proposal that I shall lay my own head on the block? You can so easily chop it off to vent any little irritation my impracticability may have caused you. However, please take it as a proof of my complete trust in your magnanimity if I answer: with pleasure—do with me whatever you think I now deserve. Only I fear I shall not be in town with any free day or hour to sit for a goodish while to come. Kindly let the matter stand over till we are gathered together again; but don't doubt meanwhile how delighted I shall be to see the copy of your series which you are so good as to promise me.

Believe me yours most truly,

HENRY JAMES

I drew Cunninghame Graham again for the series. Soon afterwards he returned to Morocco, this time travelling far into the interior, where he was arrested and imprisoned, and his mother was, for a time, very anxious. Then came a reassuring letter:

39 *Chester Square, S.W.*
November 11*th,* 1897

Dear Mr Rothenstein,

I promised to let you know as soon as I should hear of or from Robert.

A telegram came yesterday evening from Tangier, unsigned, and dated the 10th, it was as follows: 'Released by the Sultan, and all right.'

Evidently he has had some dangerous experiences though probably he will have found them very interesting. It is of course a relief to know that he is safe, but I confess I am still anxious to know what he may have had to go through.

I think you will be glad to know that your former travelling companion is as he himself says 'all-right'.

Yours very sincerely,
A. E. BONTINE

The story of Graham's experiences may be read in the remarkable book he wrote, *Mograb-el-Acksa*, a book that is too little known; for it is a classic, I think, of its kind.

Among others, I had approached Seymour Haden, who at once replied, asking me down to stay at Woodcote Manor, a beautiful Tudor house, kept in marvellous order. I had never seen such shining floors, such polished panelling and furniture, bright brass handles and sparkling silver. Haden must surely have been something of a tyrant. He was proud of his position as President of the Painter-Etchers; and if he had a marked sense of his own importance, it must be said that no one, not even Whistler, had a greater European reputation as an etcher than Haden. A big, impressive figure, whose word was law; for this reason, perhaps, Legros and Strang resigned from the Painter-Etchers.

Lady Haden was Whistler's half-sister, a gracious, dignified lady, rather quiet and subdued in manner. When her husband was out of the room, she asked me timidly if I knew her brother, and whether I was one of his supporters or not. She was pleased when I assured her of my ardent devotion; but

AUBREY BEARDSLEY AT THE HÔTEL VOLTAIRE
PARIS (1897)

it was obvious that Whistler's name must not be mentioned in the Haden household.

Haden had strong theories about Rembrandt's etchings, of which he attributed a large number to his pupils. He gave a vivid account of his meeting with Meryon, when Meryon was going out of his mind. He owned Whistler's piano picture, which I now saw for the first time. One of the loveliest of . Whistler's portraits, of Lady Haden in riding dress, called *The Morning Room*, had belonged to him also; but this no doubt he had sold, for I did not see it in the house. His workroom was meticulously orderly. I drew him making a mezzotint. It seems to me now surprising that he should not have seen what I did. Although it is unwise to allow a sitter to see a drawing before it is done, above all an unsatisfactory one, one usually shows the completed drawing; and Seymour Haden, with his dictatorial ways, was scarcely the person to let me carry anything away without first inspecting it. Yet when the print appeared, he wrote that I would be surprised .to hear he had never yet seen the portrait: 'Which I allowed you to take of me, on conditions which your publisher, it seems, has taken upon himself to disregard. This is bad enough, but to add to it, a personal account of me, which I have also neither seen nor consented to, is inexcusable.'

In reply to a letter explaining the position, he said: 'I did not accuse you of not adhering to your engagement to me. I expressed surprise at the high-handed liberty taken by your publisher with my personality, as well as the impropriety of not sending for my approval a copy of what he was saying about me.'

This was not very logical, nor very kind. If Seymour Haden had made an etching of Meryon, or of Whistler, I presume he would have felt himself free to publish it. I had written him of my intention to print a series of portrait drawings, and asked whether he would allow me to make one of him. He had courteously replied: 'I shall be most happy to give you a sitting.' There were no conditions mentioned on either side. He had shown marked interest in my lithographic work; indeed, he wanted me to submit to him, officially, a plea for membership, as a lithographer, of the Painter-Etchers on my return to town, and to approach Shannon with a view to our acting together in this. We had parted with cordial expressions. Still, on the whole I met with far less trouble at this time than I met with at Oxford.

Whistler had promised to sit for one of the *English Portraits*; but when I wrote to remind him he replied, very kindly, that 'the drawings were all right—but the moment was difficult'. He was greatly pushed and at work from morning till dusk. Besides, he thought two Napoleons at a time surely enough. The Napoleons were 'the African filibuster and the apothecary of Hants'. The last clearly was Seymour Haden; may be the first was Rhodes. 'Why then', he added, 'the champion outlander and lithographer?'

For one difficulty I had no one to blame but myself. When Oscar Wilde came out of prison, he went straight over to France. Most of his old friends and acquaintances had shown him the cold shoulder; but for my part I remembered his kindness and encouragement, and how often I had been his guest in happier days. I knew he would feel the need of friendship, and wrote offering to come over if he cared to see any of his old friends, to which he replied:

(*June 7th*, 1897)

From M. Sebastian Melmoth,

Hôtel de la Plage,

Bernaval-sur-Mer,

Dieppe,

Wednesday

My dear good Friend,

I cannot tell you how pleased I was to get your kind and affectionate letter yesterday, and I look forward with real delight to the prospect of seeing you, though it be only for a day. I am going into Dieppe to breakfast with the Stan-

nards, who have been most kind to me, and I will send you
a telegram from there. I so hope you can come tomorrow by
the daily boat, so that you and your friend can dine and sleep
here. There is no one in this little inn but myself, but it is
most comfortable, and the chef, there is a real chef—is an
artist of great distinction; he walks in the evening by the sea
to get ideas for the next day. Is it not sweet of him? I have
taken a chalet for the whole season for £32, so I shall be
able I hope to work again, and write plays or something.

I know, dear Will, you will be pleased to know that I have
not come out of prison an embittered or disappointed man.
On the contrary in many ways I have gained much. I am
not really ashamed of having been in prison; I often was in
more shameful places: but I *am* really ashamed of having led
a life unworthy of an artist. I don't say that Messalina is a
better companion than Sporus, or that one is all right and
the other all wrong: I know simply that a life of definite and
studied materialism, and philosophy of appetite and cynicism,
and a cult of sensual and senseless ease, are bad things for
an artist; they narrow the imagination, and dull the more
delicate sensibilities. I was all wrong, my dear boy, in my
life. I was not getting the best out of me. *Now*, I think that
with good health, and the friendship of a few good, simple
nice fellows like yourself, and a quiet mode of living, with
isolation for thought, and freedom from the endless hunger
for pleasures that wreck the body and imprison the soul—
well, I think I may do things yet, that you all may like. Of
course I have lost much, but still, my dear Will, when I
reckon up all that is *left* to me, the sun and the sea of this
beautiful world; its dawns dim with gold and its nights hung
with silver; many books, and all flowers, and a few good
friends; and a brain and body to which health and power are
not denied—really, I am *rich* when I count up what I still
have; and as for money, my money did me horrible harm.
It wrecked me. I hope just to have enough to enable me to
live simply and write well.

So remember that you will find me in many respects very

A cigarette box happy—and of course by your sweetness in coming to see me, you will bring me happiness along with you.

As for the silent songs on stone, I am charmed at the prospect of having society of yours. It is awfully good of you to think of it. I have had many sweet presents, but none I shall value more than yours.

You ask me if you can bring anything from London. Well, the salt soft air kills my cigarettes, and I have no box in which to keep them. If you are in a millionaire condition and could bring me a box for keeping cigarettes in, it would be a great boon. In Dieppe there is nothing between a trunk and a *bonbonnière*. I do hope to see you to-morrow (Thursday) for dinner and sleep. If not, well Friday morning. I am up now at eight regularly!

I hope you never forget that *but for me* you would not be *Will* Rothenstein: *Artist*. You would simply be *William* Rothenstein, *R.A.* It is one of the most important facts in the history of art.

I look forward greatly to seeing Strangman. His translating 'Lady Windermere' is delightful.

Your sincere friend,
OSCAR WILDE

It was a relief to find that Wilde was not embittered. He had said to me years before that I was right to put creative work before everything else; that an artist needed the strength of a steam-engine if he hoped to achieve what would last. He used to say, that of course life was the object of living; he told a story of Lazarus, whom Jesus had raised from the dead, to illustrate this. Now he admitted the waste of his gifts—the disloyalty to his artist's nature. Alas, he was more broken than at first he imagined he was, and his good resolves were based on a will that was weakened beyond repair.

Wilde met me on the quay at Dieppe. I did not know in what state I should find him, but I saw at once that the meeting would not be embarrassing. He was carrying a heavy

stick, and as I got off the boat and greeted him, saying how
well he was looking, he waved it over his head and exclaimed 'How can you say such a thing; can't you see I am
unable to stand without a stick?' He looked, indeed, sur-
prisingly well, thinner and healthier than heretofore. He was
happy at Bernaval, he assured me, full of plans for the future.
He was staying at an inn kept by M. Bonnet, who was most
attentive to all his wants; but soon, he said, he would take a
small chalet and settle down and write, living carefully
within his means. He had already made friends with his
neighbours; everyone was charming to him. Later he spoke
of his prison experiences, of the horrors of the first few
months, and how by degrees he became reconciled to his
situation. He seemed to have lost none of his old wit and
gaiety. He told how, although talking was strictly forbidden,
one of his warders would exchange a remark with him now
and then. He had a great respect for Oscar as a literary man,
and he did not intend to miss such a chance of improving
himself. He could only get in a few words at a time.

'Excuse me, Sir; but Charles Dickens, Sir, would he be
considered a great writer now, Sir?' To which Oscar replied:
'Oh yes; a great writer, indeed; you see he is no longer alive.'
'Yes, I understand, Sir. Being dead he would be a great
writer, Sir.'

Another time he asked about John Strange Winter.
'Would you tell me what you think of him, Sir?' 'A charm-
ing person,' says Oscar, 'but a lady, you know, not a man.
Not a great stylist, perhaps, but a good, simple story teller.'
'Thank you, Sir, I did not know he was a lady, Sir.'

And a third time: 'Excuse me, Sir, but Marie Corelli,
would she be considered a great writer, Sir?'

'This was more than I could bear,' continued Oscar, 'and
putting my hand on his shoulder I said: "Now don't think
I've anything against her *moral* character, but from the way
she writes *she ought to be here*."' 'You say so, Sir, you say so,'
said the warder, surprised, but respectful. Was ever so grim
a jest made in so strange a situation?

311

He enquired, of course, after his friends; I told him
that Ricketts and Shannon had now become prosperous;
Shannon especially was selling his pictures and getting
portraits to paint. Oscar appeared surprised. 'The dear
Valeists rich!' Then, after a moment's reflection, he said
'When you go to sup with them, I suppose they have *fresh*
eggs now!'

I had brought a few prints to give Wilde, among them one
or two proofs of the portraits I was doing for the Grant
Richards book; it struck me that it would be a delicate and
heartening thing to ask him to write one of the character
sketches. He seemed delighted with the idea, and offered to
write on Henley. He agreed, since the notes were to be
anonymous, that it was essential, firstly, that the criticisms
should not be unflattering, and secondly, that his lines should
not differ noticeably from the rest of the text. He assured
me that he quite understood; but when his letter-press came,
I saw at once how rash I had been:

'He founded a school and has survived all his disciples.
He has always thought too much about himself, which is
wise; and written too much about others, which is foolish.
His prose is the beautiful prose of a poet, and his poetry the
beautiful poetry of a prose-writer. His personality is in-
sistent. To converse with him is a physical no less than an
intellectual recreation. He is never forgotten by his enemies,
and often forgiven by his friends. He has added several new
words to the language, and his style is an open secret. He
has fought a good fight and has had to face every difficulty
except popularity.'

I wished I might use it; but Henley would be furious.
And the authorship would at once have been obvious. It was
an awkward situation; I hated having to reject it, and before
writing to Wilde, I consulted Max Beerbohm. He of course
recognised the quality of the lines, but agreed they would
never do. Oscar was naturally annoyed. In reply to my
letter, explaining that the text would not fit in with the rest
of the letter-press, he replied:

My dear Will,

Of course I only did it to oblige you—my name was not to be appended, nor was there to be any honorarium of any kind. It was to oblige you I did it—but with us, as with you, as with all artists, one's work est à prendre ou à laisser. I couldn't go into the details of coarse and notorious facts. I know Henley edited the National Observer and was a very bitter and in some respects a cowardly socialist in his conduct: I get the historical Review regularly and its silliness and stupidity are beyond words. I am only concerned with the essence of the man, not with his accidents—miry or other.

When I said of W. E. H. that his prose was the prose of a poet, I paid him an undeserved compliment. His prose is jerky, spasmodic, and he is incapable of the beautiful architecture of a long sentence, which is the fine flower of prose writing, but I praised him for the sake of an antithesis 'his poetry is the beautiful poetry of a prose writer'—that refers to Henley's finest work, the Hospital Poems—which are in *vers libres*—and *vers libres* are prose. The author by dividing the lines shows you the rhythm he wishes you to follow. But all that one is concerned with is *literature*; poetry is not finer than prose, nor prose than poetry—when one uses the words poetry and prose one is merely referring to certain technical modes of word-music, the melody and harmony one might say—though they are not exclusive terms—and though I praised Henley too much, too extravagantly, when I said his prose was the beautiful prose of a poet, the latter part of the sentence is a subtle aesthetic appreciation of his *vers libres*, which W. E. H., if he has any critical faculty left, would be the first to appreciate. You seem to me to have misunderstood the sentence—Mallarmé would understand it. But the matter is of no importance. Everybody is greedy of common panegyrics and W. E. H. would much sooner have a long list of his literary failures chronicled with dates.

I am still here, though the wind blows terribly—your lovely lithographs are on my walls, and you will be pleased

313

to hear that I do not propose to ask you to alter them, tho'
I am *not* the editor of a 'paying publication'.

I am delighted to hear that the Monticelli is sold, though
Obach does not say for how much. Dal Young is coming
out here to-morrow and I will tell him. He seems to be
under the impression that he bought it. Of course I know
nothing about the facts of the case....

I don't know where I shall go myself. I am not in the
mood to do the work I want, and I fear I shall never be.
The intense energy of creation has been kicked out of me.
I don't care now to struggle to get back what, when I had
it, gave me little pleasure.

Yours, O. W.

The last paragraph was ominous of what was to come.
Save for the *Ballad of Reading Gaol* his literary life was ended.
Yet he was approached from all sides for plays, and short
stories. When young poets from Paris began to pay him
visits at Bernaval, he fell into the old habit of talking what
he should have written; and what was worse, of drinking
petits verres.

It was Max Beerbohm who wrote on Henley; and, as usual,
he writes prophetically.

Berkeley Hotel,
Bognor,
Sussex

August, 1897

My dear Will,

Many thanks for your letters—I have already corrected
the proofs of Henley's innocence—and despatched them to
Grant Richards—I hope you will think them conclusive—
Also, I return your postal order—I presented it at the Bank
here, but they told me you had no account with them and
referred me to drawer—I protested feebly that you were a
lithographic-painter and could not draw—*enfin*, keep your
absurd piece of paper.

I am much amused by your difficulty with Sebastian—
I thought his lines had some witty things in them—'an open
secret' is lovely—but they were rather too antithetical and
unfriendly—and too obviously written by Oscar—I am glad
it is all right. You will now have a further set of interesting
letters for your collection. 'A few months later, he is in
Burgundy engaging in an animated controversy with the
poet, Oscar Wilde, then but lately released from prison. It
would seem that he considered one of his protégés, William
Henley, to have been unfairly treated in one of those mono-
graphs which' &c &c. I always admire your feeling for
posterity. A paragraph in the *Sketch* satisfies *me*.

I have bought a charming sign-board—a portrait of Dick
Tarlington the harlequin, dancing in an avenue, with a
memorial urn behind him, and a mask and a tambourine at
his feet. It was painted in about 1805—by one 'W. Evans',
whoever he may have been. It is very big and heavy.
I intend writing a very affected essay about it. When do you
come back? Let me know

Yours

MAX

The sign-board hung for long in Max's room at Upper
Berkeley Street; now it is one of the ornaments of his villino
at Rapallo.

Sometime during 1898 appeared Oscar Wilde's *Ballad of
Reading Gaol*. Wilde had previously written some letters to
The Daily Chronicle pleading for a humaner treatment of
prisoners, and these letters were well received. The *Ballad*
had a more mixed reception; there were some who saw
therein little change from the former Wilde, while others
were convinced of the sincerity that prompted the poem.
I had heard Wilde speak of his fellow prisoners; he had
no illusions about their past or their future, but he understood and could sympathise with their weaknesses; and I
knew how much true feeling he put into his poem. Wilde
sent me a copy of the *Ballad*, and in reply to a letter thanking
him for the gift came a generous note:

315

My dear Will,

I cannot tell you how touched I am by your letter, and by all you say of my poem. Why on earth don't you write literary criticisms for papers? I wish the Ballad had fallen into your hands. No one has said things so *sympathiques*, so full of delicate insight, so large, from the point of view of art, as you. Your letter has given me more pleasure, more pride, than anything has done since the poem appeared. Yes: it is something to have made 'a sonnet out of skilly'. (Cunninghame Graham will explain to you what skilly is. You must never know my personal experience.) And I *do* think the whole affair 'realised'—and that is triumph. I hope you will be in Paris sometime this spring, and come and see me. I see by the papers that you are still making mortals immortal—and I wish you were working for a Paris newspaper, and that I could see your work making kiosques lovely.

Ever yours,
OSCAR

There was a remarkable absence of bitterness in Wilde; as Pater said, he always had a phrase, and a happy phrase. Men said that Wilde posed up to the last; I prefer to say that even prison, with its attendant pain and humiliation, failed to break Wilde's spirit; that he was *himself* to the end. He was never a great poet, and suffering couldn't make him one; but in his strikingly intelligent outlook on life and literature, his unfailing sympathy with all conditions of men and his deliciously humorous acceptance of any situation in which he found himself he showed his genius. Watts-Dunton called him 'that harlequin Wilde'. Well, the figure of Harlequin is an immortal one; and on Watts, her solicitor, Fame turned her back, but she looked kindly on Wilde, who had lost all, even his honour. Did not Blake say something to the effect that if a fool would but *believe* in his folly, he would achieve greatness?

316

CHAPTER XXVI

RODIN

WHILE I was engaged on these lithographs, Legros had an itch to revisit Paris and see some of his old friends. Would I go with him? I was always glad of an excuse to go back to Paris; moreover, I had heard from Conder, from Dieppe: 'Aubrey Beardsley left about three weeks ago and I fear is very bad in Paris as he caught cold on arriving.' I gathered from his sister Mabel that he was seriously ill. I found Aubrey staying at a hotel on the Quai Voltaire, much changed, less in appearance—he had always looked delicate —than in character and outlook. All artifice had gone; he was gentle and affectionate, and I realised now how much I cared for him. He had found peace, he said; but how rudderless he had been, how vain; and he spoke wistfully of what he would do if more time were allowed him; spoke with regret, too, of many drawings he had done, and of his anxiety to efface the traces of a self that was now no more. Alas, that this new self, of which he was so poignantly aware, should have so frail a hold! He was going south, to Mentone, to gain fresh strength, though he foresaw, I felt, there was little hope. I had done well to come; but for this, I had never known the Aubrey whom I now loved, and would have continued to love, had he been spared. Perhaps some would say the old Beardsley was the true Beardsley. True as he had been to a former self, the new Aubrey would have been true to a finer self. I had seen a new beauty in his face,

317

felt a new gentleness in his ways; and I believed them due to something other than weakness.

I went to pay my respects to Fantin-Latour, and told him that Legros was in Paris; the idea of two old friends, long separated, keeping up an ancient quarrel, irked me, and I was eager to bring them together again. Legros was willing, but Fantin hung back—'What is the use?' he asked, 'there is nothing to be gained.' He was in a bitter mood, brooding over a recent meeting with Whistler. There had been a knock at his door, and there stood Whistler—Whistler, whom he had not seen for how many years! But, scarcely greeting Fantin, he walked back to a lady outside, saying: 'It's all right, he's here.' Then Whistler brought her with him into the studio, and seeing the *Hommage à Delacroix*, took her up to it. 'Me voilà,' he said of the frock-coated figure in the foreground of the picture, then turned to leave. 'Au revoir Fantin!' and with a wave of the hand Whistler was gone.

I could scarcely credit Fantin's story; he and Whistler had been fellow-students and, for years, devoted friends. It seemed unlike Whistler, usually so courteous, and with his French friends especially, so genial and affectionate. True, when nursing a grievance he was all eyeglass and stone; but with Fantin there had been no quarrel. I was dismayed; but for the moment it was useless to pursue the subject of a meeting with Legros.

I went with Legros to call on Degas. It was delightful to see Degas' pleasure in showing his drawings and paintings, and Legros' interest in seeing them. I have already told how Degas took us into his bedroom to show Legros one of his drawings, hanging between two studies by Ingres.

I returned with Legros to dine at the rue Victor Massé. I recall Degas saying: 'It is not difficult to get life into a six-hours' study, the difficulty is to retain it there in sixty.' In painting his practice was, he said, to keep the darks a little lighter, the lights a little darker, until the final painting. Degas was interested in photography and showed us some photographs taken by firelight. I told him how Turner

318

FANTIN-LATOUR (1897)

believed that photography, then newly discovered, would revolutionise painting—that it would help painters to a new knowledge of light. Legros said that Millais used photography for his portraits—a bad thing, for he came to rely entirely on photographs.

Degas described how Heseltine had been lately to see him—he was after his Ingres drawings, he thought. Never should any of these leave his charge, he declared emphatically; he would keep his collection intact; France should have his pictures after his death, but not Paris. He was looking out for a place not too far from Paris, where he could house it. He had the Dulwich Gallery in mind. Good things were worth taking trouble to see; to-day everything was made too easy; his pictures were well worth a pilgrimage to some quiet village. I was surprised to hear, when, during the war, Degas died, that he had made no such provision as this he spoke of. His collection was to be sold at the Hôtel Drouot.

It was Rodin, of whose eye to business Degas spoke so scornfully, who left his collection to the nation. Legros of course went to visit Rodin; Rodin was his closest friend; and I received an unexpected welcome when I found myself, with Legros, at the studio in the rue de l'Université. I had for long revered Rodin from afar: I had seen him once at the *vernissage* of the Salon, and admired his magnificent head; now I was face to face with the man, and his works.

I had heard of his greatest work, on which he had been engaged for years, *Les Portes d'Enfer*. If I was a little disappointed when I saw the actual work, I didn't confess it to myself: a colossal conception, I had thought, and I imagined a grandiose result. I was more impressed by the Victor Hugo group; the figure of Victor Hugo, nude, and with outstretched arm, was grand and arresting; equally impressive were the attendant Fates. There were other figures and busts on which Bourdelle, then acting as Rodin's assistant, was busy. All these I saw, as I saw Rodin himself, through a prism of hero-worship. Every word Rodin said seemed pregnant with meaning, as I watched him working the clay

319

with his powerful hands. When I drew him I felt I had never seen a grander head. I noticed how strongly the nose was set in the face, how ample its width between the brows, how bold the junction of the forehead with the nose. The eye was small and clear in colour, with a single sweeping crease from the corner of each and over the cheek bone, and the hair grew strongly on his head, like the hair of a horse's mane, like the crest of a Grecian helmet; and again I noticed the powerful hands, with the great thumbs, square-nailed. I think Legros must have told Rodin that I had been helpful to him; for Rodin was more than friendly, and almost embarrassed me by his attention. I must come and stay with him at Meudon, he said, before returning to London. At his house at Meudon I was able to study Rodin's work at my ease. Besides many now well-known pieces, he showed me a cupboard full of *maquettes*, exquisitely modelled. He would take two or three of these and group them together, first in one way and then in another. They gave him ideas for his compositions, he said. Many of his marbles, the works I least cared for, were inspired in this way. Rodin didn't execute these marbles; they were carried out by Italians under his direction; he never did much to them himself. He sold these marbles more easily than the much finer bronzes, and they proved his surest source of income.

The great vogue for Rodin was not yet; indeed, he complained bitterly of neglect, of being passed over, alone among contemporary sculptors, each time a public commission was given.

In the evenings we walked in his garden, and looked down on the Seine and on the distant panorama of Paris, bathed in the warm glow of the evening mist. During a walk, Rodin embarrassed me by remarking: 'People say I think too much about women.' I was going to answer with conventional sympathy—'but how absurd!' when Rodin, after a moment's reflection, added—'yet, after all, what is there more important to think about?'

I was eager to get people in England to realise Rodin's

RODIN IN HIS STUDIO (1897)

genius; Henley and Sargent would support efforts on his
behalf. I was, in fact, able to be of some service to Rodin;
and I call to mind, how, a year or two later, he said: 'I want
to do something for you in return; I have engaged the most
beautiful model in Paris; you shall come and draw her.'
What a charming acknowledgment from an old artist to a
young one, I thought. The model was indeed beautiful.
I drew her—how I longed to draw better!—under Rodin's
approving eye; but his eye was shrewd as well as approving.
For when I asked the lovely creature—what could I do less?—
to dine that evening, she promised to come, but I waited in
vain; and next day I found that Rodin knew all about it. 'She
shall sit for you, mon ami, as often as you please, but no
dining! I have lost too many models that way!'

Rodin was always drawing; he would walk restlessly round
the model, making loose outline drawings in pencil, sometimes adding a light coloured wash. And how he praised her
forms! caressing them with his eyes, and sometimes, too,
with his hand, and drawing my attention to their beauties.
I cared greatly for some early drawings which Rodin showed
me at Meudon. These were very powerful, classical and
romantic at the same time, evoking sculpture which no one,
not even Rodin himself, had attempted. They were magnificent drawings, and I was enthusiastic about them, to
Rodin's surprise—and pleasure, I think. No one, he said, had
thought much of these scraps—certainly not enough to
acquire them. I assured him that English collectors would
jump at the chance, and he confided the drawings to my care.
He would talk constantly of his ideals and his work, sometimes in a curious vein—there was an element of the Tantric
spirit in Rodin. But usually his talk was of the illimitable
perfection of nature; of praising nature he never tired. He
talked always of the Greeks; yet his sculpture, I now feel,
has more in common with the Indian spirit than with the
Greek. The calm Greek temper—with its ideal of $\mu\eta\delta\grave{\epsilon}\nu\ \mathring{\alpha}\gamma\alpha\nu$,
though he little suspected this, was directly opposed to his
temperament.

321

I was to see much of Rodin in after years, when he had become famous. At this time his friendship seemed a unique and wonderful privilege; a new asset in my life. Staying at Meudon, I became intimate almost at once with his mind, his vision and his art; he showed not his own work only, but the Greek marbles he was beginning to acquire; and since he seemed to take my artistic sensibility for granted, he gave free expression to his aesthetic views. These were often clear and emphatic—he was by temperament an objective artist. But his talk was sometimes vague and mystical, especially with critics and journalists. Perhaps because of this mysticism he held Carrière to be a great painter, greater than Degas, he believed. He owned several paintings by Carrière; others by Monet, by Sargent and by Alexander Harrison. He did full justice to Sargent's virtuosity and power; indeed, he spoke of him more generously than Sargent's friends were wont to do. To me Rodin's work combined an impassioned interest in tense and nervous form with a poetical vision—an artist's poetry. And, let it be confessed, there was added a certain paganism, a sensuality, a preoccupation with unusual sexual subject matter, a side of his temperament which became almost abnormally developed—which readily appeals to a young mind. He spoke to me of my own work, which was bound, he warned me, to be misunderstood. But never despair, and above all, never destroy; put every drawing in a drawer, some day it will serve. And I left him with an added self-respect, with an increased pride in being an artist, and with stricter resolutions to keep the small flame sheltered and constantly fed.

Maybe there are works by Rodin that will not survive the challenge of time; maybe the form, and the passion and poetry that inspire his form, convince less to-day than they did yesterday; none the less, Rodin is likely to remain one of the great European figures of his century. His influence coloured an epoch; no sculpture of the early part of this century but bore its traces.

I returned home with drawings of Rodin, of Fantin-

STUDY BY RODIN

Latour and of Beardsley—the last, I felt, I should ever make of Beardsley. I was also the richer by a lithograph of himself which Fantin gave me, and an early drawing by Rodin, also a gift. Beardsley thought the drawings of Rodin and Fantin-Latour and the one of himself an improvement on any I had yet done. Looking back, I think it was a propitious time, such as comes, perhaps, every ten years or so; a lucky moment when something crystallises into a more or less final form. This happens to most artists no doubt; but they recognise it only in retrospect.

Rodin was generous in his praise of the proofs I sent him: 'Mon cher ami,' he wrote, 'J'ai reçu un magnifique portrait et j'en suis très reconnaissant. Notre maître Legros a dû le trouver bien. Merci, ami, d'avoir fait ma commission à Henley.' I made a small medallion of Rodin. He refers to some delay in acknowledging it, and writes of the bad state of his affairs: 'quelles excuses je dois vous faire car vous ne savez que penser. Mais j'ai très certainement votre indulgence; ma position est si mauvaise que je suis accablé. Que votre medaillon m'a fait plaisir, et que je vous suis reconnaissant comme sculpteur et comme ami. Vous avez bien voulu encore ajouter un bronze qui m'a fait plaisir aussi; et pour la sculpture et pour l'intention. Pardonnez donc moi et pensez que mon cœur est à vous.' By way of return, Rodin sent me a plaster of a satyr carrying off a woman. About this plaster he wrote '*le petit plâtre ne sortira pas de chez vous*...vous me rendrez très heureux quand je reçois vos amis qui deviennent les miens. Votre amour de l'art est une des grandes règles de notre vie, et c'est cela qui nous a familiarisés si vite ensemble, aussi l'amitié de Legros pour nous deux'.

Rodin spoke to me later about his plaster figures. He feared that some day the friends to whom he gave them might get them recast, and dispose of them as bronzes. Rodin insisted that they were not suitable for casting. He expressed himself strongly on this subject, and begged me to keep his views in mind if ever I saw casts of this kind. It

Rodin forgeries happened that recently a bronze made from a plaster cast was offered to the Tate Gallery, and I was able to detect its spurious quality. I am told that many bronzes of this kind are now offered in Paris as originals, as if cast for, and approved by, Rodin himself. But no artist can be protected, after his death, from exploitation or forgery.

CHAPTER XXVII

APPEARANCE AND PAINTING

I WAS now exhibiting regularly at the New English Art *New methods*
Club. When I left Julian's my painting was slight in
quality and low in tone; now I was attempting a more solid
and a more luminous method.

My sympathies were with the Realists; but I felt there was
something accidental, a want of motive and of dignity, in
contemporary painting. To achieve the vitality which results
from direct contact with nature, with nature's final simplicity
and radiance—how unattainable! yet only by aiming at an
impossible perfection is possible perfection to be reached.

I knew myself to be wanting in imagination; yet I most
admired imaginative painters. Some artists—like Lavery for
instance—say that painting is good enough for them—all else
is 'literature'. The Louvre and the National Gallery show
that the most perfect painters have the richest minds; or to
state it in another way: those gifted with the greatest intellectual powers prove to be also the greatest craftsmen.

But I was possessed with the faith that if I concerned
myself wholly with appearance, something of the mystery
of life might creep into my work. At rare moments, while
painting, I have felt myself caught, as it were, in a kind of
cosmic rhythm; but such experiences are usually all too brief.
I was no philosopher like Fry; but nothing seemed profounder to me than appearance. Through devotion to appearance we may even interpret a reality which is beyond
our conscious understanding; in this, to my mind, lies the

325

supreme importance of the painter's art. No good artist copies merely to imitate; but because form is the discipline imposed on the universe by the hidden God, *Thy will, not mine*, is good aesthetic, as it is good moral, law. The statement 'God made man in his own image' is pregnant. Copy the image of man and you approach the face of God. Perhaps external beauty is not, after all, a merely superficial thing, but a significant answer to man's questioning of the why and wherefore of life.

I cared little for the theory of Impressionism; the methods of Seurat, Signac and von Rysselbergh seemed to me too doctrinaire to capture the dynamic character of nature. For what is technique but a net, laid to catch all the truth it will hold? and if the net be too apparent, truth that is shy and elusive is not to be caught.

I have retained my faith in the significance of appearance, and the hope that at rare moments some of that ecstasy embodies itself in my work. Not that I think raw nature is good; but nature remains the greatest of all designers, resolving her infinite detail into the austere lines of the hills, or the bewildering maze of branches into the simple contours of a tree. Man's own sense of design is derived of necessity from hers. It is nonsense to talk of 'mere realism'. Appearance is dynamic, not static; the clouds move across the heavens, trees bow before the wind, human features alter with every movement; the waves of the sea, the birds in their flight, the flowers bending in the field, change their forms from one moment to the next; each change makes a new rhythm, and without rhythm, an essential part of reality, the work of man's hands is lifeless, and comes to naught.

CHAPTER XXVIII

LIBER JUNIORUM

THE *English Portraits* duly appeared in book form; but there was no great demand for them. Only a proportion of the edition of 750 copies was bound up. Later, most of the remaining parts (they were first issued in paper covers, two at a time, like the Oxford portraits) were destroyed in a fire at Leightons', the binders. Robert Bridges wrote me two kind letters from Yattendon. The first was dated April 9, 1898:

Appearance of 'English Portraits'

'I have owed you a letter for a long time, but this month I have been busier than ever. We have all been down in Cornwall, staying in a house on the Helford river W. of Falmouth. I don't know if you know that country, the private houses are most of them (as ours was) built unpretentiously sunk in the heads of the glens which run steeply down some 200 feet to the sea. In the glens anything will grow. In our garden the camellias were in profuse bloom, and rhododendrons and laurels. With all sorts of foreign greenery such as date-palms, treeferns and bamboos. This all means a very mild and moist climate, but we saw some of the snow and had a good deal of cold wind—also we all got influenza, which has ravaged there this year, and it rather spoilt our time which I had intended to spend on the water. Fortunately the pest was only a thing of a few days, and we are now come home to be fixed at Yattendon.

'I was very busy all the month with some work which took all my attention, and this must excuse my silence.

327

I wrote no letters that I cd put off, and was lucky in getting through my work.

'I have to thank you for sending me the last number of the portraits. It is really very good of you to send them. I like to have them very much, but I don't see that I deserve them: unless indeed I promised you to subscribe to the series. If so, please tell me. I wonder whether they sell well. It amuses me to see what sort of company I am in. I like your portrait of Gissing, he looks a very good fellow. I read only one of his books—because I didn't much care for that, the manner of it, he seemed to be floundering in the mud, but I see it is not mentioned among his chefs d'œuvre. As for the other man I have always considered him as a pretentious ass—but no doubt this is very wrong of me. Since your visit here Wm. Strang has sat in the study, and (at Binyon's connivance) done an etching of me. Have you seen it? It seems to me a good piece of work, but whenever I venture to gaze upon your and his portraits of me, as I feel it is sometimes my duty to do, I find that I am quite a different person from anything that I imagined. Now this sinks into my soul, and it shd affect my general views of life, and my poetry.

'I see that Frank Harris is writing on Shakespeare in the Saturday. All very good in its way, and shows an unexpectedly delightful appreciation of poetry, but his explanation is on the wrong lines. Shakespeare in characterising his people wished to make them interesting and beautiful, and the only reasonable course was to colour them with what he accounted most interesting and beautiful, F H thinks by noting the "unintentional"! predominance of certain colours to arrive at Shakespeare's character or philosophy. Surely from the art of his ethic one may find the ethic of his art and no more?—But perhaps you haven't read F. H.

'Your portrait of me was well received in America by a friend to whom I send it.'

The second letter, dated June 2, 1898, came when the book appeared:

'I have duly received the completion of the E. Portraits, and am most grateful to you for the presentation. The book will always be of value and interest. And this morning, with your letter, I have a copy of your portrait of Canon Dixon from him. I am framing it. I like it, but I shall not know how much, till I have had it by me for a while. It is certainly a good likeness, and one which I am extremely glad to possess. It seems to me that you are getting on well, and I shall expect you to become a master in a fine style of portraiture. Strang's portrait of me had the disadvantage of not being very like me. My friends prefer yours, tho' they all say that you have given me too much nose.

'Yeats I know. He has been here, and we want him here again—he is a true poet, and delightful company, but he is in great danger of fooling himself with Rosicrucianism and folk lore and erotical spiritualisms. It is just possible that he may recover—some of his work is of the very best, both poetry and prose.

'I was in town last week for one night, for a concert. I saw the "Milanese" pictures at the Burlington Fine Arts Club. There is a *very* fine Leonardo (?), a woman, pagan, with a wreath of flowers, belonging to Chas Morrison, worth going to see —with some other good things among a lot of school stuff.

'The weather is miserable. I am sitting over a good fire— but the rain is not unwelcome if it wd only be warmer. If any time this Summer you can spare us a Sunday from London we shall be delighted to do our best to entertain you.'

I remember Oscar Wilde laughing when I told him that Robert Bridges alone had written me—that I rather expected to hear from others whose portraits appeared in the book. 'Simple Will!' he said. But I have felt much in the same way over each book of the kind.

After the *English Portraits* I published a set of portraits of younger men—*Liber Juniorum* I called it. This portfolio of prints was distinguished for one thing—no single copy of it was sold. It contained prints of Beardsley, Binyon,

Laurence Housman, Max Beerbohm, Yeats and Stephen
Phillips. I find a letter from Arthur Symons, with whom
I evidently discussed the collection: 'I have been thinking
over the *Liber Juniorum* and discussing it with Yeats, and we
both strongly feel that Watson and Davidson should *certainly*
form part of it. Why not then a dozen somewhat thus:

1. Watson	5. Horne	9. Housman
2. Davidson	6. Savage	10. Stephen Phillips
3. F. Thompson	7. Lionel Johnson	11. Binyon
4. Yeats	8. Dowson	12. A. S.

'This at once gives more weight, and allows more chance
for the one or two names which *we* think interesting but
editors may not.

'I find I have forgotten Max. I fear Dowson or Binyon
might have to go if you want the dozen.'

Housman was Laurence, not his brother A. E.; I wonder
what the present juniors think of the list.

The *Liber Juniorum* was followed by a French set which
had little more success—Legros, Fantin-Latour and Rodin—
a companion to the *Three Portraits of Verlaine* which Hacon
and Ricketts issued from the Vale Press, every copy of which
was subscribed; for 1898 was a busy year.

These portraits, like the *English Portraits*, were, as might
be expected, of unequal quality. The success of a portrait
drawing depends on many fortuitous things, on the quality
of paper and chalk, on the artist's mood at the time, but
mostly on the sitter. For the sitter helps to make or mar his
own portrait; some, the moment they pose, excite one's
pencil; others paralyse the will; some, again, cannot keep
a pose, while others, especially old people, must be kept
interested.

Sometimes, too, one is tempted to talk, and talking while
at work has spoilt many a drawing. Men, equally with
women, wish to appear other than they are—the mirror

won't lie, but the artist may be persuaded; yet if he compromises over form, his drawing suffers. Englishmen especially seem ashamed of their features; foreigners seem less sensitive about supposed defects. I have noticed too that men who affect to admire Holbein or Rembrandt are often shocked at a faithful presentment of themselves. Great works of art rarely affect their possessor's taste. What pictures have I not been asked to admire in the boudoir, in houses where Rembrandt and Bellini hang in the drawing room!

O collectors, O museum directors and other experts, your familiarity with art, the complacency and familiarity with which you speak of masterpieces, sometimes make me long to say 'Down on your knees' before a work even by a good living artist. The essential difference between the artist and the student of art lies in this: the artist is, above all other men, a man of action. For he acts each day without any action being demanded of him; and the act of creation calls for supreme energy, will and sustained effort; and this not for days, but for weeks, months, years—in fact for a lifetime. In comparison with this exercise of will, how rarely is the so-called man of action required to exercise all his faculties. It is not appreciation nor industrious scholarship; it is creative energy alone which keeps beauty immortal. To know about things is less difficult than to do them.

CHAPTER XXIX

NEWCOMERS, AND GOOD-BYE
TO WHISTLER

Fitzroy Street IN 1899 my brother Albert came to London; he also was to enter the Slade School. He was 16, the age at which I too left Bradford. I found a room for him at Mackmurdo's house in Fitzroy Street. Fitzroy Street was then a fashionable unfashionable artists' quarter; Whistler's studio was in Fitzroy Street; Sickert was shortly to migrate there. Brangwyn had until lately a studio in Mackmurdo's house; it was an Adam house, with large lofty rooms. Selwyn Image and his wife now had rooms there; so had Henry Carte and his son Geoffrey. They all had meals together at an ancient oak table, without a cloth, of course; in the middle stood a plaster figure, and four bowls of bay which, I noticed, were covered with dust. Mackmurdo believed in the simple life. He was also very unworldly, and had let a room to my brother, and to someone else, at the same time. This was awkward for each of the tenants; Mackmurdo saw this, too, and in the end my brother got the room to himself.

My brother soon became a favourite at the Slade; Brown, Tonks and Steer thought his work promising. He often spoke of two of his fellow-students who had entered the Slade before him, who drew, he said, like the old masters: John and Orpen were their names. I thought the praise was excessive, but was curious about them, so he brought them to see me. Orpen, a young Irishman, was small and shy, spoke little, called me 'sir', and looked long and carefully at

my paintings. He had grey eyes, thin rather sunken cheeks, John and Orpen
and thick brown hair, and he wore a light jacket, cut round at the Slade
at the neck, with no lappels—the kind of jacket engineers
buy in the East End. Orpen was my brother's particular
friend. John was a more arresting figure; he looked like a
young faun; he had beautiful eyes, almond-shaped and with
lids defined like those Leonardo drew, a short nose, broad
cheek-bones, while over a fine forehead fell thick brown
hair, parted in the middle. He wore a light curling beard (he
had never shaved) and his figure was lithe and elegant. I was
at once attracted to John. He brought me his drawings,
which were truly remarkable; so remarkable that they put
mine, and Shannon's too, into the shade. Here was some one
likely to do great work; for not only were his drawings of
heads and of the nude masterly; he poured out compositions
with extraordinary ease; he had the copiousness which goes
with genius, and he himself had the eager understanding, the
imagination, the readiness for intellectual and physical adventure one associates with genius. A dangerous breaker
of hearts, he would be, I thought, with his looks and his
ardour. He talked of leaving the Slade, and was full of plans
for future work; but he was poor and needed money for
models. I showed his drawings to Sargent, Furse, Conder
and Harrison; Furse chose a number of his drawings, but
was taken aback when John asked £2 for each of his nudes.
This seemed a modest price, but Furse hadn't expected a
student to ask so much. Frederick Brown and Harrison
bought drawings too, and John was able to take a small
studio.

John sometimes came with a friend, Ambrose McEvoy,
who had recently left the Slade, and was now copying a
Titian in the National Gallery. McEvoy's father had been
in the Confederate army, and was a friend of Whistler. While
John was influenced by Watteau and Rembrandt, McEvoy
was more in sympathy with the early Italians and the English
Pre-Raphaelites. He looked like a Pre-Raphaelite, with his
strikingly large eyes in a long, angular face; and he spoke in

an odd, cracked voice. I used to call John, Orpen and my brother Albert the Three Musketeers; they were always together. Not content with working all day, they used to meet in some studio and draw at night. They picked up strange and unusual models; but I was shy, after seeing John's brilliant nudes, of drawing in his company. It was stupid of me to feel so; I would have done well to practise drawing too at night. John drew nudes as no one, I thought, had drawn them in England, and his drawings of heads were remarkably fine. John's sister Gwen, a Slade student too, was also very gifted, and round these two a brilliant circle of young women gathered: Edna Waugh (now Mrs Clarke Hall), Mary Edwards, who married McEvoy, Grace Westry, Ida Nettleship, who became John's wife, Louise Salaman, Ursula Tyrwhit and Gwen Salmond (now Mrs Mathew Smith). All these fair ladies sat to John—Edna Waugh and Ida Nettleship most often; and John did their beauty full justice. Orpen, too, was a brilliant draughtsman; Conder preferred Orpen's work to John's, while for me John's drawings had more magic. John's intellect, too, was subtle and complex. He found strange people, men and women, whose surprising character or beauty he revealed in his drawings. At the Slade John was the dominating figure; whatever style he adopted, whether that of Rubens, Michael Angelo, Rembrandt or Watteau, it was imitated by all the students. Later Tonks was to develop a more thorough and scientific method than John's; but at this time John's influence was paramount.

Tonks had a story that John was quiet, methodical and by no means remarkable when he first came to the Slade. Then, while diving at Tenby (his native town) he struck his head on a rock, and came out of the water—a genius! Tonks and Steer were rather critical of John's 'genius'. For Moore didn't wear his hair long; nor did Sargent, nor indeed did either Tonks or Steer. Let an artist's work be remarkable; but he himself in their view should pass unnoticed. I thought John's appearance was splendid, and I didn't want him to

W. B. YEATS (1898)

look otherwise. Long hair, shabby clothes, even affectation
may protect an artist from idle, or so-called fashionable,
people. When an artist goes into their world, he risks his
pride and integrity. Better remain unwashed, than be wasted
on fools; better spend his evenings in cafés, than waste
them on lionising hostesses. How profound is Max's story
of Maltby haunted by the ghost, not of someone long dead,
but of his own snobbishness! It is well for the artist, like
Balzac's d'Arthez, to remain aloof until his work has earned
him a secure position in any company.

But at this time there seemed little prospect of John being
lionised. He and Orpen had discovered a troupe of street
acrobats, among which was a strange, fascinating young girl.
She might have walked out of the pages of Heine's *Florentine
Nights*, so elusively attractive was she. John and Orpen
made many drawings of her, then she disappeared, like
De Quincey's Anne, and they never saw her again.

Through Miss Terry, Henry Irving and the Trees, I got
many tickets for first nights in those days, and saw many
plays. When Pinero's *Trelawny of the Wells* was put on at
the Court Theatre, I went with Sickert to see this enchanting
piece. Here was a play which seemed written for our delight.
What fun it all was; and how enchanting the costumes! and
such a chance it provided that Sickert asked Miss Hilda
Spong—a magnificent creature who acted a part—to sit for
him; while I approached Irene Vanbrugh. Miss Vanbrugh
took infinite trouble, and endured many sittings. Sickert had
Miss Spong photographed, and from a small print and with
few sittings he achieved a life-size portrait. Miss Vanbrugh's
portrait I sent to the first exhibition of the International
Society.

This new society was started under Whistler's Presidency.
A committee was formed, with Alfred Gilbert as Chairman;
Guthrie, Lavery, Strang, Ricketts, Shannon, besides myself,
were among those invited to serve. Gilbert was charming
and considerate, and all went well until Whistler wrote
from Paris proposing that Pennell and Ludovici should be

co-opted on to the Executive. Ricketts and Shannon objected; Pennell was then writing art criticism for *The Star* under the initials A. U., which stood for 'Artist Unknown' (I used to say that his *nom de plume* would serve as his epitaph), and neither he nor Ludovici was taken seriously as an artist. But they were both his faithful followers, and Whistler insisted; the committee gave way, and I left with Ricketts and Shannon. Later Ricketts and Shannon returned, and became the most active and influential members of the Society.

It was to be a brilliant affair—Degas, Rodin and all the best foreign artists were to be invited to send works. The ice-skating rink at Knightsbridge, which was the most fashionable meeting-place of the day, was to be transformed into a gallery. Admiral Maxse, the hero of Meredith's *Nevil Beauchamp*, who was closely associated with the skating rink, was enthusiastic about the exhibition.

The first exhibition was certainly a remarkable one. Whistler showed some of his latest paintings: *The Black-smith*, and *The Rose of Lyme Regis*. There was a collection of Degas' work, and many other important French paintings. The success of the show was largely due, I think, to Francis Howard. There was to be an illustrated catalogue; but this was held up because one of Degas' paintings was reproduced before his permission had been obtained. Hearing of this he refused to sanction any such reproduction. Lavery wrote to me 'unless Degas' permission is got the plate and all the prints that have been done from it will have to be destroyed. It occurred to me that as you are a personal friend, you might see him and use your influence. I am sure he need only know that the thing is an affair of the artist and not of the dealer or middle-man, to give his consent.' When I next saw Degas he was furious, not so much about the reproduction, but because works of his had been exhibited against his wish. For Degas had a rooted objection to showing at current exhibitions. He advised me, too, to refrain from doing so. 'Show in colour shops, in restaurants—anywhere but at the brothels that picture shows are,' he advised me.

MISS IRENE VANBRUGH AS ROSE TRELAWNY

Neither Steer nor Sickert showed at the International. Meanwhile Sickert was becoming more and more estranged from Whistler. He found occasion for an attack on Pennell, who called his drawings, made on transfer paper, true lithographs. Whistler chose to regard Sickert's comments on Pennell as a veiled onslaught upon his own methods. He saw his chance, and induced Pennell to bring an action for libel against Sickert. Sickert's attack on Pennell had appeared in *The Saturday Review,* and Frank Harris promised to stand by Sickert and see him through. I at once offered Sickert my support, knowing that this action might well spell financial ruin in his case. Though my early drawings had been done directly on the stone, the greater number of my lithographed portraits were drawn on transfer paper, and I knew what risk I ran as a witness.

Soon after proceedings were instituted a telegram came from Whistler, asking me to go and see him in his studio in Fitzroy Street. When I got there Whistler talked for some time about things in general and then suddenly said: 'What is this I hear, Parson, that you are going to be on the wrong side?' I explained that I was devoted to Sickert, that he was an old and close friend; that he, Whistler, was a powerful person needing no support, and that I felt it right to do everything possible for Sickert. Whistler, forgetting that he was trying to ruin Sickert, suddenly became jealous. 'But I have known Walter longer than you have,' he drawled.

When the case came on, Sir Edward Clarke was counsel for Pennell. Among Sickert's witnesses was George Moore. He had begged to be allowed to give evidence, but never did anyone cut so poor a figure in the witness-box. When he was pressed regarding his knowledge of lithography he was completely at a loss. Finding nothing to say he at last stammered: 'But I have known Degas.' He was of little use I fear to Sickert. I was called later and severely questioned by Clarke; finally he handed me a set of my *Oxford Characters* and asked what I called them. I said that I had called them lithographs, but in the true sense of the word they were

lithographed drawings, and that is how I should have described them. Pennell says in his *Life of Whistler* that I fell
over my hat as I left the box.

During his cross-examination, Sickert suavely admitted
that there was a spice of malice in his article. Clarke, satisfied
with this, at once sat down. Pennell won his case and Harris,
true to his word, stood most of the racket. Sickert, though
his share of the expenses took most of his capital, bore no
malice against Pennell; and Whistler was so pleased with
winning the case—he considered it his case—that he too
forgot the affront. I dined with him shortly afterwards—he
was radiant. Helleu and little Jonathan Sturges were of the
party. Returning with me, Sturges talked with enthusiasm
of Whistler. 'You never get to the end of his knowledge,'
he said. 'Why, Jimmy never let on to me that he was a
classical scholar; yet there he is, he knows everything; did
you notice during dinner, he said "hinc illae lachrymae"?
amazing! *Am*azing!'

But this was, I think, the last time I was Whistler's guest.
Some time afterwards Sir William Eden decided to sell a
part of his collection of modern paintings and drawings
at Christie's; among these were several by Sickert, Steer,
Conder and myself. Steer was somewhat alarmed at our
works coming up at Christie's. He knew that they would
fetch insignificant sums; he thought Eden should be asked
to put a small reserve on our work. Eden agreed, and Steer
and I went to Christie's to meet him. While we were talking
with Eden, Whistler came into Christie's, put up his eye-
glass, stared hard at us, and then turned his back. We were
seen in Eden's company; therefore we had become 'enemies'.
There were limits to the price one should pay for Whistler's
friendship. I felt that explanation would be useless and un-
dignified. I never saw Whistler again.

CHAPTER XXX

THE END OF THE CENTURY

I DID not care much for my studio in Chelsea, and before the end of the year 1898 I found a small house in Kensington which pleased me, with a tiny cottage—a relic of the time when Kensington was a village—at the end of the garden. I went to see the landlord, a shrunken little man, wearing stays and high-heeled shoes, a person of startling appearance, but otherwise sordid and commonplace. The rent of the house was modest, only £50 a year, and I succeeded in getting the cottage, which was to be my studio, for £20 more. I was delighted with the garden: a garden of one's own in London, however small, is a precious thing. The little house was just off Edwardes Square; the houses there were built by French prisoners during the Napoleonic wars, I had heard.

A garden of my own

Opposite to me lived J. R. Lorimer, and a few doors away Andrew Bradley lodged; and nearby Henry Ford, the illustrator of Andrew Lang's fairy books, and Adrian Stokes and his Austrian wife occupied studios in the Square. In Pembroke Gardens lived Mrs Sickert, Walter's mother, with her sons, Bernard, Oswald, Robert and Leonard. Old Mr Sickert, a good, solid painter, well trained and efficient, as artists were in his time, had come to England from Munich with his young wife and family. Mrs Sickert was English, but she had acquired the kindly, patient, South-German ways. She was proud of her sons, and, happily for me, affectionately disposed towards their friends. Her house was full of her late husband's pictures; there was a portrait of old

339

Mr Sickert by Scholderer, which I greatly admired, and a
life-size painting of Walter as a child, by Füssli (a grandson
of old Fuseli) and a later, very ideal looking, portrait of
Walter with long, fair hair, by his father, I think. A few
doors away lived the Mackails; in Earl's Terrace were the
Henry Newbolts, while on the other side of the High Street
was Pringle Nichol (the son of Swinburne's old friend, John
Nichol) who, but for his inveterate idleness, should have
made his mark as a writer. So I didn't mind leaving Chelsea,
having pleasant neighbours enough in Edwardes Square.
Here I began a self-portrait, and got John to come and sit for
a painting.

I became more and more attached to John, and to his
wonderful intellect, superior in its range to that of anyone
else I knew. While his drawings and pastels got better and
better, his painting was still uncertain; he found it difficult to
control his palette, but now and again he gave promise of
astonishing genius. And what a draughtsman he was! Yet
it was hard to persuade collectors to buy his drawings. It was
not so much the indifference of the critics, of artists and collectors that angered me, as their constant assertion that John
couldn't draw, that his work was 'ugly'. These lovely things
badly drawn and ugly! were people blind? So John often
needed his friends' help:

'Its very nice of you to remember my penury. I've eva-
cuated my kopje in Charlotte Street, trekked and laagered up
at the above; strongly fortified but scantily supplied.
Generals Lawrence & Young hover at my rear. With your
timely reinforcement I hope to hold on till next Friday when
the home supplies are due. The garrison in excellent spirits.'

And Sickert too found it hard to live. He was now living
at Dieppe, working on small canvases and panels, which he
sold with difficulty, and for such small prices, that when he
sent over a number to Carfax, and Sir William Eden offered
£20 for three of his paintings, Sickert pressed us to accept.
Yet Sickert knew the value of his work well enough: 'I wish
you could see my table piled up with drawings of music-

halls, etc. Funny to think of a S—— drawing, and one
of mine, and their relative importance.' And again he wrote:
'I want another fortnight here to finish 4 or 5 pictures as
good as *Noctes Ambrosianae*, only red and blue places,
instead of black ones: The Eldorado, The Gaieté Roche-
chouart, the Théâtre de Montmartre.' The *Noctes Ambrosianae* long hung at Carfax, priced at £40. But no one
grumbled less than Sickert. His letters are full of fun, and
of plans for his future and for mine. 'I think we might
follow the Ricketts and Shannon plan and mutually confide
in each other our poor opinion of all but ourselves,' he
wrote. 'I do wish you well, *de bon cœur*. Partly affection,
partly because you are so small and so devilish earnest,
partly because of the *têtes* your success will make to all the
other damned fools.'

Whenever Sickert went to Paris, he saw Degas. 'I wish
you could see what Degas is doing now. He asked affectionately after you, in spite of his *Judenhetze* monomania. His
work seems to me absolutely sublime. He is doing some
things on a large scale.' And again: 'Degas and others; we
talked of you. I told Stchoukine you were doing an *étude sur
Goya* and would like to see his pictures. Degas said "Vous
êtes heureux de colliger les Espagnols, parce que il n'y en a
pas." Quel dommage, he said of Whistler, qu'un peintre si
fin soit doublé d'un "humbug", using the English word.'

Sickert used to see Whistler at Dieppe, in the Grande Rue,
'looking very well and very dignified' or else lunching at
Lefèvre's, where he was also painting a little panel, sending
constantly for Arnold Hannay to come and talk to him. But
of Conder, Sickert disapproved. 'Conder I think has disappeared, which relieves me. I can't drink and I am a snob.
Whistler's doctor has forbidden him to paint out of doors,
has told him it is at the risk of his life. He gets such attacks
of influenza. Poor old Jimmy. It was all such fun 20 years
ago.'

Of his troubles Sickert said but little. But Jacques Blanche
wrote, while we were at Vattetot:

*Château du Fosse
par Farges-les-Eaux,
Seine Infre.*

24 juillet 99.

Cher Rothenstein

Je vous sais, comme moi-même, ami et très ami de notre charmant Walter Sickert et je vous demande la permission de venir vous parler de lui. Vous savez sans doute qu'il a passé un mois à Auteuil avec nous; il est arrivé dans un état de dépression morale et physique, tout à fait déplorable et je l'ai vu de *si près*, qu'il me semble mieux le connaître et pouvoir le soutenir....

Walter est un vrai enfant, sous certains rapports pratiques, et je crains beaucoup qu'il ne se fixe à Dieppe et s'y enlise, comme dans un sable profond.... Je l'ai engagé à venir passer plusieurs mois chez moi. J'essaierai de lui faire faire une exposition chez Bernheim ou Durand-Ruel: il a *beaucoup* de talent, quand il ne se lance pas dans de trop grandes toiles. Son affaire, c'est de légères esquisses dans de petits panneaux. Il est né pour mettre de jolis tons sur un dessin rapide et nerveux. N'est-ce pas?

Je sens que tout ce que je vous écris vous le savez aussi bien que moi—excusez-moi donc. Mais, voici ce que je viens vous demander plus spécialement: c'est d'entretenir autour de lui le mouvement de sympathie et d'intérêt de vos amis d'Angleterre, afin qu'il ne se croie pas abandonné....

Écrivez-moi et dites-moi ce que vous pensez de tout ceci.

J'espère que vous êtes content de Vattetot et que vous y faites de belles études. Je voudrais bien pouvoir vous voir et parler d'art avec vous. Nous avons souvent causé de vous, avec Walter, à Paris, et je sais comme nous nous entendrions bien sur les choses qui nous passionnent.

Bien à vous,

J. E. BLANCHE.

I knew something of Sickert's difficulties; apparently so gay, he went through dark hours.

MISS ALICE KINGSLEY, BY AUGUSTUS JOHN

Conder, too, wrote often from Paris, hoping that I would
help him to sell his work. He wanted to marry, and badly
needed money.

I could do little to help all these gifted men; indeed, I
found it difficult to keep my own head above water; but
about this time I met a young archaeologist, John Fothergill,
who was working with Edward Warren, a distinguished
Bostonian, a classical scholar who translated Pindar, and
collected gems and Greek sculpture, both for himself, for he
was wealthy, and for the Boston Museum. Fothergill was
the youngest of Warren's fellow archaeologists, who lived
with him at Lewes House.

Lewes House was a monkish establishment, where women
were not welcomed. But Warren, who believed that scholars
should live nobly, kept an ample table and a well stocked
wine-cellar; in the stables were mettlesome horses, for the
Downs were close at hand, and he rode daily with his friends,
for the body must needs be as well exercised as the mind.
Meals were served at a great oaken table, dark and polished,
on which stood splendid old silver. The rooms were full of
handsome antique furniture, and of Greek bronzes and marbles in place of the usual ornaments. In the garden was the
famous Ludovisi throne—fellow of that whereon Venus is
seen to rise from the sea—which, by hook or by crook—
rather, I think, by crook—had been smuggled out of Italy.
There was much mystery about the provenance of the
treasures at Lewes House. This secrecy seemed to permeate
the rooms and corridors, to exhaust the air of the house.
The social relations, too, were often strained, and Fothergill
longed for a franker, for a less cloistered life.

Fothergill was not well off; but he was extremely generous,
and of an adventurous spirit. Fired by the example of Hacon
and Ricketts, he proposed to start a small gallery, where
Conder's, John's, Sickert's, Orpen's, Max Beerbohm's and
my work could be constantly shown; a gallery in fact that
would be a centre for work of a certain character. I was to
be responsible for the choice of artists, Arthur Clifton for the

business side. Premises were found in Ryder Street, St James's, and Robert Sickert, a younger brother of Walter, acted as manager, as Holmes did for Ricketts and Shannon.

I told Rodin in Paris about this new venture; he was warm in support, and sent over the collection of his early drawings, of which I spoke before, and some small bronzes. Walter Sickert too was enthusiastic, and wrote constantly, offering help, and advice.

Besides Rodin, Conder, John, Orpen, Max Beerbohm and I in turn had exhibitions at Carfax (for so the firm was named); while Conder, who there did better than ever before, proposed that Carfax should take all his paintings on silk, as in fact we did; and for the first time in his life Conder was assured of a regular source of income. I persuaded him, too, to try lithography—his pencil drawings had the quality of lithographs—and he made a number of admirable drawings, mostly illustrating Balzac, on transfer paper. He wrote to me from Stafford Terrace: 'My dear Will, I am sending 2 lithographs for the Balzac series. I hope you will like them & accept them. Two represent "Beatrix" with Calyste & with Conti—& the third "Esther" which I like the best—the two figures with the cliff behind seems to be the favourite on account of the languishing look in the young gentleman's eyes. I heard from your wife & it seems you are doing well, and have got your hand in (lucky man.) I find lithography very hard, but most interesting—If you find the "Conti & Beatrix" too slight I can touch it up with chalks. I send it because it shows more power & less difficulty than the two others. However, dear Will, I suppose you must be the judge. Yours always—C. Conder.

If you like the lithographs, please send a cheque or write to Clifton at once, because I am hard up again. C. C.'

These lithographs, and others he did, were remarkable. Carfax took them all, and Conder began to feel his feet in England. For a while all went well. Then I heard that Conder, knowing that Carfax had to ask considerably more for his fans and silk panels than they paid him (for only a proportion of what he did found buyers) told someone (he could not have been sober at the time) that I had induced him to sign an agreement with Carfax while he was drunk. This cruel statement made me furious, and I hurried to Bramerton Street, where Conder was living, and so angry was I that I seized Conder—a much stronger and heavier man—and threw him down. He complained of my attacking him thus at his own place; I replied that I could not well have invited him to come to mine in order to assault him. Conder did finally confess the baselessness of his accusation. But for long I could not forgive him, and this unpleasant experience showed me there was something equivocal in my position, and I was sorely troubled: I must at all costs withdraw from Carfax. Fortunately Robert Ross was willing to take over the business, when I was relieved from an irksome engagement; while Fothergill, who got his capital back, lost nothing by his enterprise. Carfax had been of notable assistance to all concerned, to John and Conder especially. Under Ross's and Arthur Clifton's able management, Carfax, while it continued to encourage young artists, became a serious business; for Ross and Clifton acquired and sold many interesting works, of which the most important was Rembrandt's *Polish Rider*. But I am anticipating; for my quarrel with Conder, and my leaving Carfax, happened later.

In the spring of 1899 Conder, Max Beerbohm, Robert Ross and my brother Albert accompanied me to the Kensington Registrar to witness my marriage to Alice Knewstub. Among the presents we were given was a water-colour from Walter Crane, of Pent Farm, which, two or three years later, became the home of Joseph Conrad. In the letter which Crane wrote to my wife there is a reference to Kent coal, a menace which then seemed negligible, but which has now, alas! become real enough.

My dear Mrs Rothenstein,

I have long wished to make you some little present on your marriage, & if you will not think it too belated I want you to accept the little water-colour landscape I remember you so much liked when you saw it here soon after it was done. It may also serve as a little memento of Pent Farm & your visit to us there.

In sending a picture to an artist's house one is perhaps running the risk of supplying 'coals to Newcastle'—but this at any rate is coal from Kent & I trust its fields will never be defaced by the real article. This sample if it will not feed the fire carries I hope some suggestion of the warm days; &, I trust, of a friendship, & wishes for the happiness & the prosperity of you & your husband in which, of course, my wife joins, from

Yours very truly

WALTER CRANE.

As Miss Alice Kingsley she was then playing at Her Majesty's Theatre, with Herbert Tree, in *The Three Muske-teers*. She obtained two weeks' leave, and she and I went off to Dieppe, where Walter Sickert met us. He had taken rooms for us at Lefèvre's: 'Comfort and luxury at 8 francs a head exclusive of wines, which, excellent, is to be had at 2 francs a bottle. Position dignified, carrying social prestige at Dieppe. I will be on the quay, and on the quay-vive.' Sickert lodged just outside Dieppe, in the house of a fishwife, a handsome woman, full of life and good sense, with auburn hair brushed away from a broad and intelligent brow, who looked after Walter like a mother.

We did not tarry long in Dieppe, but mounting our bicycles (which we had brought with us) said farewell to Sickert, and rode down the coast towards Étretat. We were on the look out for a place where I could paint in the summer,

346

AUGUSTUS JOHN AND THE WRITER'S WIFE (1899)
'THE DOLL'S HOUSE'

and passing through Cany, this seemed a promising spot; but farther down the coast we found a still likelier place, Vattetot, a village near the sea, where was an inn which had once been a farm, with a large *bassecour*. Nearby was a small house, with an odd little staircase leading upstairs from the single sitting room, with which we fell in love; so we rented it then and there for the summer.

On our return to London we spoke of Vattetot to John and Conder, who, with Orpen and my brother, proposed to join us there next summer. When the summer came, it was a large party which descended upon Vattetot; never had so many easels and paint-boxes been seen. It was a glorious time, divided between painting and play. Being in France, we must needs look like Frenchmen. At Yport, two miles away, lived a tailor, who sold corduroy and a coarse blue linen, such as the fishermen wear in those parts. The corduroy took John's fancy, and he presently appeared, a superb figure, in a tight jacket and wide pegtop trousers; so superb that I painted him standing beside my wife, my wife sitting on the staircase I mentioned earlier.

The village of Vattetot was uninteresting enough; but all about were farms, each with its *bassecour* and orchard, enclosed by double or triple rows of trees, to keep out the cold winds. Some of the farms were old, as were the barns and byres, and of these John and Orpen made many charming studies; but John did no painting, though his landscape drawings were remarkable. Many artists can draw figures efficiently, but few can draw landscapes well. But everything John did bore the mark of genius. In his actions as well he showed a Byronic recklessness; as when one day he suddenly leapt into a bucket that was wound to the top of a very deep well; he went down with a rush; it was all we could do to haul him up again. He was a fearless swimmer, and would swim out to sea until he appeared a mere speck in the distance; and never, I thought, had I seen so faun-like a figure as when John ran naked along the beach. Orpen, too, was as powerful a swimmer as John, though less reckless.

347

John, Orpen, and my brother Albert would sit long with
Conder listening to his stories; though Orpen would steal
away, for he loved his work, and was ambitious, I saw, to
perfect himself. He was quiet and uncommunicative, and
very modest. Conder loved to influence young men; he
liked their company, and when he sat over his wine, was loth
they should leave him.

My wife's sister Grace joined us at Vattetot later, with a
girl friend; and when we went down to the sea the ladies
undressed and dressed again in a cave under the cliffs.
Envious coastguardsmen threatened action; we took no
notice, however, and nothing happened, and we continued
our pagan ways. At night, at the inn, Conder would sit
drinking; he both charmed and frightened John and Orpen;
and John would say that if ever he felt inclined to drink,
what he had seen of Conder would be a warning. But we
were young, and feckless, and in love with life. The young
men, too, were in love with Grace; and no wonder, for she
was very beautiful.

A strange looking group, without doubt, we would walk
into Yport, Étretat or Fécamp, to invade the confectioners;
never such *pâtisserie*, we thought, as we found there. And
at night we would wander down to the sea, thinking our
ladies, in the light of the moon, lovelier than ever; and we
would bathe at the little cove at Vaucottes, and returning,
the women would hang glow-worms in their hair. Wonderful
days and wonderful nights these were; but towards the end
of the summer I fell ill. It was jaundice in a severe form;
what made matters worse, I could not now finish my paintings
as I wished to. But the autumn was coming on, the wind
blew cold from the sea, and the party was breaking up. When
I was fit to travel we went, John still with us, to spend a few
days in Paris. John had never seen the Louvre; it was, for
him, an overwhelming experience; he was drunk with excitement. Puvis de Chavannes' paintings, too, impressed him
deeply; so did Daumier's; and he was fascinated, of course,
by the life at Montmartre. Oscar Wilde, who dined with us

348

more than once, was greatly taken with John, though John was very silent.

On our return to London, I began to work on some small 'interior' subjects. At the autumn exhibition of the New English Art Club, I showed some of the pictures I had painted at Vattetot; but I sold nothing there; and being now married, and no money coming in, I was hard put to it to continue even in the modest manner in which we were living. Charles Rowley, who visited us at Vattetot, proposed I should do a set of Manchester portraits; and hinted that, if I came to Manchester, other work would follow. My youngest sister, Louisa, had married a Manchester shipper, Louis Simon, and she and her husband invited us to stay at Sale, where they lived; so I accepted Rowley's proposal. We offered our house until our return to John and his sister, who had comfortless quarters in Fitzroy Street, where Orpen too had a cellar-studio. Orpen was then painting a composition of the play scene in *Hamlet*, based on that of the Sadler's Wells Theatre, a favourite resort at this time. He invited my criticism, and the advice I gave he deemed good, for he acted upon it, to the picture's advantage, he agreed. For Orpen, at this early time, was an admirer of my work; and was perhaps rather a disciple of mine than of Brown or of Tonks, his professors.

Manchester proved a disappointment. I made 12 lithographs of Manchester people, selected by Rowley; but no other commission followed. Indeed, I felt a slight sense of discomfort in Manchester, suspecting that Rowley had chosen himself and his friends to be drawn regardless of others, on which account he had kept my presence in Manchester somewhat secret. Still, I enjoyed my job, and took pains to do the portraits as well as possible.

A pleasant letter from Laurence Housman refers to C. P. Scott, who was not on Rowley's list of those to be drawn:

349

77 *York Mansions,*
Battersea Park, S.W.
Oct. 18*th* 1900

My dear Rothenstein,

What a lot you get through in a little absence! In addition to a violent attack of jaundice, I hear that matrimony is laid to your charge. You hid that event very much under a bushel and gave me no chance of sending congratulations beforehand. Let them come now and cling as lichen to the walls of your cottage! No doubt I ought to have guessed: no permanent bachelor raves over the perfection of a small seven-roomed tenement as you did in my hearing while setting eyes of first discovery on your present abode last year, standing in the middle of the road while you did so. Your wife should have seen that first bubbling of joy: it would have complimented her genuinely.

I am glad Manchester receives you as well as me generously into its smoking bosom; are you to do local celebrities for it? In that case I suppose my Editor Mr C. P. Scott will fall a prey to you.

Surely I sent you my address and a reiterated statement of my at home evening the 13th. I find myself very comfortable thus far out of London; with a view that Corot at times might have died to look out upon: the loveliest thing I have seen in London in the way of woodland scenery.

If your Wednesdays have not died with your bachelorhood I will try to look in before many weeks are over. I too have been ill, and am aged greatly.

Ever your
LAURENCE HOUSMAN.

Among my sitters were the Misses Gaskell, daughters of Charlotte Brontë's biographer, who still lived in their parents' house. The Gaskells put me in mind of the Michael Fields; for although not artists, like Miss Bradley and Miss Cooper they were fastidious in their speech and in the choice of their friends, and their outlook on life was sensitive and humane.

The atmosphere of their house, too, had a quality and distinction that was uncommon in. Manchester; and I still remember, with peculiar pleasure, the old-world ways, and the
fine manners, of these *grandes-dames de province*. When the
Europe we know is no more, will future historians recognise
the fineness of the English character, so different in quality
and texture from that of the rest of Europe, I sometimes
wonder? I need not wonder, for the English character will
survive in literature; and not in English literature alone, for
English traits have been drawn faithfully by foreign writers.

Yet I remember how I could never convince my fellow
students in Paris that not all Englishwomen are hypocrites;
and even now French friends are with difficulty persuaded
that I know people I can trust completely. If Balzac drew a
Lady Dudley in no favourable light, Théophile Gautier, in
Jettatura, paid a generous tribute to the English character.

I made other friends in Manchester, besides the Gaskells:
Alfred Hopkinson, Oliver Elton, S. Alexander, and a cotton-
spinner named William Simpson. William Simpson was a
typical north country Quaker; grim-looking and spare of
figure, with shaven upper lip, stiff beard, and thick, upstanding head of hair. Stern and uncompromising in his
principles, he was, like many Quakers, successful in business.
He employed 3000 men in his factory; and he and his family
lived in a large house, surrounded by ample wooded grounds,
an extravagance which sometimes troubled his conscience.

When trade was bad, the care of all the men and women
who worked in his mill weighed heavily on him. What
would happen if things went ill, and he could no longer keep
all his people employed? A friend, with whom he discussed
his affairs, deemed him too austere in his dealings. 'Clients
expect to be treated well—champagne, and all that, you
know.' Such a notion had never entered Simpson's mind;
but trade being poor, Simpson, while travelling to London
on business, thought over his friend's advice; 'I have never
done such a thing, and I won't begin,' he said to himself.
But early next morning a buyer called on him at his hotel;

Simpson, thinking of his 3000 'hands', touched the bell; a waiter came: 'A bottle of champagne,' said Simpson. His client stared, surprised: champagne at nine in the morning! The waiter returned with the champagne and two glasses; Simpson poured out a glassful; 'What about yourself?' said his guest. 'Me!' said Simpson, 'I never touch the stuff.' And Simpson could not understand why his client was offended. A judgment on his own backsliding! never again! A stern, simple, lovable man, whom everyone respected.

Another of my sitters was a banker, T. R. Wilkinson, who so liked Germans (he had married a German wife) that he could never refuse them credit; whereupon his partners offered him a handsome pension, to live in retirement. He was proud of a gifted son, Spenser Wilkinson. From his father, the managing director of the great firm of Rylands, whose founder had given the Rylands Library to Manchester, I heard of another son named Spenser, Spenser Baldwin, and thereafter both Spenser Wilkinson and Spenser Baldwin made some stir in the world; Manchester has proved a teeming womb of able men. We made many friends there, although in respect of money we were no better off for our visit. The twelve portraits, published by Sherrat and Hughes, were still-born, and decently buried, and soon forgotten.

Before returning to Kensington we paid a visit to my parents at Bradford. There I fell ill with influenza. Before I had quite recovered, having to go to London for a night, I wired the Johns, who were still in our house, to expect me. For it was the middle of the winter; but when I reached Kensington I found the house empty and no fire burning. In front of a cold grate choked with cinders lay a collection of muddy boots. I managed to light a fire; and late in the evening John appeared, having climbed through a window; he rarely, he explained, remembered to take the house-key with him. There were none I loved more than Augustus and Gwen John; but they could scarcely be called 'comfortable' friends.

The next evening I took train to Bradford, when an attack of earache gave me such excruciating torture that I doubted

whether I could stay in the train. I was relieved with opium
on reaching home, and still remember how devoutly I
blessed the doctor who gave it. A second attack of influenza
left me so weak, that I was ordered change of air for a month.
Knowing little of the west of England, we went to Glou-
cester, and then to Bath; but so expensive did we find first
the hotel, and then some lodgings we took, and so uneatable
the food, that work in London seemed wiser than rest in
Bath; and we returned home. My wife, who loved the Johns
just as I did, declared that the walls must be whitewashed and
the floors must be scrubbed before the little house would be
habitable.

Having finished John's portrait, I showed it at the New
English Art Club; and soon after came a letter from Lady
Cromer asking me to paint her sister, Lady Beatrice Thynne;
it was the portrait of John which had pleased her, she explained, when she came with her sister to see me. I was eager
to do justice to my new sitter, but my old failing, that of
finding the best the enemy of the good, stood in my way.
Why couldn't I, like Orpen, discover a method which suited
my gifts, and adopt it? But I couldn't control my nerves;
moreover, I felt the radiance and subtlety of women's beauty
too acutely to succeed. With a man to sit I went more
vigorously to work, and forgot myself in concentrated
attention. But if I painted a woman thus, her charm escaped
me; so I worked hesitatingly, I lacked the courage to admit
my failure, and too often wasted my sitters' time, and my own.

At Lady Bath's house (Lady Bath was my sitter's mother)
was a drawing by Watts of Lady Bath herself; a drawing
merely, yet a drawing which possessed the distinction of
which our generation has lost the secret. I felt this again
when I drew Lady Cromer; and my admiration for Watts
was revived.

I was, at this time and for long afterwards, strongly
affected by Tolstoi's writing. Lady Beatrice surprised me by
her political knowledge: and while painting, when I should
have resisted the temptation to talk, we would argue on

353

various matters. How enlightened she and Lady Cromer were, and their sister as well, Lady Alice Shaw-Stewart, whom I met at the house of Lady Bath their mother.

Lady Bath was a noble figure, a true *grande dame*, as much as any chevalier, *sans peur et sans reproche*. My socialistic friends spoke of the aristocracy as hard and corrupt, but with a delusive veneer of fine manners. Yet traditions which could mould a woman like Lady Bath must surely be part of a sound social system. Or else are charity, graciousness, reticence and exquisite consideration for the feelings of others of no account? Surely a life dedicated to the perfection of personal conduct is a life well spent. The artist, an amateur in life, perfects what he makes; the aristocrat makes of life itself a fine art. Of course there are aristocrats who are corrupt, selfish and even ill-mannered; are there not also vulgar and trivial artists? It is, in fact, but a small number of scholars, of artists, of writers and musicians, and of aristocrats likewise, which keeps true culture alive. Some form of aristocracy must always emerge from the mass. Among the middle class, and in America, we find an aristocracy of virtue; we see this among the Quakers and Dissenters in the north.

But at this time I was, as I said, a Tolstoian. Long ago, as a child, at Scarborough, I had adored a young Evangelist, from Oxford or Cambridge, when I was convinced that my parents, who had not seen the light, must burn in everlasting fire; a fate which did not seem to disturb me much. Now I thought I must persuade Lady Bath's footman, who took my hat and coat, that his task was unworthy of one who had a soul to save. But each time I changed my mind, and followed him meekly up the stairs.

As a painter too, I attempted what was beyond me, again and again. My wife wearied of sitting, so often did I scrape out a long day's work. But somehow, something got done from time to time. I painted a portrait of my wife, and of her sister, Grace, in the sitting room of our little house; this picture I called *The Browning Readers*.

354

When the summer came, we thought of bicycling abroad; *A lady from* where should we go? As usual we were drawn to France. *Vienna* John, who was away with Conder, wrote enthusiastically about Dorset—and a lady from Vienna!

c/o Mrs Everett,
Pevril Tower,
Swanage,
Dorset.

My dear Will—

Conder is getting on with his decoration which becomes every day more beautiful. The country here is lovely beyond words. Corfe Castle and the neighbourhood would make you mad with a painter's cupidity! How are you and Alice, how is she? I have started a colossal canvas whereon I depict Dr Faust on the Brocken. I sweat at it from morn till eve.

Coggy[1] has gone back rubicond with health. Conder is his best self. I wish you were here too.

There is here a beautiful Viennese lady who has sucked the soul out of my lips. I polish up my German lore. I spend spare moments striving to recall phrases from Ollendorf and am *so* grateful for your lines of Schiller which are all that remain to me of the *Lied von der Glocke.*

Sometimes when I surprise myself not quite unhappy tho' *alone* I begin to fear I have lost that crown of youth, the art of loving fanatically, I begin to suspect I have passed the virtues of juvenescence and that its follies are all that remain to me.

Write to me my dear Will & tell me the news of the town, nay spare not those little intimacies which are the salt of friendships and the pepper of love.

Love to Alice, who should be down here to play Upsy Daisy in the waves.

Yours—JOHN.

Conder says he is writing in a day or two.

[1] Coggy was Miss Ferrier, a witty Scottish lady, who lived in Chelsea.

But neither the beauty of Dorset, nor the charms of Vienna, prevented John from attacking a large canvas; what became of his Brocken picture—whether it got done or not, I do not remember.

My brother Albert and Orpen were thinking of going to paint at Cany. John and Salaman decided to join us in France.

My dear Will—

Was glad to hear from you and to know you are getting on all right, you & your family—that is to say you & Alice and the picture—Tho' indeed you spoke of them in a very cursory fashion. I'm sorry you are not down here—Tho' for the moment it is just as well you are not for I have just had—what do you think—German Measles!! No I did not catch them in Vienna,—*German* Measles please—Conder had them some weeks ago. I had quite forgotten about it when I woke up one morning horrified to find myself struck of a murrain—I have been kept in ever since, shut off from the world. In the daylight it isn't so bad but I dread the night season which means little sleep and tragic horrors of dreams at that. I mean in the day I work desperately at my colossal task; I can say at any rate Faust has benefited by my malady. In fact it is getting near the finish. There are about 17 figures in it not to speak of a carrion-laden gibbet. Yes, you have certainly urged me to attack great works—but I suppose we must wait the psychological moment. I don't know when Salaman and I are going; he speaks of coming down here to carry me off by force! Where are Albert & Orpen going then?

> Write again to
> Yours JOHN.

How is Strang's show going?
Is your book out, do send a copy if it is.

I had seen an illustrated article by Pennell in one of the American monthlies on a place, Le Puy, in which he suggested Auvergne as a centre for work. John, too, had heard of Le Puy, and we decided to meet there; John, with Michel Salaman, a fellow student from the Slade and a patron of John, going to Le Puy by rail, while my wife and I, leaving the train at Nevers, mounted our bicycles, stopping to draw several places that attracted us on the way to Le Puy.

The country was beautiful, and we passed through many charming villages, at one of which, Billy, a village near Vichy, we met with an amusing adventure. I had been drawing all day, and towards evening we put up at the village inn. After dinner the moon being full, we strolled out of doors, and returned to the place where I had been drawing. So magical everything looked in the moonlight, I took out my sketch book to draw, while my wife, talking softly, stood by. After a time she heard strange noises, she declared, and suddenly a gun went off, and an old woman, very scantily clad, ran out of a hovel near by, a strange Daumier-like figure, in the brilliant moonlight. She at once reappeared with a struggling goose in her arms, and made a rush for the hovel, where by now another old hag stood awaiting the result of her sortie. Then the door was slammed to, and from within we heard the cackle of the goose, and the no less excited cackle of the two old women. As we returned to the inn the street was full of awakened villagers; bad characters were about, had tried to steal a goose, and they looked at us with suspicion. Billy was a perfect place for an artist during the day; but not by moonlight it seemed.

From Billy we went on to Auxerre, and from there to Clermont-Ferrand, whence we took train to Le Puy. As we approached the town, the place was surrounded with red-roofed villas, we found, and our hearts sank. Had we come so far to see this? But John and Salaman, whom we met at the station, reassured us, and indeed next morning, as we climbed the steep street to the cathedral, we saw we had done well to come. What a church, and what fascinating streets and houses, and what wonderful people!

It was the Feast of the Assumption, and sturdy women in white caps, wearing gold chains over their black bodices, and wide, pleated skirts, their men in short, black coats and black broad-brimmed hats, were pouring into the cathedral, waiting to take Communion. I had seen nothing like the religious fervour of this Auvergne crowd, pressing up to the wide communion rail.

I made many drawings of the cathedral, both inside and out, and many more of the streets of broad-eaved, tall, stone houses; of the cattle-market, too, where whiskered Auvergnats brought their beasts for sale. There was a ruined castle a mile away, the château de Polignac, which meanwhile attracted John; and every day we met at lunch in a vast kitchen, full of great copper vessels, a true *rôtisserie de la Reine Pédauque*, presided over by a hostess who might have been mother to Pantagruel himself, so heroic in size she was, and of so genial and warm a nature; so generous, too, was her table, it reminded me of a jest of Oscar Wilde, made in reply to the *cliché* about enough being as good as a feast: 'No,' said Oscar, 'enough is as good as a meal; too much is as good as a feast.' So each day, tempted and cajoled by our hostess, we ate and drank, and, thank Heaven, digested too, like heroes.

The local guide-book led us to other places: Le Monastier, almost Spanish in its austerity, with a noble early church, and Notre Dame des Neiges, the monastery where Stevenson had stayed, and which he described in his book *Travels with a Donkey in the Cevennes*. We stayed the night there, where each of us was lodged in a white-washed cell, spotlessly clean; and we joined the Brothers at table in the evening. If I remember rightly, the monks were Trappists, to whom speech was forbidden; but with the lay brothers one might talk, and we found there were still some among them who remembered Stevenson's visit. My wife stayed the night at a nunnery.

In a shop at Le Puy we saw a photograph which struck us; it was taken, the shopman said, at Arlempdes, some miles away, and we set out to find it, no easy task. 'There were evil people at Arlempdes; better not go there,' we were told when we enquired the way. But we persisted and at last drew near it along a lonely bypath. A remarkable place,

truly, this small, rough hamlet, clustered round the ruins of
a tiny stronghold, set on a high rock sheer over the Loire,
with, nearby, the remains of a small, primitive chapel. While
we were looking about, the curé approached—no strangers
had ever come to Arlempdes, he said. He had never heard
English spoken, nor indeed any foreign tongue. We enquired
after an inn; there was no inn, he answered, nor could we
get food anywhere in the village, so poor were his people;
but if we could come to his vicarage in an hour's time,
he would kill a pigeon or two. We gratefully accepted
his offer, and when we arrived there we found a table laid in
his orchard, at which we seated ourselves, when soup was
served, and then an omelette, *baveuse*, as only the French can
prepare it, and then came the pigeons; while from the first
a generous wine was offered, which our host enjoyed, it was
evident, no less than ourselves; and seeing us appreciate his
wine, from time to time he would leave the table and return
with a bottle in either hand. This was true 'Vin de Curé', he
said, laughing; for so good wine was called in those parts. He
rarely met intelligent people, his parishioners were poor,
ignorant folk, so this was a great day for him. Every three
years they acted a Passion-play, he told us, but last year the
fellow who played a Roman soldier had taken too much
wine, and had really stabbed 'Jesus' in the side, and there was
a scandal. And looking at John, seeing his long hair and
russet beard, he was struck with an idea: 'But you would
make a perfect Jesus,' he said; and the good curé called to
his sister as she came from the kitchen, 'Tell me, of whom
does this gentleman remind you?' 'Mais—de Notre Seigneur,' she answered in a matter-of-fact voice, rubbing her
greasy hands on her apron. And the curé leaning back in his
chair laughed till the tears came into his eyes. 'What did
I tell you?' he said, 'you must stay with us and play the
part.' But John, though flattered, had no desire to be
martyred; and our friend, unruffled, again disappeared, returning with two fresh bottles, heavily coated with dust.
Never had we tasted so rare a wine. We left our host with

regret, and with difficulty persuaded him to accept a small sum for the trouble and expense to which we had put them both. 'Ce sera pour les pauvres,' he said, as he bid us adieu. We laughed often over the way in which the good curé's sister said 'Mais, Notre Seigneur,' and the memory of the joyous curé lingered long. My wife and I left Le Puy reluctantly; but I wanted to make drawings elsewhere; so leaving John and Michel we pushed on to La Chaise-Dieu; then back through Burgundy, to places we had visited before. In answer to a letter from my wife, John wrote one of his wonderful letters:

Cité Titaud,

Dear Alice— *Le Puy.*

Many thanks for your letter! A simple post-card from you would have been a delightfully gratifying thing—the work of Art you have sent me is an Event!

Really, you have troubled my peace with your golden hills and fat valleys of Burgundy!

. . . . . .

How glad you must have been to be again in your beloved Vitteaux with a landlady from Tunbridge Wells! William will have a beautiful series of drawings done this summer. No! I think we will never get to Chaise-Dieu. We are not the sort of people, as you know, to wheel each other's machines up 18 miles of landscape! I must tell you I never went to Paris after all. Circumstances veered suddenly! My Viennese friend, 'inspired' I suspect by Mrs Everett's religious worldly advice, wrote to say she feared my love for her would very soon lessen if not go altogether, and thus she preferred to be wise and forgo the rash experience of coming to France to me. She says also (dear confidential Alice) 'When you will no longer have me—What will I do then? What will become of me then? Repudiated by my husband who loves me? Can you answer that?' I have answered it according to my lights, which no doubt will not be strong enough to illuminate her doubts—at this distance.

Women always suspect me of fickleness, but will they never give me a chance of vindicating myself? They are too modest, too cautious, for to do that they would have to give their lives. I am not an exponent of the faithful dog business.

I work indoors mostly now. I am painting Michel's portrait. I hope to make a success of it. If when finished it will be as good as it is now I may count on that. I am also painting Polignac castle which ought to make a fine picture.

The very excellent military band plays in the parks certain nights, and we have enjoyed sitting listening to it. It is very beautiful to watch the people under the trees. At intervals the attention of the populace is diverted from following the vigorous explanatory movements of the conductor by an appeal to patriotism, effected by illuminating the flag by Bengal lights at the window of the museum! It is dazzling & undeniable! The band plays very well. Rendered clairvoyant by the music one feels very intimate with humanity, only Michel's voice when he breaks in with a laborious attempt at describing how beautifully the band played 3 years ago at the Queen's Hall that time he took Edna Waugh—is rather disturbing—or is it that I am becoming ill tempered!

I'm glad Will is working away with his customary diligence. He will be able to look back at the summer without risking Lot's daughter's bitterness. Enviable Will! My sister tells me that Nietzsche is dead. I am so grateful for Will's loan of Balzac's *Vie Conjugale*. It pains and makes me laugh at the same time.......

Yes. Burgundy is reserved for me for another summer. All the same for my part I shall not hope for better than our visit to Arlempdes—which is not honest, for I *do* hope for better—but scarcely expect.

Michel sends much love—& I send more to you both.

JOHN.

Usually, when we were in Paris, we asked Oscar Wilde to dinner. But on our last visit he had proposed dining in an open-air restaurant, where a small orchestra played. He chose a table near the musicians; he liked being near the music, he said; but during dinner it was plain that he was less interested in the music than in one of the players. I was annoyed, and resolved not to see him again. I did not, therefore, this time let him know that we were in Paris; but the very first evening we met Wilde on the Boulevards, and I saw at once that he knew we had meant to avoid him. The look he gave us was tragic, and he seemed ill, and was shabby and down at heel. Of course we asked him to join us. He came in a chastened mood, and made himself very charming, but his gaiety no longer convinced; there was a stricken look in his eyes, and he plainly depended on drink to sustain his wit. We were never to see him again. He died later that year. Ross told me he had added my name, and my wife's, to the few he had written on the wreath he laid on Oscar's grave; I was glad he had done so. I must have written Robert Ross after Wilde's death; for I find the following letter:

> *Hôtel Belle Vue,*
> *Mentone.*
>
> *Dec. 11th,* 1900.

My dear Will—

I have been so touched by your letter, the only one of the several kind ones I have received that has given me any pleasure. I feel poor Oscar's death a great deal more than I should, & far more than I expected. I had grown to feel, rather foolishly, a sort of responsibility for Oscar, for everything connected with him except his genius, & he had become for me a sort of adopted prodigal baby. I began to love the very faults which I would never have forgiven in anyone else.

During the months I was in Paris I saw him every day & he was often in the best spirits, though he sometimes suffered a good deal of pain. One of the doctors however warned me that unless he was careful he would not live for more than *three or four years*. The night before I started for Nice on Nov. 13th he became very hysterical when I said goodbye

to him, but I never attached any importance to this: I knew
he was much worried as usual over financial matters & for
a few nights had been taking morphia by the doctor's orders.
I was rather angry at what I thought was merely nerves. But
he asked everyone to go out of the room & sobbed for a
quarter of an hour, & said he knew he would never see me
again. For several days one of his jests had been that he
would never outlive the century as the English people could
not stand him any more & that he had kept them away from
the Exhibition, so the French people would not stand him, &
I did not take his *serious* remarks more seriously than these.
Reggie promised to come & see him & keep me posted, &
during the fortnight I was absent he more than fulfilled his
promise—taking Oscar for drives & really acting as a nurse.
On Sunday night Oscar became quite suddenly light headed
& Reggie wrote to me an urgent letter, telling me that I ought
to prepare for coming to Paris. This reached me on Tuesday.
On Wednesday I was just going to move from [illegible] to
Mentone with my mother when I got a telegram from Reg.
saying 'almost hopeless,' & started for Paris at once. I could
never have got on without Reggie. The last hours were in-
expressibly painful, but I hope & believe that Oscar was unconscious. He died at 2 o'clock on Friday afternoon. You can
imagine the terrible formalities with the French authorities.
They very nearly took him to the Morgue, because no relative turned up, & did not pay any attention to my telegrams. Among the wreaths I placed a simple one of Laurels,
as 'a tribute to his literary achievements & distinction,' & on
it I put the names of those whom I thought would like to be
remembered, & yours & Alice's were among them. He was
always fond of both of you.

Always your affectionate
ROBBIE.

I admired Ross's devotion to Wilde. He says in his letter
that he felt Oscar's death 'more than he should'. But this
perfect unquestioning loyalty, continuing through so many

years, in circumstances which were often trying, sometimes dark, painful, and, at last, sordid and repulsive even, was to me, to others as well, a touching, aye, a beautiful thing in Ross. So perfect was his love, that in Ross's case a prejudice which might have been felt against one so closely associated with Wilde at the time of his downfall, was well-nigh turned into praise.

Orpen, with Conder, and my brother Albert, spent the summer at Cany while we were in Auvergne with John. Orpen wrote, after a flying visit to the Paris Exhibition, and sent me some amusing drawings, illustrating their life at Cany:

My dear Mr R.

I have just been to Paris and seen your pearl with the English swine—and send my best congratulations.[1] Paris seemed very serious as my friend Everett is hardly a suitable Parisian companion. I am very glad to hear you like Albert's work. He has sent me your book on Goya which has given me great delight. I hear from Mr C. that you have done some wonderful drawings this summer. When does the exhibition come off? I had better say nothing of what I am doing; they get worse and better, so I hope on. Augustus seems depressed. I have just had a letter from him. I sent you a few sketches to show the general aspect of Cany. I bless you for having told us of it. Its getting better every day, so I am loath to go back to London.—I suppose you have seen Conder's work. some of the best I have ever seen of his, I think—I wish you had come and drawn the town, the Market Place is splendid,—please remember me to Mrs Rothenstein.

Yours ORPEN.

The book on Goya to which Orpen refers was a small work, which I wrote for Binyon, who was editing a series of artists' biographies. Soon after my return to London I went

---

[1] A silver medal had been awarded my painting of *The Doll's House* at the Paris Exhibition.

to Bradford to finish the portrait of my parents. While I was there I heard again from John, who was still at Le Puy.

Le Puy, le 20th
Cité Titaud.

My dear Will—

Many thanks for your letter. I don't think I will allow myself any more [illegible]. My fair seems to be more cautious than fickle. I still continue to receive the most tender German missives from her. But, trifles apart, I still hang lovingly on the breasts of Puy who grows of a ripe beauty daily. I should say [illegible] perhaps, as it is in the country round that I invite my soul. I am painting beyond Espaly. The ever juvenile Michel leaves in a week. I rather expect McEvoy over then. One cannot count on the gentle dweller in Pimlico, but I have hopes. Michel pushed on by a conscientious philanthropy seeks peace with his soul in offering McEvoy his fare over and back.......

I'm glad to hear of Albert's improvement. It will be an event when the *Bathers* make their splash in an astonished world! I hear from Orpen who still remains at Cany. I want to travel again next year hitherwards and be a painter. I am, dear Will, full of ideas for work. I send you a new form of dry point. Oh, it is charming of you to send the Goya. But it has not come! Alas!......

There came a play called 'Michel Strogoff' here to which we went. What was astonishing was to see two French & English war correspondents, M. Sollivet & Mister Blount, after much comic rivalry, finally, at a moment of peril embrace and swear eternal love! To see 'La France et l'Angleterre toujours ensemble' walk off with their arms round each other's necks was a sight that stirred up the last dregs of patriotism in the clear cool Anarchistic distilled liquor of my heart! I thought it was very generous of our neighbours, putting the ridiculous Mr Blount in a heroic position! The house tempered their enthusiasm with, I thought, a regretful grain of salt.

I am going up to Paris for two or three days to see those
Daumiers etc....

It had been better, perhaps, had other ladies been as
cautious as his German 'fair'. But it was Ida Nettleship who
reigned in John's heart. We saw her on our return to town;
and often dined with her parents. Jack Nettleship was the
salt of the earth; he had an immense respect for the opinions
of young painters, and would show his canvases, begging
for criticism, criticism one was careful to avoid, lest Nettleship rush for his palette and brushes, and at once begin
changing his picture. For he had a way of accepting one's
judgment. His admiration for John was more hesitating than
mine; but my enthusiasm for John's work was, I think, a comfort to Nettleship; for he knew of darling Ida's devotion,
and he was not the man to stand in the way of true love.

In the autumn Carfax showed the drawings I made in
Auvergne and Burgundy. Charles Holmes wrote me an
encouraging letter:

Hacon & Ricketts,
The Vale Press
No. 17 *Craven St. Strand, London.*
May 5*th,* 1900.

My dear Rothenstein,

I could not help being pleased at your liking my experiments, but today your kind note was especially encouraging,
since on Wednesday and Thursday I had been greatly impressed by your drawings at Carfax. I hope you will give
the show the chance it deserves to have, and won't close it
too soon. I am sure it must be a success if people only know
of it, for even you will find it difficult to replace by another
collection of things as uniformly interesting & uniformly
artistic. You may be amused to hear that Ricketts went twice
yesterday to see them; an attention usually reserved for a
few extremely dead men.

Yours sincerely
C. J. HOLMES.

366

Carfax sold a number of the drawings; and my brother,
Charles, made me an offer for *The Doll's House* which I
gratefully accepted, as I had returned to town with empty
pockets. I received, too, a generous message from Sargent
who wished, he declared, to acquire the picture. John had
already written me: 'It may interest you to know that Tonks
& Sargent independently arrived at the same conclusion, viz.
that your Doll's House was the best painting in the Exposition. Also Tonks is enthusiastic over the portrait of
Yrs Truly, le jeune homme.' Oddly enough, *The Doll's
House* had received little notice when shown in London the
year before; but now, owing to Sargent's praise, many people
enquired about it; and some years later Staats Forbes offered
my brother a thousand pounds for the picture; but he
would not then part with it. Later, however, my brother
presented this painting to the Tate Gallery, together with
McEvoy's beautiful *The Ear-Ring*.

Meanwhile I was asked to paint a portrait of Dr Furnivall,
for Trinity Hall, Cambridge. An unusual type of scholar
was this vivacious old man, with his very human interest in
a young women's rowing club at Hammersmith, of which he
was President. Furnivall was then close on 76, and still
sculled on the river. For his years he had a wonderfully glad
eye, and a glad heart too. He liked coming to us, I think,
and while he sat in the studio, or joined us at supper, was
full of stories. As a youth he had sat at Ruskin's feet, and he
helped to start the Working Men's College. He was staying
with Ruskin when Millais came to paint Ruskin's portrait—
the one I saw at Sir Henry Acland's house. Furnivall described Mrs Ruskin minutely; he remembered the very
dresses she wore. Handsome and mettlesome, she might
cast her eye, Ruskin feared, on young Millais, whose career
was far too precious to be risked. There was no pretence of
affection, or of sympathy even, betwixt Ruskin and her.
Ruskin, according to Furnivall's story, had hoped that she
would elope with an Italian count who had stayed in the
house; but it was the count who eloped, not with Mrs Ruskin,

but with all her jewels. Ruskin was angry, not because Millais had fallen in love with his wife, but, so Furnivall said, because he believed his wife would ruin young Millais' art. Perhaps Ruskin, I said, insensitive to his wife's beauty, failed likewise to understand, and cherish, her woman's nature. As Millais' wife, was not her lot a happier one? But Furnivall rambled on, about his quarrels with Swinburne, whom he insisted on calling Piggsbrook, about Browning and the Browning Society he started, and the Early English Text Society. I found a note from W. P. Ker about Furnivall:

95 *Gower Street,*

22 *Dec.* 1900.

Dear Rothenstein

I send you a Christmas present, with good wishes.

I am grieved at my want of sense in defaulting at the Chaucer dinner—I wish I had been there, and would have been, but words spoken at midnight in the High fall easily away from the memory. It is a loss.

I hope Furnivall is shaping well. I don't think his views are quite sound about double sculling, but you needn't put that into the picture.

Very truly yours

W. P. KER.

I don't know if Furnivall's views about sculling showed in the portrait; but many years afterwards, when visiting Trinity Hall, we were shown the portrait by a college servant who observed, 'a good many young ladies from Hammersmith come to see this painting, sir!' Max was much amused by Furnivall, upon whom he once played a naughty, and successful, trick. There had been some discussion as to the meaning of certain phrases in Shakespeare; so the wicked Max wrote a letter to *The Saturday Review,* referring to a rare term of heraldry which, he believed, would throw light on the problem. Furnivall spent a whole day at the British Museum, searching for the reference which, of course, Max had invented. When the hoax was revealed to him, he burst into a charming peal of laughter, and entirely forgave Max on condition that a subscription of ten shillings should be paid to the Esperance Girls' Club.

I painted Max, too, at this time in top-hat, long coat and white gloves. Max's repute as a writer was growing daily. His *Saturday Review* articles were a delight, and he had just published his first book of prose—*The Works of Max Beerbohm* (or was it the second book—*More?*). There were still but few people who understood Max's caricatures. Max sees only the worst side of his subjects, I used to hear. *Punch* had for so long provided illustrations to harmless jokes, that the nature of true satire was wellnigh forgotten. *Vanity Fair*, too, had become a repository for amiable likenesses. People accused Max of bad form; of looking for the ugly side of men's characters. Actually, no one was quicker than Max to see the attractive side of people he met, and he preferred the gentle word which gives pleasure to the barbed phrase which hurts. But Max happened to have a genius for satire, and his integrity as a satirist equalled his fastidiousness as a writer. Once he took up his pencil he drew not with malice, nor yet with kindness, but with the intuition of a creative artist; he drew neither portraits nor poetical compositions, but caricatures, and satirical cartoons.

Satire is the poetry of laughter; the vision of what might be through the ridicule of what is; it is not for nothing that Aristophanes and Rabelais are placed among the immortals. There is a story that one day there came into Daumier's workroom an old gentleman, breathless and perturbed, who asked for M. Daumier, and then went down on his knees, saying, 'I salute the greatest historian in France'. The old gentleman was Michelet! I do not see Professor Trevelyan or Dr Gooch going down on their knees before Max; but it will now be admitted, I think, that Max will throw as much light on certain aspects of contemporary history as these distinguished writers.

It was in 1898 that Max wrote a play—*The Happy Hypocrite*—at the suggestion, I think, of Mrs Patrick Campbell. If the play were ever produced, I must design scenes and dresses, Max said. I would have loved to do this; but before the play was finished I heard from Max:

'I am distracted in the forlorn effort to write the *Hap. Hyp.* which the Lyceum people want by Tuesday or Wednesday—and I am writing to cancel various engagements—as every moment of my time will have to be devoted to drama....

'I saw Mrs P. C. and Mr F. R.[1] yesterday at Bedford Square—and Mr F. R. was so full of the way he wanted to have the Georgian dresses done (if the play were really produced) that I, a mild and embarrassed neophyte, could not introduce the idea that you ought to design the costumes. Please forgive my weakness of purpose—You are the only person who could have done the dresses really well—but I was placed in such a position that I could not make the suggestion. I will come and see you as soon as the play is definitely on—or off.'

Happily the play, when it was produced in December, 1900, was charmingly staged; the first night was a triumph; Mrs Beerbohm was the proudest mother in England. Max wrote the next day, in his modest way:

'Very many thanks for your nice, kind, amusing letters. They have greatly delighted me. I sit here among the débris of success, wondering what on earth can be the matter with my play—why it has appealed to the great heart-disease of the British Public. All the same, I am flattered. And your appreciation convinces me that the little play is not wholly awful.'

We had stayed with Rodin at Meudon on our way back from Auvergne, when he complained of his difficulties: the expenses of casting his bronzes and the cost of the marble for his *Baiser* then being exhibited. Warren promised to see *Le Baiser* in Paris, with a view to acquiring it. With Fothergill's encouragement Warren asked me to approach Rodin on the matter, and the purchase was finally arranged

[1] Mr Johnston Forbes-Robertson.

to Rodin's satisfaction, Warren agreeing to pay £1000 for *Buying a* the marble. At the same time I saw Legros, Tweed and *Rodin* MacColl, with the idea, which came from MacColl, that we should get a Rodin bronze for the Victoria and Albert Museum. I find a letter from MacColl:

Monday
Nov. 12 1900.

I saw Tweed after meeting your wife & arranged for a preliminary meeting at his studio 14a Cheyne Row....Bring Legros if you possibly can. You suffer a critic more gladly or at least more generously than anyone in my experience.

D. S. M.

Legros and Sargent both came to the meeting. Sargent was in favour of acquiring an early work, *l'Age d'Or*; he cared less for Rodin's later manner. I wrote to Rodin, who replied:

Mon cher ami

Je suis honoré et heureux de la proposition que vous me faites, et je rends grâce à messieurs Maccoll et Tweed, Legros, et vous, ami, de votre si grande sympathie.

Je crois que 4000 pour un beau bronze serait bien. Belle patine.

Pour le marbre le prix est le double peut-être plus, avec l'achat du marbre *l'âge d'airain* et *l'homme qui s'éveille* serait pour la 7e fois en marbre et je le vois dans cette matière doubler d'expression; car il y a dans cette douleur des nuances fines qui ne seraient rendues que par le marbre et, si je pouvais, du marbre grec.

Aussi bien cette figure debout, le bras sur la tête, qui a été achetée en bronze par Copenhague, serait si bien en marbre que je fais des voeux pour cela.

Amitié et présentez mes meilleurs compliments à Madame Rothenstein.

Votre dévoué
RODIN.
31 *oct.* 1900.

P.S. pour *le baiser* j'attends sans impatience de faire aussi cette sculpture, aussi par vos soins.

Again, on the 17 *nov.* 1900 he wrote:

Excusez-moi de cette feuille

Mon cher ami

Je suis heureux de savoir que vos intentions prennent de la réalité grâce à votre dévouement et à celui de vos amis.

Je crois que si Kensington prend deux bronzes, *l'âge d'airain* et *le bronze de silence*, ce serait bien, mais je dois avouer que *le silence* n'a pas encore ses bras. Voyez si cela gêne.

J'ai une très belle figure qui est d'un bourgeois de Calais qui est placée dans le petit pavillon qui précède mon expo. chez moi. *Elle est complète* quoique le morceau exposé soit sans tête et sans mains. Cette figure a une grande désinvolture.

Je ne ferai payer que les frais de fonte et quelques petits frais. Pour *le baiser* Monsieur Carfax m'a envoyé une feuille de traité pour cela. Mais je n'ai pas trouvé explicite le premier article et je lui ai demandé de bien faire mettre que mon travail était de 20,000 francs—vingt mille francs—et que le marbre de cinq mille francs 5,000 fourni par la carrière était à la charge de Monsieur Warren, c'est-à-dire 25000 en tout; les articles suivants sont très bien. . . .

à vous, cher ami; à Madame Rothenstein mes respects affectueux.

A. RODIN.

Finally, a bronze of St John the Baptist was purchased by subscription and gladly accepted by the Museum.[1] Soon afterwards *Le Baiser* was completed and sent to Lewes House.

Rodin wrote that Constantin Meunier was to be in London, and Legros brought him, with Cobden-Sanderson, to see us. Meunier was enthusiastic about London, it was so dramatic, he said; and he showed us some remarkable drawings he had

---

[1] In 1914 Rodin presented 16 bronzes, a group in marble and a mask in terra-cotta, to the Victoria and Albert Museum.

done of stark warehouses and sinister streets and courts by the Thames side, and dark archways under the bridges. It was strange, I thought, that a foreigner, during so short a visit, should do what artists living always in London failed to do. Broad-minded and large-hearted was Meunier, an austere and powerful creator. His sculpture I knew well, but not his drawings; nor have I seen his drawings since, nor heard any speak of them. Strang, too, admired the austerity of Meunier's work. Strang was now painting; he tried first one manner and then another; for the moment he was under Shannon's influence.

On Sunday evenings we often went to the Strangs at Hamilton Terrace. Laurence Binyon was a familiar there, and one evening he came, bringing a stranger, a quiet youth, with eyes that seemed surprised at the sight of the world, and hair that stood up behind like a cockatoo's feathers. As a youth he had run away to sea, Binyon whispered, and had had wondrous adventures; now he wanted to write; but he was very poor, and Binyon was helping him. After supper the stranger seated himself on the floor, and we sat round while he told us tales of adventure: how he and a few shipmates had fared in South America, where, being penniless, they nearly starved. Once, during a storm, they had fixed their jackknives in their caps, hoping the lightning might strike them and put an end to their misery, so wretched they were. Masefield—this was the young man's name—spoke in a deep and solemn voice; a serious and romantic youth, I thought; and I got to like him. Indeed, everyone liked him, and wished to be helpful; but to help is not always an easy matter. Hearing that Lawrence Hodson was planning an exhibition at Wolverhampton to show the important work being done outside the Royal Academy, Masefield successfully offered himself as secretary. And an admirable secretary and organiser he proved. He wrote, too, an introduction for the catalogue, one of his earliest pieces of prose to be published. Both Binyon and Yeats encouraged Masefield's adventures in poetry; so, I think, did Cunninghame

373

Graham. Masefield himself had a passionate admiration for Conrad. When later I got to know Conrad, I took him Masefield's *Salt Water Ballads*, and some of his stories; but Conrad had conceived one of his odd prejudices against Masefield, and indulged in a violent outburst against him. Whether his prejudice lasted I do not know.

376

384

385

389